JEWISH WOMEN PHILOSOPHERS OF FIRST-CENTURY ALEXANDRIA

Jewish Women Philosophers of First-Century Alexandria

Philo's 'Therapeutae' Reconsidered

JOAN E. TAYLOR

OXFORD
UNIVERSITY PRESS

OXFORD
UNIVERSITY PRESS

Great Clarendon Street, Oxford OX2 6DP

Oxford University Press is a department of the University of Oxford.
It furthers the University's objective of excellence in research, scholarship,
and education by publishing worldwide in

Oxford New York

Auckland Bangkok Buenos Aires Cape Town Chennai
Dar es Salaam Delhi Hong Kong Istanbul Karachi Kolkata
Kuala Lumpur Madrid Melbourne Mexico City Mumbai Nairobi
São Paulo Shanghai Taipei Tokyo Toronto

Oxford is a registered trade mark of Oxford University Press
in the UK and in certain other countries

Published in the United States
by Oxford University Press Inc., New York

© Joan E. Taylor 2003

British Library Cataloguing in Publication Data

Data available

Library of Congress Cataloging in Publication Data

Data applied for

ISBN 0-19-925961-5

1 3 5 7 9 10 8 6 4 2

Typeset by Regent Typesetting, London
Printed in Great Britain
on acid-free paper by
T. J. International,
Padstow, Cornwall

For my mother and father:
Birgit and Robert

PREFACE AND ACKNOWLEDGEMENTS

THIS book was begun in 1996, during my time as Visiting Lecturer and Research Associate in Women's Studies in Religion at Harvard Divinity School. At that stage, I believed I was writing a book that would look comparatively at material relating to women and gender in nascent Christianity, in the groups evidenced by the Dead Sea Scrolls, and in Philo of Alexandria's treatise, *De Vita Contemplativa*. However, I realized early into this exercise that such a comparative study could not be done adequately in a single volume, unless that volume were to become a very thick one indeed. It seemed preferable then to limit my study. Since I had already begun to explore aspects of *De Vita Contemplativa* and the Dead Sea Scrolls corpus, I thought at first a two-way comparative study might suffice. However, a little further down that track I realized I would have quite enough material on either topic for separate books. Therefore, this present book concerns only *De Vita Contemplativa*.

This book was continued while I was guest researcher with the Dead Sea Scrolls Initiative at the University of Copenhagen, Denmark (July to December 1999) and then substantially completed at Waikato University, New Zealand, before my departure to be an independent scholar in England in late 2000. It therefore most likely bears the marks of a threefold institutional influence. I am extremely grateful to scholars and librarians of Waikato, Copenhagen and Harvard Universities, and to the staff of Essex University library, who diligently sought the books and articles I needed to make the final amendments in the first part of 2002. Any inadequacies and mistakes in this study are of course my own responsibility.

I thank Harvard Divinity School for the year I spent (1996–7) under the guidance of the Director of the Women's Studies in Religion Program, Constance Buchanan. I thank also my associates on the programme with whom I have talked in detail about this research and historical methodologies: Lindsey Harlan,

Bonna Haberman, Joycelyn Moody, and Cynthia Scheinberg. I am grateful to Elisabeth Schüssler Fiorenza for reading and commenting upon early drafts of my chapter on method. I thank also the other members of the Department of New Testament, especially, François Bovon, Annewies van den Hoek, Helmut Koester, and Pat Tiller, for their invaluable advice at many points.

I thank Bernadette J. Brooten for discussing method and many other subjects with me and for inviting me to the Brandeis Seminar on early Jewish and Christian Studies, at which I presented a paper and received very helpful comments. My warm thanks to Rueven Kimelman for his advice and suggestions, and to Ellen Birnbaum for her excellent critique of Chapter 2.

I thank Waikato University for Research Grants which contributed to costs, and for the travel grant in 1996 which permitted Philip Davies to visit from Sheffield University in order to undertake some valuable preliminary work with me which resulted in a joint publication (for which, see the Bibliography). I thank Dennis Green for his numerous insights. I am grateful to Norman Simms, for prompting me to read a paper to the 1998 Jewish Studies Conference in Hamilton.

I thank the Philo of Alexandria Group of the SBL Annual Meeting in San Francisco, 1997, for their comments on a paper on the name and identity of the group of *De Vita Contemplativa*. I thank Holger Szesnat, for discussing key issues with me. I am extremely grateful to David Hay for reading a draft of what became the first two chapters of this book, and for his very valuable comments, and to David Runia for his advice.

I thank Fred Cryer, Jesper Høgenhaven, Greg Doudna, Thomas Thompson, Lone Fatum, Troels Engberg-Pedersen, and Søren Holst for their time and interest in discussing matters to do with Philo and the so-called Therapeutae during my period of study in Copenhagen, and for their recognition that a better understanding of these people might in some way add to our understanding of aspects of the Dead Sea Scrolls, Second Temple Judaism, and early Christianity.

I thank Pieter Van der Horst for giving me permission to reproduce his excellent translation of Chaeremon's work on the Egyptian priests, which appears as an appendix here.

I am very grateful to the Palestine Exploration Fund, for a

grant which allowed me to visit Egypt in November 1999, and thereby do some valuable site research and information-gathering. I am grateful to Hero Granger-Taylor for her invaluable advice on matters to do with clothing and textiles, and for her comments on my draft about the clothing of the Therapeutae. Very many thanks to Ross Kraemer for her extremely useful and insightful comments on this typescript, and for her support and enthusiasm for the project. Without her illuminating studies I would never have begun looking at *Contempl.*, and this book is indebted to her work in very many respects.

I thank several museums, institutions, and individuals for permissions which enable me to use photographs which appear in this book. Figure 9 appears courtesy of Dennis Green, reproduced with permission. Figures 11 and 12 are reproduced by permission of the Department of Printing and Graphic Arts, Houghton Library, Harvard College Library. The photograph of Figure 14 is made from a transparency supplied by the Réunion des Musées Nationaux Agence photographique and used with permission of the Louvre Museum, Paris. Figure 15 is a photograph provided courtesy of the Museum of Fine Arts, Boston, reproduced with permission © 2000 Museum of Fine Arts, Boston. All rights reserved. Photographs 16 and 17 are supplied and reproduced by permission, courtesy of the Museo Archeologico Nazionale di Napoli and the Soprintendenza Archeologica delle Province de Napoli e Caserta. Photograph 19 appears courtesy of the Papyrology Rooms, Ashmolean Museum, Oxford, © Egypt Exploration Fund, London. Reproduced with permission. Photograph 22 is supplied and reproduced with permission from the model-maker Alec Garrard, who retains the copyright.

Finally, as always, I thank my husband Paul and our two children Emily and Robert for their support as I indulge my passion for the past.

J.T.

July 2002

CONTENTS

LIST OF FIGURES

LIST OF ABBREVIATIONS

ANRW	*Aufstieg und Niedergang der römischen Welt: Geschichte und Kultur Roms im Spiegel der neueren Forschung*, ed. Wolfgang Haase and Hildegard Temporini (Berlin and New York: Walter de Gruyter)
BAR	*Biblical Archaeology Review*
CBQ	*Catholic Biblical Quarterly*
CIJ	Jean-Baptiste Frey, *Corpus Inscriptionum Iudaicarum*, 2 vols. (Vatican City: Pontificio istituto di archeologia cristiana, 1936, 1952)
CPJ	*Corpus Papyrorum Judaicarum*, ed. Victor A. Tcherikover and Alexander Fuks (Cambridge, Mass.: Harvard University Press, 1957–64)
CUP	Cambridge University Press
DSD	*Dead Sea Discoveries*
HTR	*Harvard Theological Review*
HUCA	*Harvard Union College Annual*
IG	*Inscriptiones Graecae* (Berlin: George Reimer, 1873–)
IGR	*Inscriptiones Graecae ad res Romanus pertinentes* (Paris: Leveux, 1911–27)
IEJ	*Israel Exploration Journal*
IES	*Israel Exploration Society*
JBL	*Journal of Biblical Literature*
JJS	*Journal of Jewish Studies*
JNES	*Journal of Near Eastern Studies*
JQR	*Jewish Quarterly Review*
JRS	*Journal of Roman Studies*
JSJ	*Journal for the Study of Judaism in the Persian, Hellenistic and Roman Periods*
JSOT	*Journal for the Study of the Old Testament*
JSS	*Journal of Semitic Studies*
LSJ	Henry George Liddell, Robert Scott, and H. Stuart Jones, *A Greek-English Lexicon*, 9th edn. with suppl. (Oxford: Clarendon Press, 1968)
NTS	*New Testament Studies*

OGIS   *Orientis Graeci Inscriptiones Selectae*, ed. Wilhelm
       Dittenberger (Leipzig: S. Hirzel, 1903–5)
OUP   Oxford University Press
PG   *Patrologia Graeca*, ed. Jacques-Paul Migne (Paris:
       Migne, 1844–)
RQ   *Revue de Qumran*
SBL   Society of Biblical Literature
SPA   *Studia Philonica Annual*
TDNT   Gerhard Kittel (ed.), *Theological Dictionary of the New
       Testament*, tr. and ed. Geoffrey W. Bromiley (Grand
       Rapids, Mich.: Eerdmans, 1964–76)
USQR   *Union Seminary Quarterly Review*
VC   *Vigiliae Christianae*
VT   *Vetus Testamentum*
WH   Ioannis Stobaeus, *Anthologius,* ed. Kurt Wachsmith
       and Otto Hense, i–iv (Berlin: Weidmannsche
       Verlagsbuchhandlung, 1958)
WHR   *Women's History Review*
ZAW   *Zeitschrift für die alttestamentliche Wissenschaft*
ZDPV   *Zeitschrift des Deutschen Palästina-Vereins*

I
Philo's 'Therapeutae' Reconsidered

When each of the choirs has sated itself by itself—as in the Bacchic rites they drink the liquor of the god's love—they blend together and become one choir from out of two, a memory of the one established of old by the Red Sea . . . [when] both men and women were filled with inspiration and became a choir singing hymns of thanksgiving to God the Saviour. The men were led by Moses the prophet, and the women by Miriam the prophetess. On this [model] most of all, the choir of the *therapeutai* and *therapeutrides* is based. They sing with [canonic] echoes and re-echoes, with men having the bass parts and women the treble, combined together, and resulting in a really musical, harmonious concord. The thoughts are lovely, the words are lovely, the choral singers are majestic, and the purpose of the thoughts and the words and the choral singers is piety.

(*Contempl.* 85, 87–8)

I

On Method

I will not add [anything] of my own for the sake of making
[my account] better, which is customary for all the poets
and chroniclers to do for want of good [historiographical]
practices, but will absolutely go about [telling] the actual
truth, even though I know the most skilled speaker would
grow weary of telling it [like this]. But nevertheless we must
persevere and fight on to the end, for the superlative virtue
of the[se] men should not be a reason to strike dumb those
who rightly think that nothing good should be passed over
in silence.

(Philo, *Contempl.* 1)

In the world of advertisement there's no such thing as a lie;
there's only the expedient exaggeration.

Roger Thornhill, in Alfred Hitchcock's *North by*
Northwest

There have been many studies on the people Philo of
Alexandria (*c.*20 BCE–*c.*50 CE) describes in his treatise, *De Vita
Contemplativa.*[1] These contemplative, mystically minded Jews,
devoted to music, meditation, and the study of scripture, who
met together for special communal meals and lived an austere,
ascetic lifestyle, are suggestive of many other more famous religious communities. Usually referred to as the 'Therapeutae',
and defined explicitly just in this one text, they are frequently
called as evidence in discussions of contemporaneous Jewish
sects, especially the Essenes and those who produced the Dead
Sea Scrolls, or of the earliest Christian churches.[2]

[1] In future cited as *Contempl.* References to Philo's works in the text are given
in accordance with the standard abbreviations of *SPA*.

[2] For a survey of literature see Jean Riaud, 'Les Thérapeutes d'Alexandrie
dans la tradition et dans la recherche critique jusqu'aux découvertes de
Qumran', *ANRW* 2: 20: 2 (Berlin and New York: Walter de Gruyter, 1987),
1189–1295. For comparison between the Therapeutae and early Christian
monastics see G. Peter Richardson, 'Philo and Eusebius on Monasteries and
Monasticism: The Therapeutae and Kellia', in Bradley H. McLean (ed.),

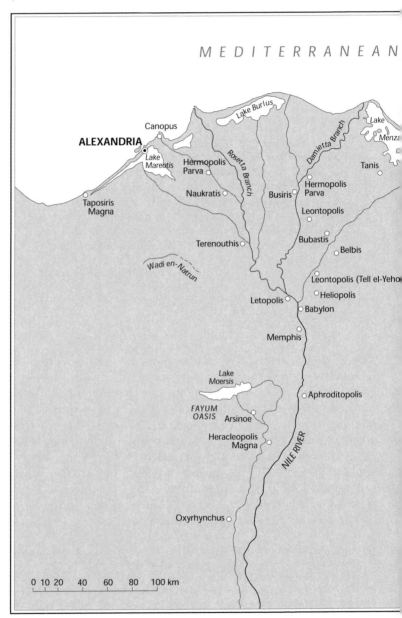

1. Map of northern Egypt in the late Ptolemaic and early Roman periods

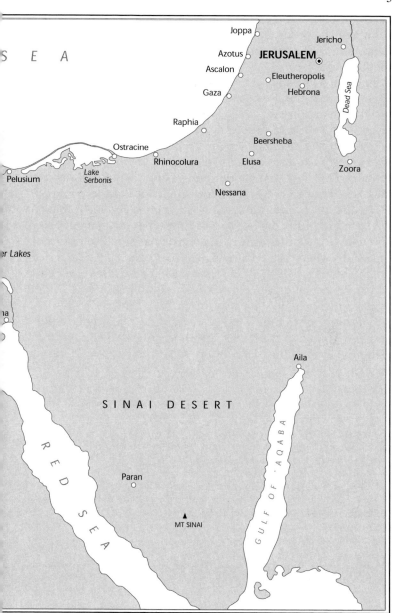

I would like here to consider various topics bearing upon the people of the group in the hope of bringing them into sharper definition, with a particular focus on women and gender.[3] I hope that this specific analysis may offer insights into various dimensions of the Jewish community of first-century Alexandria.

Having stated these goals, however, it is necessary to explain how I wish to proceed to achieve them, for at the very outset I am faced with critical issues of evidence. Historiographically, there are problems in using this text. It is generally accepted that it is not easy to make any very sure historical conclusions about what actually took place in the first century, once we move away from major political and military matters to details of social and religious history. It is certainly unwise to be too confident that one can say much with any high degree of probability when we have only one text which testifies to a particular small social group, especially when this text is highly rhetorical. The rhetorical, argumentative, nature of *Contempl.* is very clear. It is a vehicle in which Philo will drive us towards the apprehension of a single reality which will, in some way, prove his point.[4]

Contempl. champions the virtues of a quiet philosophical existence, far away from the hurly-burly of city life. Everything about the group Philo describes is good. He identifies his group as such in the first paragraph of the work, quoted above. In the

Origins and Method: Towards an Understanding of Judaism and Christianity: Essays in Honour of John C. Hurd (Sheffield: JSOT, 1993), 334–59. Studies on *Contempl.* are listed every year in the *SPA* bibliography.

[3] Interest in the women described in *Contempl.* has not been extensive, though Ross Kraemer provided a ground-breaking assessment in an article of 1989: 'Monastic Jewish Women in Greco-Roman Egypt: Philo Judaeus on the Therapeutrides', *Signs*, 14 (1989), 342–70. See also Peter Richardson and Valerie Heuchan, 'Jewish Voluntary Associations in Egypt and the Roles of Women', in John S. Kloppenborg and Stephen G. Wilson, *Voluntary Associations in the Graeco-Roman World* (London and New York: Routledge, 1996), 226–51; Holger Szesnat, ' "Mostly Aged Virgins": Philo and the Presence of the Therapeutrides at Lake Mareotis', *Neotestamentica*, 32 (1998), 191–201; id., ' "Pretty Boys" in Philo's *De Vita Contemplativa*', *SPA* 10 (1998), 87–107, cf. also id., 'Philo and Female Homoeroticism: Philo's Use of γύνανδρος and Recent Work on Tribades', *JSJ* 30 (1999), 140–7.

[4] As Chaim Perelman has defined it, rhetoric 'covers the whole range of discourse aimed at persuasion or conviction': Chaim Perelman and Lucie Olbrechts-Tyteca, tr. John Wilkinson and Purcell Weaver, *The New Rhetoric: A Treatise on Argumentation* (Notre Dame, Ind.: University of Notre Dame Press, 1969), 5.

final sentence, Philo stresses that the members of the group have received from God a reward precisely for goodness, καλοκἀγαθία (*Contempl.* 90). The only reason this group ever came to be recorded for posterity was because it was a useful model for Philo to use in his rhetorical strategy of convincing his audience of the existence of the good.

'Good' is of course a socially constructed term. What Philo or his audience perceive to be good may not be good by our definitions. Moreover, historians are concerned with what was real about the group, not what was good. We need to be very clear at the outset that our purposes are very different from Philo's, and he is not writing at all for us. In recognizing Philo's dominant concern and our own concerns, we can begin to be sensitive to the dissonance between them, and distance ourselves slightly from Philo's rhetoric, in which the people he describes are in fact pawns in an intellectual power-play between Philo and his obscure opponents. Philo himself has objectified the group of *Contempl.* as 'the good' and therefore robbed it of autonomous power. The group members are not themselves the active 'sayers' in terms of the creation of their reality. They are reified as 'that which is good'. It is fundamental that we recognize the group's own disempowered relationship to Philo's text and the role they play rhetorically before we can begin to assess their historical reality.

Philo was an expert in classical rhetoric, as this was defined by Protagoras, Antiphon, Isocrates, Aristotle, and others.[5] His work is conceptualized as a type of speech, intended to persuade a listening audience.[6] In writing about the members of this group, Philo describes things from his own social standpoint and personal interests. To put it baldly, in terms of his writing, his interest in his subjects is an exploitative one: they are to be used to prove his point. The treatise is so polemically charged that some scholars have even doubted this group had any substantial historical existence. They may have been invented out of very

[5] See Manuel Alexandre, Jr., *Rhetorical Argumentation in Philo of Alexandria* (Atlanta: Scholars Press, 1999).

[6] David A. Russell, *Criticism in Antiquity*, 2nd edn. (London: Bristol Classical Press, 1995), 96–7; David Dawson, *Allegorical Readers and Cultural Revision in Ancient Alexandria* (Berkeley, Calif.: University of California Press, 1992), 76.

little to serve Philo's purposes.[7] Can we therefore retrieve anything historical from this material?

Absolutely, for I do not think that a historian should be dissuaded from a project on account of any recognition of the rhetorical nature of the texts we may have. To set up a binary opposition between rhetoric and historical reality would be inane. We do not need to resort to defining the description of the 'Therapeutae' of *Contempl.* as fantasy, or so idealizing as to be worthless. To varying degrees, most historical evidence is embedded in rhetorical material. Evidence is found within texts designed to provide one presentation of reality for a particular persuasive purpose. In modern English, to dub something 'mere rhetoric' is to assert that it is untrue. But in the art of rhetoric—persuasion—truth functions as a very useful weapon. It is simply that this truth is not always the whole truth. It is partial, shaped truth.

In the first lines of his treatise Philo himself insists on the veracity of his account: 'I will absolutely go about telling the actual truth' (*Contempl.* 1). One could lean back cynically and suggest that this is what he might very well say, even if he were presenting a complete fabrication, for it is necessary only that his audience *believe* the account to be true. However, if it were necessary for his audience to believe his account to be true, then Philo might have situated his group much further away from Alexandria. It is characteristic of the genre of utopian fantasies

[7] e.g., Roland Bergmeier, 'Der Stand der Gottesfreunde: Zu Philos Schrift "Uber die kontemplative Lebensform"', *Bijdragen: International Journal in Philosophy and Theology*, 63/1 (2002), 46–70, argues that Philo is not describing a historical sect so much as using elements of Jewish life and customs in general and sources on the Essenes to present an image of contemplative philosophers as friends of God, and see also id., *Die Essener-Berichte des Flavius Josephus: Quellenstudien zu den Essenertexten im Werk des jüdischen Historiographen* (Kampen: Kok Pharos, 1993), 41–8; Troels Engberg-Pedersen, 'Philo's *De Vita Contemplativa* as a Philosopher's Dream', *JSJ* 30 (1999), 40–64, argues that the idealizing elements are so extensive that one could classify the treatise as 'fiction', though he does not completely doubt the existence of a real group. In this he follows Charles Guignebert, *Des prophètes à Jésus: Le Monde juif vers le temps de Jésus* (Paris: La Renaissance du livre, 1935), 320, who noted that Philo's description of the 'Therapeutae' was idealized and stylized, and that while it is likely that a group of such people did really exist, they were not necessarily as Philo described them, though cf. Doron Mendels, 'Hellenistic Utopia and the Essenes', *HTR* 72 (1979), 207–22, who pointed out that actual groups may well have modelled themselves on literary utopias.

that the ideal society is found on a very far-off island, towards the edges of the world, as in Iambulus' idealizing account of the 'children of the sun' (Diodorus Siculus, *Bibl. Hist.* 2: 55–60), written *c*.165–150 BCE.[8] No one could dispute the reliability of Iambulus' fantasy of peaceful, happy people with forked tongues, bendable bones, and amazing longevity because no one could travel far enough to the fabulous island on which they apparently lived. This type of utopian fantasy relies on the framework of a *voyage extraordinaire*, which takes the author far beyond the known world, as we find replicated in much later literary works such as Jonathan Swift's *Gulliver's Travels*.[9] The further away one went from civilization, and the closer one got to the edges of the earth, the more incredibly bizarre things became (so Herodotus, *Hist.* 3: 116).[10] But Philo locates his (decidedly

[8] See John Ferguson, *Utopias of the Classical World* (London: Thames & Hudson, 1975), 124–9. For a discussion of Iambulus, see David Winston, 'Iambulus: A Literary Study in Greek Utopianism', Ph.D. thesis, Columbia University, New York, 1956, and his summary in 'Iambulus' *Islands of the Sun* and Hellenistic Literary Utopias', *Science Fiction Studies*, 3 (1976), 219–27. The date of Iambulus' work given here follows Winston, 'A Literary Study', 38–58. Winston (ibid. 61–8) finds precedents for Iambulus' *voyage extraordinaire* in Hecataeus of Abdera's Περὶ Ὑπερβορέων (*c*.330 BCE). The exact location of this utopia—also an island—was unknown, though it was 'beyond the North Wind' (Boreas). There was also Euhemerus of Messana's Ἱερὰ Ἀναγραφή (*c*.300 BCE) about the Panchaean isles, somewhere in the Indian Ocean. Winston points out that Iambulus' utopia influenced Thomaos Campanella's *Città del Sole* (1623) and Gabriel Foigny's *Terre Australe Connue* (1676).

[9] By the end of the 2nd cent. CE, fantastic accounts of utopias—or simply odd societies—were possibly less popular than they once were, cf. Gellius, *Noctes Atticae* 9: 4: 1–4: 'We saw piles of books displayed for sale [at Brundisium] . . . including all those Greek books full of marvels and unheard of legends and remarkable things. The ancient writers were of great repute: Aristeas of Proconnesus, Isigonus of Nicaea, Ctesias, Onesicritus, Philostephanus and Hegesias, but the books had become mildewed because they had not been touched for so long.' In fact, Ctesias—who composed the *Assyriaca*, *Indica*, and *Persica*—may not have been of great repute, since more reliable ancient authors think of Ctesias and the others as mere inventors of tales: Antigonus, *Mirabilia* 15; Plutarch, *Artaxerxes* 1: 4; 6: 9; Aristotle, *Hist. Anim.* 8: 28 (606ᵃ); Arrian, *Anabasis* 5: 4: 2. Lucian parodied the genre of telling fabulous tales about remote places in his 'A True Story', which was in fact a 'pack of lies' in the grand tradition of Ctesias, Iambulus, and Homer (*Ver. Hist.* 1: 3).

[10] See James S. Romm, *The Edges of the Earth in Ancient Thought: Geography, Exploration and Fiction* (Princeton: Princeton University Press, 1992).

unfantastical) group exactly, to a particular hill (*Contempl.* 22–3) between the Mediterranean Sea and Lake Mareotis, just outside Alexandria. This city was a Roman provincial capital, the seat of the Roman prefect, station of Roman troops, and one of the greatest centres of Hellenistic civilization in antiquity. Situating a group outside Alexandria, on a busy lake, was like situating it in the suburbs of New York, rather than on the Pacific Island of Nanomana. It was reachable and verifiable.[11] No one who wished to convince an audience of the truth of total fiction would make it so easy to be found out.[12]

Secondly, the other Jewish group Philo uses for the sake of his rhetoric of 'the good', the Essenes, appears really to have existed, and his accounts of Essene characteristics in *Quod Omnis Probus Liber Sit* and the *Hypothetica* have certain parallels with the independent accounts of Pliny (*Nat. Hist.* 5: 17: 4 (73)) and Josephus (*War* 2: 119–61; *Ant.* 15: 371–3; 18: 18–22). If the Essenes were a real group, then there is every reason to suppose that the 'Therapeutae' were also.

Thirdly, there are elements in Philo's text which indicate he has massaged truth to fit his interests when the reality he perceived presented some problems for him. These will be explicated further as we proceed, but perhaps the most obvious rhetorical problem Philo has to deal with is the presence of women. As we shall see, far from being a positive trope in his discourse, Philo needs to 'explain' the presence of women in a philosophical group which could have been all the better if it had—like the Essenes—excluded women altogether. Holger Szesnat states that, in order to present the women members of the group in an acceptable way, Philo is forced into a reluctant use of the virgin motif which does not fully work: '[T]he real presence of women at Lake Mareotis seems to have forced Philo to admit that not even *all* of these women are in fact "aged virgins": they are *mostly* aged virgins.'[13] For an invented group,

[11] See Kraemer, 'Monastic Jewish Women', 347.

[12] Egypt itself could be configured as a remote land full of strange wonders in writings of the Classical world, see Georgia Frank, 'Miracles, Monks and Monuments: The *Historia Monachorum in Aegypto* as Pilgrims' Tales', in David Frankfurter (ed.), *Pilgrimage and Holy Space in Late Antique Egypt* (Leiden: Brill, 1998), 485–505 at 496, though 'Egypt' did not include Alexandria and other Hellenistic cities.

[13] See Szesnat, 'Mostly Aged Virgins', 196.

it would be easy to claim that all the women were old and un-married, which is the image Philo wants his readers to have in mind. I will return to this point in due course, but this is not the only conflict one can note in the value system of the historical 'Therapeutae' and Philo.[14] One would not invent a group with features one then had to explain away, not always very well. Philo in some ways makes a virtue out of necessity in terms of the 'woman' motif, as we shall see, but one wonders whether he would have been more comfortable excluding the women altogether.

However, scholars who are sceptical about the historicity of the text and intensely aware of the rhetorical and idealizing elements of the description are in many ways closer to my position on the text than those who have quarried it without due regard to these features. One needs to tread a middle way through this text, neither reading it as a simple repository of straightforwardly true, factual information nor as an imaginary construct bearing no or little resemblance to reality. Philo has woven his utopia with threads of reality, but in such a way as to keep us at times from seeing either the individual threads or aspects of reality he finds unimportant, useless, or problematic. In modern terms, Philo is much more of an advertising sales-person than a journalist.

In order to work out exactly where Philo presents things in a skewed way it would be helpful if there were other evidence we could use for comparative purposes. But there is no other account of the 'Therapeutae' from antiquity that we can use to assess the historicity of Philo's statements about them. Given this lack of comparative data one could either conclude that a historical assessment is impossible, since one source is not sufficient for accuracy, or else proceed on the basis of an 'if'. *If* Philo's account were in general true, what would we be able to conclude? This would not lead to verifiable facts: little here can be verifiable. It would only lead to conclusions based on the most exacting and aware reading of the text we are capable of.

[14] For more, see David Hay, 'Things Philo Said and Did Not Say about the Therapeutae', *Society of Biblical Literature Seminar Papers*, 31 (1992), 673–83, esp. 674; id., 'The Veiled Thoughts of the Therapeutae', in Robert M. Berchman (ed.), *Mediators of the Divine: Horizons of Prophecy, Divination, Dreams and Theurgy in Mediterranean Antiquity* (Atlanta: Scholars Press, 1998), 167–84.

It is then a basic presupposition of my project that for the present purposes I accept that what Philo states in regard to the group he describes in *Contempl.* is true, but not at all wholly true. Within the category of 'truth' there are some fair assessments, some exaggerations, some minimizations, and some omissions. As I noted, it is partial, shaped truth. It is axiomatic in this study that Philo has in *Contempl.* presented his reality of 'the good' with information about the group he believed to be true. However, it is his understanding of what is good that we find, and his understanding of what is truth that we must work with.

There are two levels that need to be considered in this discussion: first, Philo's highly rhetorical text itself and, secondly, the historical reality to which Philo points. What he does not say in regard to the community may be as important as what he does say.[15] His perceptions of the community might not be completely correct, and even when they are, he may be presenting things in a particular way to avoid any problems in his discourse.

We need to step back from the text, and refuse to read it as a collection of objective, factual information, even though it is still overall in the broad category of 'truth' rather than falsehood. The rhetoric itself may provide us with clues about what was real for the group, not only the supposedly informative elements of the text. When at times the rhetoric is designed to make us not see something real that Philo has already alluded to, this is highly significant for this study. This is where the rhetoric founders slightly because of a historical reality which Philo perceives but is uncomfortable with. Such instances are examples of rhetorical dissonance, and at various points in this study we shall consider them.

As I have stated, historians—all of us together engaged in consideration of the 'Therapeutae'—are concerned with what was real about the group. It does not matter to us whether the group was good, by our definitions.[16] We are very different from

---

[15] Ibid.

[16] This is not meant to indicate that historians have no concern to establish 'the good' in history. In certain historical studies, this may well be the intention. In my case, I admit that I am attracted to the group partly because there seems to be a possibility that it embraced ideals of sexual equity, and therefore I wish to see whether this notion can be sustained by means of historical analysis. So I am intrigued by the possiblity of what I perceive to be a

Philo. If we were to visit the community that Philo may have visited, what might we see? Clearly, we would ask different questions to those Philo asked, and we would present what we saw differently, for different purposes. Can we get past Philo's rhetoric and see the group, as if paying it a visit from the present? If Philo describes the 'Therapeutae' in one way, can I legitimately describe them in an alternative way, not tied to his world-view, social situation, or even his time?

Yes, indeed, but this description will of course be linked to varying degrees to my world-view, social situation, and time, and that is probably how history must be, for we ourselves are woven into the fabric of our own cultural discourses. Most historians today do not have the confidence of nineteenth-century positivists, who felt bolder about ripping through the fictions in order to rescue the facts, sure of their own purely objective stance and unbiased motives.[17] To what extent can we truly understand Philo's purposes or stand back from our own in order to create an 'objective' historical truth?[18] Such questions now bother contemporary historians of all periods and places, and they shall bother us as we progress. Yet historians will nevertheless assert that there is history to be recovered; it is only that there is not one history, but multiple histories that sometimes overlap and sometimes clash, since people have different experiences of reality and different historical memories, and historians write from their own different cultural and social standpoints.[19]

'good'. However, it is not my aim at the outset to prove that there existed in history a model of the good in terms of sexual equity, but rather to explore how this group may have configured gender in such a way as to result in Philo's text. Many other dimensions of the group are also of interest to me, but only this element has a strong ideological resonance.

[17] The influence of postmodern theory has much to do with the current situation. See for an overview of postmodernism's contribution to debates within the social sciences: Pauline Marie Rosenau, *Post-Modernism and the Social Sciences: Insights, Inroads, and Intrusions* (Princeton: Princeton University Press, 1992).

[18] In the view of Hayden White, all historical writing is an exercise in overt or covert rhetoric, so Hayden White, *Metahistory: The Historical Imagination in Nineteenth Century Europe* (Baltimore and London: Johns Hopkins University Press, 1973); id., 'The Historical Text as Literary Artifact', in Brian Fay, Philip Pomper, and Richard T. Vann (eds.), *History and Theory: Contemporary Readings* (Oxford: Blackwell, 1998), 15–33.

[19] For recent examinations of historiography, see Allan J. Lichtman and

This does not invalidate history; it simply values multiplicities. What is perceived as real now will depend on many factors, and what is perceived as real in the past will also be multiple. In terms of the group Philo describes, only Philo could have perceived and written about it in the way he does. Members of the group would have described themselves differently. An Egyptian from Bubastis would have described them in an alternative way, as would a Roman soldier, a village woman, a slave, or a child. What any observer (or self-observer) would have considered important, or believed they perceived, would all be different. And yet there would still have been a group living on that hill outside Alexandria with certain real features that all observers would be encountering, whether they were emic or etic in relation to it. As noted above, if we had independent alternative witnesses for establishing core data our chances of making secure statements about the real 'Therapeutae' would be much greater. But we only have Philo, with all of his baggage of ideas, presuppositions, and intentions.

Philo's detailed knowledge of the procedures of the community may show that he himself had visited it, learning from these people, or that he was using the account of an eyewitness. Philo notes that their special meeting is so silent that no one ventures 'to breathe too forcefully' (*Contempl.* 75), which seems a kind of awareness that only comes from personally being in a very quiet room where one becomes inordinately self-aware of the loudness of one's own breathing. Later, when he enthuses about the music (*Contempl.* 88) one detects in his detailed description and slightly exaggerated praise that he has actually heard the music.[20]

Nevertheless, even eyewitness accounts can be highly rhetorical, and present things extremely selectively. So the fundamental problem of evidence is acute. There are clues and materials that help to corroborate the evidence at certain points, but, in the end, this historical exploration will remain more of an

Valerie French, *Historians and the Living Past: The Theory and Practice of History* (Arlington Heights: Harlan Davidson, 1986), 127–39; Lawrence Stone, *The Past and the Present Revisited* (London: Routledge & Kegan Paul, 1987), 1–27, and Fay *et al.*, *History and Theory*.

[20] Kraemer thinks that Philo may indicate he had lived within the community at one time (cf. *Spec.* 3: 1–6; *Leg.* 2: 85), 'Monastic Jewish Women', 343, which is certainly very possible.

argument than a cool collection of proved points. This study is itself an exercise in rhetoric. It is aimed at convincing my colleagues in ancient history—all of those journeying with me by reading this book—of the plausibility of seeing the group as I have come to see it, by following the processes I have undertaken to explore the material. To assert that only one view of historical reality is acceptable here would be to claim a bogus absolute authority. It is common within feminist and postmodern circles to avoid such a claim.[21] There is for me, in this historical journey, the authority that comes from having carefully undertaken it with as much rigour as possible, but I am a facilitating guide only.

As noted above, I myself am particularly interested in the subject of women and gender, both within Philo's rhetoric and in the group he observed, hence the title of this book. If we are to concentrate on women and gender, on the basis of evidence that largely comprises what men like Philo write about such topics, we need expansive and radical strategies not only in terms of subject matter but also method, and we must remain modest in our expectations. Philo's account of the 'Therapeutae' is itself really a story of men, in which women feature as a slightly marginal and curious element. In the first paragraph quoted above, Philo refers to the 'the virtue of the(se) men', τῆς τῶν ἀνδρῶν ἀρετῆς, meaning males, not people. It is necessary to stand back suspiciously from Philo's rhetoric, and not accept the androcentric vision of Philo. It is by careful hermeneutical strategies employed on the text and by knowledge of the world of the text that we see things a little more clearly.[22]

---

[21] I do not wish to equate feminist and postmodernist historians, even though some methodological presuppositions may be shared. Some feminists adopt postmodern strategies, and others reject them. For the debate see Somer Brodribb, *Nothing Mat(t)ers: A Feminist Critique of Postmodernism* (North Melbourne: Spinifex Press, 1992); Joan Hoff, 'Gender as a Postmodern Category of Paralysis', *WHR* 3 (1994), 149–68; Susan Kingsley Kent, 'Mistrals and Diatribulations: A Reply to Joan Hoff', *WHR* 5 (1996), 9–18; Caroline Ramazangolu, 'Unravelling Postmodern Paralysis: A Response to Joan Hoff', *WHR* 5 (1996), 19–23; Joan Hoff, 'A Reply to my Critics', *WHR* 5 (1996), 25–30. For a critique of Foucaldian theory and practice centring on the question of sexuality in antiquity, see Amy Richlin, *The Garden of Priapus: Sexuality and Agression in Roman Humor*, 2nd edn. (New York: OUP, 1992), pp. xiii–xxxiii.

[22] For this see the hermeneutical theory developed by Elisabeth Schüssler

In configuring a key focus as being 'women and gender' here I wish to tread a middle way between polarities of women's and gender history, since I see any debate about the merits of one or the other unnecessarily dichotomous.[23] Some scholars note that the essentialist categorization of 'women' as a unified whole ignores the important differences between women which mitigates against any commonality or unified experience.[24] Scholars of women's history, however, generally accept the disruptive and undermining effects of racial and class division on women's shared experience, while affirming that 'women as a group cut through male class systems'.[25] Women in diverse social groups are different from otherwise comparable men, on account of the constructions of gender prevalent in cultures. The study of women therefore takes place within the broader study of gender.

Much of the study of women in antiquity is compensative in that it tries to make the women visible.[26] In some ways, this is precisely what I would like to do here. My interest is in balance. A focus on women serves to balance our knowledge of the world

Fiorenza in regard to early Christian texts: 'Text and Reality—Reality as Text: The Problem of a Feminist Historical and Social Reconstruction based on Texts', *Studia Theologica*, 43 (1989), 19–34; ead., 'The Rhetoricity of Historical Knowledge: Pauline Discourse and its Contextualizations', in Lukas Bornkamm, Kelly del Tredici, and Angela Starthartinger (eds.), *Religious Propaganda and Missionary Competition in the New Testament World: Essays Honoring Dieter Georgi* (Leiden: Brill, 1994), 443–69.

[23] See for some of this debate and the wider issues involved: Gisela Bock, 'Women's History and Gender History: Aspects of an International Debate', *Gender and History*, 1 (1989), 7–30; Judith M. Bennett, 'Feminism and History', *Gender and History*, 1 (1989), 251–72; Bridget Hill, 'Women's History: A Study in Change, Continuity or Standing Still?', *WHR* 2 (1993), 5–22; Judith M. Bennett, 'Women's History: A Reply to Bridget Hill', *WHR* 2 (1993), 173–84; Joan Wallach Scott, *Gender and the Politics of History* (New York: Columbia University Press, 1988), 3—ch. 1 reprints her 'Gender: A Useful Category of Historical Analysis', *American Historical Review*, 91 (1986), 1053–75.

[24] See Denise Riley, *'Am I that Name?': Feminism and the Category of 'Women' in History* (Minneapolis: University of Minnesota, 1988).

[25] Joan Kelly-Gadol, 'The Social Relation of the Sexes: Methodological Implications of Women's History', *Signs*, 1 (1976), 813–23.

[26] See Richlin, *Garden of Priapus*, p. xxi. Please see the up-to-date bibliographies for the study of women in antiquity in the excellent website www.stoa.org/diotima.

of the past. If we replicate the androcentrism of our sources, this view of history simply does not give us the resources we need for a holistic understanding of antiquity. It is therefore important not to see the study of women and gender as a ghetto in which only women live. It is not a case of accepting 'history' as already fully established and then of fitting women or any other 'others' into this pre-existent arrangement, but rather of letting the myriad voices of the past reinvent ancient history as a whole. Any focus on a group defined as 'other' (women, children, sex-workers, labourers, slaves, foreigners, and so on) in our sources is likely to open up dimensions of texts hitherto unseen, as long as we turn things around so that they are no longer 'others'.

From the foregoing comments it should be clear that my own position is neither one of extreme postmodern reality-subjectivism nor one of archaic positivism, but one which draws upon both epistemological polarities. I believe, however, that to some degree my work is still technically 'empiricist' in that it relies on the careful testing of material from the most impartial position that I am able to attain, given my constraints, if that material can be tested.[27] In the case of *Contempl.* our best method of testing is in contextualizing both the rhetoric and the historical reality to which *Contempl.* points. My strategies, stated above, are certainly not of the old school, but do rely on the collection of evidence and the careful assessment of it. Critiques of old-style empiricism, or more correctly positivism, have pointed out the false nature of claims to objectivity, and post-modernists have heralded the old fault of 'subjectivism' as now not only acceptable but inescapable. However, one does not need to claim complete impartiality in order to subscribe to the basic principles of openness and the testing of material that are the foundations of empirical method. Historians can test the limits of our own endurance and push beyond the subjective in order to accept the 'other' in history, and to let history challenge us on its own terms.

Postmodern, or post-structural, theory has done much to address issues of power relations and multiple realities in

[27] Empiricism takes its name from the *Empeirikoi* or *Empirici*, a school of ancient physicians who stressed the importance of noting observable phenomena and experience, and drawing conclusions from these. They are considered to be among the founders of scientific method.

the world of antiquity, and our own entrapment in cultural discourses, which I completely accept. The very fact that communication about 'reality' takes place by means of language itself indicates to some post-structuralists that we are stuck in the present, for language itself is a system of signifiers and concepts which reflects cultural ideology, which the individual cannot help but replicate in discourses.[28] Despite acknowledging this, it seems necessary for me to assert that language reflects more than cultural ideology, and can be used both to transcend ideology and express realities with neutral cultural valences. Good historical method, of whatever form, can encourage us to value all evidence openly, and listen to all the voices of the past, acknowledging no single hegemonic model of evidence, therefore creating dissonances which can move us beyond our own time and culture. The languages of the ancient world constantly undermine our own 'culturalism' by refusing to bend to our current words and phrases, and it is with the excitement of discovery that we allow their words and concepts to challenge us. If the women of antiquity appear to be like foreign words for which there is no modern English equivalent, then all well and good. As all this discussion I hope indicates, I subscribe completely to empiricist ideals of an open-minded view of history, as far as I am able to attain it, and the freedom to ask questions.

Given the paucity of my primary evidence, I am concerned in this study to establish context in various different areas. Historians' methods are often determined by the nature of the evidence we are dealing with. By means of contextualizing elements in Philo's discussion, and drawing out the wider worlds of meaning in the text and its background, more historical information seems to come to light which may increase our knowledge of the world of the text and therefore our ability to understand both Philo's rhetoric and the historical reality he points to.

Along with this process of contextualization, I approach the text with a strong focus on rhetorical criticism, which allows the alternative realities Philo wishes to ignore or suppress to come to

---

[28] For a good overview of postmodernism (including post-structuralism) and history, see: Joyce Appleby, Lynn Hunt, and Margaret Jacob, *Telling the Truth about History* (New York and London: W. W. Norton & Co., 1994), 198–237, and see Franklin R. Ankersmit, 'Historiography and Postmodernism', in Fay *et al.*, *History and Theory*, 175–92.

the fore. In these strategies, the central axis on which the discussion revolves is Philo's text. Historical reconstruction works *via* Philo's text, since this is the road we need to travel down in order to find anything about our subject, but in walking down this road we may discover new ways of seeing that enable us to gain a better insight into realities that Philo wished us not to notice. In all these manœuvres, I am seeking more evidence. Ultimately, all historical work relies on an assessment of what evidence is sound and what is not.

In terms of the structure of this book, I begin by looking at Philo and the reasons why he may have written *Contempl*. This is perhaps the most 'historical' of all the chapters, in that it establishes a certain sequence of events and rationale for the text. It is through this analysis that I present a context for the rhetoric, which forms the foundation of everything else that follows. I then consider the name of the group commonly known as the 'Therapeutae', and the rhetorical nature of this name. After this I consider the group's geographical situation and socio-economic character, especially in terms of Alexandrian society.

Next, I move out again to consider the way Judaism was conceptualized as *philosophia* in the Graeco-Roman world (not only by Philo), which is necessary before considering not only Philo's construction of the group but its own self-identity. The group's use of an (extreme) allegorical method of interpreting scripture, their asceticism, and their particular type of solar calendar will be considered as indicating the wider milieu from which they are drawn. This examination provides evidence that at least some Jewish women in Alexandria were educated, learning scriptural interpretation and seriously following the life of philosophy.

In writing about the group of *Contempl.*, Philo works with the recognition that this is a kind of philosophical school of thought, a αἵρεσις (*Contempl.* 29). In identifying the group as such, certain preconceived notions of 'the life of philosophy' and 'philosophical women' will obtain. I then explore concepts of philosophical women in Graeco-Roman society as evidenced in extant literature, in order to contextualize the ideas Philo and his readership may have had about them. Following on from this, I focus on how Philo constructs the women of *Contempl.* and why.

There is then a chapter on spatial arrangements, including the topic of clothing. The interest here is in how the group defined space—both public and private and personal—in terms of gender. We then turn to spirituality. Philo's own understandings of spirituality and his interpretations of the Exodus traditions enable us to gain considerable insight into the central significance of the group's celebrations of the crossing of the Red Sea every forty-nine days. The group appears to preserve lost traditions of the inspired song and prophecy of Miriam, which surface in fragmentary form in later haggadic literature or pseudepigraphical material, and in a fragment from the Dead Sea Scrolls.

There is no one neat 'rhetorical' section and another 'historical' section, but explorations in both areas are found throughout this book. While I have divided the analysis into two main parts, the first in which I focus on matters of the group of people called the 'Therapeutae' as a whole and the second in which I focus on issues of women and gender, I would strongly caution against anyone trying to read one section alone. General conclusions about the group as a whole are found within the second section, and vice versa: observations regarding women and gender are found in the first. Overall, this book is much more than a study of the Jewish women philosophers who lived as members of this group. It is a proposal that we try to see the people known as the 'Therapeutae' in a new light, within the diversity of Alexandrian Judaism in the Roman period. It is a beginning rather than an end.

2
Philo's *De Vita Contemplativa* in Historical Context

Philo became known as a remarkable man to many, not only among us, but also among those who had sprung from outside [i.e. classical] education. He was ethnically Hebrew by origin, and second to none in terms of the illustrious men in Alexandria. It is clear to all concerning the work [he did], how hard he toiled in the Scriptures and the nation's learning. It is hardly necessary to speak of his position in regard to philosophy and the liberal arts of outside education, especially in his zealous study of Plato and Pythagoras, in which it is related that he surpassed all of his contemporaries.

(Eusebius, *Hist. Eccles.* 2: 4: 2–3[1])

What we know about Philo 2000 years after his birth is little more than what Eusebius tells us at the beginning of the fourth century. We can determine almost as much as what Eusebius writes from the internal evidence of Philo's own copious writings and, like Eusebius, we can look to Josephus for some additional scanty information. For example, Josephus writes that Philo was the brother of the wealthy and influential Alexander, who became Jewish alabarch,[2] that he was 'not ignorant of philosophy' and that he was the leader of an Alexandrian Jewish delegation to Gaius Caligula (Josephus, *Ant.* 18: 259). All these assertions seem consistent with Philo's writings.

Philo was a member of an elite, Alexandrian Jewish family, and he lived in the first part of the first century CE.[3] We have only

[1] My translation from the Greek text given by Kirsopp Lake, *Eusebius, The Ecclesiastical History*, i (Loeb Classical Library; Cambridge, Mass.: Harvard University Press, 1926), 116.

[2] A term indicating leadership of the Jewish community in regard to the Roman administration of Alexandria.

[3] For introductions to Philo and his writings see Erwin R. Goodenough, *An Introduction to Philo Judaeus* (Oxford: Basil Blackwell, 1962); Samuel Sandmel, *Philo of Alexandria: An Introduction* (New York: OUP, 1979); Jenny Morris,

a sketchy idea of the dates of his birth and death. Philo was writing of events concerned with the reign of Caligula when he was, apparently, old (*Legat.* 1); he was already the eldest of the five men who went to visit the emperor (*Legat.* 182). He may then have died sometime in the mid to late 40s or possibly as late as the 50s, and may have been born perhaps as early as 30 BCE[4] (the more usual dates being 10–20 BCE[5]), but we can only really give possible outside parameters for his chronology. He apparently did not live to see the destruction of Jerusalem in 70 CE, or else there would probably have been some comment from him about this event. There are extant 36 treatises by Philo, and several more parts and fragments of treatises, all of which have been scrutinized for any possible factual information about his life, but little more is sure in terms of history.

From what we do know, we can identify that Philo's perspective was of one who was wealthy and extremely well-educated, not only in Judaism but also in classical scholarship.[6] Philo's extant work comprises treatises which present Jewish law and lore in a form comprehensible to those familiar with concepts deriving from Graeco-Roman philosophy.[7] This recognition is

---

'The Jewish Philosopher Philo', in Emil Schürer, *The History of the Jewish People in the Age of Jesus Christ* (175 B.C.–A.D. 135), iii/2, rev. and ed. by Geza Vermes, Fergus Millar, and Martin Goodman (Edinburgh: T. & T. Clark, 1987), 809–70; Ronald Williamson, *Jews in the Hellenistic World: Philo* (Cambridge: CUP, 1989); Peder Borgen, *Philo of Alexandria: An Exegete for his Time* (Leiden: Brill, 1992).

[4] Williamson, *Philo*, 1.

[5] Morris, 'Philo', 816.

[6] He claims himself to have been the best educated of the delegation to Gaius (*Legat.* 182) and seems to have had a basically positive attitude to Greek education. This does not mean he accepted all of what it taught him. For an exploration of Philo's perspectives on the Greek *encyclia*, see Alan Mendelson, *Secular Education in Philo of Alexandria* (Cincinnati: Hebrew Union College Press, 1982).

[7] For explorations of Philo's philosophy and its relationship with Platonism and other philosophies see the discussions in *SPA* 5 (1993), and, in particular: James Drummond, *Philo Judaeus or the Jewish Alexandrian Philosophy in its Development and Completion*, 2 vols. (London: Williams & Norgate, 1888; Amsterdam: Philo Press, 1969); Thomas H. Billings, *The Platonism of Philo Judaeus* (Chicago: University of Chicago Press, 1919); Harry A. Wolfson, *Philo: Foundations of Religious Philosophy in Judaism, Christianity and Islam*, 2 vols. (Cambridge, Mass.: Harvard University Press, 1947); Arthur D. Nock, 'Philo and Hellenistic Philosophy', in Z. Stewart (ed.), *Essays on Religion and*

basic in terms of an initial approach to any text from his corpus of work.

We gain a greater understanding of Philo and his works when we place him within the context of the city in which he lived. Some understanding of Alexandria and the problems facing the Jewish community of this city helps further to illuminate the man himself and the terrible events in which he found himself embroiled, and also helps to explain the context in which *Contempl.* was written.

In Philo's day, Alexandria was one of the greatest cities in the world. Founded as a Greek colony by Alexander the Great in 331 BCE, it had become a major port on the trade route between Europe and Asia. Consequently, the city had grown to be cosmopolitan and ethnically mixed, a place where new ideas would be exchanged and intellectual achievement was highly valued, amid a Hellenistic cultural milieu. Despite being located in Egypt, and the area capital, Alexandria was a quintessentially 'Greek', post-colonial, Roman-ruled *polis* which was in many respects unique in antiquity.[8] It was outward-looking towards the Mediterranean and the East rather than inward-looking to the rest of Egypt, and the Roman provincial capital. Aptly, its official title in Roman times was Ἀλεξάνδρεια πρὸς Αἰγύπτῳ, *Alexandria ad Aegyptum*: 'Alexandria-by-Egypt'.[9] The Roman

---

the *Ancient World*, 2 vols. (Cambridge: CUP, 1972), 559–65; David T. Runia, *Philo of Alexandria and the Timaeus of Plato* (Leiden: Brill, 1986); Robert Berchman, *From Philo to Origen: Middle Platonism in Transition* (Chico, Calif.: Scholars, 1984); A. P. Bos, 'Philo of Alexandria: A Platonist in the Image and Likeness of Aristotle', *SPA* 10 (1998), 66–86.

[8] One may refer to Alexandria in the 1st cent. as 'Roman' in terms of administration and government, though it would not be correct to consider it 'Roman' culturally, or even 'Graeco-Roman' at this early stage. It remained essentially Hellenistic in terms of its cultural identity. For discussion of Egypt's 'Romanity' see Naphtali Lewis, '"Greco-Roman Egypt": Fact or Fiction?', in Deborah H. Sandmel (ed.), *Proceedings of the Twelfth International Congress of Papyrology* (Toronto: A. M. Hakkert, 1970), 3–14.

[9] For the title in Philo see *Prob.* 125; *Legat.* 250, cf. Ptolemy, *Geogr.* 4: 5: 56; Strabo, *Geogr.* 5: 17; P. Oxy. I: 35. For an extensive examination of Alexandria see Peter M. Fraser, *Ptolemaic Alexandria*, 3 vols. (Oxford: Clarendon Press, 1972), and, for a briefer overview, Dorothy Sly, *Philo's Alexandria* (London and New York: Routledge, 1996). For a concise summary, see Eleanor Huzar, 'Alexandria ad Aegytpum in the Juleo-Claudian Age', *ANRW* 2: 10: 1 (1988), 619–68, and H. I. Bell, 'Alexandria ad Aegyptum', *JRS* 36 (1946), 130–3.

prefect of the province was likewise titled 'Prefect of Alexandria and Egypt'.

Only very recently, Alexandria had been the seat of the Ptolemaic rulers, the line of one of Alexander's Macedonian generals. It was not long before Philo's birth that the last queen of the Ptolemaic line, Cleopatra VII, committed suicide after her defeat with Mark Antony at the battle of Actium (31 BCE). Direct rule from Rome thereafter ensured that Alexandria—and the rest of Egypt—was kept in control by the *augusti*. Roman prefects took the place of the Ptolemaic administration and gradually Romanized administrative and fiscal government.[10]

It was a large city, with a population of around 500,000.[11] From a variety of different sources, literary, papyrological, and epigraphic, we know that this population of Alexandria comprised a large melting-pot of different ethnic groups which were broadly divided—for the purpose of administration—into the categories of 'Greek' (Hellene) and Egyptian.[12] 'Greek' was not

---

[10] There was probably not a very radical change in terms of city administration, but there was some progressive alteration, see Huzar, 'Alexandria', 620. The city *boulē* had been removed prior to the Romans, possibly under Ptolemy VIII Euergetes II, who expelled the intellectuals of Alexandria, see Alan K. Bowman, *Egypt under the Pharaohs 332 BC—AD 642, from Alexander to the Arab Conquest,* 2nd edn. (London: British Museum, 1996), 211. Despite the removal of the *ethnarches* in 11 CE some would argue that much continued the same, see Claire Préaux, 'Les Continuités dans l'Egypte gréco-romaine', *Actes du Xe Congrès internationale de Papyrologiques* (Warsaw: Zaklad Narodowy Im. Ossolinskich, 1961), 231–48. Nevertheless, progressive Romanization brought significant changes that would ultimately reduce the status and unique position of Alexandria, see Alan K. Bowman and Dominic Rathbone, 'Cities and Administration in Roman Egypt', *JRS* 82 (1992), 107–27.

[11] See Diana Delia, 'The Population of Roman Alexandria', *Transactions of the American Philological Association,* 118 (1988), 275–92.

[12] Fraser, *Ptolemaic Alexandria,* 38–92; Huzar, 'Alexandria', 630–8, see *Apion* 2: 71–2. In terms of families in the Fayum, papyrological evidence indicates that the majority of men had Greek names but that they often married women with Egyptian names, see Sarah Pomeroy, *Families in Classical and Hellenistic Greece* (Oxford: Clarendon, 1998), 119–20, esp. 123–4 and see for a perceptive analysis of issues of ethnicity: Roger S. Bagnall, 'The People of the Roman Fayum', in Morris L. Bierbrier, *Portraits and Masks: Burial Customs in Roman Egypt* (London: British Museum, 1997), 7–15, who argues that *Hellenes* in the Roman *Gnomon of the Idios Logos* are really a kind of subcategory of *Aiguptioi*, the residents of the (Hellenized) chief towns of the nomes. In Ptolemaic law there was a distinction between people designated Hellene and

so much an ethnic but a cultural and administrative term, and Jews may have been part of the administrative category. The 'Greek' population was further divided into citizen *Alexandreis*, who enjoyed certain privileges like exemption from the poll-tax, and non-citizens. The Jewish situation in Alexandria during the first century CE has been much discussed, especially in regard to the question of status and rights, and only the most critical points for our subject will here be considered.[13]

It seems clear that the Jewish population of the city was large and spread out in all of the five areas (*A, B, Γ, Δ, E*), but mainly in areas *Δ* and *B* (*Flacc.* 8; *War* 2: 494–8; *Apion* 1: 33–5). Debate concerning the history of the Jews in first-century Alexandria has focused on what the Jewish community wanted to achieve and what their political and legal status was in the city.[14] If Jews had citizenship, for example, what would this mean in terms of their participation in civic cults and associations?[15]

Philo himself claims that Jews had been fully *Alexandreis* but that their citizen status had been attacked by the prefect

---

Egyptian, and within the Hellene category were not only those who could trace their ancestry to Greek immigrants but immigrants from elsewhere also: Thracians, Paeonians, Judaeans (Jews), and Idumaeans. In other words our distinction, useful in modern scholarship, between 'Greeks' and 'Jews' does not necessarily reflect the terminology of the 1st cent., see Ellen Birnbaum, 'Philo on the Greeks: A Jewish Perspective on Culture and Society in First-Century Alexandria', *SPA* 13 (2001), 37–58.

[13] See Fraser, *Ptolemaic Alexandria*, 54–8; Victor A. Tcherikover, *Hellenistic Civilisation and the Jews* (New York: Jewish Publication Society of America, 1959), 320–8; E. Mary Smallwood, *The Jews under Roman Rule from Pompey to Diocletian: A Study in Political Relations* (Leiden: Brill, 1981), 220–50; Joseph Mélèze-Modrzejewski, *The Jews of Egypt: From Rameses II to Emperor Hadrian* (Philadelphia: Jewish Publication Society of America, 1995); Ariyeh Kasher, *The Jews in Hellenistic and Roman Egypt* (Tubingen: J. C. B. Mohr [Paul Siebeck], 1985); Borgen, *Philo of Alexandria*, 14–45.

[14] See esp. Kasher, *The Jews*, passim, and Erwin R. Goodenough, *The Jurisprudence of the Jewish Courts in Egypt: Legal Administration by the Jews under the Early Roman Empire as Described by Philo Judaeus* (New Haven: Yale University Press, 1929).

[15] See E. Mary Smallwood (ed. and tr.), *Legatio ad Gaium* (Leiden: Brill, 1961), 13–14. Smallwood doubts that most Jews could have had full citizenship because they would have had to participate in public institutions that would have caused problems for their religion. Only those Jews who had become very Hellenized (i.e. the modernists) would then have been counted as fully *Alexandreis*.

A. Avillius Flaccus in 38 CE (*Legat.* 194; 363; *Flacc.* 53–4).[16] Philo clearly saw himself as that class of real 'Greek' Alexandrians different from the inferior Egyptians and 'Barbarian' visitors, but many pagan 'Greeks'—if one can call them that—seem to have held different views about Jewish claims. Eleanor Huzar has noted that, given the ethnic mix of the city, to be a 'Greek' signified language and culture, not blood, and presumed a basic elementary education for boys in the *palaestra* and gymnasium.[17] Citizenship seems to have depended on boys' enrolment in the *ephebeia*.[18] An edict of Claudius in 41 CE (see below) presupposes that Jews participated in the gymnasium,[19] and Philo indicates he was educated as a Greek (*Congr.* 74–6). Actually, whatever Jewish status was, it is unlikely that Jews were forced to participate in any cults that would have compromised their sense of the proper worship of God, since in *Apion* 65–7 Josephus indicates that the Jews' refusal to participate in the city cults was one of the charges *against* them. It seems quite likely that our difficulty in trying to establish the precise legal status of Jews in Alexandria in the first century reflects the ambiguity of the Jews' actual position in regard to citizenship at that time. That is the whole point of the dispute. Jews were apparently *Alexandreis* while not necessarily full citizens. They had a special status with certain exemptions and a degree of legal autonomy, and were administrated by a Jewish *gerousia*—council of elders—and the Jewish alabarch.[20]

[16] See also Josephus, *War* 2: 487–8. Strabo does not say that Jews were citizens, but he does indicate they had a special position in the city, with an area set aside for them and an ethnarch who presided over the courts.

[17] Huzar, 'Alexandria', 633. See also Mendelson, *Secular Education,* 25–6.

[18] Bowman and Rathbone, 'Cities and Administration', 115.

[19] *CPJ* 2: 153, ll. 92–3, and see Harold A. Harris, *Greek Athletics and the Jews* (Cardiff: University of Wales Press, 1976); Allen Kerkeslager, 'Maintaining Jewish Identity in the Greek Gymnasium: A "Jewish Load" in *CPJ* 3.519 (= P. Schub. 37 = P. Berol. 13406)', *JSJ* 28 (1997), 12–33.

[20] To what extent the Jewish community was collectively a *politeuma* is debated, see Mélèze-Modrzejewski, *Jews of Egypt,* 82. The term is found in the *Letter of Aristeas* 310, copied by Josephus (*Ant.* 12: 108). For the standard definition of the *politeuma* and the Jews' status in Alexandria see Tcherikover, *Hellenistic Civilization,* 296–329; Smallwood, *The Jews,* 224–35. Sylvie Honigman has critiqued assessments of this *politeuma* as being too influenced by a 'ghetto' model from medieval Europe, see her 'Philon, Flavius Josèphe, et la citoyenneté alexandrine: Vers une utopie politique', *JJS* 48 (1997), 62–90, esp. 63–4.

Whatever the status of the Jews, it is clear that they had once enjoyed special exemptions and privileges which ensured a degree of autonomy (*Flacc.* 78–80) and that they felt in some way deprived of them by 38–9. Jews had been among the earliest settlers in Alexandria, during the time of Ptolemy I (304–283 BCE), according to Josephus (*Apion* 1: 186–9; *Ant.* 12: 8). Their special position may have been obtained through military services: Jews had a special militia that could be used in support of (and sometimes against) Ptolemaic rulers (*Ant.* 13: 353–64; cf. *War* 1: 33; 7: 421–36; *Ant.* 13: 62–73; *Apion* 2: 49–56).[21] This involved them also in dealings with Rome. In 55 BCE the Jewish militia aided Ptolemy XII Auletes, who was affiliated with the Roman commander Gabinius (*War.* 1: 175; *Ant.* 14: 98–9). A little later, the Jewish militia acted in support of Roman interests, aiding Caesar in 48 BCE (*War* 1: 187; *Ant.* 14: 127–32), and gaining certain privileges from him (*Ant.* 14: 188–9; *Apion* 2: 37).[22] Augustus apparently thanked the Jews for services against Cleopatra VII (*Apion* 2: 60) and guaranteed Jews' special status and privileges (*Flacc.* 50; 74; *Ant.* 14: 188).[23] Philo's own writings indicate he was favourable to the Roman Senate and the imperial family—the house of Augustus—though this may be differentiated from his feelings regarding the realities of Roman (mis-)rule in Alexandria, and his distaste for Gaius Caligula.[24]

In Philo's day the Jewish alabarch was his brother, Gaius Julius Alexander (*Ant.* 18: 259), who is known to have lent money to Cypros, the wife of Jewish king Julius Herod Agrippa I (*Ant.* 18: 159–60), and managed Antonia's estates (*Ant.* 19:

---

[21] This military role for Jews in Egypt is found in texts stretching back to the 7th cent. BCE, see Kasher, *The Jews*, 1–12; Mélèze-Modrzejewski, *Jews of Egypt*, 83–7. The Jewish community of the 2nd cent. BCE would have been part of the category of 'mercenaries' described by Polybius (*Hist.* 34: 14: 1–5 = Strabo, *Geogr.* 17: 1: 12/797), who settled in the time of Ptolemy VIII Euergetes II, 145–116 BCE. On the military role for Jews see also John M. G. Barclay, *Jews in the Mediterranean Diaspora: From Alexander to Trajan (323 BCE–117 CE)* (Edinburgh: T. & T. Clark, 1996), 35–41.

[22] See Kasher, *The Jews*, 13–17.   [23] Huzar, 'Alexandria', 635–6.

[24] He praises Augustus in particular (e.g. *Legat.* 143–51; *Flacc.* 74), see below, though (rather oddly) against this see Erwin R. Goodenough, *The Politics of Philo Judaeus: Practice and Theory* (New Haven: Yale University Press, 1938), who argued that Philo was generally critical of Roman rule, and see his *Introduction*, 52–74. See further R. Barraclough, 'Philo's Politics: Roman Rule and Hellenistic Judaism', *ANRW* 2: 21: 1 (1984), 417–553.

276, cf. 20: 100).[25] Both factors indicate that he was very wealthy. Philo's nephew, Tiberius Julius Alexander, became Roman prefect of Egypt under Nero.[26] To what extent all the leading Jewish families of Alexandria were basically pro-Roman in the first century is difficult to assess, but a collection of writings known as *The Acts of the Pagan Martyrs* (*Acta Alexandrinorum*) associates Jews with the Roman authorities, who violently oppress the 'Greeks' of the city, from the time of Claudius to Septimius Severus.[27] Having this 'other side' to the dispute is very valuable in terms of understanding the resentments of the conflict, and may be read along with Philo and Josephus to illustrate the bitter feelings on both sides, which continued long after Philo's day. Josephus indicates that the Jewish authorities of Alexandria did not support the Jewish revolt against the Romans in Judaea: Judaean *sicarii*, dagger-men, in Alexandria were handed over to the Roman authorities after they had retaliated against prominent Alexandrian Jews who denounced their cause (*War* 7: 409–20). Whatever the case, one should probably not look to find complete cohesion among Jews in Alexandria (or among the 'Greeks'), given that there appear to have been a number of different groups, with different interpretations of law and a variety of political perspectives (see *War* 2: 487–93).

The specific events in which Philo found himself embroiled appear to have been prompted by the visit of Agrippa I—whom the Emperor Gaius Caligula had installed as king of the northern region of (wider) Judaea—in 38 CE.[28] According to Philo, certain

---

[25] He is probably to be identified as the Gaius Julius Alexander in papyri of 26 CE (*CPJ* 2: 420a) and 28/9 CE (420b), see Morris, 'Philo', 815. Alexander was imprisoned in Rome by Gaius and probably released by Claudius (*Ant.* 19: 276).

[26] The Roman name is striking. The brother of this prefect, named Marcus Julius Alexander, married Berenice, daughter of Agrippa I (*Ant.* 19: 276–7), a fact that indicates both his wealth and enormously high social status. For all the diverse evidence relating to Tiberius Julius Alexander, see Viktor Burr, *Tiberius Iulius Alexander* (Bonn: R. Habelt, 1955) and Alberto Barzanò, 'Tiberio Giulio Alessandro, Preffetto d'Egitto (66/70)', *ANRW* 2: 10: 1 (1988), 518–80; S. Étienne, 'Réflexion sur l'apostasie de Tibérius Julius Alexander', *SPA* 12 (2000), 122–42.

[27] For which see Herbert A. Musurillo, *The Acts of the Pagan Martyrs: Acta Alexandrinorum* (Oxford: Clarendon Press, 1954), and see Smallwood, *The Jews*, 250–5. Parts of this work which refer to Jews are found also in *CPJ* 2: 152–9.

[28] See for questions concerning the precise dating of Agrippa's visit Alla

anti-Jewish Alexandrians congregated in the gymnasium and paraded a fool, Carabas, revering him as the Jewish king. The Roman prefect Flaccus took no reprisals, even when Jews were driven from their homes and killed. The accusation was made that Jews were anti-emperor in not installing statues of the divine Gaius in their synagogues, which were thereafter burnt and desecrated (*Flacc.* 32–40; *Ant.* 18: 257–8). From Josephus' use of the word *stasis* ('civil dissension') we may surmise that the Jews did not remain entirely passive victims. At any rate, Flaccus responded to the events by punishing the Jews, relegating them to the class of 'aliens and foreigners' rather than *Alexandreis*. Some elders of the Jewish community were brutally whipped in public.[29] Jews were told to move into one area of the city only (*Flacc.* 41–96; *Legat.* 115–37; *Ant.* 18: 257).[30] Probably partly on account of gross mismanagement of such civil strife, Flaccus was removed in chains, exiled to the island of Andros, and, in due course, executed. A new prefect, Vitrasius Polio, arrived and some order was restored. Representatives of the Jewish and the Greek sides went to Rome to appear before Gaius, a deputation which included, as we saw, Philo himself. Gaius, according to Josephus, was impressed by the anti-Judaic words of a representative of the Greek side, Apion, and angrily cut short Philo, who had to leave (*Ant.* 18: 259–60; cf. Eusebius, *Hist. Eccles.* 2: 5: 2–5).[31] Josephus' account preserves the essence but probably not quite the reality of what actually took place. Philo's own very valuable eyewitness version of the audience with Gaius is found vividly told in his *Legat.* (180–98; 349–72). He indicates that the farcical meeting took place while Gaius was surveying various villas adjacent to the gardens of Maecenas and Lamia. The delegations from both sides of the Alexandrian dispute were forced to trail behind the emperor, who had already

Kashnir-Stern, 'On the Visit of Agrippa I to Alexandria in AD 38', *JJS* 51 (2000), 227–43.

[29] There is no mention of Philo suffering this humiliation, though he must surely have known personally those who were scourged.

[30] See for discussion Barclay, *Jews*, 48–81; Smallwood, *The Jews*, 235–42; Kasher, *The Jews*, 20–3.

[31] Josephus' own response in *Contra Apionem* provides us with a good idea of what Apion stated, and what Philo apparently needed to address. Apion clearly provided a case against the notion that Jews should have Alexandrian citizenship.

decided against the Jews, while Gaius contented himself with
tormenting the five-man Jewish embassy as an aside while
engaged in the apparently more important problem of ordering
building renovations.

Nothing was formally decided by Gaius regarding the Jewish
situation in Alexandria. After his assassination on 24 January
41 CE further rioting broke out in the city, and the new
emperor Claudius received further deputations (*Ant.* 19: 278).[32]
According to Eusebius, Philo travelled to Rome again in the
reign of Claudius, undoubtedly as a member of another deputation (*Hist. Eccles.* 2: 18: 8).[33] According to Josephus, the result
was that two edicts were issued by Claudius regarding the status
of the Jews (*Ant.* 19: 280–91). One granted Jews political and
religious rights. The other, concerning Jews of the empire,
granted these with the proviso that Jews also exhibit religious
toleration and cooperation.[34] Papyrological evidence confirms
the gist of Josephus' report, in the form of a purported letter
from Claudius dated 10 November 41 CE, addressed to the
Alexandrians, and apparently published by the new Roman prefect L. Aemilius Rectus. In this 'letter' form of the edict,
Claudius orders the Greeks to grant to Jews the rights promised
by Augustus, and orders the Jews neither to disturb athletics,
nor to seek reinforcements from 'Syria' or the rest of Egypt.[35]
But the edict resolved little for very long. According to Josephus,
violence continued. In 66 CE the prefect (Philo's nephew)
Tiberius Julius Alexander was responsible for using Roman
troops against his own ethnic community, with much blood-
shed (*War* 2: 290–8, 387, 489–90; 7: 409–19).[36] In 115 CE the

[32] *CPJ* 2: 153, ll. 90–2.
[33] See also *CPJ* 2: 153, ll. 16–20, 90–2, 96–8.
[34] See *Ant.* 19: 280–9; *CPJ* 2: 153, l. 88; Tcherikover, *Hellenistic Civilisation*,
413–15.
[35] For the letter see P. London 1912 = *CPJ* 2: 153, esp. ll. 23–5; 82–95; and
discussion in Smallwood, *The Jews*, 248–50; Mélèze-Modrzejewski, *Jews of
Egypt*, 180–3, cf. *Legat.* 27–31. This 'letter' was copied by a village tax collector
named Nemesion, and is probably a pro-Greek version of the same edict to the
Alexandrians mentioned by Josephus, see Ann E. Hanson, 'Village Officials at
Philadelphia: A Model of Romanization in the Julio-Claudian Period', in Lucia
Criscuolo and Giovanni Geraci (eds.), *Egitto e storia antica dall'ellenismo all'età
araba: Bilancio di un confronto* (Bologna: CLUEB, 1989), 429–40.
[36] See also *OGIS* ii. 669; P. Berol. 11601. After the death of Nero, Alexander
actually admitted many abuses of Roman power in Alexandria and stressed that

animosity between Jews and Greeks would erupt again in bloody civil war.[37]

While details of the conflict are not our concern here, the image we get from the evidence indicates that Alexandria was in social turmoil. It is in this context that Philo wrote his later works, and it is this strife that most likely drew him from an introverted philosophical lifestyle into an active political involvement as a spokesman for his community, as the erudite brother of the alabarch and a member of an illustrious family. In a famous passage in *Spec.* (3: 1–6) Philo writes of how he once spent all his waking hours devoted to philosophy and contemplation, but the choice to enter politics was thrust upon him. He entered 'a sea of troubles', one in which he gasps and sputters and almost drowns.

We do not know exactly all the reasons for the unrest, or the precise sequence of events, and the foregoing comments are designed only to sketch the situation as broadly as possible, given the evidence we have. The ancient texts read as so many descriptions and comments read in today's newspapers, with different parties each telling their own stories of heroism and martyrdom in a bloody ethnic conflict. We need to recognize, however, the situation in Alexandria as we approach Philo's 'historical' material. It is not written with calm objectivity. It has a political purpose.

DE VITA CONTEMPLATIVA AND *ON VIRTUES*

The text of *Contempl.* has long been considered fascinating, ever since Eusebius happily concluded that Philo was describing early Christians in the work (*Hist. Eccles.* 2: 16–17) and quoted extensively from it, assuming everyone would recognize the similarities between the practices of Philo's 'Therapeutae' and

---

these would now be rectified under Galba. The text of his decree is found in stone inscriptions and a papyrus of the 2nd cent., see *BGU* 7: 1563; *OGIS* ii. 669, cf. *Ant.* 18: 259, 276, see Mélèze-Modrzejewski, *Jews of Egypt*, 186–90.

[37] For which, see the discussion in Christopher Haas, *Alexandria in Late Antiquity: Topography and Social Conflict* (Baltimore and London: Johns Hopkins University Press, 1997), 99–109.

Christians. The inclusion of women in the group was a particularly clinching matter for Eusebius, since women's participation in such a group was, apparently, something 'found only in the evangelical worship of the Christians' (*Hist. Eccles.* 2: 17: 18).

No one today seriously entertains the idea that the group was Christian. It is rather to be identified as Jewish (cf. *Contempl.* 64, where the group follows the sacred instructions according to the prophet Moses). But we should not be too amused at Eusebius, for in reading the text there are indeed elements which strike chords with those aware of diverse types of early Christians, Graeco-Roman philosophical schools, and Jewish sects, and it is by no means clear exactly where this group stood in relation to other contemporary congregations, associations and schools. They were, moreover, living their life of 'very philosophical and vehement asceticism' (*Hist. Eccles.* 2: 16: 2) at the time that the seeds of Christianity were first being cast into Alexandria. St Mark is traditionally associated with the city. We know from the evidence of later Christian scholars such as Clement of Alexandria (150–215) and Origen (185–254) that in due course Christianity continued elements of the Jewish allegorical exegetical tradition, in the catechetical school, whose earliest known head was Pantaenus (died *c.* 190),[38] but the period between Philo and Pantaenus is little known in terms of Jewish and Christian relations. The Alexandrian Church would be largely responsible for the conservation of Philo's works. Eusebius was noting similarities between a type of Jewish community and later Christian communities that are distinctive.

Fortunately, few would dispute that Philo did in fact write the essay, though in the past some doubt was expressed on this point. The great proponent of its spurious authorship was Ernst Lucius, who agreed with Eusebius that the work must surely refer to early Christians, but then argued that, if this were the case, *Contempl.* could not be a genuine work of Philo's, but was composed a little before the time of Eusebius (who is first to

[38] For the use of Philo in early Alexandrian Christianity and elsewhere see David T. Runia, *Philo in Early Christian Literature* (Assen: Van Gorcum, 1993), esp. 119–211; Annewies van den Hoek, *Clement of Alexandria and his Use of Philo in the* Stromateis: *An Early Christian Reshaping of a Jewish Model* (Leiden: Brill, 1988); ead., 'The Catechetical School of Early Christian Alexandria and its Philonic Heritage', *HTR* 90 (1997), 59–87; ead., 'Philo and Origen: A Descriptive Catalogue of their Relationship', *SPA* 12 (2000), 44–121.

mention it) for the sake of claiming an ancient precedent for Christian monasticism.[39] Refuting Lucius and others, the authenticity of the work was persuasively defended by Frederick Conybeare.[40] More awareness of the diversity within Hellenistic Judaism and a better appreciation of Philo's literary style and themes have led recent scholars to consider it very much a part of Philo's corpus of genuine writings.

It exists in various Greek codices, an early Armenian version, an Old Latin translation in two recensions (fourth–fifth century), and a more recent Latin recension.[41] It is found in collections of Philo's works produced by Adrianus Turnebus in 1552[42] and Thomas Mangey in 1742.[43] A major critical edition of the Greek text was produced by Frederick Conybeare in 1895,[44] and thereafter by Leopold Cohn in 1915.[45] A Greek text closely modelled on that of Cohn, with English translation by Francis H. Colson, was published in 1941 in the Loeb series.[46] For the Greek text used here, I refer the reader to Colson's edition. I will not provide a full translation of the work myself, since English

[39] Ernst Lucius, *Die Therapeuten und ihre Stellung in der Geschichte der Askese: Eine kritsche Untersuchung der Schrift* De vita contemplativa (Strasbourg: F. Bull, 1879), and see Riaud, 'Les Thérapeutes d'Alexandrie', esp. 1191–1210.

[40] Frederick C. Conybeare, *Philo About the Contemplative Life* (Oxford: Clarendon Press, 1895; repr. New York: Garland, 1987), 326–53.

[41] Morris, 'Philo', 856–8; Conybeare, *Philo*, 1–24, with stemma p. 9; Old Latin version pp. 139–53; Armenian version pp. 154–80. The Armenian version and the Greek text used by Eusebius share a common lacuna at *Contempl.* 78 while all other Greek manuscripts have lacunae at *Contempl.* 18 and 33. For a recent discussion of the text in the light of the Armenian version, see Romano Sgarbi, *Problemi linguistici e di critica del testo nel* De Vita Contemplativa *di Filone alla luce della versione Armena* (Milan: Istituto Lombardo di Scienze e Lettere, 1992).

[42] Adrianus Turnebus, *Philonis Iudaei in libros Mosis, de mundi opificio, historicos, de legibus; Eiusdem libri singulares* (Paris: Apud Adr. Turnebum typographum regium, 1552).

[43] Thomas Mangey, *Philonis Judaei opera quae reperiri potuerunt omnia*, ii (London: G. Bowyer, 1742), 471–86.

[44] Conybeare, *Philo*, 25–135.

[45] Leopold Cohn, Paul Wendland, and Siegfried Reiter, *Philonis Alexandrini opera quae supersunt*, vi (Berlin: George Reimer, 1915), 46–71 (editio minor: vi. 32–50).

[46] Francis H. Colson, *Philo ix* (Loeb Classical Library; Cambridge, Mass.: Harvard University Press, 1941), 112–69, henceforth abbreviated to 'Colson, *Philo ix* (Loeb)'.

versions are so easily accessible,[47] but all passages quoted here in English are my own translations from the Greek text as established by Colson unless otherwise stated. A partial translation of *Contempl.* appears in Appendix 1.

The manuscript versions of the title seem to suggest a compilation of different traditions. The usual title reads: Περὶ βίου θεωρητικοῦ ἢ ἱκετῶν ἀρετῶν τὸ δ', *On the Contemplative Life or On the Suppliants, On Virtues no. 4*, a heading given also by Eusebius (*Hist. Eccles.* 2: 17: 3; 2: 18: 7), though without the identification of it being the fourth part of a larger work.[48] There seem to be two alternatives introduced by the word ἢ which suggests an attempt by the copyists to utilize all available information. Some evidence for this possibility is found in the Cod. Paris. 435(*c*), which has only ἱκέται ἢ περὶ ἀρετῶν δ', *Suppliants or On Virtues no. 4*, with the first part *On the Contemplative Life* omitted.[49]

The heading indicates that the text forms the fourth part of a discussion of the virtues, a work therefore titled Περὶ ἀρετῶν, *On Virtues*.[50] This is to be distinguished from another work

---

[47] See the early versions of Charles D. Yonge, *The Works of Philo Judaeus, the Contemporary of Josephus, translated from the Greek* (London: Henry G. Bohn, 1854–5; repr. Peabody Mass.: Hendrickson, 1993), 698–706 and Frederick Conybeare, 'Philo Concerning the Contemplative Life', *JQR* 7 (1894), 755–69. More recently, there is not only that of Colson, but also translations by David Winston, *Philo of Alexandria: The Contemplative Life, The Giants and Selections* (Classics of Western Spirituality; New York and Toronto: Paulist Press, 1981) and Gail Paterson Corrington, 'Philo On the Contemplative Life: Or, On the Suppliants (The Fourth Book on the Virtues)', in Vincent L. Wimbush (ed.), *Ascetic Behavior in Greco-Roman Antiquity: A Sourcebook* (Studies in Antiquity and Christianity; Minneapolis: Fortress, 1990), 134–55. David Hay's new translation and commentary of *De Vita Contemplativa* is eagerly awaited.

[48] For some variants see Colson, *Philo ix* (Loeb), 518.

[49] For which, see Conybeare, *Philo*, 25.

[50] The MSS read either: ἀρετῶ τὸ δ or ἀρετῆς τὸ τέταρτον. The subheading is missing only in the Armenian version and also in the Caesarea library text used by Eusebius, another factor that suggests they are part of the same textual tradition, in which there is a common lacuna, see above n. 41. The Latin MS published by Jean Sichard in 1527 has a completely different title, identifying the subjects as Essene monks who lived at the time of Agrippa I: *De Essaeis et Philonis Iudaei liber de statu Essaeorum, id est Monachorum qui temporibus Agrippae regis monasteria sibi fecerunt*, see Jean Sichard, *Philonis Judaei, Libri antiquitatum, Quaestionum et solutionum in Genesin. De Essaeis. De nominibus Hebraicis. De Mundo* (Basil: Adam Petrus, 1527). This may be derivative of Eusebius' comments, see for discussion Caroline Carlier, 'Sur un titre latin

similarly titled, which is still extant and known in Latin as *De Virtutibus* (Eusebius, *Hist. Eccles.* 2: 18: 2), in Greek fully, Περὶ τριῶν ἀρετῶν ἃ σὺν ἄλλαις ἀνέγραψε Μωυσῆς, *Concerning the Three Virtues which with Others have been Described by Moses*, a kind of appendage to *De Specialibus Legibus.*[51] Since the issue of whether *Contempl.* is part of *On Virtues* is, I think, critical for understanding the purpose of the work and rhetorical elements in the text which will bear upon historical inquiry, we need to consider the question in some detail at the outset.

To begin with, all except one of the extant manuscripts of *Legat.* indicate that this treatise is the first part of *On Virtues.*[52] Despite various alternative structures that have been given over the years,[53] the identification of *Legat.* as forming the first of the treatises comprising *On Virtues* is quite strong, since it is supported not only by the manuscript tradition, but also by Eusebius. Eusebius writes that Philo related in five books what happened to the Jews in the time of Gaius (*Hist. Eccles.* 2: 5: 1). He cites the story that Philo read out this work to the Roman Senate in the reign of Claudius, and that it was titled—ironically—*On Virtues* (*Hist. Eccles.* 2: 18: 8). In *Hist. Eccles.* 2: 5: 6 he introduces the work by terming it the Πρεσβεία, reflecting the Greek title of *Legat.*: Πρεσβείας πρὸς Γάιον. Eusebius indicates that he will pass over most of the things in it and cite only the points which relate to the misfortunes which came upon the Jews, meaning that there was much more to the whole work than simply these misfortunes. He notes that Philo relates that in the time of Tiberius Sejanus took measures to destroy the Jewish people (cf. *Legat.* 159–61) and that Pilate made an attempt on the Temple (*Legat.* 299–305)[54] and then he quotes from *Legat.* 346

du *De Vita Contemplativa*', *SPA* 8 (1996), 58–72, and see Conybeare, *Philo*, 281–2.

[51] Morris, 'Philo', 850–3.

[52] Colson, *Philo x* (Loeb Classical Library; Cambridge, Mass.: Harvard University Press, 1962), p. xiv.

[53] See Morris, 'Philo', 859–64, regarding Eusebius' comments on *Legat.* and the theories which would account for the relationship between *Legat.* and *Flacc.* Colson discusses the ancient title and also that of *Legat.* in *Philo ix* (Loeb), 112, the appendix on p. 518 as well as in *Philo ix* (Loeb), pp. xiv–xxvi.

[54] Colson, *Philo x* (Loeb), pp. xix–xx, explains that Eusebius considers Pilate's actions to have concerned the Temple (*Dem Evang.* 7: 2: 123), even when Philo himself does not state this. Josephus also makes no connection

(*Hist. Eccles.* 2: 6: 2). It seems therefore fairly clear then that Eusebius sees *Legat.* as part of this longer, five-part, discussion *On Virtues*. This gives us a definite historical context for *On Virtues* as a whole.

Eusebius then goes on to the second treatise of *On Virtues* as describing innumerable other atrocities in the reign of Gaius (*Hist. Eccles.* 2: 6: 3).[55] Such other atrocities are found in *Flacc.*, some overlapping with *Legat.* (*Flacc.* 33–96, cf. *Legat.* 120–39), and in Eusebius' *Chronicon*, *Flacc.* is listed as the second of the five-part work called Πρεσβεία (after the first treatise only).[56] However, here, while it is apparent that Eusebius himself linked *Flacc.* with *Legat.*, it may not be correct to follow his lead.[57] In the text of *Flacc.* it is indicated that another work preceded it: it follows on from an account of the charges against the Jews by Sejanus (so *Flacc.* 1) and the suffering of a persecutor, mentioned in the final sentence (*Flacc.* 191). But the suffering of this persecutor is not found in the extant *Legat.*, and mention of Sejanus is quite brief (cf. *Legat.* 159–61). In order to argue that *Flacc.* followed *Legat.* one would need to establish that our manuscripts of *Legat.* are incomplete. Philo does refer to a παλινῳδία, 'recantation', in the final sentence of *Legat.* (373), which may have described the sorry fate of Gaius, now missing, but probably not Sejanus, since he is not the main subject.[58] The references at the

between a similar incident and the Temple (*Ant.* 18: 55–9; *War* 2: 169–77), though Eusebius also cites Josephus in support of his interpretation. The issues concerned having items (dedicated shields in Philo, busts of the emperor attached to military standards in Josephus) connected with imperial/military Roman religious rites in the holy city of Jerusalem, not within the Temple as such. In other words, Eusebius is referring to *Legat.*, but he has misinterpreted what Philo has stated, just as he misinterpreted Josephus.

[55] The Greek is not entirely certain here, but Eusebius should possibly be read in the light of Rufinus' Latin translation: 'In the second of the books which he entitled *On Virtues* . . .'

[56] See Alfred Schoene (ed.), *Eusebi Chronicorum libri duo*, ii (Berlin: Weidmann, 1875–6), 150–1 and see Morris, 'Philo', 860 n. 198.

[57] For discussion see Morris, 'Philo', 859–64. Colson suggests that all the five books referred to by Eusebius were part of the extant *Legat.* (four parts) along with the Palinode, *Philo* x (Loeb), pp. xxiv–xxvi. Conybeare, *Philo*, 284–5, thought that all five books were from *Legat.* but that our extant version of *Legat.* is truncated, with *Contempl.* cut out. He notes that in Codex 435 *Legat.* is followed directly by *Contempl.* without a break.

[58] See Morris, 'Philo', 860–1; Colson, *Philo* x (Loeb), xvi–xvii.

beginning and end of *Flacc.* naturally read that the preceding
work was another of the same type as *Flacc.*, about the evils of
Sejanus, not Gaius, who persecuted the Jews and who then
suffered a premature end. Moreover, *Flacc.* is fundamentally
different in theme to *Legat.* Thematically, *Legat.* is indeed concerned with virtue (see below), but the theme of *Flacc.* is that
those who do terrible things to the Jews will receive divine retri-
bution in accordance with their sins, which provides 'undoubted
proof that God has not withdrawn from the Jewish people'
(*Flacc.* 191), a theme which is presumably the same as the
preceding work on Sejanus. There is no significant mention of
virtue.[59]

If *Legat.* is the opening section of *On Virtues*, then this would
indicate that Philo began this project after the deputation to
Gaius Caligula (*c.*39–40 CE), which he led (*Ant.* 18: 259), and
shortly before he went again to Rome in 41 as part of the delegation to Claudius (if we take Eusebius' comments as sound in
regard to this visit to Rome). We would possess two out of the
five sections of this work: (1) *Legat.* and (4) *Contempl.* If the
reference to a παλινῳδία is to a work following on from *Legat.*
and in *On Virtues*, then this may have concerned Gaius' fate
and the glorious choice of Claudius as his successor. We also
have a strong indication of another in the sequence of treatises.
According to the opening lines of *Contempl.*, a discussion on the
Essenes formed the preceding (third) treatise. He writes:

I have discoursed on Essenes, who were zealous for and who worked
hard at the active philosophical life, excelling in everything or—at least
to say it more moderately—in most parts. Going on directly, and indeed
carrying on in accordance with the plan [of my subject] I will say what
is required about those who embrace contemplation [as a philosophical
lifestyle]. (*Contempl.* 1)

This indicates that *On Virtues* comprised: (1) *Legat.*, (2) the
Palinode, 'recantation', (3) a treatise on the Essenes, (4)
Contempl., and (5) an unknown conclusion.

In regard to *Contempl.* it should be noted that Eusebius does
not refer to the subtitle which would connect the treatise with the
larger work *On Virtues* (*Hist. Eccles.* 2: 17: 3; 2: 18: 7) and in the

---

[59] For more on *Flacc.* see Herbert Box, *Philo Alexandrinus, On Flaccus* (New
York: Arno Press, 1979).

Philonic texts which he lists, he places *Contempl*. separately after the linked texts 'Every wicked person is a slave' (a lost treatise) and 'Every good person is free' (*Prob.*, concerning the Essenes). Eusebius himself indicates that the work was a late composition, written after *On Virtues*, probably because of his conviction that it was praising *Christians*. He states that Philo wrote it *after* he was in Rome during the reign of Claudius, where not only did he read out *Legat*. to the Roman Senate, but luckily met St Peter (*Hist. Eccles.* 2: 17: 1; 18: 7–8).[60] Implicitly then, in Eusebius' thought, St Peter has somehow influenced Philo to think favourably towards the Church, and this explains why Philo has written *Contempl*. about Christians. In fact, it was logically impossible for Eusebius to ascribe *Contempl*. to the period before Philo met Peter, since he believed that it was only after this meeting that Philo could have written about Christians. Even if Eusebius had seen a manuscript title linking *Contempl*. to *On Virtues* he would not have been able to accept such an identification, since *On Virtues* was, he thought, written prior to Philo's meeting with Peter.

Overall, regarding Eusebius' evidence, the difficulty lies in establishing to what extent he knew Philo's treatises in terms of their exact origins as parts of larger wholes, and to what extent he wished to give a complete and comprehensive catalogue. For example, it is very likely that the passage Eusebius quotes in

[60] For Eusebius it was sufficient that both Peter and Philo were in Rome sometime during the reign of Claudius (*Hist. Eccles.* 2: 17). I have suggested this was in 41 CE, when a Jewish delegation was there, a delegation that may largely have replicated that of 38 CE, which Philo led. However, from Acts 12: 3–10, it seems that Peter was in Judaea in the reign of Herod Agrippa I (41–4), and he is noted as participating in a church council in Jerusalem (Acts 15: 20–2), usually dated *c*.48. Eusebius' evidence is not to be rejected as intrinsically improbable, since he is apparently relying on what is 'recorded' in a very early witness, namely, Clement of Rome (30–97 CE), cf. *Hist. Eccles.* 2: 14. It is widely accepted that the chronology of Peter's many missions is very little known, since there is minimal positive evidence. Both Eusebius and Jerome (cf. *De Viris Illustribus* 1) knew of an episcopal list that had Peter as founder and leader of the Roman church for 25 years before his death, dated to the fourteenth year of Nero (Oct. 67–8), which would have him in Rome from as early as Oct. 42, though an earlier date for his death following the fire in Rome of 64 (cf. Tacitus, *Annals* 15: 44) is often suggested, and may mean that Peter established a community in Rome as early as 39. Like many other apostles, he appears to have been extremely peripatetic.

Praep. Evang. 8: 6–7 derives from a work he identifies elsewhere as ὑπὲρ Ἰουδαίων (*Praep. Evang.* 8: 11) and περὶ Ἰουδαίων (*Hist. Eccles.* 2: 18: 6). The latter is listed in his catalogue as a single work, like *Contempl.*, but in *Praep. Evang.* 8: 5: 11 he states that it derives from a much larger multipartite work—answering those (like Apion) who accused the Jews—known as the *Hypothetica.*[61] The assumption may be that in the library in Caesarea which Eusebius used they possessed some 'floating' single treatises from larger works, and that Eusebius did not necessarily always know where they belonged.[62] 'Floating' treatises could also have been placed together with works of similar subject matter, when they were part of different rhetorical fields (e.g. *Flacc.* and *Legat.*), or left unrelated to other texts they actually belonged with, if the whole work was known by several different names. Eusebius' evidence can be very helpful, but we cannot trust him completely, given his own presuppositions and the possibly incomplete, damaged, or hotchpotch nature of the Caesarean library holdings.

It was Erwin Goodenough who suggested that *Legat.* was

---

[61] Morris, 'Philo', 266–8.

[62] This Philonic collection may possibly have been an assemblage of rolls which were part of Origen's personal library, brought with him to Caesarea from Alexandria in 215, see David Runia, *Philo in Early Christian Literature* (Assen: Van Gorcum, 1993), 119–31. The Caesarean library was comprised of codices with papyrus pages which, by the end of the 4th cent., were greatly damaged owing to the friability of papyrus as it ages; Jerome comments on how it was renewed with parchment pages (*Epist.* 34), see Lionel Casson, *Libraries in the Ancient World* (New Haven and London: Yale University Press, 2001), 131. This means particularly that the first, much-used pages of papyrus codices were in danger of being damaged, the very pages which contained valuable information about where a piece belonged. From the time when codices replaced rolls as the normal form of reading material, there was also the problem that disparate rolls could be copied into one book, thereby locking them into an association that may not have been right. In ancient catalogues, including that of Alexandria, rolls tended to be classified by subject under the main author heading (Casson, *Libraries*, 40, 59), and labelled accordingly by tag (which, in an age before super-glue, could fall off). While some of Philo's longer works may well have existed on long rolls, thereby ensuring their integrity, smaller rolls were much more manageable, but also more vulnerable. If both the *Hypothetica* and *On Virtues* originally existed as a collection of small rolls (making them easier to read from), with library tags indicating author and subject matter if they were intact, then this would explain why the individual treatises on diverse subjects became dispersed, linked with other works, or lost.

designed for the Emperor Claudius.[63] This, in my opinion, is
very plausible. Eusebius' story of Philo reading out *Legat.* to the
Roman Senate may be slightly awry, but that there was an
Roman audience would certainly explain some of the absolutely
extraordinary rhetorical features it exhibits.[64] For example, as
noted above, the treatise is clearly concerned with virtue, especially *andreia* and the faculty of *logismos*, reason (*Legat.* 2, 112,
196).[65] But Philo uses as prime examples of virtue—which Gaius
should have emulated but did not—the Graeco-Roman *gods*:
Heracles, Dionysus, the Dioscuri, Hermes, Apollo, and Ares
(*Legat.* 81–113). Augustus, defined as a 'philosopher', was given
his honorific title because of his virtue (*Legat.* 143, 309, 318).[66]
In the post-Gaius world, Romans would have found the intense
character assassination of the mad emperor and his associates
pleasing, given that it was also coupled with great esteem for
Augustus and his line. This work was then a document to accom-
pany the embassy to Claudius. We know that such documents
also preceded and accompanied the embassy to Gaius (*Legat.*
178–9).[67]

There is no absolute proof of this to be gained, but certain
other features of *Contempl.* and *Legat.* are suggestive of this
context. The metaphor of healing which we find in *Contempl.*
concerning those who live a contemplative life may well have
struck chords with the new emperor. As Barbara Levick writes:

---

[63] Goodenough, *Introduction*, 59–60. Conybeare, *Philo*, 291, likewise
believed it was brought to Rome but that Philo wrote it earlier (22–3 CE) and
'when he was suddenly called upon to go and plead the cause of his country men
before the Emperor simply went to his repertory and took it out'.

[64] One wonders though whether he read a shortened version. Philo writes of
an almost identical but shorter version of a long supplication made to Gaius in
Legat. 178–9.

[65] Even reason is not enough, but is inferior to the ability to see or ascend to
God, see *Legat.* 4–7.

[66] Augustus is said to have transcended human nature in all the virtues
(*Legat.* 143). This may be because part of Augustus' religious reforms involved
a stress on morality, see John H. W. G. Liebeschuetz, *Continuity and Change in
Roman Religion* (Oxford: Clarendon, 1979), 90–100.

[67] On the other hand, *Flacc.* may have been written for the new Roman
prefect of Egypt, Vitrasius Polio, since here Philo indicates that M. Aemilius
Lepidus was still alive (*Flacc.* 151, 181) and Lepidus was executed on Gaius'
northern campaign late in 39, see Goodenough, *Introduction*, 58–9. *Flacc.* then
preceded *Legat.*, and should be dated to early–mid 39.

'Claudius' prime task as Princeps was, as he saw, to heal the wounds of seventeen years, in particular those of Gaius' reign, and the terror of 24–5 January, 41. Restoring an empire scorched and ruined was how Seneca put it, but Claudius, so often in the hands of physicians, favoured the metaphor of healing.'[68] The name of Philo's ideal group—the θεραπευταί (m.) or θεραπευτρίδες (f.)—is described as possibly having some double-entendre which resonates with healing. They are called by this name perhaps 'because they profess medical skill better than in the cities—for that [in the cities] heals bodies alone, while their *therapeia* heals souls' (*Contempl.* 2). I shall consider further the meaning of this designation in the next chapter. For the moment it is interesting only that Philo uses the medical association of the name in the introductory part of his treatise.

The first edict of Claudius, as documented by Josephus, has striking allusions to the subject matter of *Legat.*, in noting that the Alexandrians 'rose up in insurrection against the Jews in their midst in the time of Gaius Caesar, who through his great folly and madness humiliated the Jews because they refused to transgress the religion of their fathers by addressing him as a god' (*Ant.* 19: 284).[69] In Claudius' purported letter to the Alexandrians the emperor refers to the 'war against the Jews' in the city.[70] Whatever was communicated to Claudius was apparently very much like what we have in *Legat.*, and it convinced the emperor.

The striking 'Roman-friendly' features of *Legat.* are not so apparent in *Contempl.* but there is, at the very start, evidence that *Contempl.* was formulated as a spoken address for a particular occasion. This was to some degree conventional, but in *Legat.* he

[68] Barbara Levick, *Claudius* (New Haven and London: Yale University Press, 1990), 89. For Claudius' need for doctors, see Suetonius, *Div. Claud.* 2: 1. Seneca uses the medical metaphor in his letter to Polybius, *Ad Polybium, de Consolatione* 13: 1: 'Suffer him to heal the human race, that has long been sick and in evil case, suffer him to restore and return all things to their place out of the havoc the madness of the preceding prince has wrought!', cf. 14: 1, quoted from John W. Basore's translation in *Seneca, Moral Essays* (Loeb Classical Library; Cambridge, Mass.: Harvard University Press, 1965), 395. This letter was written at some time in the period 41 to 49 CE.

[69] English text quoted from Louis H. Feldman, *Josephus ix* (Loeb Classical Library; Cambridge, Mass; Harvard University Press, 1981), 349, 351.

[70] See esp. *CPJ* 2: 153, ll. 73–8.

makes his opponents visible by addressing them directly, as 'you who of all people are the most idiotic', as if they are really listening to his words, and will 'now' reply (*Legat.* 140), which goes beyond convention.[71] The same kind of immediacy is found in *Contempl.* in that the written text has words appropriate for an oral delivery at a particular time. Philo writes that 'having discoursed' (διαλεχθείς) on the Essenes, 'I will say' (λέξω) what is required regarding his next subject, and he implies that he is giving an oration in noting that 'the most skilled speaker' would grow weary of telling the truth, '[b]ut nevertheless we must persevere and fight on to the end, for the superlative virtue of these men should not be a reason to *strike dumb* those who rightly think that nothing good should passed over in *silence*' (*Contempl.* 1). His opponents are not directly addressed, though they are alluded to: 'I know that some hearing this will laugh, but they are people who do things worthy of tears and lamentation' (*Contempl.* 73). While rhetoric of any kind in antiquity was written down as if it were to some degree oral, it remains very striking that Philo has then designed his written text as if he is speaking aloud on the virtue of his subjects to an audience not entirely on his side. His unaddressed opponents are still obliquely indicated as idiotic, for in many places he goes on the offensive in order to savage features of Hellenistic (Alexandrian) banquet practice and heroes of the Greek philosophical tradition in a manner that indicates Philo was angrily denouncing ideas and cultural elements dear to those responsible for the atrocities inflicted on his people (*Contempl.* 3–10, 14–15, 40–63). While it is common to see Philo as quietly intellectual and esoteric, carefully accommodating Judaism to Greek philosophy, in *Contempl.* his tone is sometimes snide, disrespectful, and furious towards this same philosophy. More than a third of *Contempl.* is taken up with invective against the bad practices of the Greeks (mainly)[72] and Egyptians (thirty-four out of ninety sections).[73]

---

[71] If this treatise was read out as part of the petition to Claudius, this direct remark would be understandable, for the opposition would presumably have been part of the audience.

[72] Philo does not address his Alexandrian opponents directly in *Contempl.* but their Greek and Egyptian norms can be shown to be inferior to Jewish ways.

[73] See Kraemer, 'Monastic Jewish Women', 348; Hay, 'Veiled Thoughts', 174–7. Birnbaum, 'Philo on the Greeks', 51–2, notes that Philo associates the Alexandrian opponents of the Jews with animal worship in *Legat.* 138–9; 162–4.

In *Contempl.* there is a carefully balanced interplay which contrasts the 'bad' of Greek and Egyptian culture with the 'good' of the virtuous 'Therapeutae' and, by implication, the Judaism in which they are to be located. The tone itself may be understood in the light of the political context of *On Virtues* as a whole.

On practicalities too, Philo indicates that he is composing his piece for those who live outside Egypt. They are not that familiar with Egyptian administrative divisions. The division of Egypt into nomes was a tradition which stretched back as far as the Old Kingdom. There were twenty-two nomes in Upper Egypt and twenty in Lower Egypt. Philo writes: 'in each of the nomes, *as they are called*' (*Contempl.* 21) as if he hopes people will understand that the regions are 'called' this locally. Porphyry does exactly the same thing in *De Abstin.* 4: 9, writing about Egyptian customs. He mentions 'and one district of Egypt, which is called a nome (ὅ καλοῦσι νομόν)'. Porphyry was writing this in Rome in the third century. You would not use such language to residents of Egypt.[74] It seems clear then that the primary audience of *Contempl.* was considered to be resident outside Egypt.

Philo also assumes that his hearers do not understand the significance of the Sabbath day (*Contempl.* 30, 32, 35–6, 65) and have to be told the basic story of the Red Sea (*Contempl.* 86). We get a sense then that not only is his primary audience not Greek-Egyptian, but it is not even Jewish.

In defining a 'primary audience', I mean to imply also that there is a secondary audience. Let us assume that the primary audience is that which Philo planned to address in Rome, comprising the Emperor Claudius and Roman officials, though bracketed into this primary audience there is also the Greek delegation from Alexandria, who would have been present, as they were when he and his Jewish team met with Gaius. The secondary audience would be those he expected to read his treatise afterwards. Therefore, an Alexandrian Jewish readership is

---

Egyptian animal worship is attacked as if to appeal to Roman notions of its absurdity, see Klaas A. D. Smelik and Emily Hemelrijk, ' "Who Knows Not What Monsters Demented Egypt Worships?": Opinions on Egyptian Animal Worship in Antiquity as Part of the Conception of Egypt', *ANRW* 2: 17: 4 (1984), 1853–2337.

[74] Cf. Herodotus, *Hist.* 1: 192, 'The governorship, which the Persians call 'satrapy', of this land . . .'

probably also to be considered in the rhetoric, even though they are not, I think, explicitly addressed.

In terms of the Greek delegation to Claudius, the writings about and by Chaeremon are particularly illuminating. Chaeremon himself is identified as being one of the Alexandrian ambassadors to Claudius, and the papyrus version of Claudius' *Letter to the Alexandrians* mentions him specifically as 'Chaeremon son of Leonidas' who 'presented me with the decree and spoke at length about the city'.[75] He is described as a Stoic philosopher and a *hierogrammateus*, one of a scholarly class of sacred scribes in Egyptian temples,[76] a cultural blend that was quintessentially Alexandrian.[77] He was later hired as tutor to the young Nero.[78] That Chaeremon spoke 'at length about the city' is very interesting. I have suggested that Philo is defining the Jewish story for Claudius in *On Virtues*. It would then have followed that the Alexandrian Greeks would have told their side of things, with a focus on the city of Alexandria itself and Greek–Egyptian practices.

Given this context, it is particularly striking that Chaeremon wrote a work on the Egyptian priests, for which only epitomes survive (cf. Porphyry, *De. Abstin.* 4: 6–8; Jerome, *Adv. Iovinianum* 2: 13), that has such striking parallels with *Contempl.* Both *Contempl.* and Chaeremon's work use a real religious group in order to argue that their lifestyle was philosophical and good. Chaeremon asserted, as Philo did of the 'Therapeutae', that Egyptian priests—of which he was apparently one—used allegory as a means of interpreting their scripture and tradition. They are 'philosophers among the Egyptians', choosing temples

---

[75] *CPJ* 2: 153, ll. 14–21; Pieter van der Horst, *Chaeremon: Egyptian Priest and Stoic Philosopher* (Leiden: Brill, 1987), 3.

[76] Van der Horst, *Chaeremon*, p. x.

[77] The appropriation of Egyptian cult in Greek Alexandrian religion, and its subsequent transport outwards to the entire Mediterranean in the form of the Greek–Egyptian Isis (and Serapis) cult, is well-documented, see, among a number of excellent overviews, R. E. Witt, *Isis in the Graeco-Roman World* (London: Thames & Hudson, 1971) and Sarolta Takacs, *Isis and Sarapis in the Roman World* (Leiden: Brill, 1975). The Greek and Egyptian cultural mix one finds in Hellenistic and Roman period Alexandria is obvious in the tomb remains found in the city and elsewhere in Egypt, where there is an evocative blend of Greek and Egyptian motifs.

[78] Van der Horst, *Chaeremon*, p. ix.

as their places of residence because 'to live close to their shrines was fitting to their whole desire of contemplation'. They 'devoted their whole life to contemplation and vision of the divine'. Their lifestyle is abstinent, esoteric, and ascetic. The specific correspondences between Chaeremon's text, as described by Porphyry, and *Contempl.* are striking down to small details concerning their diet. It appears that (*a*) either Philo knew Chaeremon's work and tried to better it[79] or (*b*) Chaeremon knew Philo's and tried to improve on that[80] or (*c*) both works drew on common tropes of discourse in terms of a presentation of the ideal contemplative life, the kinds of tropes we find also in Iambulus and other utopian writers.[81] Scholarly consensus, configured in various terms, has favoured option (*c*). We would then have two members of opposing delegations to Claudius who wrote independently on the theme of the virtuous contemplative life. Again, this does not provide any proof that they were pitting their wits against each other in these treatises for a Roman audience, it remains only suggestive. But it is an extraordinary overlap. For the Greek–Egyptian Chaeremon the ultimate examples of 'the good' in terms of the contemplative life are to be found in the Egyptian priests; for Philo they may be found within a Jewish milieu. Both argue that pre-eminent virtue is to be located on their side of the dispute.

Let us consider now an objection to placing the primary audience of *Contempl.* within the framework of Rome. The most obvious consideration is that Philo is so dismissive of banqueting practices which a Roman audience would have relished just as much as a Greek–Egyptian one. Philo even goes as far as to decry 'Italic expensiveness and luxury emulated by both Greeks and

[79] The view that Philo was trying to outdo Chaeremon's work was expounded by Paul Wendland, 'Die Therapeuten und die philonische Schrift von beschaulichen Leben', *Jahrbücher für classische Philologie, Suppl.* 22 (1896), 693–772, esp. 753–6; and see Gregory Sterling, 'Philo and the Logic of Apologetics', *Society of Biblical Literature Seminar Papers 1990* (Atlanta: Scholars, 1990), 412–30.

[80] Hans-Rudolf Schwyzer, *Chairemon* (Leipzig: Harassowitz, 1932), 41–3, 78–9.

[81] Isaak Heinemann, 'Therapeutae', *Pauly's Realencyclopädie der classische altertumswissenschaft*, 5a (1934), 2337–8, cf. Andre J. Festugière, 'Sur une novelle édition du "De Vita Pythgorica" de Jamblique', *Revue des Études Grecques*, 50 (1937), 470–94, at 476–89, see Van der Horst, *Chaeremon*, 56.

Barbarians who arrange things for ostentation rather than for festivity' (*Contempl.* 48) in their banqueting, a form 'prevalent everywhere'. This might appear something of an 'own-goal' at first sight. It is interesting here that 'Roman' is a word not used. There is a kind of bracketing out of Roman considerations elsewhere in the treatise, where the focus is very much on what Greeks do, or have done: true athletes have 'the eyes of all Greece (or: all the Hellenic world) upon them' (*Contempl.* 42) and 'among the symposia of Greece, two of these are widely known and notable' (*Contempl.* 57).

Chaeremon apparently wrote similarly of the Egyptian priests who, according to Porphyry, were 'on guard against *foreign* luxury and pursuits' (*De Abstin.* 4: 8). Decrying luxury and ostentation is something an audience would have expected of a philosopher extolling the virtues. Seneca denounced wealth and luxury (*Ep.* 17: 3; 20; 2; 108: 9–12). Epictetus associated wealth with misery (3: 22: 27, cf. Plutarch, *De Cupiditate*). This could have an ascetic twist: Musonius Rufus stressed the importance of self-control and abstinence from pleasure (*On Training, Discourse* 4).[82] The Cynic epistles champion a very austere life.[83] Tacitus could identify the elegant banquet as something through which the Romans corrupted and rendered servile the British (*Agr.* 21). The banquet as a vehicle for corruption was a commonly used trope in the writing of antiquity to point to someone's moral weakness.[84] A Jewish philosopher decrying 'Italic luxury' may have provoked some smiles in Rome, but it would probably have been what people expected.

---

[82] See Vincent Wimbush (ed.), *Ascetic Behaviour in Greco-Roman Antiquity* (Minneapolis: Fortress, 1990), 129–33.

[83] See Abraham J. Malherbe (ed.), *The Cynic Epistles* (Missoula, Mont.: Scholars, 1977).

[84] See William J. Slater, *Dining in a Classical Context* (Ann Arbor: University of Michigan, 1991), 157–69. Claudius himself seemed concerned to promote moral order in meal situations, and insisted on the sons and daughters of distinguished families being present, sitting at the foot of couches (Suetonius, *Div. Claud.* 32, cf. *Div. Aug.* 64), though Quintilian thought the presence of youngsters might be far from educative or moral, rather the reverse, since the children would be corrupted by the depravity of the situation (*Inst. Orat.* 1: 2: 6–8). Suetonius in fact believed that Claudius was a horrendous glutton (*Div. Claud.* 33).

VIRTUE AND THE PHILOSOPHICAL 'LIVES' TRADITION

Philo is clearly much concerned about expounding virtue, ἀρετή, in *Contempl.*, and all historical information is put at the service of this fundamental objective.[85] In discussing virtue, or excellence, Philo can draw upon recognized virtues known from Graeco-Roman philosophy, particularly as found in Aristotle and Stoicism.

Both David Runia[86] and Troels Engberg-Pedersen have profitably explored the internal evidence of the text itself to highlight Philo's purposes. Engberg-Pedersen also points out that Philo has presented his work in terms of a genre invented by Aristotle, the *pragmateia*, 'systematic or scientific treatise';[87] in *Contempl.* 1 Philo refers to his own work as precisely that.[88] It is a systematic treatise on the subject of a virtuous life.

Focusing his attention on the reading of the final paragraph of the work, Runia has pointed out key terms that underlie Philo's presentation and themes. Since the study is offered as a corrective to current translations, I take the opportunity to publicize Runia's version of the conclusion, based on textual, philological as well as interpretative considerations:

Let this account suffice for the Therapeutae, who have embraced the contemplation (θεωρίαν) of nature and what it contains, and have lived a life of the soul alone, citizens of heaven and the cosmos, truly commended to the father and maker of the universe by their excellence[89] (ὑπ' ἀρετῆς), which has procured for them his friendship and set it before them as the most fitting reward for their goodness (γέρας καλοκαγαθίας[90]) a gift superior to all prosperity and attaining to the very summit of felicity. (*Contempl.* 90)

---

[85] See Hay, 'Things Philo Said and Did Not Say', 677 and his note 24.

[86] David T. Runia, 'The Reward for Goodness: Philo, *De Vita Contemplativa* 90', *SPA* 9 (1997), 3–18.

[87] Aristotle, *NE* 2: 2.

[88] Engberg-Pedersen, 'Philo's *De Vita Contemplativa*', 41. Engberg-Pedersen goes on, however, to suggest that another preferable answer in terms of genre is to consider *Contempl.* as being purely a 'philosopher's dream', which seems a less likely solution, see Ch. 1 above.

[89] Runia prefers this term 'excellence' to the more usual 'virtue'.

[90] See for the translation of this expression Runia, 'Reward for Goodness', 7–8.

We can note here the reference to virtue (ὑπ' ἀρετῆς) as an excellence loved by God. Runia points out that in *QG* 3: 8 a single man saves the city through this virtue/excellence, and that this ability to save the city itself is given as a reward for his goodness by God, who loves such excellence.[91] Likewise, in *Mos.* 1: 148 we find that Moses is given leadership as a reward for excellence and goodness. Thus ἀρετή and καλοκἀγαθία are almost synonymous,[92] and the two words are linked elsewhere in the text (*Contempl.* 72). Philo has designed the closing paragraph to link with the opening one: 'I will say what is required about those who embrace contemplation (θεωρίαν) . . . for the superlative virtue (ἀρετῆς) of the[se] men should not be a reason to strike dumb those who rightly think that nothing good (καλὸν) should be passed over in silence' (*Contempl.* 1). The repetition of the link between contemplation, virtue, and goodness establishes the central theme of the work. This snake-biting-its-tail technique is used in order to stress Philo's main purpose of extolling the virtue and goodness of those who live a life of contemplation (θεωρία). The word ἀρετή appears at key points in the text to ensure we stay on course in terms of thematic development. The 'Therapeutae' dream of divine virtues (*Contempl.* 26). They aspire to the summit of virtue (*Contempl.* 72). Most particularly, we find the specific virtue of ἐγκράτεια, 'self-control'—the fourth of the Stoic cardinal virtues—strongly emphasized, and linked with the 'Therapeutae' as a vital part of their definition: they establish ἐγκράτεια as the foundation of all the virtues (*Contempl.* 34).[93] It would follow then that this essay would form an appropriate part of the work *On Virtues*, as the subheading indicates.

The initial reference to a previous discussion on the Essenes (*Contempl.* 1) is significant in that it situates the present discussion in at least a run of two works. Engberg-Pedersen notes that the discussion on the Essenes cannot be taken to refer to either *Prob.* 75–91 or *Hypoth.* 11: 1–18 (which is preserved in Eusebius,

---

[91] Ibid. 10.

[92] Runia notes that the conception of καλοκἀγαθία is equated with ἀρετή in Aristotle's *Eudemian Ethics* 1248ᵇ10; 'Reward for Goodness', 11 n. 26.

[93] See Goodenough, *Introduction*, 31–2; Winston, *Philo*, 315 n. 1. The virtue of ἐγκράτεια is also found in the account by Chaeremon: the Egyptian priests 'practised frugality and restraint, self-control and endurance, and in all things justice and freedom from avarice' (Porphyry, *De Abstin.* 4: 6).

Prep. Evang. 8: 11: 1–18)[94] since the Essenes in these texts are not specifically mentioned as having a practical as opposed to a contemplative life.[95] There are some very significant thematic overlaps between *Prob.* and *Contempl.*, as Runia points out, for in the text of *Prob.* there is at the beginning and the end of the description of the Essenes the mention of ἀρετή and καλοκἀγαθία (*Prob.* 74–5, 88, 91–2). Both conclude with the stress on happiness (εὐδαιμονία).[96] The two texts read so relatedly that it would seem that Philo cut and pasted into *Prob.* something of a previous discussion on the Essenes designed to focus more on virtue/ excellence than on the ostensible theme of the treatise: the freedom of the good.

Likewise, it seems quite possible that Philo used his description of the contemplative community outside Alexandria in his lost work 'Every Wicked Person is a Slave'. Philo refers to his previous argument during *Prob.* and mentions how his opponents will scoff at what he has presented, for example at his comment that those who are materially rich are actually poor, when those who are truly 'rich' live on air like grasshoppers (*Prob.* 8). This is exactly what he says in regard to some of the 'Therapeutae' of *Contempl.* (35). Philo calls them rich for they have received the 'wealth of perception' (13), leaving behind blind wealth to those who are still blind in mind. The reference in *Prob.* to 'friends of God' (42, cf. 44) recalls *Contempl.* 90 when he refers to those who have procured God's friendship.

In the discussion of the Essenes taken from the treatise concerning the Jews in *Hypoth.* (often termed *Apologia pro Iudaeis*) there is a tone which suggests that it 'should be seen in the context of the anti-Judaism known from Josephus' *Against Apion*, as Jenny Morris notes.[97] The *Hypoth.* was apparently

---

[94] In regard to the *Hypothetica*, Eusebius may have harmonized some elements with the description of the Essenes found in Josephus' works. For example, while Philo states in *Prob.* that the Essenes live in villages, in the *Hypothetica* he apparently states that they live also in towns. Josephus states they live in towns (*War* 2: 124).

[95] Engberg-Pedersen, 'Philo's *De Vita Contemplativa*', 42.

[96] Runia, 'Reward for Goodness', 10. Aristotle had defined this as the purpose of human life (*NE* 10: 6: 1–3), a point with which Philo agrees (*Mos.* 212). Virtue is therefore related to the purpose of human existence, and in *On Virtues* we get (at least) two alternative ways of achieving this.

[97] Morris, 'Philo', 817.

composed by Philo, on behalf of the Jews, πρὸς κατήγορους αὐτῶν, 'against their accusers', which would then mean that the work derives from the same period of political unrest as *On Virtues*, and the use of the Essenes in the *Hypothetica* to counter the accusations of people like Apion illustrates Philo's rhetorical strategy of using specific Jewish schools of thought to make general points about the nature of Judaism as a whole. Whereas in the *Hypoth.* we seem to have a distinctive *apologia*, however, in *On Virtues* the theme is different and the apologetics are much more subtle. A certain amount of repetition may nevertheless be expected. The inter-textual linkages and distinctions between *Contempl.* and material on the Essenes are very clear in our material, leading to a conclusion that whatever formed the fourth part of *On Virtues* was composed of text very similar to what we have on the Essenes elsewhere. As Runia suggests, 'the description of the Essenes at *Prob.* 75–91 (and perhaps also that in *Hypoth.* 11) is very likely a summary of the contents of the lost treatise that preceded *Contempl.* which has been adapted to the special theme of the liberty of the sage.'[98]

The pairing of the subject matter may have seemed natural to Philo, who wrote elsewhere of the balance between the philosophical lifestyles of action and contemplation, the two 'best lives' (*Dec.* 101). It was in fact a philosophical commonplace which would have been familiar to any educated audience. Engberg-Pedersen points out that in Aristotle's *Nicomachean Ethics* (1: 5) four virtuous lives are listed as possibilities for happiness, the foremost two being the active life, βίος πρακτικός,[99] and the life of those who have welcomed contemplation, βίος θεωρητικός,[100] and he explicitly discusses whether

---

[98] Runia, 'Reward for Goodness', 10 n. 23. Interestingly, Eusebius records the existence of these two works, but while he quotes from *Prob.* in *Praep. Evang.* 8: 12 he never quotes from the other. If the 'Therapeutae' were indeed used as examples in the companion work, Philo must have written of his subjects in such a way that led Eusebius to decide they could not be identified with those he described as Christians in *Contempl.*

[99] The translation of πρακτικός here should be 'active', but it should be remembered that the term derives from the verb πράσσω, 'work, do'. The sense is that those engaged in this philosophical lifestyle are engaged in labour of some kind while they practise philosophy.

[100] Likewise, the translation of θεωρητικός is usually 'contemplative', deriving from the Greek θεωρέω, 'look at, view, contemplate'. One might also translate it 'meditative'. Those practising this form of philosophical lifestyle withdraw

happiness consists in the life of contemplation or in action (10: 7–8).[101] Ultimately, the contemplative life is superior (*NE* 10: 7). Among Aristotle's students, Dicaearchus apparently preferred the active life and Theophrastus the contemplative (Cicero, *De Finibus* 5: 57). According to Diogenes Laertius, Panaetius the Stoic divided virtue into two kinds: contemplative and active (*Lives* 7: 92), though other Stoics divided it differently, determining there to be three types of philosophical lives: 'Of the three kinds of life, the contemplative, the active and the rational, they (i.e. the Stoics) state that we should choose the last one, because a rational being is expressly produced by Nature for contemplation and action' (*Lives* 7: 130). The ideal Stoic integration of the contemplative and active modes of virtuous life in the rational (λογικός) life is actually what we find in Philo's writings. For Philo true virtue comprises both contemplative and active lifestyles. In Philo's allegorical interpretation of Genesis, the trees planted in Eden are virtues, which are both contemplative and active, for what is desirable to look at (contemplative) is also excellent to be enjoyed (active) (*Leg.* 1: 57–8). In philosophy one seeks the perfection of two modes of life, contemplative and active, which once attained makes one happy (*Praem.* 11). In the perfect plan of Moses, people should follow God by devoting six days to the active and the seventh to the contemplative side of virtue (*Decal.* 100, cf. *Spec.* 2: 64). The ultimate integration of both is to be found in the example of Moses. Moses could live a virtuous life that was truly an example in which the contemplative and active were integrated (*Mos.* 1: 48).[102] One may wonder then whether the final treatise in *On Virtues* concerned Moses and his rational virtue, following the Stoic division of three virtuous lives of which the final one was that of the λογικός: an integration of contemplative and active lives in accordance with Nature. This βίος λογικός would then be represented in the books of Moses: the foundations of Jewish life. It would make perfect sense if Philo went from (*a*) 'particular Jewish group i (the

---

from the activities of ordinary work and focus on 'vision of the [Divine] Being' (*Contempl.* 11, cf. Plato, *Rep.* 582c).

[101] Engberg-Pedersen, 'Philo's *De Vita Contemplativa*', 41.

[102] However, at times Philo clearly feels the contemplative life is the superior one: 'For what life is better or more suitable for a rational being than a contemplative one?' (*Migr.* 47, cf. *Fug.* 36).

Essenes)' to (*b*) 'particular Jewish group ii (the Therapeutae)' to (*c*) 'all Jews (Moses and all who abide by the Law)', using the three virtuous lives as a theme: active, contemplative, rational. Whatever the case, the final *telos* of *On Virtues* is to be found in this missing final treatise, and we should not expect everything rhetorically from *Contempl*. In *Contempl*. we have one step along the way in the whole rhetorical project.

Overall, then, the ancient subtitle of *Contempl*. would fit with the theme, which is definitely concerned with virtue. Given the foregoing considerations as a whole, I accept that this treatise is part of a greater one which specifically discusses the virtues, a work in which we find both *Legat*. and its Palinode, and also a missing discussion of the Essenes which bears some resemblance to extant discussions of the Essenes.[103] *On Virtues* was most likely written as material which might be presented in the course of the Jewish deputation to Claudius, in the wake of terrible social unrest in Alexandria. This work and also its overlap with other separate texts indicates that Philo had a flurry of activity late in his life concerned with a much more direct confrontation with the pagan world in regard to 'explaining' and extolling Judaism. It may not be too speculative to suggest that the shock of events in Alexandria, combined with the painfully humiliating experience of his audience with Gaius, led to the very different type of writing we have from Philo in the above-mentioned texts to the esoteric and apparently apolitical texts we find in most of his extant corpus.

The historical context of *Contempl*. would be the bitter hostilities between Jews and 'Greeks' in the city of Alexandria. The 'Greeks' had been favoured by Gaius Caligula. Now, under Claudius, there was a chance for a fairer assessment of the social strife and a more positive appraisal of Jews and Judaism. As we saw above, Claudius did in fact issue edicts safeguarding Jewish rights after delegations came to him from Alexandria. The work

---

[103] Grammatical features of the text of *Contempl*. may also point to it being followed by a further discussion, not only preceded by one on the Essenes. Engberg-Pedersen notes that the last paragraph is introduced by μὲν δή which should be followed by δέ but is not ('Philo's *De Vita Contemplativa*', 42). After noting this, however, Engberg-Pedersen suggests that Philo only presented his work as part of a larger whole when it was in fact a stand-alone text.

On Virtues may be seen then as part of the propaganda he received in order to convince him of the necessity of restoring Jewish rights.[104]

On Virtues would then have had an immediate political relevance, in that Philo was seeking to prove the excellent virtue that is to be found among the Jews,[105] who were at that time in fear of their lives. One should not, after all, demand the deaths of those who are virtuous. *Contempl.* is designed to show that a pinnacle of human moral existence—manifested in a truly philosophical, contemplative, good life—was experienced by a group of Jews living outside Alexandria.

[104] This is not to say that Claudius was pro-Jewish. His attitude to Judaism was clearly mixed. While Claudius acted fairly positively in regard to the Jews of Alexandria, he apparently acted with much greater harshness towards the Jews of Rome. In the very same year that Philo's deputation met with the emperor, Claudius apparently forbade Roman Jews the right of assembly (Cassius Dio, *Hist. Rom.* 60: 6: 6) and expelled (some of?) the Roman Jewish community in 49 CE, because of their rioting about 'Chrestus' (usually identified as 'Christ'): Suetonius, *Div. Claud.* 25: 4, cf. Acts 18: 2. See Arnaldo Momigliano, *Claudius: The Emperor and his Achievement*, tr. W. D. Hogarth (Oxford: Clarendon Press, 1934), 29–38.

[105] Conybeare, *Philo*, 279, notes that *Contempl.* was designed to show that 'Jewish religion could furnish types of excellence in both aspects of life, in the practical as well as in the contemplative'.

3
Identity: The Name 'Therapeutae' and the Essenes

> The more one works in Philo, the stronger is apt to arise the suspicion that the account of the Therapeutae is hardly one of restrained, accurate reporting. In recent years a variety of 'communes' have arisen, and comparable idealization has seemed to me present in the glowing reports I have heard or read on the part of participants, and especially on the part of would-be participants.[1]

As noted in the foregoing chapters, it is important to recognize at the very start that our information about the community described by Philo in *Contempl.* is embedded in rhetoric. Philo is proving points. However, this awareness of Philo's rhetorical interests should not lead us to suppose Philo was making up his community out of thin air. Philo both tells and distorts the reality he perceives, and can only do so from his particular vantage point in his time and place. In order to understand both history and rhetoric, what Philo does not say may be as important as what he does say. Already, in naming his subjects, there are rhetorical issues at work.

It is usual in scholarship to refer to the group Philo describes in *Contempl.* as a particular Jewish sect that can be designated by the Latinized term 'Therapeutae'. In this chapter, I will explore the meaning of Philo's Greek word θεραπευταί (m.)/ θεραπευτρίδες (f.) and problematize the designation. The question we will be considering is as follows: in naming his subjects is Philo using the terminology of the group he describes or is he inventing this term to enhance his argument?

---

[1] Sandmel, *Philo of Alexandria*, 39.

THE MEANING OF THE TERM θεραπευταί/ θεραπευτρίδες

In the first part of *Contempl.*, Philo establishes that he is going to discuss those who follow a philosophical lifestyle, the *bios theoretikos* (*Contempl.* 1), who are devotedly-attending people (*Contempl.* 11), whose devotion (*therapeia*) consists in striving to see a vision of the (Divine) Being. He states that those who embrace the contemplative lifestyle are found all over the world: 'Now then the type of people [I describe] is in many parts of the inhabited world, for it was necessary that perfect good be shared by the Greeks and the Barbarians. But in Egypt, in each of the "nomes" as they are called, it is superabundant, and especially around Alexandria' (*Contempl.* 21). We may get an image of a large satellite picture, from which it is possible to view now the world, now Egypt, and then Alexandria, and then one tiny particular location.[2] This consideration of universal virtue ties in well with his comments in *Prob.* 73–4 when he notes that people who are truly just and good are found in many parts of the world, both among the Greeks and the Barbarians. Philo identifies 'seven' philosophers of ancient Greece, the Persian magi, and the 'gymnosophists' of India as special examples, drawing on a widely evidenced philosophical tradition of citing exemplary philosophers of other cultures. This acknowledgement of other cultural ideals of excellence in philosophy or wisdom is found in Diogenes Laertius, *Lives* 1: 1–11, and Clement of Alexandria, *Strom.* 1: 71–3. Laertius indicates that 'some say the study of philosophy had its origins among the barbarians' and cites: the Persian magi, the Babylonian and Assyrian 'Chaldeans', the Indian gymnosophists, and the Celtic and Gallic druids. He cites as authorities for this view Aristotle's *Magicus* and Sotion's *Succession of the Philosophers*. Clement is clearly deriving his discussion from similar sources, though in his case they are unaccredited. Strabo (*Geogr.* 15: 1: 59–60) cites Megasthenes' *Indika* as the source of his information on Indian philosophers: Brahmins and Sarmanae (Pali: *samana*; Sanskrit: *sramana*), the latter term referring to non-Brahminic ascetics, including Buddhists.[3] In

---

[2] See Ch. 4 for further consideration of the precise localization.
[3] For which see Bardesanes in Porphyry, *De Abstin.* 4: 17–18. For discussion,

Apollonius of Tyana's *Life of Philostratus* (books 1–6), there is a lengthy narrative of how the philosopher visits Persia and India, consulting with Brahmins, and then goes to Egypt and visits gymnosophists by the Nile. There was a story that Alexander the Great met a gymnosophist in India (*Prob.* 92–7), probably called Calanus (Plutarch, *Alexander* 65). Josephus cites Clearchus, *On Sleep*, in stating that Jews are in fact descended from Indian philosophers called Calani (*Apion* 1: 179).[4] It is interesting that Philo has identified the practitioners of the contemplative life as being superabundant in Egypt at this stage. He acknowledges here that perfect good in terms of lifestyle is found widely in Egypt, particularly around Alexandria. Here one thinks not only of Philostratus' Egyptian gymnosophists, but also of Chaeremon's claims regarding the Egyptian priests.

At the beginning of his treatise Philo sets out that he will 'say what is required about those who embrace contemplation [as a philosophical lifestyle], (who) . . . truly are called (καλοῦνται) *therapeutai* and *therapeutrides*' (*Contempl.* 1–2). The passive tense is important; they are called by this designation. Read with *Contempl.* 11–12 and 21, this implies that all those in the world who embrace the philosophical lifestyle of contemplation—the devotedly-attending type of people (θεραπευτικὸν γένος)—are called such. This is simply not so. There is no instance in any other extant Greek sources in which philosophers practising a meditative/contemplative life are called *therapeutai*. In fact, Philo seems to be purposely ambiguous in the first part of the treatise so that we get an appeal to the universality of virtue and the practice of the contemplative life intermixed with the intro-duction of a very specific Jewish group.

Philo introduces and tackles the name of the specific group of people he wishes to use as examples of 'the good' before he goes on to describe them, and immediately gives their name a double meaning. Philo notes that 'they profess medical skill better than in the cities' because they heal the soul by their specific spiritual

see Philip C. Almond, 'Buddhism in the West: 300 BC–AD 400', *Journal of Religious History*, 14 (1987), 235–45, at 236–40.

[4] Calanus was the Indian gymnosophist who followed Alexander the Great and self-immolated himself in front of the army (*Apion* 1: 179; Plutarch, *Alexander* 65).

'therapy' (cf. θεραπεία), or because they have learnt how to serve (θεραπεύειν) God. The verb θεραπεύω is slippery, and provides Philo with ample opportunity to play on a double entendre. It means to 'wait on' or 'serve', 'attend to', 'take care of, 'provide for', somewhat like διακονέω, but it may mean, 'observe (a day)', 'keep (a fast)', 'tend the sick', 'heal', or 'cultivate (land)' among other things.[5] Philo notes that the term θεραπευταί could refer to the fact that they heal the soul (*Contempl.* 2), drawing on the same threads as the Stoic philosopher Epictetus (*c.*55–135 CE), who wrote that true philosophy was the cure of the soul, offered to one who was aware of being ill (Epictetus, *Diss.* 2: 9: 19; 3: 21: 30–8, cf. Seneca, *Ep.* 15: 1).[6]

Other Greek literature and epigraphy can help us here get a better sense of Philo's usage and what his hearers would have understood him to mean. While the word θεράπων (m.)/θεράπαινα (f.) was found commonly to refer to a household servant or attendant (a free person differentiated from a slave), the word θεραπευτής is found in Plato's famous *Phaedrus* to describe one who serves the gods (252c).[7] More specifically, in one Egyptian papyrus the term signifies devotees or cultic attendants of Isis and Serapis.[8] In two inscriptions from Pergamon, a θεραπευτής is an attendant or worshipper of Asclepius and

---

[5] LSJ 722–3. In Acts 17: 25, Paul—addressing the Council of the Areopagos in Athens—claims that God does not need to be served (θεραπεύεται) by human hands, an allusion to the cultic service of deities in temples, but in the Gospels the main meaning of the word is 'heal': Matt. 4: 23–4; 8: 16; etc.; see Joseph Comber, 'The Verb *therapeuō* in Matthew's Gospel', *JBL* 97 (1978), 431–4. A remarkable study of this word and other healing terms in antiquity has been undertaken by Louise Wells, *The Greek Language of Healing from Homer to the New Testament* (BZNW 83; Berlin and New York: de Gruyter, 1998). Wells identifies that in terms of the healing aspect of the word *therapeuō* there is a spiritual meaning present.

[6] Seneca could also use the metaphor of healing to refer to Claudius healing the Empire after the reign of Gaius (*Ad Polybium, de Consol.* 13: 1, cf. 14: 1) and see above, p. 41.

[7] The θεραπευταί here are those who serve Ares, who are linked with the devotees of Zeus. See also *Leges* 740c. A 'server' or 'devotee' of the body is also referred to at *Gorgias* 517e, *Rep.* 369d.

[8] Ulrich Wilcken, *Urkunden der Ptolemäerzeit* (Berlin and Leipzig: Walter de Gruyter, 1922), 8: 19 (2nd cent. BCE). It was also the title of a play by Diphilus Comicus, see Theodor Kock (ed.), *Comicorum Atticorum Fragmenta*, 3 vols. (Leipzig: Teubner, 1980–8), ii. 541, see LSJ 792.

Hygeia[9] and also Serapis.[10] In Magnesia ad Sipylum, the devotees of Serapis and Isis are termed θεραπευταί,[11] as they are also in inscriptions from Demetrias[12] and Cyzicus.[13] The term θεραπευταί appears numerous times in inscriptions from Delos, relating to Egyptian cult.[14] The term is found frequently in the *Sacred Tales* of Aelius Aristides (2nd. cent. CE) referring to the worshippers or cultic attendants of Asclepius (5: 104; 39: 5; 48: 47; 50: 16, cf. 19: 50; 47: 23).[15]

The masculine word θεραπευτής is probably close to the word θεραπευτήρ, which also means 'attendant' (Aristoxenus, *Frag. Hist.* 15; Plutarch, *Lycurgus* 11; Charito, *Erotici* 4: 1). The feminine form, θεραπευτρίς, is also found as θεραπεύτρια.[16] The Suidas has, under the entry for θεραπευτῆρες: οἳ τῶν ἱερῶν προϊστάμενοι, θεραπευταὶ ἴσιδος παρ Ἀιγυπτοις, 'those who stand before the holy places/temples, devotees of Isis of the Egyptians'.[17] Also inter-

---

[9] Christian Habicht (ed.), *Altertümer von Pergamon 8.3: Die Inschriften des Asklepieions* (Berlin: Walter de Gruyter, 1969), no. 71, 108–9; LSJ supplement, 150.

[10] Ladislav Vidman, *Sylloge inscriptionum religionis Isiacae et Sarapiacae* (Berlin: Walter de Gruyter, 1969), no. 314, p. 161. The inscription is dated 1st to 2nd cent. CE. I am grateful to Prof. Helmut Koester for this and the following four references, and see his 'Associations of the Egyptian Cult in Asia Minor', in Peter Scherrer, Hans Taeuber, and Hilke Thür (eds.), *Stein und Wege: Festschrift für Dieter Knibb zum 65 Geburtstag* (Vienna: Osterrichisches Archäologisches Institut, 1999).

[11] Vidman, *Sylloge*, no. 307, p. 158, marble stele dated to the 1st to 2nd cents. CE.

[12] Ibid., no. 102, p. 46, dated *c.*117 CE.

[13] Ibid., no. 318 and no. 319, p. 163, probably to be dated to the 1st cent. CE and cf. nos. 200 and 201 from Lindus (p. 113, dated to the 3rd cent.), where there are references to τὰν θεραπείαν τῶν ἱερῶν τοῦ Σαράπιος.

[14] Pierre Roussel, *Les Cultes égyptiens à Délos du IIIe au 1er siècle avant J.-C.* (Nancy, Paris: Berger-Levrault, 1916), nos. 3, 21, 105, 115, 117, 151, 160, 164, 175, cf. 2, 41, 42.

[15] For this see Harold Remus, 'Voluntary Association and Networks: Aelius Aristides at the Asclepieion in Pergamon', in J. S. Kloppenborg and S. G. Wilson (eds.), *Voluntary Associations in the Graeco-Roman World* (London and New York: Routledge, 1996), 146–75, esp. 152–3.

[16] See Thomas Gaisford (ed.), *Etymologicum Magnum* (Oxford: E. Typographico Academico, 1848), 47: 45.

[17] Suidas 229, Ada Adler (ed.), *Suidae Lexicon* (Stuttgart: Teubner, 1967–71), ii. 706. I am grateful to Dominic Montserrat for this reference, and his help with the following one. The previous entry in the Suidas summarizes Philo's description in *Contempl.*

esting is the use of the term θεραπευτήρια (pl.) in some third-century Egyptian papyri.[18] The term seems to refer to a private feast in celebration of unmarried girls who have completed some kind of ritual event or cultic duty. As Dominic Montserrat writes: 'The *therapeuteria* could . . . be the festival marking the end of the girl's ritual seclusion as a temple servant, in which case it should not surprise us that the festivities take place in private homes rather than temple dining rooms.'[19]

The word θεραπευτής is strikingly not found in the Septuagint to refer to the cultic attendants in the Jerusalem Temple: the priests and Levites. When the word θεραπεύω is used it is in regard to Memphibosthe not 'attending to' his feet (2 Kingdoms 19: 24) and θεραπεία refers to a group of attendants serving Pharaoh (Gen. 45: 16). The Hebrew word that would have been closest to θεραπευτής is שֵׁרֵת, but this is not found in the Hebrew scriptures as a noun, and the verb שֵׁרֵת tends to be translated in the LXX by the verb λειτουργέω. Philo is clearly not deriving his use of the word from the LXX.

When we turn to Philo's language specifically it is interesting to see that Philo uses the word θεραπευτής in numerous places in his extant writings with precisely the meaning determined above, to mean '[cultic] attendant'. It is frequently coupled with the word ἱκέτης, 'suppliant'. In *Leg.* 3: 135, regarding Aaron and his sons, 'the θεραπευτής and minister of holy things is subject to discipline and hardship'. The Levites are appointed as θεραπευταί of God, understood allegorically as Reason 'who has found refuge with God and become his suppliant' (*Sacr.* 118–19). The Levites stand for ὁ θεοῦ θεραπευτὴς, 'the attendant of God' (*Sacr.* 127, cf. 120). Phineas is 'the priest and θεραπευτής of the only good [God]' (*Post.* 182). Potiphres, the father of

---

[18] P.Oxy. Hels. 50: 17 cf. LSJ Suppl. 150; P.Oxy. 66: 4542 and 66: 4543, cf. P. Lond. Inv. 3078.

[19] Dominic Montserrat, 'An Edition, with Translation and Commentary, of Thirty Unpublished Papyrus Texts of the Roman Period from Oxyrhynchus', unpubl. thesis, University College London, 1991, p. 190, and see discussion pp. 188–93, cf. id. 'P.Lond.Inv. 3078 Reappraised', *Journal of Egyptian Archaeology*, 76 (1990), 206–7; id. *Sex and Society in Graeco-Roman Egypt* (London and New York : Kegan Paul, 1996), 45–6. Montserrat also points out that in a glossary compiled by the Alexandrian scholar Hesychius (θ: 370), there is an entry θερτήρια which should probably be restored to θεραπευτήρια. It is defined simply as a 'festival'.

Aseneth, is a 'priest and θεραπευτής of Mind' (*Somn.* 1: 78). In *Ebr.* 126 Philo notes 'for it is the task of priests and θεραπευταί of God alone, hardly any others, to offer abstemious sacrifices'. The θεραπευτικὸν γένος, 'attending type of people' (cf. *Contempl.* 11) is a 'dedicated offering' to God, 'consecrated for the High Priesthood to him alone' (*Fug.* 42). An angel is a 'servant and θεραπευτής' of God in the heavenly realm (*Conf.* 174).

In *Mos.* 2: 67 it is specifically identified that θεραπεία is the business of the priesthood. In *Mos.* 2: 149, in the context of a discussion of the functions of the priesthood, proper rites and sacrificial ceremonies are befitting 'to the θεραπευταί and ministers of God into which they were to be initiated (by Moses)', and the priests are themselves 'θεραπευταί of holy rites' (*Mos.* 2: 274). As High Priest and initiator of ritual functions Moses is himself a cultic attendant of God: the θεραπευτής (=Moses) is the servant of God, who must lay hold of the truth (*Sacr.* 13). In *Det.* 160 Moses pitches his tent outside the camp (body) for only then can he be a perfect suppliant and θεραπευτής of God (and see *Mos.* 2: 135).

Philo can also use the word ironically. When Gaius Caligula decks himself out in the regalia of Mars, believing himself to be the god, Philo scoffs at how his minions had to be the 'θεραπευταί of this new and unknown Mars' (*Legat.* 97). He refers to 'θεραπευταί of the intemperate and incontinent soul', the gluttonies that attend the desire for bread, meat, and drink (*Ebr.* 210). He can mention 'the θεραπευταί of the sun and moon, and all the host of heaven', who are in error (*Decal.* 66).

On the basis of this meaning of '[cultic] attendant'—with a specific reference at times to priests and Levites—Philo can use the word θεραπευτής to refer to someone who 'attends' God by means of a good, perfect, wise, and devoted life (cf. *Plant.* 60). In *Ebr.* 69 the 'θεραπευταί of the only wise [God] must alienate themselves from everything in creation, and look upon all such things as enemies and thoroughly hostile' (cf. *Fug.* 91). Playing on the submeaning of the word he toys with in *Contempl.*, Philo notes that God extends spiritual healing to all his suppliants and θεραπευταί and asks them to employ it to heal those whose souls have been wounded by folly, injustice, and vices (*Migr.* 124, cf. *Sacr.* 127). The perfect man longs to be suppliant and θεραπευτής of God (*Congr.* 105). A θεραπευτής attends to justice and righteousness (*Mut.* 106). Proselytes have forsaken their own country and national customs to become 'lovers of simplicity and truth', i.e. 'suppliants and θεραπευταί of the living [Divine] Being' (*Spec.* 1: 309). God takes the suppliant to be his own, and goes forth to meet the person who hastens to do him service (θεραπεία): 'the true θεραπευτής and suppliant' of God is a wise man defended by piety towards God (*Virt.* 185-6).'The holy and genuine θεραπευταί and friends of God are those who apprehend God by himself without reasoning, and God reveals his existence to his suppliant' (*Praem.* 43–4).

The feminine form θεραπευτρίς is found in *Post.* 184: 'for the consecrated intelligence, being minister and attendant [of God], must do everything in which the Master delights'. In *Somn.* 1: 232 θεραπευτρίς is used to refer to incorporeal souls who are 'attendants' of God, and to them he reveals himself as to friends. Later on in the same treatise, Philo identifies the 'Levites' alle-gorically as suppliants; 'proselytes' as people who have left their homes and taken refuge with God, and 'orphans and widows' as people who are orphaned and widowed to creation, whose 'attendant' soul has adopted God as lawful husband or father (*Somn.* 2: 273).

The θεραπευ- word group would have been used in regard to medical treatment on the basis of a primary meaning of the word as 'attend to' or 'look after', a meaning that lies at the basis of its many nominal developments. All the subsidiary meanings of the verb θεραπεύω may be traced to this primary semantic root: 'observe (a day/fast)' = 'attend to (a day/fast)'; 'tend/heal (the sick)' = 'look after/attend to (the sick)'; 'cultivate (land)' = 'look after/attend to (land)'. Those who 'attend to' or 'look after' a god are servicing that god in some way, while a doctor may attend to a patient, and service the patient's needs. Curiously, without an object in *Contempl.* 2, the designation is rather vague, which suits Philo's interests. What exactly are these people attending to or servicing? The vagueness is there because, if he had been more specific and defined them as 'attendants of God' he could not have made the medical allusion, because God could not be the object of doctors' attention! Philo does not dwell long on the notion of his philosophers as 'healers', perhaps because he was aware of certain semantic difficulties that could arise, but the imagery clearly appealed to him at the start.

With this widespread use of the term as 'servers' or 'attendants' in a cultic context, Philo's text may be translated:

> I will say what is required about those who embrace contemplation [as
> a philosophical lifestyle], (who) . . . are truly called 'attendants', male
> and female, either because they profess the medical skill [to attend the
> sick] better than in the cities, for that of the cities attends bodies alone
> . . . or else because they have been instructed by Nature and the sacred
> laws to attend to the [Divine] Being who is better than a Good, purer
> than a One, and older than a Monad.

It is not possible to include all the resonances of the Greek in an
English translation here, and a better word than 'attendants' or
'servers' in English would be 'devotees', since this carries a little
of the cultic/religious dimension of the Greek word, but keeping
to the 'attendant' translation shows more of what Philo was
doing in terms of word-play than one that does not translate
θεραπευταί/ρίδες and leaves the word purely as some kind of
sectarian name.

When Philo used this word in the context of contemplative
philosophers he would have immediately set up a rhetorical
dissonance. His audience would have associated the word with
cultic attendants, particularly of the Egyptian gods: he initially
introduces the word in the context of true service of God, or the
philosophical power to heal the soul. He takes a word with a wide
cultic application, which he uses also to refer to the cultic attendants of the Jewish Temple, and uses it as a term for a particular
type of philosopher.

Philo provides both the masculine (θεραπευταί) and feminine
(θεραπευτρίδες) forms of his noun, presumably not only with an
awareness that women as well as men were included in the group
he is to focus upon, but also because women as well as men could
be cultic attendants of the gods in general, especially in the cult
of Isis, and engage in contemplative philosophy.[20] It should be
remembered that Serapis was the special god of the Ptolemaic

---

[20] For women's participation in the cult of Isis see: Sharon Kelley Heyob,
The Cult of Isis among Women in the Graeco-Roman World (Leiden: Brill, 1975);
Ross Shepard Kraemer, *Her Share of the Blessings* (New York: OUP, 1992),
71–9. The inclusion of a specific reference to women in the very term he uses for
the group is surprising given that the masculine plural form θεραπευταί could
have included women anyway. At the very start Philo wishes to signal his interest in the women here, giving some indication that he will discuss them specifically in the course of his essay.

dynasty, and that the Serapeion was the most magnificent build-ing in Alexandria.[21] Those devoted to the temple service of Isis and Serapis were the practitioners of θεραπεία, devotion to a god.

In the epitomes of Chaeremon's description of the Egyptian priests, there is no clear evidence that he used the term θεραπευταί at any point, though it would fit with the evidence if the term θεραπευταί was applied to both priests and laypeople in the Egyptian cult. Philo and Chaeremon might well not only both have been writing about people dedicated to the contemplative life, but people (in Chaeremon's case, men only) who would have been called θεραπευταί.[22] Even without definite proof of the same terminology, both Chaeremon and Philo go conceptually from the cultic to the philosophical in one fell swoop.

When we consider what Philo states regarding the Essenes as 'servers/attendants of God' (*Prob.* 75) we see exactly the same process at work. Philo configures them in the light of attendants in the Temple of God, dedicated to his service. He is using imagery to explain their devotion to their way of life. He is not giving them a name 'Therapeutae' here. The whole context reads: 'Certain [Jews of Syria Palaestina] are called *Essaioi* . . . which I believe . . . is [a designation] formed from [the word] *hosiotes* (holiness). They are worthy [of this designation] since they are attendants of God (θεραπευταὶ θεοῦ), not through sacrificing animals, but through preparing to sanctify their minds' (*Prob.* 75). Here Philo deliberately addresses the implied cultic resonance of his usage of θεραπευταὶ θεοῦ by adding that they are attendants of God 'not through sacrificing animals'.

In summary, Philo's use of the word θεραπευταί owes much to common usage associated with the cult of Serapis and Isis, as well as usage in currency at least from the time of Plato, which referred to those who were devoted to the service of the gods (or God) as θεραπευταί.[23] The word θεραπευταί would have been generally

---

[21] Huzar, 'Alexandria ad Aegyptum', 627. The library was in the 1st cent. housed in part of the Serapeion. The foundations of part of the Serapeion struc-ture are visible in the area of the so-called 'Pillar of Pompey' (actually erected by Diocletian) in Alexandria today. According to Suetonius, *Claudius* 42: 2, the Emperor Claudius added an extension to the Alexandrian library.

[22] Chaeremon apparently distinguished between those who truly followed the contemplative and ascetic life he describes and the lower orders of the priest-hood whose purity and self-control were not as great (Porphyry, *De Abstin.* 4: 8).

[23] The view that the Greek word is a loan from Sanskrit/Pali *theravada*, from

understood in a cultic sense. Philo understands the word in this way, and can apply it to the priests and Levites in the Jewish Temple, but also uses it metaphorically to refer to those living very pious lives, and here to lives of contemplative philosophy.

Philo in fact appears to provide his own definition of the term θεραπευταί in *Contempl.* He asks (rhetorically) who of 'those who profess piety' is worthy of comparison with the θεραπευταί, meaning the latter are those who (like the Essenes) are truly pious, not simply those professing to be so (*Contempl.* 3).[24] He discusses people who revere the elements, worshippers of heavenly bodies, of demi-gods, of images, and of Egyptian animal gods as all hopelessly misguided, and comments (*Contempl.* 10):

> But these people infect with foolishness not only their own compatriots, but also those [living in regions] nearby, and they remain incurable (*atherapeutoi*), for they are incapable of sight, the most vital of the senses. And I talk not of the body, but the sight of the soul, which alone gives knowledge of truth and falsehood.

This passage is paralleled in *Decal.* 66 (see above) where he does use the word θεραπευταί of those who are devotees of astrological powers. The opposite of the true θεραπευταί—dubbed here the ἀθεράπευτοι[25]—are foolish, incurable, sick in the soul, incapable of apprehending the knowledge of truth and falsehood, and essentially impious. There is an implication that, while such

Buddhist missionaries who followed the *theravada* 'teachings of the old ones', seems unlikely in that it does not recognize the priority of the verb. At any rate it does not connect the group of *Contempl.* with Buddhists even if the term originated as a loan-word, contra Zacharias P. Thundy, *Buddha and Christ* (Leiden: Brill, 1993), 245; Elmar R. Gruber and Holger Kersten, *The Original Jesus: The Buddhist Sources of Christianity* (Shaftesbury: Element, 1995), 183. However, the influence of Buddhism and other Indian philosophies on the intellectual world of Alexandria as a whole is certainly likely, and seems to have been linked with the discovery of the 'Monsoon Passage' and subsequent direct trade between Alexandria and the East from the end of the 2nd cent. BCE onwards.

[24] This definition may then relate to constructions of the so-called 'pious' movement (cf. 1 Macc. 2: 42–4; 7: 13–17), but I would strongly resist lumping all the Jewish 'pious' together as some kind of sect. Different people can claim to be pious, or be called pious, for different reasons, at different times, for different purposes.

[25] This is an adjective rather than a noun, but a pun is clearly intended. The opposite therefore defines what Philo means.

devotees of demi-gods and animal gods may profess to be pious, and therefore would then have been dubbed θεραπευταί, this was completely wrong. True θεραπευταί are as Philo configures them. It is unlikely that any of the examples of the ἀθεράπευτοι would have offended elite Roman sensibilities, as Philo appears to be appealing to cultic forms that the Roman elite would have dubbed *superstitio*,[26] though they would have offended Chaeremon's. Philo pours scorn on Egyptian worship as the opposite of true piety.

As noted above, keeping with the universalist theme of the beginning of *Contempl.*, Philo notes that the θεραπευτικὸν γενός, 'the devotedly-attending type of people', wish to see the Divine Being and seek the spiritual experience of true bliss (*Contempl.* 11). This statement reinforces the notion that the true θεραπευτικὸν γενός is a worldwide phenomenon and essentially philosophical. Philo is not only referring to Jews, even though he elsewhere possibly refers to Jews as a contemplative γενός (*QE* 2: 42–3). What needs to be established for Philo's rhetoric is the acceptance of a universal virtue. The motivation for this virtue is equally universal: 'those who are going about θεραπεία[27] [do so] . . . not from custom, or from advice or recommendation of anyone, but because they are seized by a heavenly passion' (*Contempl.* 12). They leave their possessions to their families and dwell in places outside urban communities: this they have in common (cf. *Mut.* 32). Such a universal acknowledgement of the type of persons committed to the pursuit of Wisdom is found also in *Spec.* 2: 42–8. Here Philo notes that all those who live according to Wisdom 'whether among the Greeks or Barbarians' avoid cities, choose a life of peace and tranquillity, raise themselves above the passions and needs of the body, and pass their time happily celebrating the bliss of their life. He also notes that such people are few (47).

This again is probably conventional discourse on the good life of true philosophy, since the same kinds of ideals are to be found

[26] For Roman tetchiness about *superstitio*, see Mary Beard, John North, and Simon Price, *Religions of Rome*, 2 vols. (Cambridge: CUP, 1998), i. 211–44. Claudius was apparently very concerned to correct cultic abuses (Tacitus, *Annales* 11: 15; Suetonius, *Claudius* 22: 25: 5). For Roman views of Egyptian animal worship, see Smelik and Hemelrijk, 'Demented Egypt'.

[27] Here, perhaps literally 'attendance', but clearly 'devotion to god(s)' is meant rather than the other meaning of 'medical treatment'.

in the utopian fantasies of Iambulus, Euhemerus, and others, as well as the idealizing descriptions we have of philosopher communities such as the Essenes (Josephus, *Ant.* 13: 171–3; 15: 371–9; 18: 11, 18–21; *War* 2: 119–61; Pliny, *Nat. Hist.* 1: 15: 73), or the aforementioned various accounts of philosophers of other nations, and much later in Iamblichus' *De Vita Pythagorica* (late third cent.). There must have been a kind of constellation of motifs that people expected to find in evidence in any group of people going about a virtuous philosophical ('good') existence. In Festugière's analysis of these motifs, he noted particularly that the two characteristic traits were ἐγκράτεια, 'self-control' or 'continence', and ἀναχώρησις, 'separation from the world'.[28] The decision to live away from urban life is characteristic of nearly all true and good philosophers, according to Philo (see *Prob.* 63; *Abr.* 22–3; *Spec.* 2: 44 cf. *Mos.* 2: 34). The motif occurs in Chaeremon's work on the Egyptian priests: they have chosen temples as their quiet sanctuaries away from the world (Porphyry, *De Abstin.* 4: 6). Doron Mendels has pointed out in regard to the Essenes that a certain range of ideal features is far more than a literary convention; actual groups such as the Essenes may really have modelled themselves on the set of ideals established as common features of virtuous philosophical lives.[29] Indeed, it seems safe to assume that there were cultural paradigms of virtue that would influence not only how certain groups were described in discourse for the sake of idealizing strategies and rhetoric but also how those groups actually behaved or sought to behave. They were themselves participants in this discourse.

The designation, 'suppliants', ἱκέται, in the heading of *Contempl.* is, like the term θεραπευταί, a cultic one. I have noted some of the instances of the word's occurrence in Philo above, and that it is often associated with the term θεραπευταί. The word ἱκετεύω means 'to approach as a suppliant, entreat, beseech'.[30] Philo generally understands that the ἱκέτης is someone who has taken refuge at a temple, close to the altar (e.g. *Conf.* 160; *Fug.* 80, *Ios.* 229; *Spec.* 1: 159–61; *Virt.* 124; *Prob.* 148–51; *Somn.* 2: 299), though one can also make supplication of a king or ruler for

---

[28] Festugière, 'De Vita Pythagorica', 476.
[29] Mendels, 'Hellenistic Utopia'.
[30] See LSJ 826.

refuge or justice (*Mos.* 1: 34–6; 1: 142; *Legat.* 228, 276). But, more specifically, as with θεραπευταί, the ἱκέται are the Levites who have 'taken refuge with God as genuine suppliants and servants' (*Det.* 62, cf. 63). The genuine suppliants, the Levites, raise hymns of thankfulness in their hearts (*Ebr.* 94). To be a suppliant is 'the job of the consecrated tribe of Levi' (*Her.* 124). This is because the tribe of Levi has collectively taken refuge at God's footstool. They were allotted no territory in the division of Canaan between the twelve tribes of Israel, but rather were given 'the privilege of priesthood' (*Plant.* 63, cf. Deut. 10: 9; Num. 18: 20). A suppliant is one who does God's service (θεραπεία) (*Somn.* 2: 99), who 'begs for grace at the altar by prayers, vows and sacrifices' (*Somn.* 2: 299). Ultimately, however, Philo treats the suppliant tribe of Levi as symbolic of the mind which renounces all things of creation, concentrating on God alone, the mind that states 'God alone is [everything] to me'; that is the 'Levite mode' (*Plant.* 63), for the suppliant is positioned by the altar that is 'the place of innocent and purified souls' (*Fug.* 80). Real suppliants are those who 'love a life of virtue', who quench their search for wisdom with water drawn from holy fountains (*Virt.* 79). We again take a loop from the cultic to the philosophical. In Philo, Moses is one who, above all, makes supplication to God, because of his fervent desire for Wisdom (*Spec.* 1: 41–50).

It is rather curious how the subtitle ἱκετῶν came to be applied to the treatise rather than the more understandable θεραπευτῶν but the unflinching focus of the group on God seems to be at the heart of this designation. Given both terms are cultic in usage, it is striking that the 'reality' Philo constructs in the text is philosophical. Only at the end of the treatise does the cultic break in once more in a way that does not cohere with this philosophical project. Philo writes of the bread eaten by the group in their festive meal as being 'in deference to the sacred table in the vestibule of the holy Temple court. For upon this [table] are loaves and salt, without flavouring, and the bread is unleavened, and the salt is not mixed in' (*Contempl.* 81). Their singing is also on the pattern of the Temple singers: their songs are 'hexameters, trimeters, hymns for processions, [hymns] relating to libations, [hymns] relating to the altar' (*Contempl.* 80). By implication the special meals appear to constitute cultic service. Philo can use cultic language—especially of the mystery cults—for the sake of imagery in his work.[31] Allegorical interpretation of scripture is itself, according to Philo, for the 'initiated' who see Moses as their chief hierophant.[32] But whose terminology is being used in regard to the sacred meal: the group's or Philo's? It should be remembered that he has, at the outset, defined the designation as something placed upon the group either by themselves or by other people but not by himself alone: they 'are called attendants, male and female'. In terms of the festive meal, the bread 'is in deference of the sacred table'. While Philo may pun on the word they are called by, and focus on the self-control exhibited when these people ate simple bread only, the cultic dimensions surge out of the text despite Philo's philosophical project. Philo's use of the cultic term θεραπευταί/ρίδες for what he otherwise indicates is a philosophical reality is therefore an example of rhetorical dissonance that points to some aspect of the real project of the group he describes. By the end of the text it is actually quite clear that this one specific group itself goes by the name of 'attendants' or 'devotees' (of God): 'On this model most of all the choir of the attendants/devotees, male and female, is based' (*Contempl.* 88), though Philo concludes by asserting his more generalized philosophical definition: 'So then let this suffice for matters of the attendants [of God] who embrace contemplation of Nature and what it contains, and of those living in the soul alone' (*Contempl.* 90).

'THERAPEUTAE' AND ESSENES

Modern scholarship has often associated the group Philo describes in *Contempl.* with the Essenes,[33] and the foregoing remarks concerning the name of the group may not be sufficient

---

[31] *Leg.* 3: 219; *Cher.* 42, 48–9; *Gig.* 54; *Deus* 60–1; *Somn.* 1: 164–5.

[32] See David Hay, 'Philo's References to Other Allegorists', *Studia Philonica*, 6 (1979–80), 41–75, at p. 45.

[33] For a survey of those who link the 'Therapeutae' with the Essenes, see Riaud, 'Les Thérapeutes d'Alexandrie', 1189–1295 at 1241–64 and see also Marcel Simon, *Jewish Sects at the Time of Jesus*, tr. James H. Farley of *Les Sectes juives au temps de Jésus* (Paris: Presses universitaires de France, 1960; Philadelphia: Fortress, 1967), 120–30; Geza Vermes and Martin Goodman (eds.), *The Essenes According to the Classical Sources* (Sheffield: Sheffield

to dislodge this conception. The identification of the group as Essene is caused by the fact that at the very beginning of *Contempl.* (1), Philo writes ambiguously. He states:

I have discoursed on Essenes, who were zealous for and who worked hard at the active life, excelling in everything or—at least to say it more moderately—in most parts. Going on directly, and indeed carrying on in accordance with the plan [of my subject] I will say what is required about those who embrace contemplation . . .

Given this, one could read it that Philo is now going to write about 'those Essenes' who embraced contemplation, rather than anyone else. However, if Philo intended to write about people of the Essene school alone who were contemplative rather than active, we would surely have something further about the relationship between the two branches of the school. Despite his ambiguity at the start of his essay on the contemplative life, Philo himself does not directly equate the community of θεραπευταί/ρίδες in *Contempl.* with the sect of the Essenes (Ἐσσαῖοι) he had just described (cf. *Prob.* 75–91 and *Hypothetica* 11: 1–18).

Philo's project is to illustrate the active and contemplative philosophical lives by illustrations from Judaism that ultimately would prove how virtue is found within the community he represents. To focus on one school of Judaism only would have made his argument weak, since virtue would be concentrated in the Essenes, of all Jewish groups. Philo's purpose is to focus on the superlative virtue of certain Jewish groups as representing key aspects of Israel's relationship with God, while indicating that such superlative virtue should in fact be shared by all those who follow the Mosaic law. The groups are not then singled out as exceptional so much as indicated as representational of the perfect ideals of Judaism. In *Virt.* 64 Philo identifies that Jews have the greatest of professions: 'the supplication of He who is'. In other words, he can take one specific example or another of a Jewish group that seems in some way to be particularly pious or devotional, but Philo's ultimate interest is in representing Judaism as a whole as having these essential characteristics.

In *Prob.*, while acknowledging the universal manifestations of devotional type of people, Philo provides a pre-eminent Jewish example as the ultimate illustration: the Essenes, who live in Syria Palaestina (*Prob.* 75). In *Contempl.*, while the θεραπευτικὸν γένος exists in many parts of the inhabited world, he specifically identifies a Jewish group outside Alexandria as being his pre-eminent example of philosophers who have embraced ἐγκράτεια, quitted society, and disbursed their possessions[34] in order to contemplate Nature. Outside Alexandria, the 'best of them' (i.e. of the θεραπευτικὸν γένος, *Contempl.* 11) come to dwell. Since Philo associates the Essenes with Syria Palaestina, they cannot be the same group he places outside Alexandria.

As Philo presents the matter at the beginning of *Contempl.*, he is *contrasting* the two examples of Jewish groups rather than linking them together,[35] in order to represent them as undertaking different forms of virtuous lives. On the one hand there are the prime attendants of God who live an active life—the Ἐσσαῖοι—and then on the other hand there are those who live a meditative/contemplative life: the members of this group outside Alexandria.

Further, we should note that the most striking difference made between Philo's description of *Essaioi* and his attendants of God outside Alexandria comes in regard to women's membership of the two respective groups. In the *Hypothetica* 11: 14–18 Philo states that the all-male *Essaioi* do not marry, and this aversion to marriage is expressed by means of a caricature of married life. Philo does not address the issue of celibate 'Essene' women at all and, with Pliny, *Nat. Hist.* 5: 17: 4 (73) and Josephus, *War* 2: 120, describes a sect composed entirely of celibate and tending-to-elderly men (*Hypoth.* 11: 3). He appears not to know about the case of married Essenes described by Josephus (*War* 2: 160–1). The combination of the testimony of these three separate authors would appear to be conclusive as hearsay: it was generally believed that there was a sect named the *Essaioi* composed of celibate males who did not admit women into their group. Even when Josephus describes a marrying type of Essenes, he does not

---

[34] Leaving aside possessions and neglect of the things of the body are common characteristics of all who are 'virtuous and wise', so *Mut.* 32.

[35] So Conybeare, *Philo*, 192, who also notes (pp. 278–9) that grammatically there would need to be τῶν before Ἐσσαίων for any equation to work.

indicate that the women they marry are included within the sect, only that the men belonging to the Essene school happen to marry (and only for the purposes of procreation). For Josephus, the sect remains male. In the second century, the Christian author Hippolytus would base himself on Josephus in describing the Essenes, but note additional points also, one of these points being that, even if women wanted to adopt the same discipline (including celibacy), the Essenes would not let them in because they 'do not trust women in any way' κατα μηδένα τρόπον γυναιξὶ πιστεύοντες (*Ref. Haer.* 9: 18). Here Hippolytus may directly address the question of female celibates because of the model of Christian women celibates known to him, and identifies what is implicit in all the extant accounts of the Essenes (even if this were untrue): there were no Essene women, only women married to certain Essenes.

Therefore, when Philo used the Essenes in his third treatise of *On Virtues*, he would have presented them as an all-male group, as he did in *Hypoth*. It would not be logical if immediately following on from this Philo stated: 'I will say what is required about those [Essenes] who embrace contemplation, (who) . . . are called *therapeutai* (masc.) and *therapeutrides* (fem.)'. Those who wish to read Philo as referring to contemplative Essenes here are, in fact, strikingly woman-blind. In the group outside Alexandria, women have adopted the contemplative life, 'having the same zeal and purpose' as the men (*Contempl.* 32). Philo writes that they have adopted the contemplative lifestyle:

because of a zeal and yearning for Wisdom, which they are eager to live with. They take no heed of the pleasures of the body, and desire not a mortal offspring, but an immortal one, which only a soul which is loved by God is able to give birth to, by itself, because the Father has sown in it lights of intelligence which enable her to see the doctrines of Wisdom. (*Contempl.* 68)

Relations between men and women in the community are presented as being harmonious, and the two sexes inter-react by 'making beautiful music together' (literally!) which provides Philo with an opportunity to give them superlative praise. Whether his description of the Essenes or the 'Therapeutae' near Alexandria is accurate is not the issue; what is important is that Philo himself describes them as being definitively different on a main, distinctive feature relating to the groups: the admission of women. Therefore, Philo believed the groups to be distinct.[36]

Geza Vermes has made an interesting linkage of the Greek words Ἐσσαῖοι and θεραπευταί/ θεραπευτρίδες by identifying the underlying Aramaic of the former as אסא, meaning 'healer'.[37] But since the basic meaning of θεραπευταί was 'attendants' and was cultic in application, we no longer have in Philo's work a distinct sect who may be designated 'healers'. It is Philo's speculations on double entendre that lead him to wonder if the word refers to those who heal the soul. Moreover, Philo tries to make the word θεραπευταί in *Contempl.* apply not only to the Jews he wishes to focus upon, but, by implication, also to all those who appear to live the contemplative life of philosophy. He takes the word he found applying to one Jewish group and makes it stand for all those who follow a type of meditative philosophy that would enable them to see the Divine Being. In *Prob.* 75 he uses the term to indicate the special 'service' of the Essenes in sanctifying their minds, but he does not say they 'are called' θεραπευταί, rather their name is *Essaioi.* Philo can use the term θεραπευταί here figuratively, but in *Contempl.* he has people who *are called* θεραπευταί 'cultic servers' of God. In this case Philo reconfigures their actual name to give it a non-cultic figurative meaning, which is not the same as in *Prob.* In *Contempl.* it applies to all engaged in contemplative philosophy, which would rule out the Essenes in this case, because they are being used in *On Virtues* as exemplars of a different form of philosophical life, the *bios prak-tikos.* Nevertheless, while we need to have consistency between *On Virtues*, no. 3, and no. 4, which occupy one rhetorical field, we do not between *Prob.* and *Contempl.*, because these two works occupy different rhetorical fields.

Given that the Greek term θεραπευταί/ρίδες refers to cultic attendants/devotees of gods, then it cannot have been an exclu-sive sectarian name for a single Jewish group that could easily be identified by using this name. If the group of *Contempl.* did indeed use this term to refer to itself, then it would have serious ramifications for its self-understanding: the name would be

---

[36] Ibid. 215.

[37] See Vermes and Goodman, *Essenes*, 1–2; Geza Vermes, *Jesus the Jew: A Historian's Reading of the Gospels*, 2nd edn. (London: SCM, 1983), 59–63.

making a claim for the group's relationship with God, as names like *hasidim* (Heb.) 'the pious' (1 Macc. 2: 42–4; 7: 13–17) also did. If other people referred to them in this way, this would also be interesting. The name of the group, I think, continues to need to be problematized if we are to go further. I have noted here that there was a cultic dimension to the group's festive meal. I will return to the issue of what it might have meant for the group later on in this study. In order to avoid emphasizing the designation 'Therapeutae' in its usual sectarian sense, I will for the moment generally avoid using it. In accordance with the precedent set in Dead Sea Scrolls scholarship, in which a group resident at Qumran (which may or may not be Essene) is defined as 'the Qumran community', I will refer to the historical group Philo describes in *Contempl.* not by the designation 'Therapeutae' but as 'the Mareotic community' or 'the Mareotic group', since these people lived close to Lake Mareotis. It is to their location that we now turn.

4

Placements: The Geographical and Social Locations of the Mareotic Group

> Like the monasteries on the Chinese Silk Road oases, the Indian monks' retreats were usually located near ancient trade routes. Because of salt marshes along the coast, these routes passed from the western seaports near Bombay, through the Western Ghats . . . to the inland center of Ujjaini (Ujjain) or to Bharukaccha (Broach) on the coast.[1]

It is easy to configure the Mareotic group in the light of later Christian monasteries, and become blind to the evidence that Philo provides in his text. As we have seen, for Philo and for others in the Graeco-Roman world the stories of Indian sages and Buddhist monks and nuns provided examples of those who lived a contemplative life. To what extent those who followed the contemplative life copied any forms or ideas from the norms of Eastern philosophy cannot be known, but Eastern types of philosophical/religious lifestyles may be used to challenge our preconceptions, based so strongly within the Christian tradition. In early Christian monasticism, ascetics such as St Antony went far away from human society into the wilderness. Our proto-typical image of a monastery in Egypt is St Catherine's, deep into the Sinai desert. This kind of isolation is not usual in Buddhist monasticism. Traditionally, in Theravada Buddhism, the

[1] Sally Hovey Wriggins, *Xuanzang: A Buddhist Pilgrim on the Silk Road* (Boulder, Colo.: Westview Press, 1996), 139. This describes the one hundred Buddhist monasteries—many of which were ancient—in the north-western district of India, as noted by the Chinese traveller, Xuanzang, who visited here in 641 CE, and who went on further north, to Malva (now in Madhya Pradesh), where there were hundreds more. Between 20 and 240 CE the north-west was part of the Kushana Empire, in which trade—especially with the Persian Gulf—and a cosmopolitan ethos were strong. For more see Sukumar Dutt, *Buddhist Monks and Monasteries in India: Their History and Contribution to Indian Culture* (London: George Allen & Unwin, 1962).

sangha (the community of monks and nuns) has a special relationship with the wider Buddhist community, which supports those who live in the monastery: the wider community supplies the *sangha* with food, when the monks[2] come to beg, and the *sangha* gives advice to the wider community. The location of a monastery is often right in the heart of a town. In this chapter we will consider the geographical and social location of the group Philo describes in order to define more precisely how it might be placed in terms of the community from which it came. We will also consider how it places different members of the group in terms of status.

GEOGRAPHICAL LOCATION

Philo seems to be very careful to situate the group he describes with great precision. He writes:

The best of them from anywhere set off as to a homeland settlement, to a very suitable place[3] which is above Lake Mareotis, lying upon a flattish, low hill, very well situated, because of safety and temperate air. The safety is supplied by the encircling dwellings and villages. And the continual breezes which arise from both the lake which flows into the sea and the open sea nearby [result] in the pleasant temperature of the air. For those [breezes] of the sea are slight, but those coming up from the lake are stronger, so the mixture creates a very healthy climate. (*Contempl.* 22–3)

Philo seems to be working with a clear understanding of the exact place where the group lived. No one has as yet determined exactly where this community was located, though Philo is extremely

---

[2] I use only the word 'monks' here deliberately, because full nuns in the Theravada Indian tradition gradually grew fewer and eventually disappeared, see Nancy Auer Falk, 'The Case of the Vanishing Nuns: The Fruits of Ambivalence in Ancient Indian Buddhism', in Nancy Auer Falk and Rita Gross, *Unspoken Worlds: Women's Religious Lives* (Belmont, Calif.: Wadsworth, 1989), 155–65.

[3] The word here is χωρίον not τόπος. This term is a common one, the diminutive form of χῶρος and χῶρα, which has agricultural or rural associations. It applies to a small tract of land. See the discussion in Joan E. Taylor, *Christians and the Holy Places: The Myth of Jewish–Christian Origins* (Oxford: Clarendon Press, 1993), 198–9, where I note that χωρίον is translated at times into Latin as *villa* or *praedium*.

precise. He describes a flattish, low hill which lies above Lake Mareotis, close to the open sea. Later on, Philo also mentions that the Mareotic group drink 'spring water' (*Contempl.* 37), which indicates the close proximity of a natural spring.

Rhetorically, this description appears to indicate the good sense of the people who have come together at this site. They have chosen their position well, and therefore at the very start we gain the impression that they form good judgements.[4] Moreover, the speculations Philo has made about the name *therapeutai/rides* having an association with health are here alluded to, for the location itself is extremely healthy. Philo himself is very conscious of the benefits of good air (*Gig.* 10). Here is a site which is well-aired both from the sea and the lake, promoting well-being, and it is also safe. This description of their location is not then given to satisfy our historical curiosity, but to make a rhetorical point in favour of a positive appraisal of the Mareotic group from the very moment we meet them. That is, even a passage that appears to supply us with straightforward historical evidence is in fact highly rhetorical when one considers the treatise as a whole. Its rhetoricity, however, does not invalidate its historicity,[5] since to make the assertion that what is rhetorical is not historical only creates a simplistic binary opposition and nothing more substantial. In stating that the group go to this exact place 'as to a homeland settlement' Philo is clearly stressing that they have a natural predilection for a perfect location, defined in contrast to the hurly-burly of the city where people who do not have the same sensibility live (*Contempl.* 19). They divest themselves of their belongings by giving them to

---

[4] For the rhetorical issues at work here, see Bergmeier, 'Der Stand der Gottesfreunde', 49–51.

[5] Contra Bergmeier, 'Der Stand der Gottesfreunde', 49–50, and n. 24. It was mentioned in Joan E. Taylor and Philip R. Davies, 'The So-Called Therapeutae of *De Vita Contemplativa*: Identity and Character', *HTR* 91 (1998), 3–24, at 12 n. 45, that Alexandrians could verify the existence of the people Philo describes by an excursion from Alexandria by boat. This is not the transference of a 'moderne Jachtklubvorstellungen auf die Antike', as Bergmeier suggests, but rather acknowledges the large amount of traffic on Lake Mareotis in antiquity (see below): an interested observer could get passage on a trading boat to visit a site on the lake. Given that Philo was a native of the area, it is unlikely that he made a mistake with his geographical siting. If part of his audience was composed of his Alexandrian 'Greek' opposition it would have been especially important to get the easily verifiable details correct.

friends and family and 'flee' (*Contempl.* 18), not to another city, but to this very suitable spot. Their physical home in the city is not their real home; their real home is the most ideal location imaginable for those with a philosophical consciousness, who are truly those who are 'good'. They are the best of all contemplative philosophers, and they have chosen the best location, which they go to as people would go to a special homeland. This is the place they belong. The best people go to the best spot.

As already noted, if Philo were inventing a group, he should have located them vaguely in a faraway location that could not be verified. In locating them so precisely, close to the Roman city of Alexandria, he almost invites his audience to pay the group a visit, or at the least implies that he himself has visited them. If you want to invent a group, it seems wasteful to identify them not only as living on a hill, but specifically 'on a flattish low hill', ἐπὶ γεωλόφου χθαμαλωτέρου.[6] The adjective and descriptive noun provide a visual image far more precise than would be necessary for an invention. It is not some ill-defined 'island' far away, or even any 'hill' outside a city. One apparently sees the hill like this as one nears it from the Lake Mareotis, which would have been the natural way of reaching it from the Mareotic (southern) port of the city of Alexandria, since it was faster to travel by boat than by foot.

The words ἐπὶ γεωλόφου χθαμαλωτέρου describe a place on one of the hills comprising the low, limestone ridge which stretches north-east to south-west on the south-western side of Alexandria. This ridge only rises to a maximum height of about 30 m (see Figure 2).[7] The limestone ridge beyond Alexandria was in ancient times known as ἡ Ταινία, 'the Strip' (Ptolemy, *Geogr.* 4: 5: 24). While Peter Richardson has recently suggested that the group should be located south of Lake Mareotis,[8] I would dispute this localization. The suggestion that the community may have been on the south shore of Lake Mareotis relies on a reading of ὑπέρ λίμνης Μαρείας as 'beyond Lake Mareotis' or

---

[6] The noun γεώλοφος itself indicates a hill of low height.

[7] The long, limestone spur runs from Bahig to Aboukir. For the archaeology in this region see Mieczslaw Rodziewicz, 'Taenia and Mareotis: Archaeological Research West of Alexandria', *Annual of the Egyptian School of Greek and Roman Studies*, 1 (1990), 62–78.

[8] Richardson, 'Philo and Eusebius', 337, 346 n. 37.

2. The limestone ridge which runs south-west from Alexandria. View from across slim arm of Lake Mareotis. Note encroachment of modern buildings to the right

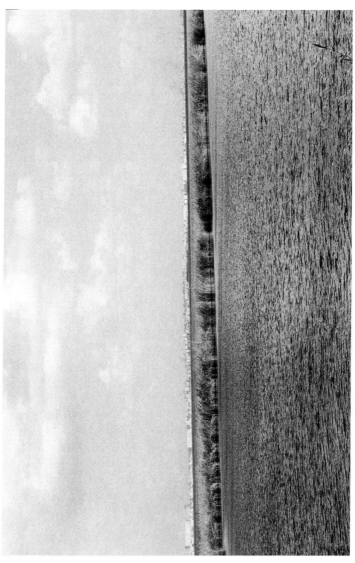

3. View over Lake Mareotis to modern Alexandria from the south, looking northwards

'farther inland' from it. This suggestion has been rejected by
Annewies van den Hoek, who notes that the first meaning of ὑπέρ
with the genitive is 'over, 'above', or 'on higher ground'. The
second meaning, favoured by Richardson, is more common with
an accusative, and indeed Philo uses it with the accusative when
he wishes to indicate 'beyond' (*Leg.* 1: 2; *Somn.* 1: 54; *Spec.* 86:
4). Otherwise, particularly in a geographical context, Philo uses
ὑπέρ with the genitive to mean 'above' a location, as in ὑπέρ γῆς
(*Sacr.* 25; *Her.* 226; *Fug.* 57; *Abr.* 140: 1; *Mos.* 1: 175; *Dec.* 56:
2).[9] Given this, there seems no reason to situate the Mareotic
group anywhere other than on 'the Strip'.[10]

Philo identifies two types of breezes: those of the sea and those
of the lake, indicating that the site was close to both lake and
sea—a matter which Philo also specifically states—along 'the
Strip'. He states also that the two types of breezes could be distinguished, that is, they came from different directions, which is
the case on the ridge. The locality is 'above Lake Mareotis'
somewhere on this ridge, and subject more to the lake breezes
than those of the sea. South of the lake one only feels a general
breeze that blows from the sea over the lake (when there is not the
hot and dusty Khamsin wind in March and April, which is anything but refreshing), and it would be impossible to state that the
lake breezes are stronger than those of the sea as the impression
is only of a general light sea breeze. Furthermore, there is no time
that the lake breezes are stronger than those of the sea in the
Alexandria region, and the only way to experience stronger lake
breezes would be if the sea breezes were blocked off in some way.
Strabo notes that the air from the lake is healthy and that the
Etesian breezes from the sea (in mid-summer) cool the city of
Alexandria (*Geogr.* 17: 1: 7), but they can also be too much in
autumn. If we locate the site of the group a little down the slope
of the hill so that it faces the lake, it would have been closer to the
lake breezes than those of the sea, since the spur of the hill would
have protected the site from the blustery sea wind. In fact, a situation right at the top of the hill would have been too exposed,

---

[9] See van den Hoek, 'Catechetical School', 84–5, n. 124.

[10] Sly, *Philo's Alexandria*, map 3, has the 'city [sic] of Therapeutae' squeezed
in between the southern walls of Alexandria and Lake Mareotis, which seems
unlikely, given this was where necropoleis were located (see below) rather than
'dwellings and villages'.

since sometimes the wind is very powerful, even lightly destruc-
tive, and subsequently not very pleasant if you meet it at full
force. It seems unlikely that the community was located far down
the coast, because for the lake breezes to be experienced as
significant it must have been sited where the lake was reasonably
broad, even though a finger of Lake Mareotis stretched some 47
km south-west from Alexandria to culminate in the city of
Taposiris Magna (Abu Sir).[11]

An approximate localization for the Mareotic group as being
on 'the Strip' was proposed over thirty years ago by François
Daumas, who identified in this region 'des bourgs et des vallons
qui ont pu contenir, à une époque où la végétation était moins
désertique, quelques filets d'eau douce'.[12] This was not isolated
wilderness. Strabo stresses that Lake Mareotis was heavily
populated. There were eight islands in it and 'all the shores
around it are well-inhabited' (*Geogr.* 17: 1: 14). This region was
known for its wine. Papyrus and Egyptian bean grew beside the
lake.[13] The papyrus plant grew abundantly in the marshy
borders. Papyrus was one of Alexandria's largest manufactured
products. 'The Strip' gave its name to a particular kind of
papyrus.[14] According to Philo, the Mareotic group used this
papyrus for their couches when they ate together (*Contempl.* 69).

Strabo (*Geogr.* 17: 1: 14) noted certain towns named Plinthine
and Nikios (Nicium, probably located at Sidi Kreir) as well as a
guardpost Cherrhonesos (or Chersonesus) some 13 km from
Alexandria, which is to be identified in the vicinity of the El
'Agami el Qibilya Fort.[15] Across the lake was the town of Marea/

---

[11] Strabo notes that Lake Mareotis was 150 stadia (32 km) broad and just less
than 300 stadia (64 km) long (*Geogr.* 17: 1: 14), which is a slight exaggeration.

[12] François Daumas and Pierre Miquel, *De Vita Contemplativa* (Les Œuvres
de Philon d'Alexandrie; Paris, Éditions du Cerf, 1963), 44–5. Daumas also notes
the presence of numerous wells in this region, which indicate ancient settle-
ments. Conybeare, *Philo*, 294–7, discusses the pros and cons of a north-east or
south-west location and ultimately decides that the latter is more probable,
given that it would have been on this side that the lake debouched into the sea via
a channel (or channels) below El Mex and this is described as being 'nearby' in
Contempl. 23.

[13] Strabo, *Geogr.* 17: 1: 15, cf. Pliny, *Hist. Nat.* 13: 69, 76 cf. Socrates, *Hist.
Eccles.* 1: 27. See Fraser, *Ptolemaic Alexandria*, i. 144–6; Mieczslaw Rodziewicz,
'Alexandria and the District of Mareotis', *Graeco-Arabia*, 2 (1983), 199–216.

[14] See Haas, *Alexandria*, 34.

[15] See Daumas and Miquel, *De Vita*, 45 and Anthony de Cosson, *Mareotis,*

Philoxenite, which was identified in 1977. The lake was connected by canals to the Nile. According to Strabo, the traffic on
the lake was heavy, even more so than that from the sea, and the
harbour on the lake side of Alexandria was consequently also
richer (*Geogr.* 17: 1: 17). Far from giving us a picture of this
group situated in a wilderness, Philo insists on the close proximity of villages and other establishments, since the locality's very
lack of isolation satisfied the need for security. In the Byzantine
period also, this region continued to be inhabited. Several ruins
of Christian monasteries were noted in this area in the survey
done by Anthony de Cosson, published in 1935,[16] and, as
Daumas noted, '(t)oute cette côte jusqu'à Taposiris Magna est
pleine de vestiges antiques'.[17] Wealthy Alexandrians had built
resort villas in this region,[18] but the main character of the area
was agricultural, with many small villages. Philo writes that the
place where the Mareotic group lived was rendered safe by virtue
of encircling ἐπαύλεις and κῶμαι. A κώμη was a village, which
could at times be quite a large unwalled country town. The word
ἔπαυλις has the meaning of an enclosure, used for cattle, but it
could also be a dwelling for people.[19] In the Greek papyri from
Egypt it has the sense of a building with agricultural land around
about it. These buildings could also be in clusters.[20] In other

*Being a Short Account of the History and Ancient Monuments of the North-
Western Desert of Egypt and of Lake Mareotis* (London: Country Life, 1935),
106–13.

[16] De Cosson, *Mareotis*, 106–7; Daumas and Miquel, *De Vita*, 45–6. The
monastery of Enaton (Deir el Hanatun) was located at the ninth milestone from
the western (Moon) gate; and at the eighteenth milestone was a monastery aptly
named Oktokaidekaton (El Deir). These were the second and third monasteries
west of Alexandria. The first was Pempton at the fifth milestone. In 1935 de
Cosson commented that the remains of Enaton had almost completely disappeared, but were close to the village of El Dikhela. Now the village itself has
been swallowed up by the urban sprawl of the modern city of Alexandria.

[17] Daumas and Miquel, *De Vita*, 45. The very important monastery complex
of St Menas was constructed 55 km from Alexandria in the 4th cent. The
remains of the monastery, basilical church, water reservoir, and bath are visible
near the town of Borg el Araba el Gedid.   [18] For the wealthy resorts, ibid. 42.

[19] P.Oxy. ii. 248, 29–70, dated 80 CE. See for discussion Geneviève Husson,
Oikia: Le vocabulaire de la maison privée en Égypte d'après les papyrus grecs
(Paris: CNRS and Sorbonne, 1983), 45–54, 77–80.

[20] Husson, *Oikia*, 77–80 and see p. 78 n. 2 where she notes that in the LXX of
Lev. 25: 31 the word ἐπαύλεις designated a little group of houses (in a hamlet) as
opposed to those of towns.

words, Philo defines a placement for the group which is populated rather than isolated. Here we do not have a community
situated in the desert, far from human habitation, but one which
was rural and yet not isolated. People living in the area would
have known of it. It was in a prime, fertile, quite well-inhabited,
agricultural location. It should also be remembered that it was a
farm too: there were cattle that should be untied on a Sabbath
(*Contempl.* 36), presumably from their work ploughing fields
and turning mills.

Conybeare thought it unlikely that the site of the settlement
could be identified,[21] but he wrote long before modern map-
making and archaeological discoveries improved our knowledge
of the area. The detailed maps produced by the British Survey of
Egypt (Department of Survey and Mines) from the 1920s to
1940s give us a great deal of information, and there is really only
one very likely general location of the Mareotic group.[22] This
area is shown in Figure 4. Since Philo mentions dwellings and
villages around the site, arable land and territory sufficient to
support villages and dwellings should be found close by, and
here we have it, whereas elsewhere the lake abutted the ridge too
closely, especially if we allow for a higher water level.[23] Philo
writes also of a single hill, rather than a locality just anywhere
along the ridge. The ridge is subdivided into distinguishable
hills in places, and so here. Moreover, there is a spring at the foot
of the hill.

In October–November 1999 I visited Alexandria and went to
this area to see what now remains. Unfortunately, the entire
region is heavily developed, with suburbs of Alexandria blending into each other and consuming the countryside with each
passing year. Little has been done here to conserve the archaeological heritage of this vicinity. The suburb occupying the area
around the hill is called Abu Yousef, and has been built up
largely in the last ten years. The specific hill itself has been so

[21] Conybeare, *Philo*, 294. He was not averse to making general suggestions,
however, and opted for the ridge south-west of Alexandria.

[22] These maps are the most detailed geographical plans of the region available
in English and exist down to a scale of 1:25000.

[23] The lake went to the southern walls of the ancient city, see Forster,
Alexandria, 10, and a bit of the lake in fact breached the wall. For the shape of
ancient Lake Mareotis see the beautiful plans and drawings in Jean-Yves
Empereur, *Alexandria Rediscovered* (London: British Museum Press, 1998).

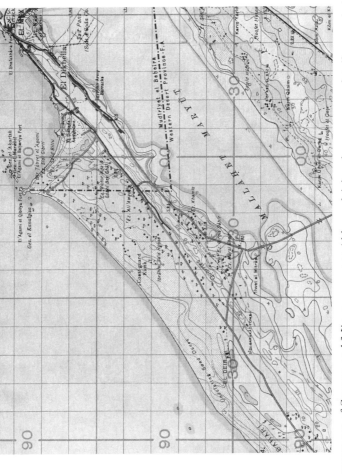

4. British Department of Survey and Mines map 1939 'Alexandria' scale 1:100,000, detail expanded. Each square measures 1 km. Black dots indicate wells. The most probable location for the Mareotic group is on the quarried hill

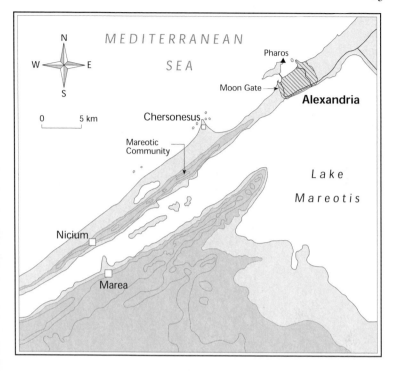

5. Area south-west of Alexandria in the 1st century CE

extensively quarried for stone to build this new suburb that it is
almost completely obliterated (see Figures 5 and 6). Where the
Mareotic group may have lived, there is now an enormous hole.
I was able to walk along the eastern arm of what remains to take
photos, and found a few Roman and Byzantine potsherds.
Evidence of the spring, used for water (*Contempl.* 37), is found at
the foot of the hill, where there are reeds and plants growing and
a water channel. One can still look out over palm trees to the
more distant Lake Mareotis (Figure 7) and use one's imagination
to see what it may have been like in a previous age.

Even if others are not confident of so precise a localization,
there does not seem to be any other convincing alternative
site for the community other than somewhere along this ridge
south-west of Alexandria. There was most likely some distance

6. 'Therapeutae' hill, looking westwards. The hill is now almost completely obliterated by quarrying

7. 'Therapeutae' hill: view southwards over Lake Mareotis, with spring channel and reeds visible at the foot

8. 'Therapeutae' hill: view from foot of ridge over reeds to show height

between the site and the city. Too close and it would have abutted necropoleis. There were necropoleis of tombs and gardens beyond the south-eastern and south-western walls (Strabo, *Geogr.* 17: 1: 10),[24] and several tomb areas have now been uncovered.[25] To the east of ancient Alexandria, there were low-lying fields, as in some parts today where the city has not yet spread. Also to the east was the Hadra lake, the route to Canobus, along the busy Canobic canal, and the town of Eleusis (Abu Qir). Both Eleusis and Canobus were identified by Strabo as localities in which 'both men and women' indulged in the rather licentious 'Canobic lifestyle' which would not be the right environment for Philo to place the group of *Contempl.*! Moreover, the lake and the sea were adjacent to the south-west rather than to the north-east. It is here, on and around the limestone ridge, that we find ancient wine presses, wells, villas, farms, and villages, which are dotted along the coast for some 60 km.

As for the city, Philo mentions Alexandria by name in the localization of those who embrace the contemplative life in general, who are found abundantly not only in all the nomes of Egypt but especially 'around Alexandria' (περὶ τὴν Ἀλεξάνδρειαν, *Contempl.* 21). The devotional aspect of their lives requires, it appears, quiet. The city is there, just close by, and yet distant enough. It is, nevertheless, the city of Alexandria they have rejected in order to live their quiet, focused existence. Philo writes:

And they do not move into another city, like the unfortunate or worthless slaves who beg to be sold by their owners, exchanging masters, not procuring freedom for themselves. For every city, even the best governed, is full of noise and innumerable disturbances which no one who has ever once been led by Wisdom can endure. Outside [city] walls,

---

[24] See Sly, *Philo's Alexandria*, 37.

[25] To the east we have the Chatby cemeteries (4th–3rd cent. BCE), Alabaster tomb (3rd cent. BCE), Hadara tomb (3rd cent. BCE), Antoniadis tomb (3rd cent. BCE), the necropolis of Mustafa Kamel [Mustafa Pasha] (2nd cent. BCE), and further east the Montazah tombs (3rd–1st cent. BCE); and to the west the Wardian tomb (2nd cent. BCE), Shounat Stagni tomb (2nd cent. BCE), Gabbari tombs (2nd cent. BCE), cemetery of Saleh Fort (2nd cent. BCE); on Pharos Island: the necropoleis of Anfouchi (3rd–2nd cent. BCE). In the south, there is the necropolis of Kom el Shogafa, dating to the 2nd–3rd cents. For details, see *The Archaeological Sites of Alexandria (331 BC–1801 AD)* (Alexandria: The Alexandria Preservation Trust Historical Map Series, No. 1, 1992).

they pass their time in cultivated or uncultivated land, pursuing solitude, not because they are practising any contrived misanthropy, but because the custom of mixing with dissimilar things is [something] they know [to be] unprofitable and harmful. (*Contempl.* 19–20)

Their origins are clearly within the city. They do not move to *another city* (εἰς ἑτέραν πόλιν) but rather they reject the city because of the disturbances and noise of city life. They are not of the countryside; they are city people who decide not to move to another city, but to the land outside it.[26]

Philo identifies here that the places the contemplative philosophers choose to live in are κήποις, cultivated tracts of land or gardens, and μοναγρίαις, single tracts of uncultivated land (fallow land), where they dwell for the purpose of ἐρημίαν μεταδιώκοντες, 'pursuing solitude'. The solitude they pursue is not possible in the city, which is so noisy and full of disturbances. The presence of the word ἐρημία has most likely been the reason that scholars have thought of 'wilderness' in regard to the Mareotic group,[27] since it can mean this, but here clearly it is found in the sense of isolation from the bustle of city people rather than a desert with no one around for miles. Lake Mareotis was busy with traffic, and the countryside here was dotted with towns, villages, dwellings, and farms. Workers were busy with papyrus and wine production, and other agricultural activities. It was not, however, the city.

The Mareotic group go to a place which is very well situated near water in a safe and breezy spot, which is also close by dwellings and villages: a prime piece of real estate! It was accessible to Alexandria by land and lake. It would have been a good place for a country villa. In contrast to what we may expect, then, Philo now seems determined to stress that there is no luxury involved.

The little houses of those who have come together [in this place] are very frugal, providing shelter against the two most urgent things: against the blazing [heat] of the sun, and the chilly [cold] of the air. They are neither close together, like those in the towns —for close neighbourhood is troublesome and displeasing to those who are zealous for

---

[26] Apparently, in order to leave Alexandria one needed an exit visa (*prostagma*), see Strabo, *Geogr.* 2: 3: 5; Huzar, 'Alexandria', 631.

[27] But already Conybeare, *Philo*, 210, noted that 'the Therapeutae were far from retiring into the desert, although they sought solitude'.

9. Simple stone dwellings, dated to the Roman period, located above En Gedi, by the Dead Sea, Israel (Photo: Dennis Green)

solitude and pursue it—nor far apart, because of the sense of community they adhere to and [also] in order that, if robbers make an attack, they may help one another. (*Contempl.* 24)

It is interesting that this is the second time Philo mentions fear of robbery. There is protection from theft afforded by the dwellings and villages around the site, and also within the site itself because people's little houses are located fairly close together. Each person lives in his or her little house separately, not in a common house. Philo also notes here that they have a sense of community (κοινωνία) which is another reason for close proximity. These huts would probably have looked like farm labourers' dwellings. In the famous Nilotic mosaic from Palestrina there is a small hut like this depicted in the centre, close to a *columbarium* and not far from a very splendid country villa. Interestingly, above En Gedi in Israel, simple stone huts have been discovered dating to Roman times that could also be simple workers' dwellings.[28]

[28] See Yitzhar Hirschfeld, 'The Archaeology of the Community of Hermits', *Cathedra*, 99 (2001), 197–201, who identifies the huts as being Essene dwellings.

The ideal of living in such simple places in the countryside, secluded to a degree, could have been realized by many different groups. If we believe Philo, in fact, there were numerous people who went off to live a philosophical lifestyle in the countryside close by Alexandria. Given the prevalence of the notion of there being something good to be gained by living a contemplative life of virtue, and Alexandria's character as a place where education, culture, and philosophy were vigorous, we may well expect this. The particular philosophical characters of all those who undertake such lifestyles would surely have been diverse: Stoics, Platonists, Pythagoraeans, Jews, or those that blended various different philosophical streams.

As we saw, the word *therapeutai/rides* should be associated with temples rather than quiet localities in the countryside. We can feel the dissonance between Philo's use of the word *therapeutai/rides* in *Contempl.* and the wider apprehension of what *therapeutai/rides* were. Moreover, in Chaeremon's description of the Egyptian priests, he apparently made it clear that it was not in fact necessary to remove oneself to the country in order to live a contemplative life. It could be pursued perfectly well within a cultic setting (where we would expect to find people designated as *therapeutai/rides*). Porphyry writes:

Chaeremon the Stoic tells in his exposé about the Egyptian priests who, he says, were considered also as philosophers among the Egyptians, that they chose the temples as the place to philosophize. For to live close to their shrines was fitting to their whole desire of contemplation, and it gave them security because of the reverence for the divine, since all people honoured the philosophers as if they were a sort of [sic] sacred animals. And they were able to live a quiet life, as contact with other people occurred only at assemblies and festivals, whereas for the rest the temples were almost inaccessible to others. (Porphyry, *De Abstin.* 4: 6[29])

It seems here that Chaeremon knew that the contemplative life should strictly speaking be pursued away from other people or even cities, but he would insist that temples afforded this isolation. Philo does the opposite: he knew that *therapeutai/rides* should be located in temples, but he places them in the countryside. True *therapeutai/rides*—those who are attending to god(s)

---

[29] Van der Horst, *Chaeremon*, 17.

—are philosophers who have gone out to live in the countryside rather than those who are attending to deities in city temples and in pilgrimage shrines. The philosophers are the exponents of 'perfect good' (like gymnosophists and Brahmins). They are Jews who live far away from the Temple, in the most excellent, well-chosen locality imaginable close to Lake Mareotis.

THE SOCIO-ECONOMIC LOCATION OF THE MAREOTIC GROUP

Having discussed their physical situation, let us turn now to consider the group's social situation. We have seen that the group was from Alexandria. Was the group Philo describes one from elite circles in Alexandria, or was it comprised of people from less advantaged sectors of society? There seems to be strong evidence that points to the group coming from affluent circles.

First, considering Philo's rhetorical purposes, it is very likely that Philo himself would not have used the community as a model of excellence and virtue had the members come from the lower echelons of Alexandrian society. It is important to recognize that for many of the elite of the Hellenistic and Roman worlds, the poorer sectors of society were without *moral* standing. Wealth was associated with good character, honesty, and virtue.[30] As such, with a few exceptions, only the wealthy could philosophize, truly conceptualizing themselves as 'the moral minority'. The elite view of the poor had direct consequences in the legal sphere. People in trade and craftworkers were considered to be dishonest as it was believed that their livelihoods depended on lying about their products, while the poor were unreliable witnesses in court because their poverty incited them to lie, cheat, and steal. As Ramsay MacMullen has noted, 'The rich frankly confessed that only themselves could afford to be honest!'[31] Moreover, '[a] final, circular argument was . . . commonly invoked: the poor deserve to be held in contempt because they have no money. Poverty in and of itself is "vile",

---

[30] See Peter Garnsey, *Social Status and Legal Privilege in the Roman Empire* (Oxford: Clarendon Press, 1970); Ramsay MacMullen, *Roman Social Relations* (New Haven: Yale University Press, 1974), 117.

[31] MacMullen, *Social Relations*, 116; Garnsey, *Social Status*, 208, 212

"dishonoured", "ugly".'[32] Slaves were assumed to be dishonest (Cicero, *Pro Sulla* 48). In Rome, a slave was always examined under torture for judicial proceedings, since his or her testimony was considered invalid otherwise.[33] We see this played out in texts concerning the nascent Church. The amount of poor people involved in the Church directly undermined its moral credibility among the wealthy. If it was a movement of the poor, it was by definition contemptible (see Origen, *Contra Celsum* 3: 18, 75; 4: 31, 50).

This suggests that Philo would have been wise to avoid praising a group with low socio-economic credentials or using them as a prime example of virtue if he was addressing his 'speech' to wealthy Romans. It would have been almost essential that Philo used people who were of a high social class or else his point would easily be countered by class prejudice. Moreover, there are various indicators in Philo's treatise that point to the contemplative Jews he describes as coming from an educated elite in Alexandria.

The literacy of the group members is the most telling evidence. Alexandrian boys were expected to attend the *palaestra* and gymnasium, in order to receive a basic Hellenistic education, and it seems Jews also participated in this, even if not in the advanced research institute of the Museion, given that it was a 'temple of the Muses' and under the authority of a priest of the Muses. In parallel, it seems likely that Jewish boys were educated in synagogue-related schools.[34] However, not only the men, but also the women of *Contempl.* are able to read: this seems

[32] MacMullen, *Social Relations*, 116 and see his appendix B, 138–41 on terms of contempt the rich used for the poor.

[33] Arnold H. M. Jones, *The Criminal Courts of the Roman Republic and Principate* (Oxford: Basil Blackwell, 1971), 114; James L. Strachan-Davidson, *Problems of Roman Criminal Law*, 2 vols. (Oxford: Clarendon Press, 1912), ii. 126. It was thought that a slave would be expected to give favourable testimony to his or her master or mistress; denial of guilt could only be accepted if it had been maintained under torture. I am grateful to a paper by Jeannie Constantinou, for the New Testament Seminar at Harvard Divinity School on 23 Apr. 1997, for these references. See also Pliny's letter to the Emperor Trajan, which refers, almost incidentally, to the torture of the Christian slave girls he has arrested, Pliny, *Ep.* 10: 96: 8.

[34] See S. Safrai and M. Stern, *The Jewish People in the First Century: Historical Geography, Political History, Social, Cultural and Religious Life and Institutions*, ii (Assen: Van Gorcum, 1976), 945–70.

to indicate that they come from wealthy families in which literacy was acquired by female members of the household.[35] Elsewhere in the Graeco-Roman world, female literacy appears to have been linked with affluence and social status. Educational opportunities had been expanding for women throughout the Hellenistic period, subject to some regional variations.[36] As Sarah Pomeroy has noted in regard to Roman Egypt, '[a] minority of daughters acquired an education'.[37] Egyptian papyri from the Hellenistic and Roman periods indicate that some women could sign their names on contracts,[38] but it was still the privilege of the affluent few. A wife of a literate cavalryman from Upper Egypt had difficulty in writing.[39] In another papyrus a son writes for his illiterate mother.[40] Illiterate women in families where other members are literate are found in a number of papyri,[41] though a literate woman with an illiterate husband is found.[42] Later, in a papyrus from 263 CE, a woman claimed special consideration because she was literate.[43] Depictions of women with stylus in hand from Pompeii also tend to show affluent women,

[35] See for discussions of the education of women: Susan Guettel Cole, 'Could Greek Women Read and Write?', *Women's Studies*, 8 (1981), 129–55; Sarah B. Pomeroy, '*Technikai kai Mousikai*: The Education of Women in the Fourth Century and in the Hellenistic Period', *American Journal of Ancient History*, 2 (1977), 51–68; Kraemer, 'Monastic Jewish Women', 350. For Jewish contexts, see Tal Ilan, *Jewish Women in Greco-Roman Palestine* (Peabody, Mass.: Hendrickson, 1995), 191–3.

[36] So Pomeroy, *Technikai kai Mousikai*.

[37] Sarah B. Pomeroy, 'Women in Roman Egypt: A Preliminary Study Based on Papyri', *ANRW* 2: 10: 1 (1988), 708–23, at 715. Note that this article is substantially the same as her 'Women in Roman Egypt: A Preliminary Study based on Papyri', in Helene B. Foley (ed.), *Reflections of Women in Antiquity* (New York: Gordon Bread and Science Publishers, 1981).

[38] For discussion of women's literacy, in the context of literacy in general, see William V. Harris, *Ancient Literacy* (Cambridge, Mass.: Harvard University Press, 1989), 142–3. The literacy of the men is itself significant. As Harris notes, in the Egyptian papyri 'there are no revelations of lower-class literacy', p. 142.

[39] P.Grenf. i. 15.

[40] P.Rein. i. 16 (109 BCE). See for this and the preceding papyrus, Harris, *Literacy*, 143.

[41] Sel.Pap. i. 16; P.Mich. ix. 554; P.Fayum 100; P.Oxy. 17: 2134; P.Amh. ii. 102; P.Tebt. ii. 399. See Harris, *Literacy*, 279 n. 516.

[42] P.Oxy. 12: 1463. See Harris, *Literacy*, 279 n. 517.

[43] P.Oxy. 12: 1467. Papyri themselves do not always indicate whether the person who sent the letter was literate, because of the use of scribes. Therefore,

and most of the pictures were found in very affluent houses.[44]
William Harris concludes that 'in a certain number of reasonably
prosperous Pompeian families . . . a woman's ability to write was
thought to be an attraction or an asset' and 'a woman of this social
class was not presumed to be literate—it was a definite attribute
if she was'.[45] Small terracotta figurines and tombstone reliefs
found in Alexandria depict girls with wax tablets, and possibly
relate to a picturesque upper-class ideal.[46] As Pomeroy has
noted, '[a]lthough membership in a privileged class does not
necessarily guarantee that women were literate, the converse is
likely to be true, for a girl's parents would have had to be able to
pay for her tuition'.[47] Ross Kraemer notes rightly of the women
in the community Philo describes: '[f]ew women, Jewish or
otherwise, would have been so highly educated'.[48]

   In addition, Philo describes those who have made the decision
to go into the contemplative life as leaving their possessions to
friends and family. The implicit assumption is that they had
significant possessions to leave. They give them 'an advance
inheritance', having received the 'wealth of perception', and the
blind wealth they had previously enjoyed was now passed over
(*Contempl.* 13). Philo can write critically of Anaxagoras and
Democritus who were so taken with philosophy that they left
their fields to be eaten by sheep (*Contempl.* 14, cf. 15) and
recommend rather that those who were (relatively?) poor among

even when we have someone writing without mention of literacy, we do not necessarily know whether the letter was written by that person, or read out by an
intermediary at the other end. In 3rd-century Alexandria, Origen could assert
that the majority of the population was unlettered (*Contra Celsum* 1: 27).

[44] See Harris, *Literacy*, 163. Funerary reliefs showing girls and women
carrying book-rolls most likely indicate according to Harris that 'some literary
education was thought to be desirable for a woman of good family' (p. 252).

[45] Harris, *Literacy*, 263.

[46] For examples see Sarah Pomeroy, *Women in Hellenistic Egypt from
Alexander to Cleopatra* (New York: Schocken, 1984), fig. 7. Such terracottas are
a common type in the Hellenistic world and date from the 2nd to 1st cents. BCE.
A selection of these are on display at the Graeco-Roman Museum in Alexandria.

[47] Pomeroy, 'Women in Roman Egypt', 720; As Jane Rowlandson writes:
'[l]iteracy in Greek was an accomplishment possessed by some (particularly
upper-cass) women, although one to be boasted about, rather than taken for
granted', in ead. (ed.) with Roger Bagnall *et al.*, *Women and Society in Greek and
Roman Egypt: A Sourcebook* (Cambridge: CUP, 1998), 14, and see 299–308.

[48] Kraemer, *Blessings*, 114; ead. 'Monastic Jewish Women', 350.

their friends and companions could show themselves as rich (14, 16) upon receipt of philosophers' possessions.

Once divested of their familiar wealth, an elite group would be rather vulnerable. Either this is, in the case of the Mareotic group, an exaggeration, or else there were people in Alexandria who supported the group's activities. As Kraemer notes, they must have been dependent on endowments and benefactors for their survival, for their buildings, books, clothing, food.[49] This is an important point, since this would place them within a framework of dependency, as in the case of Buddhist monks and nuns.

Did someone wealthy from Alexandria own the land on which the Mareotic group lived, where they could exist for free? Probably not, because in Roman-administered Egypt, full ownership of private land did not exist. As Alan Bowman and Dominic Rathbone point out, the two categories of land—royal land and sacred land—were rented out by the secular and religious authorities of the state to private individuals.[50] A dwelling in such a place would have been like the Roman villa excavated near Marea.[51] Such a residence may easily have been adapted to a philosophical purpose, as was the country house of Verecundus, where Augustine went after his conversion to Christianity (*Conf.* 9: 3). In order to pay for the rent of this house and land, there must have been some kind of financial support from people who did not devote their entire lives to contemplation, perhaps from friends and family who had received donations of possessions, or from a wider community sympathetic to the goals of the group. It should be noted that Philo does not state that the group gave their possessions into a common fund for group needs, which was a philosophical commonplace,[52]

---

[49] Kraemer, 'Monastic Jewish Women', 366.

[50] Bowman and Rathbone, 'Cities and Administration', 109.

[51] This is a 4th-century peristyle villa rustica at Huwariya; Rodziewicz, 'Alexandria and the District of Mareotis', 204–7.

[52] Plato, *Leg.* 739c, *Rep.* 424a; Aristotle, *NE* 1159b; Diogenes Laertius, *Lives* 8: 10; 10: 11; Iamblichus, *Vita Pythag.* 30: 167–70; Diodorus Siculus, *Bibl. Hist.* 5: 9: 4, and also the Essenes, *Ant.* 18: 20; *War* 2: 122, see Matthias Klinghardt, 'The Manual of Discipline in the Light of Statutes of Hellenistic Associations', in Michael O. Wise, Norman Golb, John J. Collins, and Dennis G. Pardee, *Methods of Investigation of the Dead Sea Scrolls and the Khirbet Qumran Site: Present Realities and Future Prospects* (New York: New York Academy of Sciences, 1994), 251–70, at p. 255 and n. 20. Augustine clearly saw it as part of

especially given the model of the Alexandrian Museion, whose members ate together in a common dining room and held all their property in common (Strabo, *Geogr.* 17: 1: 8/793–4; Vitruvius, *De Arch.* 5: 11: 2). The Mareotic group gave their possessions to friends and family; they did not pool them to create a communal fund. How then did they exist economically in a world of rent, and, moreover, poll-tax?[53] There has to be more than the contemplative philosophers themselves in this picture.

The Mareotic group compose 'psalms and hymns to God in all kinds of metres and melodies which they have to write down in dignified rhythms' (*Contempl.* 29). The composition of music in various metres and melodies would also possibly indicate that those who have come here have had the advantage of a classical education, in which the learning of music was still probably of some importance.[54] Education in choral singing was critical, since choirs were required for many religious ceremonies. While most choral singing was done by men and boys, women and girls could also form separate choirs, and mixed choirs were also known.[55] Such choral singing was also connected with dancing, as is evidenced in the Mareotic community (80, 84–8). Again, in this community, women also compose music, which indicates they had been well-educated.

Philo characterizes the members of the group as being 'people of good birth and erudite (conversation) who are trained in philosophy' (*Contempl.* 69). Philo notes that they have 'from early youth matured and grown up in the contemplative part of philosophy, which indeed is the most beautiful and godly' (67). Such statements reinforce the impression that the Mareotic community was comprised of people who came from the affluent and rather refined circle *Philo himself* came from, a point I will explore further below in terms of their exegetical tradition. He is

what one did to pursue a philosophical lifestyle, *Conf.* 6: 14, where he imagines about ten members of such an *ad hoc* philosophical 'community'.

[53] Bowman and Rathbone, 'Cities and Administration', 112–13, 116, note that Alexandrian citizens were exempt from the poll-tax—the *tributum capitis* or *laographia*—instituted in the mid–20s BCE. This tax fell on all adult males between the ages of 14 and 62.

[54] Henri I. Marrou, *A History of Education in Antiquity* (London: Sheed & Marou, 1956), 134–7. Marrou notes, however, that it had declined in value since classical antiquity, pp. 138–41.

[55] Ibid. 135–6.

clearly using their good birth and their intellectual, educated character to score points in terms of proving their virtue. They are poor in that they have given away their wealth, but they are not of the poor, any more than they are of the country.

In terms of the wider socio-economic context of the group, we can conclude that Philo actually presents us with an educated Jewish Alexandrian elite, who, for philosophical reasons, had chosen to forsake their affluent urban lifestyles in order to embrace a contemplative life of reading, music, and meditating on scripture.

SENIORS AND JUNIORS: PLACEMENTS WITHIN THE MAREOTIC GROUP

We find Philo's rhetoric very apparent when we try to concern ourselves with the internal organization of the group. We need not assume that there were very many people involved in the Mareotic group, no matter how exemplary it was as far as Philo was concerned. In the symposium the group holds on the forty-ninth day[56] Philo writes of a single table brought into the room (*Contempl.* 73, 81).[57] On this table the food for their special meal was placed: loaves of bread and salt mixed with hyssop. A single table may suggest a smallish group rather than a large number of people.

There is a hierarchical order in terms of people's placements at the symposium which reflects the social ordering within the group. The seniors are those who recline and the juniors are those who serve. The seniors lie on very basic couches (*Contempl.* 69) in order of their seniority (67, 75) and they are waited on by the juniors who bring them food from the central table (71–2, 75). Philo seems not to be very interested in the juniors. Anything that would require the subjects of Philo's discourse to be active or practical is given short shrift. Philo tells us almost nothing of any activities apart from those focused on spiritual matters, but someone had to cook and clean. All the

---

[56] They do not eat a communal meal on the Sabbath, contra Kraemer, 'Monastic Jewish Women', 345.

[57] Colson wrongly translated τράπεζαν in the plural here (p. 163). Those reclining would have been served from the table that was brought into the room.

practical arrangements appear to be in the hands of the juniors in the community who are not actually accorded the luxury of a fully contemplative lifestyle. According to Philo, there are no slaves present as members of the community or as people who serve at table; all are free (71–2), and the juniors take the place of slaves in terms of manual labour. The juniors—the 'dailies' (ἐφημερευταί),[58] or rather 'servers' (διάκονοι)[59]—are also like children, for they regard the seniors as their parents in common. The juniors may themselves be quite old, and the seniors could be young, but older people would still be 'children' of the seniors if they had only recently come into the community (67). The juniors provide the support structure needed to ensure that the contemplative seniors are entirely undisturbed and looked after.

If we peek behind the text, the juniors must have been quite busy. Every evening food would have been prepared and served to those who lived in the isolated simple houses (even if they neglected to eat it!). In Philo's description, food seems rather magically to appear inside the doorstep, for the contemplative seniors 'do not cross over the main (outside) door or even see it from a distance' for six days (*Contempl.* 30), and yet they eat (or at least have the option of eating). Philo indicates that the contemplative seniors normally attend to food and drink after sunset (33), some do not think of food for three days (35), and others eat only after six (35). The incidental appearance of food in Philo's description must make us aware of his rhetoric: he is only interested in the treatise in the senior members of the Mareotic community. He focuses only on those whom he wishes to hold up as examples of perfection, not on the question of who makes the food or gives it to them. Only in the special forty-ninth day symposia do all the group members gather together, in a hierarchy based on length of time they have been in the group (rather than age, though also divided along gender lines) and he is almost forced to mention the juniors to explain the circumstances.

---

[58] This word is rare, and is related to others in which someone takes on a special task for the duration of a day (from ἐπί + ἡμέρα), see LSJ 743: ἐφημερεύω: keep guard by day; ἐφημερευτήριον: the (day-)guards' lock-up room; ἐφημερία: a division of guards on duty; ἐφημερεύοντες: (daily) cleaners in a temple.

[59] The word διάκονοι here, as in Christian contexts, may be male or female, cf. Phoebe in the church of Cenchraea, a suburb of Corinth, in Paul's letter to the Romans (16: 1), who is a διάκονος.

Philo does tell us that these junior people have been appointed after being 'chosen on merit with all care, which is fitting for the manner of good character and good birth of those eager to reach the summit of virtue' (*Contempl.* 72). Once more, there is a reference to good birth. This comment also indicates that there must have been some kind of admission procedure: the community was not open to anyone who just happened to want to come into it. We are told nothing about this.

The juniors are clearly in charge of arranging things so that the seniors are free of responsibility. Concerning the special festive meal Philo writes that 'a certain person from the "dailies"—as it is the custom to call those performing these services—gives a sign' (*Contempl.* 66). The junior people have clearly worked out the organization of the evening. Only now, in the treatise, does it become clear that it is only the seniors who recline: 'the seniors recline following the order of [their] admission' (67). The juniors too listen to the speech (77), and they participate in the clapping and probably in hymn singing, before they bring in the food. But the mention of the juniors in this passage is not meant to lead us into any further consideration of their role in the community, or their work, but only to provide an indication of their relationship to the seniors. It is the issue of their not being slaves, and their loving service like children to parents, that is of concern to Philo. Accordingly, blindly following the flow of Philo's rhetoric, modern scholarship also generally neglects to consider them further. Just as children may be ignored as being not so important, Philo chooses to ignore these 'children'.

Further consideration of practicalities also points to the large role played by the juniors in the maintenance of the community. Philo tells us that this community has cattle: on the seventh day they release the cattle from the continuous labour (*Contempl.* 36). This leads to all kinds of other considerations. Who released the cattle? Who ploughed the fields with cattle and worked with them? The seniors Philo focuses on do no physical labour at all, but are entirely devoted to their philosophical discipline. But in order that they can be free to live an undisturbed contemplative existence devoted to the pursuit of spiritual excellence they need to be maintained. In *Contempl.* Philo is not writing about the whole group. He is writing about the seniors, not the junior members who seem to run the community in a practical sense.

In his discussion of virtue, Philo was aiming to give a presentation of a contemplative life rather than an active one. He had just described the Essenes of Syria Palaestina as the most brilliant exemplars of an active philosophical life. Philo tells us in *Prob.* (75–91, cf. *Hypoth.* 8: 6–7) that Essenes work at agriculture or crafts in order to earn money. It is implied that this work is outside the community, for any payment they get is brought in and placed in a communal fund. They live in communal houses, eat *daily* food communally, and have no personal clothing.[60] If he now digressed to mention that his Jewish exponents of the contemplative life were in fact an elite group of seniors maintained by a support structure of juniors—who clearly are engaged in an active life of labour—this would have muddied the waters of his rhetoric. Instead, in terms of his portrayal of the contemplative life, we have a sudden dissonance when the juniors appear. The juniors are ignored completely until they appear in the symposium to illustrate the fact that the contemplative seniors do not have slaves but rather spiritual children, and to explain the basic circumstances of the feast. They are then quickly packed away again.

The highest position in the hierarchy of the Mareotic group appears to be the president, or most senior of the seniors. Ross Kraemer wonders whether women could perhaps not speak in the assembly or at the feast as 'president' of the meeting, while noting that the text is ambiguous.[61] The words used for the most senior speaker are indeed masculine: πρεσβύτατος (*Contempl.* 31) and πρόεδρος (79–80), but it is unnecessary to assume that this person was always male. Given that ranking in the community was in order of their admission, it would follow that at some points the most senior person (the one who had been longest in the community) was a woman. One who is most experienced in the doctrines may likewise be female (*Contempl.* 31). Philo may have written about the president as male, though the reality was

---

[60] Josephus also stresses that they have communal property and engage in agricultural labour (*Ant.* 18: 18–22, cf. *War* 2: 119–61).

[61] Kraemer, 'Monastic Jewish Women', 344, 346 n. 16: 'it may be that women were excluded from some participation in the communal life, such as the delivery of public lectures, which might suggest that they did not sing solos'. But Philo writes that 'each person' (ἕκαστος) sings a hymn (81), and there seems no reason to think they were excluded from any functions.

not necessarily patriarchal.[62] A masculine noun can function as inclusive of women in Greek, even in singular form. We know of instances in which a female subject is given a masculine 'function', as in the case of Iulia Crispina, in the Babata archives (P. Yadin 20) who is described as an ἐπίσκοπος, or Phoebe in Rom. 16: 1 who is διάκονος. Women represent about half of those mentioned as *sacerdos* of the Idean mother of the gods in Rome and Latium.[63] In a papyrus from the sixth century, found in Oxyrhynchus, a woman serves in public office as λογιστής, πρόεδρος and 'father of the city' (P.Oxy. 36: 2780).[64] If there is specific evidence of a woman being termed a πρόεδρος elsewhere in Egypt,[65] even if it is from a later context, then we cannot say that a woman could not be a πρόεδρος in this instance.[66] Philo's mention of a 'wise woman', Skepsis, who teaches him (*Fug.* 55) may refer to a woman such as this, a matter I will return to in due course.

The overall impression we gain from having examined Philo's description in *Contempl.* is that the community was not particularly large, and composed of certain people from an affluent, educated circle in Alexandria. Such people withdrew from the noise of the city to follow their own particular type of philosophy in a tract of land—comprising buildings and fields—located on a low-lying hill in the limestone ridge which extends south-westwards from Alexandria. Like the Buddhist monasteries of

[62] One part of the text concerning the identification of the 'president of the meeting' is, moreover, corrupt, and the Greek has been supplied in the Loeb edn. of the work by recourse to the Armenian. See Colson, *Philo ix* (Loeb) 158 n. 1.

[63] Kraemer, *Her Share*, 223 n. 27, cf. her reference to Tata of Aphrodisias being *stephanophorus*, p. 84 and see p. 183 where Kraemer notes a 4th-century epitaph from Jerusalem in which a woman calls herself a διάκονος, a masculine form with a feminine article, and other examples.

[64] See Rowlandson, *Women and Society*, 204.

[65] Any attempt to dismiss this evidence because of the lateness of the date would still have to account for numerous other contemporaneous instances of a woman being given a masculine title, only some of which are given here.

[66] Moreover, when Philo writes of the Sabbath assembly that men and women both listen to the elder (*presbutatos*) 'who is very experienced in the doctrines' (*Contempl.* 31), and 'women customarily participate in listening (like the men), having the same zeal and purpose' (32), this also need not lead to a conclusion that women *only* listen and never speak.

the East, this group of meditative philosophers situated themselves close to other people, in an agricultural environment. Their community was hierarchical, with the principal division being between seniors, who lived an ultra-ascetic, contemplative life, and juniors, whose life was to some extent active, practical and supportive of the seniors. Within these two categories, there was a precise pecking order based on the date of their admission to the group, which implies some kind of entry procedure not discussed by Philo. In terms of gender, it appears that the membership of this community was open fully to men and women. It is not necessary to assume that the highest position in the community could only be held by a male, since seniority was defined in terms of the date any member was (fully?) admitted into the group and expertise in the doctrines. The Mareotic group have left Alexandria, the city that is their home, for a new 'real' home, but an Alexandrian community that supports them seems somehow to be close at hand. Any supportive community is ignored, just as the juniors are ignored for most of the text, since such details are unnecessary to Philo's rhetoric. Nevertheless, the Mareotic group are essentially Alexandrian, located away from the city, but understandable within the philosophical life of the city.

5

The *Philosophia* of *Ioudaismos*

Philosophy is not a formal learning, fixed and rigid, abstracted from all feeling. It is a quest for love, love of beauty, love of wisdom, which is one of the most beautiful things. Like love, the philosopher would be someone poor, . . . a sort of barefoot waif who goes out under the stars seeking an encounter with reality, the embrace, the knowledge . . . of whatever benevolence, beauty, or wisdom might be found there.[1]

Jesus said to his students: 'Compare me to someone and tell me whom I am like.' . . . Matthew said to him, 'You are like a wise philosopher.'

(*Gospel of Thomas*, Logion 13)

As we have seen, Philo names his subjects as θεραπευταί/ρίδες. They 'are called' this. The designation is cultic, signifying the pious attendants or devotees of certain gods, active in temples and shrines. However, we meet, in *Contempl.*, a group of philosophers. Philo does not expect his audience to think of his philosophers as being associated with cultic activities at an actual temple, but rather he uses them as exemplars of the *bios theoretikos*, the classic meditative/contemplative life. Philo uses the verb θεωρέω as meaning 'see, behold': 'the [divinely] attending type of people' are 'taught always to see' and 'desire a vision of the [Divine] Being' (*Contempl.* 11). In order to achieve this they embrace a life of philosophy (16).

The Mareotic group are those who truly are 'the good', the very image of perfect philosophers. He constantly defines them in philosophical terms, leaving the cultic designation θεραπευταί/ρίδες to the beginning and ending of his treatise only. The members of the Mareotic group follow a αἵρεσις or

---

[1] Luce Irigaray, 'Sorcerer Love: A Reading of Plato, Symposium, "Diotima's Speech" ', in ead. *An Ethics of Sexual Difference*, tr. Carolyn Burke and Gillian C. Gill of *Ethique de la différence sexuelle* (Ithaca, NY: Cornell University Press, 1993), 20–33.

προαίρεσις,[2] a philosophical 'school' (*Contempl.* 2, 17, 29, 32, 67, 79). They are explicitly called 'philosophers' (2). They are driven by impulses for philosophy (16), trained in philosophy (69), living and cultivating a life of philosophy (16, cf. 89), led by Wisdom (Sophia) (19, cf. 35, 68). Their activity is to philosophize (34). They call out the decrees of the sacred philosophy while dreaming (26), interpret allegorically the inherited philosophy (28), follow the contemplative part of philosophy (67). We get constant repetitions of the term φιλοσοφία to emphasize the reality Philo perceives or wishes his audience to apprehend. Philo jumps from cultic language to philosophical language. This would have seemed perhaps more striking to his audience than to us, for cult and philosophy were two discrete conceptual categories in antiquity. To understand how Philo could make the jump, and how he could expect his audience to do so, we need to look at 'religion' as a whole, and basic understandings of Judaism, in the Graeco-Roman world.

CULT AND PHILOSOPHY

The presentation of the group of *Contempl.* as following a certain school of thought within wider Judaism rests on a basic presupposition that Judaism itself is fundamentally *philosophia*. This may seem strange to us, since we are more accustomed to seeing Judaism as a religion. The problem is that, in terms of ancient conceptual categories, our modern concept of 'religion' was unknown to people of the first century.[3] Steve Mason has

---

[2] The word αἵρεσις itself means a 'choice', from the verb αἱρέομαι, 'take for oneself, choose', LSJ 42. One chooses to follow a philosophical school of thought and lifestyle. David Runia has concisely explored the use of the term αἵρεσις in currency during Philo's day in 'Philo of Alexandria and the Greek Hairesis-Model', *VC* 53 (1999), 117–47, esp. 118–24, and noted that '[i]t is of vital importance to recognize that *haireseis* were primarily "schools" or "directions" of *thought*', p. 120, following John Glucker, *Antiochus and the Late Academy* (Gottingen: Vandenhoeck & Ruprecht, 1978), 174–92. This needs to be stressed in order that we avoid conceptualizing this group along the lines of a 'sect'.

[3] Our modern concept of religion is not easy to define, but it encompasses certain beliefs about the nature of reality and the universe, especially belief in supernatural controlling forces, and actions consistent with these beliefs that

perceptively explored how *philosophia* functioned as a group designation in the literature of Graeco-Roman society,[4] Judaism, and Christianity, and in turn bases himself on the classic study, *Conversion* (1933), by Arthur Darby Nock.[5] The studies of Nock and Mason will be used as the bedrock of the following discussion.

Nock pointed out that neither in Latin nor in classical Greek is there any term for 'religion' as we use this word today.[6] When we talk about 'religion' in antiquity, we are imposing a useful mental construct on the past for the sake of our own subject divisions. There is nothing wrong with contemporary mental constructs; these can be very helpful and in fact we can only really think coherently in ways our time and place and language permit. Nevertheless, we may recognize different mentalities which may challenge those we take for granted. Nock argued that, in the Graeco-Roman world, there were two main conceptual categorizations available for what we may understand as a 'religion' or 'religious movement'. On the one hand, there was the category of 'cult', summed up under the Greek word ὁσία, which may be defined as the service or worship owed by human beings to the gods by means of rites and offerings.[7] This is generally what is covered under the category *religio* in Latin. On the other hand there was φιλοσοφία, the love of wisdom, which involved a lifestyle and conversion to a set of ethical and philosophical

usually involve community rituals, festivals, and forms of prescribed and moral behaviour, as well as taboos. To some degree, the definition of 'religion' becomes problematic in our own day, given the multiplicities of 'eastern philosophies' and 'new religious movements' that exist.

[4] Steve Mason's important paper was read out to the Canadian Society of Biblical Studies AGM in May 1990, and then appeared on the internet via the *Ioudaios* site. Following this it was published as 'Greco-Roman, Jewish and Christian Philosophies', in Jacob Neusner (ed.), *Approaches to Ancient Judaism*, NS 4 (Atlanta: Scholars, 1993), 1–28. The final version appears as '*Philosophiai*: Graeco-Roman, Judean and Christian', in Kloppenborg and Wilson (eds.), *Voluntary Associations*, 31–58, and only this version will be cited in the footnotes. I am indebted to Mason for many references.

[5] Arthur D. Nock, *Conversion: The Old and the New in Religion from Alexander the Great to Augustine of Hippo* (Oxford: OUP, 1933).

[6] Ibid. 10. The word εὐσέβεια means the performance of due worship in the proper spirit, while ὁσιότης refers fundamentally to ritual purity.

[7] LSJ 1260–1. Some parallel to this is found in Latin *pietas*, which involves *cultus*.

principles.[8] For a large part of his book, Nock concentrated on understanding the nature of Graeco-Roman cults, the mystery cults (τελεταί) included. He noted on the basis of his sifting through classical literature how cultic devotion generally did not seem to require by necessity any belief in a certain ideology or code of moral behaviour.[9] In participating in a public cult people showed their religious devotion to a god, by attendance at a temple or shrine, ritual practices, sacrifice, processions, and so on, but such activity did not usually involve exclusivity. There was no real teaching or preaching tradition. A person used a cult to venerate a god and hoped in return for protection from the perils in this life, or security in the next. A person did not 'belong to it body and soul', as Nock puts it.[10]

On the other hand, writings about philosophy present a different perspective. In these, philosophy is articulated as a lifestyle based on certain practical and metaphysical principles which would result in knowledge of the universe and well-being (εὐδαιμονία). The fundamental premise appears to have been that people should be pious in regard to the gods and just or righteous in regard to fellow human beings. Piety (εὐσέβεια) and righteousness (δικαιοσύνη) are the backbone of the philosophical life.[11] Students of philosophers are described as forming a kind of group, what Nock called a 'sodality'.

Philosophy could become a cult—of a private type[12]—and cult could become curiously philosophical[13]—especially by the

---

[8] Purportedly (given the Greek fascination with origins) the first person to call himself a *philosophos*, 'lover of wisdom', was Pythagoras, Diogenes Laertius, *Lives* 1: 12, see Mason, *'Philosophiai'*, 31, 56 n. 3; Nock, *Conversion*, 28.

[9] Nock, *Conversion*, 11.

[10] Ibid. 14. One could be initiated into any number of cults, as Apuleius states in the *Metamorphosis* 55.

[11] Plato, *Gorgias* 507b; Polybius, *Hist.* 22: 10: 8; Diodorus of Siculus, *Bibl. Hist.* 1: 92: 5; Xenophon, *Mem.* 4: 8: 7,11, so Mason, *'Philosophiai'*, 33, 56 n.16.

[12] Neopythagoraeanism, according to Nock, *Conversion*, 116.

[13] Orphism and some of the later Dionysiac rites, among others, ibid. 116. See also Nock's discussion of Orphism at pp. 26–8. In this he notes that salvation and personal religion emerge, and we find 'a theology and a way of living which claimed to be based on a sacred literature passing under the names of Orphaeus and Musaeus, singers of the mythical past', p. 26. Orphic initiates espoused vegetarianism, abstinence from woollen clothing and contact with birth or death, respect for holy writings, contempt for the body, and

second century BCE when blends were more in evidence—
but Nock suggests that the conceptual distinctions were still
apparent. A blend would then not invalidate the fundamental
conceptual categorization evidenced in the literary sources, but
would mean that the boundaries of the categorizations could be
fluid, in different places and times, and in accordance with
different informants. A cult could develop a philosophical
dimension and a philosophy could develop a cultic one.
Moreover, those who participated in a philosophical school
would show piety by participating in a cult, or various cults;
sacrifice to the gods was considered part of piety. Those who participated in cultic activities as part of a proper, pious life would
not necessarily feel at all that a single philosophical position was
required. Unlike in the case of cultic piety, for philosophy it
was important to make a choice about what you believed.

Nock concentrated on the notion of conversion which related
to entry into a philosophical school. He noted that one of the
terms used for a philosophical path was ἀγωγή, which means 'a
way of teaching' or 'way of living', from the verb ἄγω, 'lead'.[14]
Plato wrote of a 'turning around' (ἐπιστροφή) of the soul coming
to philosophy (*Rep.* 518c–d).[15] Philosophy was a βίος, a life.
Those who embraced a life of philosophy did so with passion and
zeal (Seneca, *Ep.* 108: 17). It involved a decision to adopt an
ascetic or disciplined praxis, and here also we find the moral
justification for doing good, but philosophy in the literature is
not simply about lifestyle, virtue, and reason; it also encom-
passed a metaphysical dimension, what we today might call
'spirituality'. Especially in Pythagoraeanism and Platonism, it
had a profoundly mystical side, in that the soul was to encounter
ultimate reality.[16] In this, ancient Western philosophy paralleled
ancient Eastern philosophy: the Vedic philosophy of India and
Buddhism. The parallel is much more than coincidental. The
West was clearly interested in Eastern philosophy, and the East

a belief in a happy afterlife (cf. Diogenes Laertius, *Lives* 1: 12). Nock rightly
wonders about its link with Pythagoraeanism and whether it may be called a
'sect'.

[14] Cf. the word συναγωγή, see Mason, '*Philosophiai*', 33.

[15] Also Cicero, *Nat. Deo.* 1: 77.

[16] See Plato's *Timaeus* 47a–c; *Rep.* 507–9, 529–31. One ascends to a vision of
divine beauty (*Symp.* 210d–212a, cf. *Phaedrus* 246e–247e, 249c).

encouraged the interest. The thirteenth rock edict inscription of the great King Asoka (264–228 BCE) records how he sent Buddhist missionaries to the great Hellenistic kings, including Ptolemy in Egypt.[17]

Cultic forms of philosophy evolved during the course of the Hellenistic and Roman periods. Pythagoras was thought by some to be a manifestation of the god Apollo (Diogenes Laertius, *Lives* 8: 11). Certain devotees of Plato participated in something very like a cult, in which there was almost an apotheosis of the philosopher.[18] Epicurus could be regarded as divine.[19] Philostratus' *Life of Apollonius of Tyana* reflects the notion of the philosopher as a kind of superbeing (cf. 3: 50: 335).

Even when not considered divine, philosophers were exemplary. In certain stories, philosophers could perform thaumaturgical acts and be immune to magic.[20] Philosophers could be exemplary ascetics.[21] Philosophers may also be martyred for their beliefs and practices, the pre-eminent example of this being Socrates. Zeno of Elea was reputed to have died under torture, inflicted upon him in order that he should divulge a secret, and, upon death, apparently bit off his tongue and spat it out at his

---

[17] Devadatta R. Bhandarkar, *Ashoka*, 4th edn. (Calcutta: University of Calcutta, 1955), 43–4. The Ptolemy here is Ptolemy II Philadelphus (285–247 BCE). Another inscription refers to missionaries being sent on 256 occasions. Dio Chrysostum (*c*.40–112 CE) refers to Indian members of his Alexandrian audience (*Orat.* 32: 40). Epigraphic remains in Egypt, some with Buddhist symbols, show that Buddhist/Indian traders were active here, see R. Saloman, 'Epigraphic Remains of Indian Traders in Egypt', *Journal of the American Oriental Society* 111 (1991), 731–6; Ludwik Sternbach, 'Indian Wisdom and its Spread beyond India', *Journal of the American Oriental Society*, 92 (1972), 97–123; Almond, 'Buddhism in the West'. For Pythagoras and Vedic/Buddhist philosophy see the classic exploration: Leopold von Schroeder, *Pythagoras und die Inder: Eine Untersuchung über die Herkunft und Abstammung der Pythagoreischen Lehren* (Leipzig: O. Schulz, 1884).

[18] See Marcus Tod, 'Sidelights on Greek Philosophers', *Journal of Hellenic Studies*, 77 (1957), 132–41, at 134–5.

[19] Lucretius, *Rer. Nat.* 5: 8; Cicero, *Tusc.* 1: 48; Diogenes Laertius, *Lives* 10: 18, see Runia, *Hairesis*, 123–4.

[20] Porphyry, *Ad Marcellam* 11.

[21] Apollonius: Philostratus, *Vita Apol.* 1: 13; Porphyry: Eunapius *Vita Soph.* 457, cf. Porphyry, *Abstin.* 2: 52; and see what Diogenes Laertius says of Epicurus, *Lives* 10: 118–19, that ideally a wise man will not fall in love, marry, have a family, or care about funeral rites. The Cynic Epistles expound the same kind of ascetic ideal.

persecutor.[22] According to Clement of Alexandria (second century CE), other martyr philosophers include: Theodotus the Pythagoraean, Paulus the friend of Lacydes,[23] Posthumus the Roman, Anaxarchus, Zamolxis the student of Pythagoras (*Strom.* 4: 56: 1–4: 57: 2). Musonius Rufus apparently avoided martyrdom, but endured successive persecutions, torture, and banishments by emperors (Nero, Vespasian) in holding fast to his ethical principles, and once almost lost his life trying to talk peace to frenzied soldiers.[24] As Mason comments, 'The litmus tests of genuine philosophic practice were clear to everyone: utter simplicity of life, tranquillity of mind in all circumstances; disdain for common values, opinions and sensual delights; disregard for social conventions and status . . . and, especially, fearlessness in the face of death'.[25]

The traditions of the heroic founders of the school were passed down through a chain of teachers in succession (Diogenes Laertius, *Lives* 1: 13–15 cf. Seneca, *Ep.* 40: 3), through διάδοχοι, 'successors'.[26] Students of philosophers were expected to memorize large portions of their teachings and speeches by rote, just as boys may learn the Qur'an today in some societies. Socrates, in the *Menexenus* of Plato, notes how he was made to memorize the entire funerary oration of Aspasia as she went along. He jokes that he was threatened with physical punishment if he made a mistake—caricaturing her as a stern *paidagogos* teaching a child (*Menexenus* 236b–c)—but nevertheless this indicates that students attempted earnestly to remember the work of a revered teacher.

---

[22] Diogenes Laertius, *Lives*, 9: 25–8, who tells other versions of the martyrdom also; Clement of Alexandria, *Strom.* 4: 56: 1, quoting Eratosthenes, *On Things Good and Evil*.

[23] Citing Timotheus of Pergamus, *The Fortitude of Philosophers* and Achaicus, *The Ethics*.

[24] For which see Tacitus, *Hist.* 3: 81, cf. *Ann.* 14: 59; 16: 21; Cassius Dio, *Hist. Rom.* 65: 18, 19; Philostratus, *Vita Appol.* 4: 46, see Cora E. Lutz, *Musonius Rufus: 'The Roman Socrates'* (New Haven: Yale University Press, 1947), 14–18.

[25] Mason, '*Philosophiai*', 35.

[26] Ibid. 32; Runia, *Hairesis*, 122–3.

JUDAISM AS PHILOSOPHY

Given all this, it is no surprise that a number of Jews, including Philo, understood Judaism as *philosophia*. It would seem likely that by the fourth century BCE, there was a notion among some Greek authors that the Jews were collectively 'philosophers', and descendants of ancient Indian sages (*Apion* 1: 179).[27] Theophrastus refers to Jews as 'a people of philosophers', and Megasthenes includes them in a list of non-Greek philosophers who also understand Nature.[28] Clement of Alexandria cites such ancient sources to prove the point that Judaism was the oldest philosophy by far, pointing also to Philo as one who argued the matter persuasively.[29] Regarding Moses, Clement stresses 'the great antiquity of the philosophy according to him'.[30]

For Philo it was fundamental that philosophy is the origin of all that is good (*Opif.* 53) and that Moses was the greatest philosopher, who acquired the clearest and most perfect knowledge by his encounter with God on Sinai (*Leg.* 3: 97–101; cf. *Mos.* 1: 21–4). Moses is prime διδάσκαλος 'teacher' (*Gig.* 54; *Spec.* 1: 59). Moses is also king, lawgiver, and prophet, but these are offices he can undertake because he is a *philosophos* (*Mos.* 2: 2).[31] This quality of being an exemplary *philosophos* is linked with sanctity, of great closeness to God: Moses is called 'most holy', ἱερώτατος, twenty times in the extant Philonic corpus.[32] This sanctity arises because, ultimately, the teacher of (Jewish) *philosophia* is God, also identified as Wisdom. One who follows Moses is an ἐραστὴς σοφίας, a 'lover of Wisdom' (*Her.* 102, cf.

---

[27] Josephus cites Clearchus' report of Aristotle's story found in the first book of his work 'On Sleep' and notes that Hermippus concluded his presentation of Pythagoraean philosophy by stating that Pythagoras imitated the ideas of the Jews and Thracians (*Apion* 1: 165, cf. 2: 287). See also Hecataeus of Abdera in Diodorus Siculus, *Bibl. Hist.* 40: 3; Strabo, *Geogr.* 16: 2: 35–9.

[28] Theophrastus, *On Piety*, in Porphyry, *Abstin.* 2: 26; for Megasthenes, *Indica* (3rd book), see Clement of Alexandria, *Strom.* 1: 15: 72: 5.

[29] Clement, *Strom.* 1: 15: 72: 4–5. Clement interestingly dubs Philo here a 'Pythagoraean'.

[30] *Strom.* 1: 15: 73: 6. For a detailed analysis of the figure of Moses in non-Jewish sources see John G. Gager, *Moses in Greco-Roman Paganism* (Nashville, Tenn.: Abingdon, 1972), esp. 25–79.

[31] Ibid. 129.

[32] Ibid. 133 n. 75, e.g. *Leg.* 3: 185; *Cher.* 39; *Det.* 135, 140; *Spec.* 1: 59; *Virt.* 175.

Sacr. 65; *Congr.* 114). One is taught also by the (divine) law of Nature (*Agric.* 66; *Her.* 182) and the Mosaic law (*Post.* 80), which are all in perfect harmony. For Philo, synagogues are schools of piety, holiness, and virtue in which the duties to God and people are discerned and rightly performed (*Mos.* 2: 16; *Spec.* 2: 62; *Opif.* 128; *Legat.* 155). What others learn from Greek philosophy Jews learn from their customs and laws (*Virt.* 65). Judaism is not just *a* philosophy for Philo, but *the* philosophy of God. Those who truly love Wisdom should follow Moses. Ultimately, as David Runia writes, Philo identifies Mosaic (divine) philosophy as 'something which will eclipse and supersede the Greek model'.[33]

It is not surprising that Philo could formulate Judaism in this way and expect acknowledgement on the part of his audience, given that the notion that Moses was a philosopher was accepted in the Graeco-Roman world;[34] in the second century Galen would cite Moses along with Plato and Epicurus as an authority (though a flawed one) on medical matters[35] and the Pythagoraean philosopher Numenius would allegorize Mosaic tradition to find it remarkably similar to Greek philosophy.[36] As Mason points out, the cultic aspects of Judaism were visible only in Jerusalem; Jews in the Diaspora may well have seemed more like participants in a philosophical school than cultic practitioners. Jews followed a carefully prescribed ethical way of life, involving disciplines of various kinds, and joining the group 'Israel' did involve conversion unless you were born and brought up in its ways. The synagogue may have seemed more like a building for a gathering of a philosophical school than a temple, which was conceptually a god's house rather than a meeting hall. In the synagogue the writings governing the school were read and studied.[37] The normal cultic manifestations—sacrifice, processions,

---

[33] Gager, *Moses*, 143.

[34] See above.

[35] Galen, *On the Usefulness of Parts of the Body* 11: 4, and see Gager, *Moses*, 87–91. As Gager notes: 'Galen, Celsus and Julian continued to recognize Moses as a philosopher, much as Hecataeus and Strabo before them, but as one who needed to be criticized for serious philosophical deficiencies', p. 88.

[36] See Gager, *Moses*, 63–9. The fragment from Numenius is found in Origen, *Contra Celsum* 4: 51.

[37] Mason, '*Philosophiai*', 42, and see Nock, *Conversion*, 62. Mason also notes, however, that some Roman sources of the 1st century define Judaism as a

choral singing, and so on—were not in evidence. This is not to say that the sacred activities of Jews were not understood along cultic lines at times by the Romans, who were worried about the introduction of new gods which would threaten traditional customs. Judaism could seem another terrible foreign cult which was not socially healthy.[38]

In terms of the synagogue,[39] it appears likely that gatherings for teaching and worship were classified in Rome and its empire as *collegia*, 'clubs' or 'associations'. Later, in the Theodosian Code, it is clear that the synagogue is conceptualized as a *collegium* from which the *fiscus Iudaicus* was collected (*Cod. Theod.* 16: 8: 14, 29). Synagogue meetings were conceptually understood as *collegia* in extant writings reflecting Roman policy in the first centuries BCE and CE: Julius Caesar prohibited all *collegia*, excepting Jewish meetings (Suetonius, *Divus Julius* 84: 5; Josephus, *Ant.* 14: 213–16), as did Augustus (*Legat.* 156–8; 311–17). Tiberius had been ruthless with foreign cults in Rome, which here included Jewish and Egyptian (Serapis–Isis cult) worship (Suetonius, *Tib.* 36). Flaccus banned sodalities and clubs in Alexandria, which would have included synagogues (*Flacc.* 4, cf. 136). Gaius had allowed a proliferation of clubs in Rome, but these were apparently disbanded by Claudius, who had a more severe attitude, and forbade Jewish assemblies (Cassius Dio, *Hist. Rom.* 60: 6: 6).[40] The clearly apologetic tone of *Legat.* 311–12, where Philo insists that Jewish *collegia* are 'not based on drunkenness and merry-making but are schools of temperance and righteousness', may reflect an attempt to convince Claudius of his error in banning Jewish assemblies. If *Contempl.* and *Legat.* are to be linked, then we see further in *Contempl.* a

dangerous foreign cult, not as a philosophy (Valerius Maximus and Suetonius, *Tiberius* 36), and see n. 38.

[38] See Plutarch, *De Superstitione* 8; Strabo, *Geogr.* 16: 2: 37; Tacitus, *Hist.* 4: 81: 2; 5: 13: 1. It was also considered riduculous: Tacitus, *Hist.* 5: 4–5; Juvenal, *Satires* 14: 96–106; Horace, *Satires* 1: 5: 96–105. See Beard *et al.*, *Religions of Rome*, i. 221–2.

[39] For the synagogue in Graeco-Roman Egypt, see Allen Kerkeslager, 'Jewish Pilgrimage and Jewish Identity in Hellenistic and Early Roman Egypt', in Frankfurter (ed.), *Pilgrimage and Holy Space*, 99–225, at 115–22.

[40] Wendy Cotter, 'The Collegia and Roman Law: State Restrictions on Voluntary Associations, 44 BCE–200 CE', in Kloppenborg and Wilson (eds.), *Voluntary Associations*, 74–89.

very powerful argument that this group, in some way representative of the highest ideals of Judaism as a whole, are truly pious
and good in their common assemblies. The concentration on the
symposium of the Mareotic group has a political dimension: the
contrast between the Greek symposia (*Contempl.* 40–7) and
those of this group may also be a plea to Claudius for a positive
appraisal of the Jewish case. Unlike in other *collegia*, the banquet
(symposium) is entirely restrained.[41]

Chaeremon's focus on the moderation of Egyptian priests may
also be interesting in the light of the suspicion in Rome of the
Serapis–Isis cult and its associated assemblies. According to
Tacitus, the people of Alexandria were 'subject to superstitions',
with *superstitio* as a category including not only the Serapis–Isis
cult (that had been promoted by the Ptolemies), but also Judaism
(*Hist.* 4: 81: 2; 5: 4–5; 5: 13: 1). Both Judaism and Egyptian
religion could be understood in Rome as wacky cults/societies
which were therefore particularly attractive to women (on Isis,
see Juvenal, *Satires* 6: 522–41). Augustus had banned Egyptian
rites within the *pomerium* of Rome (Cassius Dio, *Hist. Rom.* 53:
2: 4; 54: 6: 6). In 19 CE there was a scandal involving a Roman
lady who was a special devotee of the cult of Isis, when she was
duped into adultery in the temple. Tiberius responded by
destroying this temple, having the statue of Isis thrown into the
Tiber, and crucifying the priests (Josephus, *Ant.* 18: 65–84, cf.
Tacitus, *Annales* 2: 85).[42] It is interesting that Chaeremon makes
Egyptian cultic worship philosophical and argues for its superi-
ority in terms of virtue.

If the Romans saw Judaism as philosophical, and Jewish
assemblies in synagogues as *collegia*, then the cultic language
Philo uses in *Contempl.* may have seemed rather curious at first
sight. The philosophical reading of the situation would have
made better sense. Philo ensures in his work that even the properly cultic aspects and objects of Temple ritual are remade in
philosophical terms (for example, the menorah: *Heres.* 216–23;

---

[41] See also what he states about the Passover feast in *Spec.* 2: 145–6. For discussion of how Philo attempts to deal with Jewish associations and differentiate
them from others in Alexandria, see Torrey Seland, 'Philo and the Clubs and
Associations of Alexandria', in Kloppenborg and Wilson (eds.), *Voluntary
Associations*, 110–25.

[42] See Beard *et al.*, *Religions of Rome*, i. 230–1.

the altar and tabernacle, *Ebr.* 134–5: sacrifices, *Sacr.* 72–111), and blends the language of cult with the language of philosophy into one whole: to follow Moses was indeed to follow the way and lifestyle of the *hierotatos philosophos*.

Philo was not alone. We know that Hellenistic Jews in Alexandria understood Judaism to be *philosophia*. Artapanus (third–second centuries BCE) asserted that Moses invented philosophy, and was the figure identified by the Greeks as Musaeus, the 'teacher' of Orpheus,[43] In the so-called *Letter of Aristeas* (second century BCE), Jews astound the king, Ptolemy II Philadelphus, with their wisdom (200–1, 293–4, 312). Using the terms of Greek philosophy, Jews accept the centrality of piety (εὐσέβεια)[44] and righteousness (δικαιοσύνη).[45] Moses' main concerns, it asserts, were precisely for piety and righteousness (131, 144). In the philosophical symposia described within the work, the king and the court philosophers acknowledge the excellence of Jewish opinions.

The Jewish scholar Aristobulus (second century BCE) explained that Torah is the pinnacle of philosophy and in fact numerous Greek philosophers and poets are dependent on Moses (Eusebius, *Praep. Evang.* 8: 10: 4; 13: 1–16), a view held later by both Philo and Josephus (*Apion* 2: 168). Aristobulus, associated with the Egyptian King Ptolemy VI Philometor (180–145 BCE), is described in 2 Maccabees 1: 10 as the king's teacher (of Jewish philosophy)—his διδάσκαλος—and a member of 'the family of the anointed priests'.[46] In his writings he appears to be familiar with Stoicism, Aristotelianism, and

---

[43] Artapanus inverts the identification of Musaeus as the pupil of Orpheus. For the surviving fragments of his work, found in Eusebius, *Praep. Evang.* 9: 18: 1; 23: 1–4; 27: 1–37, see John J. Collins's translation and commentary in James Charlesworth (ed.), *Old Testament Pseudepigrapha* (London: Darton, Longman & Todd, 1985), ii. 889–903.

[44] *Aristeas* 131, 215, 229 etc.

[45] *Aristeas* 193, 195, 197 etc.

[46] His work is in fact dedicated to Ptolemy VI Philometor (*Praep. Evang.* 8: 9: 38). For issues of identification see Nikolaus Walter, *Der Thoraausleger Aristobulus: Untersuchungen zu seinen Fragmenten und zu pseudepigraphischen Resten der jüdisch hellenistischen Literatur* (Berlin: Akademie-Verlag, 1964), 35–123, who is negative about the historicity of 2 Macc. though see the positive assessments of Kasher, *The Jews*, 62, Hengel, *Judaism and Hellenism*, ii. 105–7, nn. 373, 378, and Adela Yarbro Collins, 'Aristobulus', in Charlesworth (ed.), *Old Testament Pseudepigrapha*, ii. 831-42, at 833.

Pythogoraeanism and can formulate his discourse in the terminology of Greek philosophy (cf. the 'seven-fold *logos*' of 12: 12,
15).[47] For Aristobulus, 'Judaism' is a 'school of thought', αἵρεσις,
which prescribes a way of life one chooses to follow. He articulates the essential nature of Judaism in this way: 'For it is agreed
by all the philosophers that it is necessary to hold holy opinions
concerning God, a point our philosophical school makes particularly well, and the whole constitution of our Law is arranged
with reference to piety and justice and temperance and the rest of
the things that are truly good.'[48] As John Barclay has pointed
out, we can see this Jewish philosophical consciousness breaking
out at times even in the literalist translation of the Septuagint. In
God's declaration in the burning bush, ἐγώ εἰμι ὁ ὤν (Exod. 3:
14), 'the potential for a Jewish Platonizing theology is already
clear'.[49]

We do not even need to stay within Alexandria in order to find
Jews conceptualizing Judaism as something essentially philosophical. The very use of the Greek term 'Judaism', may have its
conceptual origin in a fundamental classification of the 'religion'
of Judaeans as philosophy. The first attestation of the term
Ἰουδαϊσμός in 2 Maccabees occurs at a time when Greek notions
of philosophy are beginning to permeate Judaean religion.
Strictly speaking, the word Ἰουδαϊσμός means 'Judah-ishness'
and is extremely vague. What does it mean to be 'Judah-ish'
when the term designates more than regionality?[50] A comparison
from philosophy may be helpful. Πυθαγορισμός ('Pythagoras-
ishness') designated the ideas and practices of Pythagoras.[51] To
'Pythagorize' was to be like Pythagoras in your lifestyle.[52] In the

---

[47] Barclay, *Jews*, 153 n. 59. For a full examination of Aristobulus' philosophy,
see Roberto Radice, *La filosophia di Aristobulo: I suoi nessi con il 'De mundo'
attributo ad Aristotele* (Milan: Vita e Pensiero, 1994) and David Dawson,
Allegorical Readers and Cultural Revision in Ancient Alexandria (Berkeley,
Calif.: University of California Press, 1992), 77–81.

[48] Frag. 4; Eusebius, *Praep. Evang.* 13: 13: 8; Yarbro Collins, 841.

[49] Barclay, *Jews*, 126.

[50] The regional connotation of the term should not be ignored, however, see
Ross S. Kraemer, 'On the Meaning of the Term "Jew" in Greco-Roman
Inscriptions', *HTR* 82 (1989), 35–54.

[51] LSJ 1551, which cites Antiphanes Comicus 226: 8; Alexis Comicus 220: 1.

[52] Cf. Philostratus, *Vita Apol.* 7: 'So you go and live your own life', he said,
'and I will live that of Pythagoras.' The term Μηδίζω may also be looked to for
comparison, since in Herodotus, *Hist.* 4: 144 it means to 'side with the Medes'

case of Judah we have a region, while in the case of Pythagoras there is a proper name, but the principle of making some identifying noun or name represent a lifestyle occurs in both instances. It was not possible to use the term Μωυσαϊσμός, for this would have included the Samaritans ('Israelites'). Ἰουδαϊσμός is distinguished from Samaritanism, since Samaritans, while accepting the Mosaic scriptures, did not accept the authority of the Judaean Temple, even though they shared an Israelite/Hebrew past with Judaeans. Ἰουδαῖοι are those who live in the region of Judah/Judaea,[53] but more so they are those who practise the philosophy-cum-cult of Judah, whether they live in the Land or not, just as Πλατώνειοί are those who practise the philosophical system of Plato.[54] The term appears to have arisen in an environment in which people understood the cult, praxis, and beliefs of those who accepted the authority of the Mosaic scriptures and the Temple in Judaea as comprising the philosophical system of the Judaeans, namely, 'Judah-ishness'. If so, the very concept of Ἰουδαϊσμός is probably (and somewhat ironically) derived from Greek philosophical patterns of thinking.

Perhaps the neatest examination of the origin of the word Ἰουδαϊσμός is that of Yehoshua Amir, who notes the early examples of this term, and concludes that it had associations with philosophical conceptualizations.[55] He identified seven early instances in which the term Ἰουδαϊσμός appears: 2 Maccabees 8: 1; 14: 38; 2: 21; 4 Maccabees 4: 26; 2 Galatians 1: 13–14; a dedicatory inscription in the synagogue in Stobi (Yugoslavia) from the third century BCE,[56] and the funerary inscription from the cemetery of Porto, Italy, in praise of a woman 'who lived with her spouse for thirty-four years a gracious life in Judaism'.[57] To this

and therefore behave as they do. Μηδισμός is to go along with the Medes in general, see LSJ 1125. The word βαρβαρίζω means 'behave like a Barbarian' (Herodotus, *Hist.* 2: 57) or 'side with the Barbarians' (Xenophon, *Hist. Graec.* 5: 2: 35), see LSJ 306 and Suppl. 66 on βαρβαριζμός, 'siding with non-Greeks', *SEG* 22: 506: 9.

[53] So Aristotle, quoted by Clearchus of Soli in Josephus, *Apion* 1: 179.
[54] e.g. Philostratus, *Vita Apol.* 7.
[55] Yehoshua Amir, 'The Term Ἰουδαϊσμός: A Study in Jewish-Hellenistic Self-Identification', *Immanuel*, 14 (1982), 34–41.
[56] Frey, *CIJ* 694.
[57] Frey, *CIJ* 537; Noy, no. 584 (now in the Vatican Museum) dated 3rd to 4th centuries, though this is unsure.

list should be added also 2 Maccabees 2: 21. Amir notes the reference to life 'in Judaism' in the inscriptions and in that of 2 Maccabees 8: 1, and stresses that Ἰουδαϊσμός means living one's life according to a νομός (2 Maccabees 6: 6) within a πολιτεία, system. One therefore enters into this system by becoming Jewish (cf. LXX Esther 8: 17, ἰουδάϊζον) and one can leave it by 'going away from the laws of the ancestors' (2 Maccabees 6: 1). To follow Ἰουδαϊσμός is essentially to follow the philosophical life of the Judaeans. One dwelt in the Judaic *politeia* centred on the Judaic law.[58] Alon notes that in 2 Maccabees Ἰουδαϊσμός is defined against those who follow 'the ways of a foreign nation' (2 Maccabees 4: 12–14), namely the Greeks. Jews invented the term to indi-cate that which was truly of the nation in the situation they were faced with. As Amir concludes, 'preliminary examination of the sources as given above would appear to lead to the conclusion that our word denotes the complex of behaviour which is entailed by the fact that someone is a Jew, and that that behaviour is held to be of such value that it is worthy to fight, even to die, for its sake.'[59] As we have seen, such commitment to philosophy is precisely what was expected of true philosophers.

For Josephus, a Judaean, Jewish religion is quite clearly a kind of philosophical system, with a concern for well-being, εὐδαιμονία.[60] The major concern is to live in accordance with the same Graeco-Roman philosophical virtues: piety (εὐσέβεια) and justice (δικαιοσύνη) (e.g. *Apion* 2: 168–71). As already noted, Josephus believed that Greek philosophy was founded on Mosaic philosophy (*Apion* 2: 168, 281). Josephus repeatedly uses philosophical terms to highlight the philosophical nature of Jewish religion, at times extolling certain individuals by reference to these and thereby implying that they are exemplary teachers of philosophy. For example, in the case of John the Baptist, Josephus describes him as 'a good man who was exhorting the Jews to practise virtue and righteousness towards each other and piety towards God' (*Ant.* 18: 116). He says that all Jewish customs are concerned with 'piety and righteousness'

---

[58] See also Honigman, 'Philon', 73–8.

[59] Amir, 'Ἰουδαϊσμός', 36.

[60] Mason, '*Philosophiai*', 57 n. 46, notes how Josephus introduces this word 47 times in his paraphrasing of the LXX (*Ant.* 1–11).

(*Ant.* 16: 42).[61] Righteousness and piety are the particular characteristics of good Jewish kings (*Ant.* 7: 338, 342, 356, 374, 384; 9: 236). Moreover, the Jewish philosophy had three (or four) major philosophical schools, αἱρέσεις, just as the alternative system of Graeco-Roman 'philosophy' had such schools (*War* 2: 137; *Ant.* 13: 171) or philosophies (*War* 2: 119; *Ant.* 18: 9, 11), where a distinctive way of life was followed (*War* 15: 371). The Pharisees are the equivalent of the Stoics, the Essenes are the equivalent of the Pythagoraeans,[62] though he could not quite stretch to portraying the Sadducees or his 'Fourth Philosophy' as Cynic, Epicurean, or anything else. Nevertheless, as Diogenes Laertius would do in his third-century history of Greek philosophy, the schools could be divided between the polarities of 'sceptic' (Sadducees) and 'dogmatic' (Pharisees).[63]

All this evidence tends to suggest that Jews in Alexandria and elsewhere were comfortable with seeing Judaism as philosophical, and that this conceptualization of Judaism may well have been fairly common in the Diaspora. It was not an apologetic strategy so much as a cognitive essential for those living in the Hellenistic world. This was already proposed in the 1950s by Morton Smith, who noted that 'when Judaism first took shape and became conscious of itself and its own peculiarity in the Hellenized world of the later Persian Empire, it described itself with the Hellenic term meaning the wisdom of its people' (Deut. 4: 6).[64] In fact, the conceptualization may have happened as much in Israel as in the Diaspora; for Smith, any notion that Palestinian Judaism was impervious to Hellenization was absurd. The 'long roll call of the wisdom literature' testified to the philosophication of Judaism in the Land as well as beyond it.[65] The Egyptian Jews who would do so much to conceptualize

---

[61] To Josephus, piety, *eusebeia*, was ideally centred in the Temple cult (cf. *Ant.* 8: 122–4; 10: 45; 14: 65). It involved obedience to God/Torah (*Ant.* 6: 148; *Contra Apion* 2: 184), the observance of food and purity laws (*Life* 14, 75, cf. *War* 7: 264), Sabbath observance (*Apion* 1: 212), circumcision (*Ant.* 10: 44–8), and sacrifice (*Ant.* 14: 65).

[62] See *War* 2: 119–62; *Ant.* 13: 171–3; 15: 371; 18: 11–22; *Vita* 12 cf. *War* 2: 118.

[63] See Mason, '*Philosophiai*', 44–6; Runia, 'Hairesis-Model', 136–8.

[64] Morton Smith, 'Palestinian Judaism in the First Century', in Moshe Davis (ed.), *Israel: Its Role in Civilization* (New York: Jewish Theological Seminary of America, 1956), 67–81, at 79.   [65] Ibid.

the law as philosophy would draw greatly on the Wisdom literature to explain the fundamentals of the system. As Aristobulus
explains, Wisdom is 'first' in creation because: 'all light has its
origin in her . . . and wisdom holds the place of a lantern, for
as long as they follow her unremittingly, they will be calm
throughout their entire life'.[66] With the adoption of Wisdom
terminology, we find an integration of the vast reservoir of the
prophetic tradition into what it means to be a lover of Wisdom.
As Wisdom of Solomon 7: 22–8: 1 has it, Wisdom is the pure
breath and power of God who 'passing into holy souls . . . makes
them into God's friends and prophets' (7: 27). To be a prophet is
therefore to be somehow united with Wisdom, a lover of
Wisdom, a *philosophos*.

This 'philosophication' of the religion of ancient Judaea is of
course precisely what Jacob Neusner has argued as having taken
place by the second century CE. The Mishnaic system, Neusner
repeatedly points out, is a philosophical one, highly indebted to
principles expounded by Aristotle in his *Natural History*, which
aims at the hierarchical classification of all things.[67] In Neusner's
analysis, the entire Mishnaic system is conceptualized and
articulated in the form of an Aristotelian philosophical work.
This vast systemic analysis could perhaps only be done with such
precision by Neusner, but already nearly thirty years ago Elias
Bickerman noted how Mishnah Avot 1 used the language of a
'chain of tradition' or succession of the *diadochoi* just as philosophical schools used it.[68] Traditions are handed down, as
traditions were handed down within the philosophical schools
of ancient Greece and Rome.[69] He noted that references to the
'house of Hillel' or the 'house of Shammai' have parallels in

---

[66] Frag. 5; Eus. *Praep. Evang.* 13: 12: 10.

[67] Jacob Neusner, 'The Mishnah's Philosophical Method: The Judaism of
Hierarchical Classification in Graeco-Roman Context', *SPA* 3 (1991), 192–206;
id., *The Transformation of Judaism from Philosophy to Religion* (Urbana and
Chicago: University of Illinois Press, 1992); id., *Judaism as Philosophy: The
Method and Message of the Mishnah* (Columbia: University of South Florida
Press, 1991); id., *The Philosophical Mishnah*, 4 vols. (Atlanta: Scholars, 1989).

[68] Elias Bickerman, 'La Chaîne de la tradition pharisienne', in his *Studies in
Jewish and Christian History*, ii (Harvard: Heinemann, 1979), 256–69.

[69] Seneca, *Ep.* 40: 3: 'People speak of "handing down" precepts to their
students', cf. Justin, *Dial.* 2.

philosophical literature. Other motifs which have parallels with philosophy were: the ideal of teaching without pay, while accepting gifts; a group of students who followed teachers about and served them; exemption from taxation; distinctive clothing; asceticism and, as Smith puts it, 'they discussed the questions philosophers discussed and reached the conclusions philosophers reached'.[70] K. H. Rengstorf has stressed the huge similarity between what he distinguishes in rabbinic literature and the philosophical schools of Hellenism, a factor he puts down to an 'apologetic debate with Hellenism'.[71] He finds this in the fellowship of students, the chain of succession tradition, the disputative methods of teaching, memorizing teaching, the citing of previous authorities, and other matters.[72]

This is not to say that Judaism was understood always as *philosophia* rather than a cult in some kind of absolute sense. We do not have to jump into one or the other of these categories, formulated as binary oppositions. It may be best to see Judaism as a kind of blend. Judaism could very well be seen as a cult (or a *superstitio*), with its cultic centre in Jerusalem. The cultic aspects of Judaism united Jews throughout the Diaspora by drawing them to Jerusalem, if possible, for festivals, and functioned as a unifying idea and centre of holiness. Prior to 70, the Jerusalem Temple was a point of holiness on earth, ideally an *omphalos* of all Jewish life and worship. The point is only that Judaism was not 'just' a cult in the Graeco-Roman understanding of what cult was, for it involved more than what Graeco-Roman cult would generally entail. Judaism was a cult *and* philosophy, both wrapped into one. But whereas those living in Judaea might find the cultic aspects of Judaism very much in evidence, those living further away might find the philosophical aspects more relevant.[73] This combination of cult and philosophy is precisely what made Judaism so strange and appealing to the Graeco-

---

[70]   Smith, 'Palestinian Judaism', 80.

[71]   K. H. Rengstorf, '$\mu\alpha\theta\eta\tau\dot{\eta}\varsigma$' in Gerhard Friedrich (ed.) *TDNT* iv. 438.

[72]   Rengstorf notes: 'We may venture to say that the *talmid* as such came into Judaism from the educative process of the Greek and Hellenistic philosophical schools' (p. 439). In Rengstorf's discussion of the verb $\delta\iota\delta\acute{\alpha}\sigma\kappa\epsilon\iota\nu$ in the LXX and the New Testament he finds it deeply indebted to the Hebrew לִמֵּד and correspondingly can argue that a $\delta\iota\delta\acute{\alpha}\sigma\kappa\alpha\lambda o\varsigma$ is 'one who indicates the way of God from the Torah' (*TDNT* iii. 151).

[73]   See Mason, *Philosophiai*, 46–55.

Roman mind, and Christianity would in due course also take over this dual identity and become a kind of quasi-Jewish Graeco-Roman answer to what was already there in Judaism: the philosophical cult which united ethics and piety in a total package of salvation.[74]

In summary, Jews in the centuries following Alexander the Great's conquests were using the inescapable cultural mental technology of the Hellenistic world, especially in Alexandria, where Judaism was understood as *philosophia*. More specifically, Philo may have presented the Mareotic group as philosophical not so much because it was a clever rhetorical device, but because he really had no other way of presenting his group. So Philo makes his case. For Philo, this Mareotic group of philosophers is the pinnacle of (cultic) piety: θεραπευταί/ρίδες and ἱκέται of an invisible shrine. They are the true cultic devotees, servers and suppliants of God, constantly focused on divine things as priests in a temple will constantly focus on cultic sacra and ritual. They attend to divine things, but the divine things are not in the usual physical cultic situation, but in the realm of the soul. They are then the contemplative type of philosophers who endeavour to see those things truly worth seeing in the metaphysical universe.

A jump from a cultic term—or a cultic reality—into philosophy was a natural one to make for Philo, even if not for his audience. One might argue that it was not a very strong rhetorical card to play, unless Philo knew that some of the leading figures he was addressing were pro-philosophy in principle, perhaps taking some lead from an emperor with scholarly leanings. It is clear that at various times some of the elite of Rome were uncomfortable about *collegia* and the banqueting that took place as part of association meetings, and 'philosophy' added to the mix did not necessarily spell 'virtue' in the way Philo implies. Ever since Plato's account of the death of Socrates—killed partly for the disruption he caused to cultic devotion on a public level (Plato, *Apology* 29c)—philosophies could be seen as adopting a dangerous stance, and become associated with criticism of

---

[74] The mystery cults of the Egyptian gods, particularly Isis, or the Persian god Mithras were to some degree moving in the same direction, but they lacked the great corpus of theological writing which was the foundation of the Jewish lifestyle.

rulers.[75] Philosophers were those who may at times accept death rather than stoop to flatter cruel and wicked rulers (Epictetus, *Diss.* 1.29: 10). Seneca himself was reportedly killed by Nero.[76] Vespasian allegedly expelled all philosophers from Rome except for Musonius Rufus, and Domitian executed prominent citizens on the charge of 'philosophy' and evicted the rest (Cassius Dio, *Hist. Rom.* 65: 12: 1–2 and 13: 1–2) in 89 CE.[77] The spiritual and intellectual commitment to the truth of the philosophy is exemplified by these stories; the martyr would rather die than accept that the philosophy is wrong. Rulers in turn could both respect and despise philosophers. There might be philosophers at court, but there might also be philosophers outside the court who acted as moral critics on the behaviour of the ruler and government. They were dangerous precisely because of their elite position in society. Not without reason, the men who killed Julius Caesar were understood to be 'philosophers'.[78]

Methodologically, I have defined that there is no way of assessing the historicity of Philo's statements in *Contempl*. We cannot say here empirically that Philo is providing us with either true or false information. In terms of this investigation, it is therefore a presupposition that Philo is presenting truth, broadly defined, and conclusions are drawn on the basis of this. The identification of a rhetorical project in the work does not invalidate its historicity, but rather the rhetoric itself may help us determine elements of truth in the text. If Philo is turning cultic language into philosophical language, then the cultic language is important to recognize, for it may provide clues to aspects of the group we may have failed to note when carried along by Philo's rhetoric. I shall return to this later on. However, we could not say that because of the rhetoric the group were the opposite of what Philo defines: cultic rather than philosophical, for this would be a simple inversion of rhetoric ungrounded in any logical necessity.

Our best benchmark lies in contextualization. If we think of the

---

[75] See Mason, *'Philosophiai'*, 35–7. Also, Ramsay MacMullen, *Enemies of the Roman Order* (Cambridge, Mass.: Harvard University Press, 1966), 46–94.

[76] On Seneca, see Cassius Dio, *Hist. Rom.* 62: 24: 1, cf. 62: 26: 1 (Thrasea and Soranus); see also Nock, *Conversion*, 176.

[77] Mason, *'Philosophiai'*, 36.

[78] Ibid. Cato was a Stoic, Brutus was an Academic, and Cassius an Epicurean, cf. MacMullen, *Enemies*, 1–45.

group contextually within Alexandrian Judaism, the evidence suggests that they would have shared many of Philo's own presuppositions: that Judaism was *philosophia*, that their meetings were in line with kinds of *collegia*, that the cultic aspects of Judaism as a whole could be interpreted in accordance with philosophical ideology. Philo's rhetoric is then placing additional emphasis on ideas that he himself found within the group, selecting those elements that particularly supported his rhetoric and ignoring those that did not.

To what degree were Philo and the group he describes in *Contempl.* following a very similar philosophical ideology? He writes here as if he stands in complete agreement with them, but, as we shall see, that is not quite so. In terms of the group's particular philosophy within wider Alexandrian Judaism we venture down a path Philo himself was not particularly concerned to mark out. Whatever he does say is designed to illustrate the group's virtue, not difference. They are peculiarly exemplary, not examples of peculiarity. However, Philo saw this group as following a particular school of thought within the milieu of the true *philosophia*, Judaism. The more we explore this school of thought, the stranger these people seem. We will consider first of all their allegorical interpretation of scripture and unusual calendar.

6

Allegory and Asceticism

Philo could hardly have been single-handedly responsible for the exuberantly rich exegesis exhibited in his scriptural commentaries. The enormous variety, the great subtlety, and the sheer quantity of his exegesis, in addition to his own many attestations of his predecessors, make it virtually certain that much of his commentary derived from a rich body of scholastic tradition.[1]

Philo was an allegorizer. For him, in scripture, things were not as they seemed. Allegorical interpretation rests on the assumption that the writer intended a piece of literature to function on two levels: an obvious one and an obscure one that can be understood only by the adept, skilled at seeing true reality. *Allegoria* is, basically, 'to say something other that what one seems to say'.[2] For Philo the corpus of scripture was encoded, and the codes could be deciphered to indicate the great path of the soul to God, and the teaching of Wisdom. In it one could discern the *logos*— reason, message—that God meant humanity to understand. The hazards we should be warned of are all brilliantly exemplified in ancient tales, which refer to universal archetypes and the world of mind and soul. Scripture is fundamentally metaphysical. Philo was not averse to interpreting scripture fairly literally, or at least not allegorically, when it suited him, but it is for his allegorical interpretations that he is known.[3]

Philo was not alone in his enterprises in Alexandria, for Philo's writing indicates that there were other intellectual Jews like himself who looked beyond the literal meaning of scripture to a spiritual or hidden meaning.[4] Allegorical interpretation had a

---

[1] David Winston, 'Philo and the Contemplative Life', in Arthur Green, *Jewish Spirituality from the Bible through the Middle Ages* (New York: Crossroad, 1986), 198–231, at 200.

[2] Dawson, *Allegorical Readers*, 3.

[3] For a careful examination of Philo's allegorizing exegesis, ibid., 73–126.

[4] See *Abr.* 217; *Spec.* 3: 178; *QG* 4: 196, and see Gregory Sterling, ' "The

rich history in the city, but not all allegorizing led to the same results Philo obtained. Philo writes of other Jewish allegorizers perhaps as many as seventy-four times in his writings, sometimes positively and sometimes critically.[5] Overall, however, it is the allegorizers who are on the right track, not the literalists.[6] As David Hay notes:

They examine the biblical text closely and observe its subtle nuances. . . . In contrast to literalists, they are persons who can contemplate incorporeal facts and live in the soul rather than the body.[7] They have spiritual vision, being both willing and able to see immaterial reality. Their ears are open and purified, receptive to spiritual things. Their exegesis tends to make their religion joyful and centered in the love of God.[8]

Among these other Jewish allegorizers, we find the members of the Mareotic group. Philo writes:

The entire interval from morning until evening is for them an exercise, for they philosophize by reading the sacred writings and interpreting allegorically the inherited philosophy. They consider the words of the literal text to be symbols of Nature which has been hidden, and which is revealed in the underlying meaning. (*Contempl.* 28)

The interpretations of the sacred scriptures are through the underlying meanings [conveyed] in allegories. For these men, all the law book seems to be like a living being, with a body made up of literal words,[9] and the invisible mind of the wording constitutes its soul. The soul above all begins to consider the things similar to it. As it were through a mirror of names, it sees the transcendent beauty of concepts which are reflected [there], bringing what is perceived naked into light for those able with a little reminding to see the unseen things through the seen. (*Contempl.* 78)

In describing them in this way, Philo would have expected his audience to have some inkling about what the group was trying

School of Sacred Laws": The Social Setting of Philo's Treatises', *VC* 53 (1999), 148–64.

[5] See Hay, 'Philo's References', esp. 42–3. Some of these may be to imaginary conversation partners, but these must be grounded in the kind of interpretations Philo believed his actual conversation partners to have held.

[6] For which see Montgomery J. Shroyer, 'Alexandrian Jewish Literalists', *JBL* 55 (1936), 261–84.

[7] See below for the ascetical aspects of the allegorizers.

[8] Hay, 'Philo's References', 44–5.   [9] Cf. Plato, *Phaedrus* 264c.

to do. Stoic philosophy, in seeing the *logos* as the fundamental principle of everything, sought to find it in literature as elsewhere. The first-century grammarian Heraclitus applied allegorical exegesis to the writings of Homer to ensure that the Homeric tales were truly moral,[10] and could trace his allegorical approach to Crates (second century BCE).[11] But this tradition probably stretched back further than that. In the late third century BCE the Alexandrian rulers Ptolemy IV Philopator and Queen Arsinoe founded a temple of Homer. In a relief from this temple, now in the British Museum, Arsinoe is identified as Oikoumene—the world—and Ptolemy with Chronos—time. In embodying such universal concepts some allegorical consciousness may have been at work. Homer would have been seen as the divine producer of literary works, and it would follow then that his works contained divine truth that needed to be sought out by allegorical exegesis. Philo himself allegorizes Homer in *Contempl.* 17 (cf. *Iliad* 13: 5, 6). This method was not always popular, at least in some circles at Rome, but criticisms of the practice by Cicero and Seneca[12] indicate at least that it was well-known in the Roman world that you could read literature—particularly Homer—as meaning something quite different to what it apparently means, especially if you were a Stoic. Chaeremon, Philo's opponent, the Stoic Egyptian priest who went on to become Nero's tutor, was an allegorizer himself. According to Porphyry, the Alexandrian Christian allegorizer Origen used Chaeremon's allegorical method of interpreting the 'mysteries of the Greeks'.[13] Chaeremon in fact appears to have claimed that allegory as a method was introduced first by Egyptian priests 'since they wanted to teach the great and lofty

---

[10] See Dawson, *Allegorical Readers*, 38–52; Sandmel, *Philo*, 19–21; Winston, 'Philo', 205. The allegorizing of Homer would continue, especially in Neoplatonic tradition, see Robert Lamberton, *Homer the Theologian: Neoplatonist Allegorical Reading and the Growth of the Epic Tradition* (Berkeley and Los Angeles: University of California Press, 1986) and John Dillon, 'Philo and the Greek Tradition of Allegorical Exegesis', in the *SBL 1994 Seminar Papers* (Atlanta: Scholars Press, 1994), 69–80.

[11] Heraclitus, *Quaestiones Homericae* 43.

[12] See Cicero, *De Natura Deorum* 1: 39–63; Seneca, *On Benefits* 1: 3; Dawson, *Allegorical Readers*, 52–72.

[13] Porphyry, *Contra Christianos*, frag. 39 = Eusebius, *Hist. Eccles.* 6: 19: 8, see van der Horst, *Chaeremon*, 4–5.

things to the uninitiated by means of allegories and myths'.[14] In Chaeremon's work on the Egyptian priests, he stated that the rituals associated with the cult were themselves each 'an indication of some allegorical truth'.[15] Given this, the Ptolemaic temple to Homer may be seen within the context of the blending of Egyptian and Hellenistic concepts, and must make us pause again to wonder at the peculiarities of Alexandrian culture.

Allegorizing clearly could make a bridge between the cultic and the philosophical, between the mythical and the ontological, but it fell foul of those who thought that there was a proper place to the categories that was being blurred by allegorical methods. Perhaps a common attitude to the uses and abuses of allegory is best summed up in the writings of Plutarch, who lived a generation after Philo. Plutarch considers the value of ancient myths, some of which are overtly immoral, in his discussion of the tales of Isis and Osiris. For Plutarch, the Egyptian allegorizing exegeses of such myths point to physical truths: Osiris is the Nile uniting with Isis, the earth, and so on (*Is. et Os.* 363d) or mystical meanings about the soul's release to behold formless beauty (*Is. et Os.* 382e–383a). However, Plutarch is not so much in favour of similar allegorical interpretation of Homer, and is a major advocate of treating poetic stories as exactly that: fictions.[16]

If the Mareotic group were allegorizers, then that tells us that they participated in something that had a wide interest in Alexandria, among both Jews and 'Greeks'. That Philo and this group allegorized would suggest that they may have shared some common methods and traditions. The preserved writings of the famed Jewish philosopher Aristobulus may be the most informative for placing the Mareotic group within a particular Alexandrian Jewish milieu of thought, very close to that of Philo, but not necessarily identical.[17] These writings give us an example of a scholar whose exegesis could have given rise to the entire school of allegorical interpretation, and also divergences

[14] Tzetzes, *Exegesis in Iliadem* 1: 193, quoted from van der Horst, *Chaeremon*, 7. This type of allegory is itself associated with the mystery of hieroglyphic writing, see Tzetzes, *Exegesis in Iliadem* 1: 97; Chiliades 5: 395–8 for which see van der Horst, *Chaeremon*, 24–5.

[15] Porphyry, *Abstin.* 4: 6.

[16] His argument is expounded in *De aud. poet.*, see Dawson, *Allegorical Readers*, 58–66.

[17] For summary, ibid. 150–8.

within the school. It is clear that both Philo[18] and the Mareotic
group had writings from predecessors on which to base their
own allegorical exegesis. As regards the latter, 'men of old . . . left
behind many recollections of the form of interpretations [they
used]. These [writings] are sort of like models used [by the
group] in order to imitate the method of the practice [of allegorical interpretation]' (*Contempl.* 29).

Aristobulus seems to have adopted into Judaism the allegorical methods pioneered by the Stoics.[19] Barclay senses that
Aristobulus is testing the ground in adopting an allegorical
approach to scripture, and appeals to no one before him to
justify his methodology.[20] Winston notes that, while Aristobulus
knew how one could allegorize Homer, and did so, he does not
apply allegory to scripture in the same 'playful manner'.[21]
Rather, Aristobulus seems a novice; he does not know the later
standard vocabulary of allegory, which means he is 'aware of
using a relatively new exegetical method and that he could not
rely on a well-established tradition'.[22] By the time of Philo there
were firm canons of allegory and exegetical rules. Still, excerpts
illustrating Aristobulus' allegorical method serve to show how
similar he was to Philo and to the people of *Contempl.*, as far as we
know (tr. Yarbro Collins):

And I wish to exhort you to receive the interpretations according to the
laws of nature and to grasp the fitting conception of God and not to fall
into the mythical and human way of thinking about God. For our lawgiver Moses proclaims arrangements of nature and preparations for
great events by expressing that which he wishes to say in so many ways,
by using words that refer to other matters (I mean matters relating to
outward appearances). Therefore, those who are able to think well
marvel at his wisdom and at the divine spirit in accordance with which
he has been proclaimed as a prophet also. . . . But to those who have no

---

[18] *Spec.* 1: 8; *Prob.* 82.

[19] See Yarbro Collins, 'Aristobulus', 832, 834.

[20] Ibid. 156: 'The hesitant and inconsistent way in which Aristobulus
employs his allegorical method indicates his pioneering role in its application to
the Pentateuch.' The *Letter of Aristeas* may also indicate approval of an allegorical approach to scripture, when the high priest Eleazar points out that Jewish
purity laws reflect a deeper logic (*Aristeas* 143), see Dawson, *Allegorical
Readers*, 76.

[21] Winston, 'Philo', 205.

[22] Ibid. 204.

share of power and understanding, but who are devoted to the letter alone, he does not seem to explain anything elevated. (Frag. 2; *Praep. Evang.* 8: 10: 2–5)

As in Stoic philosophy, Nature is indicative of God. God's greatness permeates Nature. Therefore, one may have thought, contemplation of Nature would be a way of understanding God. Indeed, apparent contradictions in the scriptures can be overcome by interpreting texts in accordance with the laws of Nature (Frag. 2: 8: 10: 2). This is of course precisely what the Mareotic group does according to Philo: they have 'dedicated their personal lives and themselves to the understanding and contemplation of the facts of Nature, according to the sacred instructions of the prophet Moses' (*Contempl.* 64). Wisdom also is esteemed as the goal of contemplation in Aristobulus' philosophy:

All light has it origin in it [wisdom]. And some of those belonging to the Peripatetic school have said that wisdom holds the place of a lantern; for as long as they follow it unremittingly, they will be calm through their whole life. And one of our ancestors, Solomon, said more clearly and better that wisdom existed before heaven and earth; which indeed agrees with what has been said. (Frag. 5; *Praep. Evang.* 13: 12: 10–11)

It is to Wisdom that the group has dedicated its life in *Contempl.* (19, 28, 34, 35, 68). For Philo Wisdom can be identified with the *logos*, which is, as Winston describes it, 'the pattern of all creation and the archetype of human reason'.[23]

The allegorical interpretation of scripture is a means by which the soul can be encouraged to contemplate Nature, for it enables those dedicated to this goal to see better. Again, we remember that the Greek word θεωρία, usually translated as 'contemplation', has its root in the verb 'behold, see'. Those who contemplate are those who see, the beholders of divine things, in Philo's view. Allegorical interpretation is the method 'dear to people with open eyes' (*Plant.* 36). Since allegorizing serves contemplation of divine things, allegorizers continue the succession of inspired persons who are lovers of the soul (*Deus* 55). They are people of understanding and wisdom (*Mut.* 140). The contemplative life is essentially the allegorically interpreting life.

For Philo, Moses was a model to be followed, not only as a

---

[23] Ibid. 201, and see pp. 202–4, esp. n. 4.

teacher of wisdom and the true philosophy of the nation, but as one who entered into the place where God is: into the unseen, invisible, incorporeal, and archetypal essence of existence. Moses saw what is hidden from the sight of mortal nature. Those who follow Moses strive to imprint that same image in their souls (*Mosis* 158–9). For the allegorizers, the task is a spiritual as much as an intellectual one. Runia points out that in fact Philo indicates that the extra Pentateuchal scriptural texts were written by disciples of Moses or one initiated into his mysteries (*Somn.* 1: 164; *Cher.* 49; *Agr.* 55; *Plant.* 39; *Conf.* 39, 44; *Congr.* 177),[24] and that Philo himself claims to have been initiated into the mysteries by Moses and Jeremiah (*Cher.* 48–9; *Post.* 173). The realm of cultic mystery-religion is used figuratively to explain mystical processes. Philo himself describes the frenetic inspired writing phases he experiences, when he is unpacking the truths of scripture via allegorical interpretation, as an instances of being 'under divine possession' (ὑπὸ κατοχῆς ἐνθέου) (*Migr.* 35).[25]

Philo therefore undoubtedly approves of the group's enterprise in terms of its allegorical interpretation. Philo describes the members of the group as being counted among 'the pupils of Moses', οἱ Μωυσέως γνώριμοι (63): 'those who have dedicated their personal lives and themselves to the understanding and contemplation of the facts of Nature, according to the sacred instructions of the prophet Moses' (64). It is their allegorical interpretation of scripture which marks them as philosophers, not simply their espousal of Judaism. Elsewhere in his writings this term, 'the pupils of Moses', can refer to those who try to follow the philosophy of Moses,[26] but more specifically it refers to those who interpret scripture allegorically (*QG* 3: 8),[27] those who are able to reconcile (allegorically) apparent inconsistencies of language in scripture (*Her.* 81). As Runia notes, 'allegorical exegesis is a *sine qua non* if a deeper understanding of Moses' thought is to be attained'.[28] It is a special group who are really οἱ

[24] Runia, 'Hairesis-Model', 132.

[25] See John R. Levison, 'Inspiration and the Divine Spirit in the Writings of Philo Judaeus', *JSJ* 27 (1996), 271–323, esp. 282–4, 294–5.

[26] So Runia, 'Hairesis-Model', 128.

[27] *Det.* 86; *Post.* 12; *Conf.* 39; *Cong.* 177; *Mos.* 2: 205; *Spec.* 1: 319, 345; 2: 88, 256; *Hypoth.* 11. 1; *Heres* 81; *QG* 3: 8. See Hay, 'Philo's References', esp. p. 45.

[28] Runia, 'Hairesis-Model', 131.

κατὰ Μωυσῆν φιλοσοφοῦντες, 'those who follow the philosophy of Moses' (*Mut.* 223), or 'the pupils of the most excellent philosophy' (*Virt.* 65). As already noted, Moses is their *didaskalos*, 'teacher' (*Gig.* 54; *Spec.* 1: 59), but beyond Moses is God, who is described as the διδάσκαλος of ἐραστὴς σοφίας, the teacher of 'a lover of wisdom' (*Her.* 102, cf. *Sacr.* 65; *Congr.* 114).[29] In using the verb ἐράω, rather than φιλέω, Philo connects his understanding with both Platonic ἔρως[30] and the 'lover of beauty' we find in the *Symposium*, and what it means to 'love wisdom' in the Wisdom tradition, where Wisdom is personified as a beautiful woman a man aspires to marry (cf. Wisdom 8: 2–16). Philo compares the learning of a pupil of God with drinking water drawn from a well (*Post.* 146–52). The teaching is not from human beings but divine: τὸν γὰρ θεοῦ φοιτητὴν ἢ γνώριμον ἢ μαθητὴν ἢ ὅ τί ποτε χρὴ θεμένους ὄνομα καλεῖν αὐτὸν ἀμήξανον ἔτι θνητῶν ὑφηγήσεως ἀνέξεσθαι, 'for the scholar or pupil or student—or whatever name one decides to call him—of God is without means to sustain any longer mortal leadings' (*Sacr.* 79). Unlocking the mysteries of allegorical interpretation is very much the aim of all true students of Moses. In using the expression Μωυσέως γνωριμοί (63) Philo identifies the allegorizers as a kind of school that adopts a philosophical approach to Moses as the philosopher-teacher who not only wrote the text of Torah but also transmitted to his pupils, over the ages, an allegorical way of interpreting it, a method that would provide the means of understanding and undertaking one's spiritual journey.

This school of the allegorizers is distinguished from the simple literalists, whom Philo snidely dubs 'provincials', literally 'citizens of a small town', μικροπολῖται (*Somn.* 1: 39), indicating they exemplify parochial narrow-mindedness. Philo considers

[29] The reference to God as a teacher of Israel is found implicitly also in the Second Blessing of the Shema, deriving ultimately from the presentation of the teaching God in Psalms (25: 4–5; 71: 17; 94: 12; 119; 132: 13; 143: 10) and Isaiah (48: 17–18), see Rueven Kimelman, 'The Shema' and its Rhetoric: The Case for the Shema' Being More than Creation, Revelation and Redemption', *Jewish Thought and Philosophy*, 2 (1992), 111–56.

[30] See esp. *Symp.* 203e–204a where Eros is defined as a philosopher and *Symp.* 210a–212a in which the *erastes* ultimately gives birth to philosophical discourse and virtue. Though cf. his negative presentation in *Contempl.* 59, where Plato's *Symposium* is scorned as being almost completely 'about (erotic) love'.

them inadequate and ignorant in many respects.[31] Aristobulus before him was unimpressed by those who were 'devoted to the letter alone' as showing no insight or understanding (*Praep. Evang.* 8: 10: 5).[32] The literalists are not even identified as a kind of school, and it may be that Philo really only accepts one true school of Mosaic philosophy, for which allegorical interpretation is essential. If you are a disciple of Moses you cannot accept a literal reading of the text alone. However, the literalists appear to be the most predominant Jewish group in Alexandria; they are the 'many' while those who study according to allegorical methods are the 'few' (*Migr.* 147). This is important, since we should then probably not see in Philo's approach to scripture any kind of normative Alexandrian Judaism, but rather a method of exegesis for an elite few who were skilled in sophisticated approaches to Greek language and literature.[33] David Dawson has argued in regard to Philo's allegorical methods that he is in fact trying to integrate Hellenism into Alexandrian Judaism as a form of cultural revisionism for the sake of the Jewish community, not because he was interested very much in what people outside Judaism thought. Allegorical interpretation was a strategy of survival in a Hellenistic cultural universe.[34] But many Jews in Alexandria simply did not accept the necessity for this type of approach.

Philo himself is a *gnorimos* of Moses (*Det.* 86; *Spec.* 1: 345) and in *Spec.* 1: 59 Moses is identified as the founder of a philosophical school, teaching his disciples, who are distinct from all of Israel (cf. *Virt.* 65).[35] A rather narrow definition of 'pupils/ students of Moses' proper is not peculiar to Philo. Despite the conceptualization of Judaism as a whole as philosophy, there is some hesitation in calling all Jews 'students of Moses'. In the Aramaic translations of the scriptures—the targums—the

---

[31] For a catalogue of their inadequacies, according to Philo, see Shroyer, 'Alexandrian Jewish Literalists'. The worst form of literalists are those who reject Judaism on account of a literal interpretation of scripture (e.g. *Conf.* 2): 277–9.

[32] Dawson, *Allegorical Readers*, 77.

[33] See further, Louis H. Feldman, 'The Orthodoxy of Jews in Hellenistic Egypt', *JSS* 22 (1960), 215–37.

[34] Dawson, *Allegorical Readers*, esp. 74–9, 112–13.

[35] Runia, 'Hairesis-Model', 128, and see also *Post.* 12; *Spec.* 1: 319; 2: 88, 256; *Congr.* 177.

Hebrew בְּנֵי הַנְּבִיאִים 'sons of the prophets' of 2 Kings (2: 3, 7, 15; 4: 1, 38; 5: 22) are תַלְמִידֵי נְבִיא 'students of the prophets', מִשְׁפָּחוֹת, 'guilds' of 1 Chronicles 2: 53 and 55 are תַלְמִידַיָּא, 'the students'.[36] This seems to show a clear conceptual link between the prophets and the philosopher-teachers of the Graeco-Roman world, and the identification of a fairly small and inspired group of students learning from the sages. Josephus himself indicates that these ideas were known in the first century, since he too translates 'sons of the prophets' of 2 Kings as 'students of the prophets' (*Ant.* 9: 28, 68).[37] Josephus identifies Joshua as the student of Moses (*Ant.* 6: 84) and Elisha is to Ἐλίᾳ μαθητὴς καὶ διάκονος (*Ant.* 8: 354, cf. 9: 28, 33) and γνώριμος καὶ διάδοχος (*War* 4: 460), as in Lucian's *Macrobius* 19, where Cleanthes is Zeno's γνώριμος καὶ διάδοχος. The Q saying of Jesus in the Gospels concerning the 'sons of the Pharisees' (Matthew 12: 27; Luke 11: 19) seems also to represent an Aramaic idiom that could refer to students of certain sages as 'sons' or 'children', and therefore we may also look to the expression 'sons of Moses' in Mishnaic Hebrew to find the concept. In the Babylonian Talmud the sons of Aaron are also the sons of Moses (Num. 3: 1–4), for while Aaron fathered them physically, Moses as prophet-teacher instructed them (b.Sanh. 19b). In the Tosefta, Elisha is the *talmid* (student) of Elijah in the same way (t.Sota 4: 7) even though Elijah is a *talmid* of Moses. Philo also presents Joshua as Moses' disciple and successor (*Virt.* 55, 66). In the Gospel of John 9: 28, *Ioudaioi* (Judaeans) define themselves exclusively as τοῦ Μωυσέως μαθηταί. The term is paralleled in the Babylonian Talmud (b.Yoma 4a; 53a): תַּלְמִידָיו שֶׁל מֹשֶׁה. But who was specifically a 'student of Moses' at any time might depend on one's perspective.

The allegorizing 'school of thought' did not exist as a sectarian entity in the sense of an exclusive, self-defining group of people who saw themselves as having certain beliefs that set them apart from everyone else and a distinctive way of life different from that of other Jews. Allegorical exegesis of various types was probably taught in Alexandrian synagogues and private homes by Jewish exegetical scholars,[38] and people would have formed

---

[36] Rengstorf, 'μαθητής', 434.
[37] Ibid. 443. The LXX keeps faithfully to the Hebrew.
[38] Hay, 'Philo's References', 46–7. Philo at times vehemently disagrees with certain allegorical interpretations propounded by other teachers, e.g. *QG* 1: 10;

ad hoc interpretative groups for different purposes, within the
rubric of an allegorical tradition that was handed down, scholar
to scholar. The existence of the Mareotic community is possibly
testimony enough to the formation of such *ad hoc* groups.

Runia has pointed out that, even in identifiable schools in
the Hellenistic world, like Platonism, Pythagoraeanism, and
Stoicism, there could be different interpretations of the tradition, because creative exegesis led to divergences of opinion.[39]
We know Philo disagreed with other allegorizers at times. Philo
explains where he does not agree with a particular kind of allegorical interpretation in *Migr*. 86–93. In this text, it serves his
rhetoric to be quite clear about the differences between one view
and his own on the issue of following distinctive Jewish praxis.
The curious thing is that there are some significant overlaps
between the group Philo praises in *Contempl*. and the one he
criticizes in *Migr*. In *Migr*. Philo indicates that there were people
in his circle of allegorizers who considered the words of the law
as symbols of the mind and therefore neglected the observance of
the ritual law. They concentrate on Nature in its naked absoluteness and the inner meaning of things so intensely that they neglect the Jewish established customs; they are careless about the
regulations governing the Sabbath; they bypass the Jewish festivals during the year, and they do not bother to circumcise their
sons. These people are known by Philonists as 'extreme allegorizers'. Were they the same people Philo praises in *Contempl*.? For
ease of reference, this passage appears in Appendix 2.

David Hay has adeptly explored the context of this passage,
which concerns not only *being* good, but *seeming* good to others.
You should not do things that cause others to talk about you negatively. In neglecting observances specified in Torah, some good
people invite just such negative talk from fellow Jews. Virtuous
people should aim to look good as well as be good (*Migr*. 12).[40]

Post. 41–2; *Her*. 300; *Leg*. 1: 59. See also Hay, 'References to Other Exegetes in
Philo's *Quaestiones*', in David M. Hay and Ernest S. Frerichs (eds.), *Both
Literal and Allegorical: Studies in Philo of Alexandria's Questions and Answers on
Genesis and Exodus* (Atlanta: Scholars, 1991), 81–97.

[39] Runia, 'Hairesis-Model', 122.

[40] Here Philo refers to 'very many' who are virtuous but are held to be not so
(*Migr*. 86), a category of unfortunate people of which the extreme allegorizers
are one case study. This does not mean there are many extreme allegorizers.

One can be completely devoted to virtue, but attract the criticisms of 'the many' who are less virtuous (*Migr.* 86, 90, 93, 107) by doing things they feel to be wrong.[41] Directly after this passage, Philo points to the figure of Leah, who states in Gen. 30: 13: 'Happy am I, for the women will call me happy.' 'Female praise' is that which goes purely on appearances. It can be purely superficial, and not reflect what is true, but it is necessary in the case of those who deserve praise (*Migr.* 95). It is characteristic of the perfect soul 'both to be [virtuous] and to be thought to be [virtuous]' (*Migr.* 96). Having said all this, however, Philo admits that to be in reality *praiseworthy* is superior to being praised (*Migr.* 108), but he is clearly irritated that certain allegorizers—who are truly good—neglect the literal laws in their quest for perfection, and therefore invite criticism. He accuses them of being 'new' in their lifestyle; the interpretations which lead to extreme allegory and neglect of distinctive Jewish praxis are the result of 'people of our time', and not ancient (*Migr.* 90).

Implicit in this discussion is the presupposition that the extreme allegorizers are indeed praiseworthy and virtuous, but that they invite criticism rather than praise by being lax with the literal law, because most Jews cannot understand why they are doing this. Are they then to be identified with the Mareotic group? Clearly, it would not have been wise to hold up a group of extreme allegorizers as examples of virtue if Philo's audience was composed entirely of Alexandrian Jews, comprising a large contingent of literalists. However, if we identify that Philo's primary audience was largely Roman, this would not be a problem. His Alexandrian pagan opponents might not have been aware of fine details concerning Jewish opinions on different Jewish exegetical groups, and would probably have been more sympathetic to the allegorizers anyway, standing as they did in a tradition of exegesis the Stoics and the Egyptian priests themselves employed. This rhetorical anomaly does not seem a reason to completely rule out a possible connection between those Philo describes in *Migr.* and *Contempl.* given that we have two different rhetorical fields. If Philo were using the extreme allegorizers as figures exemplifying virtue, for his rhetorical purposes in

---

[41] See discussion in David Hay, 'Putting Extremism in Context: The Case of Philo, *De Migratione* 89–93', *SPA* 9 (1997), 126–42.

Contempl., then he would have chosen to emphasize the points on which he agrees with them, and downplay anything with which he disagrees.

Let us consider certain the key points of correspondence. In *Migr*. Philo uses the issue of the seventh day as a prime example of the error of the 'extreme allegorizers': one should not light a fire or carry a load on the Sabbath, along with other 'work' activities, even if one knows it is actually meant to teach the power of the 'unoriginated one' and that a creature is entitled to rest from labour (*Migr.* 91).[42] The implication is that these 'extreme allegorizers' did indeed carry a load on the Sabbath, and light a fire, till the ground, go to court, and so on, because the symbolic meaning of the Sabbath is what is important. Interestingly, the catalogue of things one should not do on a Sabbath includes country activities (tilling the ground) and city activities (conduct proceedings in court, etc.); an indication that the extreme allegorizers of *Migr.* are to be found in town and country.

When Philo writes of the Mareotic group's appreciation of the seventh day, he commends them for believing exactly the right thing about the Sabbath, as he commends the 'extreme allegorizers' for sharing the same view:

They consider the seventh day to be something all-sacred and all-festive, thinking it worthy of special honour. [On this day], after the care of the soul, they also nurture the body, just as they of course also release the cattle from their continuous labour. (*Contempl.* 36)

First of all, these people assemble on [every] seventh seventh-day, holding in awe not only the simple number of seven, but also the square of it. For they know its purity and eternal virginity. And it is also the eve of the great special day which the number fifty has been assigned; fifty being the most holy and natural of numbers, since it is the square of the right handed triangle which is the origin of the composition of the whole universe. (*Contempl.* 65)

Philo himself believed wholeheartedly that the Sabbath existed from creation for all people (*Opif.* 89; *Dec.* 98), though only after the Exodus did Israel learn how to date it correctly (*Mos.* 1: 207;

---

[42] See E. P. Sanders, *Judaism: Practice and Belief 63 BCE—66 CE* (London: SCM, 1992), 208–11. Observance of the day of rest is found in the first ten commandments Exod. 20: 8–11; Deut. 5: 12–15, cf. Exod. 34: 21; Lev. 19: 3 and see Jer. 17: 19–27 on the rule against carrying burdens.

2: 263). It is the birthday of the world (*Opif.* 89; *Mos.* 1: 207; *Spec.* 2: 59), a day of light (*Spec.* 2: 59), that is the divine light which is virtue (*Leg.* 1: 16–18). It is a day of contemplation and the pursuit of wisdom (*Dec.* 97–101; *Opif.* 128), the day for exposition of the law in synagogues (*Mos.* 2: 215–16; *Hypoth.* 7: 12–13; *Legat.* 156–7; *Prob.* 80–2).[43] Aristobulus, two centuries earlier, had also insisted on the inherent importance of the number 7 and the seventh day, 'which might be called first also, as the genesis of light in which all things are contemplated'. All things in the universe apparently revolve in series of sevens.[44]

In *Contempl.* the honouring of the seventh day as holy and the rest from labour is specifically stated. He is comfortable about this. He does not specifically indicate that the Mareotic group does anything wrong, in his eyes, but the language is curiously similar to that of *Migr.* This group rests from the activity of exegesis, contemplation, musical composition with which they engage, in order to come together as a group and hear an instruction. They (that is, the junior members, whose activities are more practical) also untie their cattle, which is consistent with the view that the Sabbath is supposed to reflect the 'inactivity of created beings', which we find in *Migr.* 91. The trouble with the people of *Migr.* is that they may accept the ideal, and go so far along the way of inactivity, but still make allowances for certain necessary things. The legal system of Alexandria did not close on the Jewish Sabbath, and therefore if it were necessary for these people, they would indeed go to court, act as a juror, prosecute a claim, and so on. According to Josephus, the Ionians did not exempt Jews from going to court on this day, much to their displeasure (*Ant.* 16: 45–6). But here in *Migr.* the suggestion is that some Alexandrian Jews were not particularly bothered if this occurred.

In *Contempl.* we must make the connection that this group is described as having a sacred dinner on a Sabbath day (the ultraholy Sabbath, of a week of weeks or forty-ninth day) and that it is on this day that all the food is carried into the dining room on a single table. Where from? They appear to be carrying a load

---

[43] Roger Beckwith, *Calendar and Chronology, Jewish and Christian* (Leiden: Brill, 1996), 14–16. See also *Deus* 12, *Her.* 216, *Migr.* 28–9.

[44] Frag. 5, Eusebius, *Praep. Evang.* 13: 12: 9–16, in Yarbro Collins, 'Aristobulus', 842–3.

on the Sabbath. Did they light a fire? Did they bake bread? Ordinarily, a Sabbath dinner is cooked during the daytime because the Sabbath normatively begins with sunset, but this group sees the new day as beginning at sunrise (see following chapter), and therefore the table would have been carried in on the Sabbath. Philo here does not present any clear infringement of the law; he simply leaves us asking questions.

In *Contempl.* there is also an omission of any action pertaining to ritual purity. Presumably, with a community located so close to Lake Mareotis and the sea, the members of the group had access to water for ritual purification, though nothing is stated concerning any purification rituals. The food is considered to be especially 'pure' (*Contempl.* 81–2) but it is hard to know exactly how Philo means this. The main point about the food is that it is extremely basic and simple. Philo can refer also to the Sabbath as being especially pure and virginal, though this is clearly metaphorical (65; cf. *Spec.* 2: 56–62). One could argue that lack of mention of purity rituals proves nothing, since this was not a concern in terms of presenting his community as virtuous for a Roman audience, but in *Contempl.* 66 Philo uses the language of ritual purity when one might expect *actual* hand-washing, as if he himself is conscious of the omission: 'Before they recline, they duly stand in order in a row, with their eyes and hands lifted up to heaven. The eyes have been trained to see things worth look-ing at, and the hands are *clean* of income, and are *not defiled* by any gain. They pray to God that they might meet according to his mind and that their feast will be pleasing [to Him].' This lan-guage of ritual purity seems to reflect the rhetorical dissonance of Philo's attempt to prove the virtue of the group at a moment when he might have felt their virtue was able to be questioned. The group is described as praying prior to eating here, but Philo thinks they should also have washed their hands. It is not at all certain to what extent hand-washing was a norm prior to eating in Hellenistic Judaism, or for that matter in Israel itself,[45] despite the comment in the Gospel of Mark that 'the Pharisees, and all the Jews, do not eat unless they wash their hands' (Mark 7: 3). The omission in regard to the hand-washing may have been connected more with the prayer. In the *Letter of Aristeas* Jews

---

[45] See Sanders, *Judaism*, 437–8.

wash their hands in the sea in the course of prayers to God (*Aristeas* 304–6; cf. *Ant.* 12: 206). In the *Sibylline Oracles* 3: 591–3 Jews lift up their hands to heaven to pray, and wash their hands. In 4: 163–70, Jews are told to 'wash your whole bodies in perennial rivers' prior to stretching out the hands to heaven in prayers for forgiveness. In the *Testament of Levi* 2: 3 bathing occurs prior to prayer.[46] Philo, like other Jews, believed it was important to purify the body by splashing or sprinkling prior to entering the Temple (*Spec.* 3: 89, 205–6, cf. 1: 261), before sacrificing (*Spec.* 1: 256–66), after sex (*Spec.* 3: 63), after contact with a corpse (*Spec.* 3: 205–6), and presumably on other occasions which the law indicated.[47] For him, ritual purity was relevant and efforts should be taken to maintain it. As E. P. Sanders has pointed out, synagogues were often built close to the sea (cf. also Acts 16: 13; *Ant.* 14: 258), which may reflect a concern to wash prior to or during prayer.[48] Since we know of a connection between ritual hand-washing and prayer in the Diaspora, then it is striking that in this passage the Mareotic group are described without any mention of actual hand-washing, and yet with an emphasis on the metaphorical purity of their hands (that is, innocence).

Chaeremon, in his description of the Egyptian priests, discusses purity at length, which only serves to make the silence in *Contempl.* seem deeper. Purity and piety might, to some, be considered matters that go together, not only in a Jewish context but also in a pagan one. According to Chaeremon, people who approached the special Egyptian priests in the temples would purify themselves and abstain from certain things (so as not to contaminate them). There were particular times (seven to forty-two days) for purifications and fasts, prior to the performance of sacred rites, when they did not have contact with anyone—even their nearest relatives—but only those who were pure and fasted with them in special rooms which were inaccessible to those who were not pure. During these periods of purification they did not eat bread, vegetables, and pulses, or eat animal products. They

---

[46] See discussion in Joan E. Taylor, *The Immerser: John the Baptist within Second Temple Judaism* (Grand Rapids, Mich.: Eerdmans, 1997), 91–2.

[47] See E. P. Sanders, *Jewish Law from Jesus to the Mishnah: Five Studies* (London: SCM, 1990), 238–9; id. *Judaism*, 223–4.

[48] Sanders, *Jewish Law*, 214–27.

abstained from sex and washed themselves in cold water three times a day, and had a bath if they had an ejaculation in their sleep. The importance of purification is stressed in that Chaeremon notes that lesser priests also practise the same rites of purification but not with such accuracy and self-control, implying their rites are inferior (Porphyry, *De Abstin.* 4: 6–8).[49] Other evidence of Egyptian priests in the cult of Isis confirms how important purity was in this context. The Egyptian word for 'priest' was based on the verb *web*, 'to cleanse', with the hieroglyphic sign showing a vase from which flowed water.[50] The priest was washed clean and hallowed by the holy Nile River, and honoured the source of his sacerdotal power with pure water drawn from the Nile.

The extreme allegorizers of *Migr.* have sons whom they fail to circumcise (*Migr.* 92), an omission resulting from an allegorical reading of the command to Abraham.[51] If circumcision means the excision of the pleasures that delude the mind (so also *Spec.* 2: 9), then what is the point of actual, physical circumcision? Since circumcision (and clitoridectomy) was widely practised among the Egyptians (Herodotus, *Hist.* 2: 104: 1–3; Diodorus Siculus, *Bibl. Hist.* 1: 28: 3) it would not have served as a distinguishing mark of the Jewish community in the same way as it would have done in the wider Graeco-Roman world. It was something that the Jews of Egypt took note of: Philo himself remarks on the Egyptian practice of circumcising both males and females (*Spec.* 1: 2; *QG* 3: 47). This shared practice may have contributed to the tendency of Roman authors to lump Jews and Egyptians together (Tacitus, *Annals* 2: 25–8; Suetonius, *Tib.*

---

[49] The details of the rites are not given in Porphyry's epitome.

[50] Witt, *Isis*, 89.

[51] Gen. 17: 10–14, cf. Exod. 12: 48, Deut. 10: 16, and in Philo, *QG* 46–52 and *Spec. Leg.* 1: 2–2: 11 where he explains the allegorical meaning shared by those in *Migr.* While Philo agrees with them that circumcision is essentially symbolic and represents the excision of the pleasures which delude the mind, the extreme allegorizers would have argued that it is better to excise these pleasures than perform the actual circumcision. Despite the allegorical meaning, Philo considers actual circumcision something healthy; it stops inflammations of the penis, secures cleanliness of the body; it signifies on the outside of the body the excision of thoughts of pleasure from the heart; it helps the flow of seminal fluid (*Spec.* 1: 2–11). See John M. G. Barclay, 'Paul and Philo on Circumcision: Romans 2: 25–9 in Social and Cultural Context', *NTS* 44 (1998), 536–56, at 538–43.

36), and it is interesting that both groups were expelled together by Tiberius in 19 CE. Jews neglected to circumcise their sons for different reasons, in different places and times, sometimes because of simple apostasy, or Hellenization, or fear of reprisals by unsympathetic rulers, or—apparently in Alexandria—extreme allegorizing. In the Book of Jubilees (15: 25–34) there is a passage directed against such neglectful Jews, where the idea is put forward that even the angels were circumcised.[52] Jewish anti-circumcision exegesis has not survived. In the second century, the Christian scholar Justin Martyr points out that it was indeed only a sign, and had to be, because it did not benefit women (Justin, *Dial.* 23: 5, cf. Cyprian, *Adv. Iud.* 1: 8), though to what extent he was drawing on the Jewish exegesis with which he was familiar is unknown in this instance.[53] The Mareotic group are said to have had children (*Contempl.* 18), but nothing in *Contempl.* is stated about the issue of circumcision. Actual children are not part of the group.

Philo states in regard to the extreme allegorizers that they do not celebrate the usual feasts of Judaism: 'It is true that the feast is a symbol of the happiness of the soul and thankfulness to God, but we should not for this reason spurn the general gatherings of the year's seasons.' This will require further elucidation, and I will turn to matters of the calendar in the following chapter. For now, we can note that Philo states nothing whatsoever about the Mareotic group celebrating any of the usual feasts of Judaism. Conybeare tried to make the Mareotic group's celebration of the '50th eve' into a celebration of Pentecost, the Jewish festival taking place fifty days after the *omer* sacrifice of Passover, but this is never said by Philo and in fact it simply cannot be right, for the Mareotic group celebrates a festival *every* 49th day, continually. If this is the only festival they do celebrate—as Philo indicates—then it does not conform to any normative Jewish feast. Philo protests that 'we shall be ignoring the sanctity of the Temple and a thousand other things, if we are going to pay heed to nothing

---

[52] The Book of Jubilees was probably written in Palestine in Hebrew, *c.*160–140 BCE, see O. S. Wintermute, 'Jubilees', in Charlesworth (ed.), *Old Testament Pseudepigrapha*, ii. 35–142, at 45–6.

[53] See Judith M. Lieu, 'Circumcision, Women and Salvation', *NTS* 40 (1994), 358–70, at 359. Lieu points out that Justin shows knowledge of contemporary Jewish exegesis, even when this has survived independently only in later sources, p. 360.

except what is shown us by the inner meaning of things' (*Migr.* 92). Did the Mareotic group ignore the sanctity of the Temple?

Philo himself was only just in the camp of those who acknowledged the continuing importance of Temple sacrifices and procedures. It is necessary for people as a kind of training (*Her.* 123), and one should participate so as not to cause offence to others (*Ebr.* 87). One could imagine that Philo's family would definitely have been offended had he rejected ordinary Temple sacrifices, since they gave money for the Temple gates (Josephus, *War* 5: 205), and it is clear that Philo went at least once to the holy city (*Prov.* 2: 64; *Spec.* 1: 67–78). However, for Philo, sacrifice is actually about bringing oneself to God (*Spec.* 1: 269–72) and he can at times move into the 'no-sacrifice-necessary' camp. In *Mos.* 2: 107 he identifies the real and true sacrifice as being the piety of a soul who loves God. In *Plant.* 108, those who have innocent minds will be received by God, even if they have never sacrificed at all, 'for God takes pleasure from altars on which no fire is burned, but which are visited by virtues'.

In several places in *Contempl.*, it seems that things of the Temple are transformed into processes and artefacts in the group's own system. For example, the huts in which the senior members live are defined as mini-temples with the back part functioning like a 'holy of holies', where there is a sacred room (οἴκημα ἱερόν), which is *called* a reverence-place and place-for-one (*Contempl.* 25). This is not Philo's innovation here; he is observing what they do and what they call things. The meeting room they come to on seventh days is a 'common reverence-place' (32), the meal is a 'sacred symposium' (71). Most particularly the language of the sacred cult erupts around the forty-ninth-day celebration, in regard to the singing and the food (80). The music the group sing is actually related to procedures of the Temple: processions, libations, hymns relating to the altar. Furthermore, the sacred meal that is consumed is laid out on a table which is representative of the table of shewbread (81) in the vestibule of the holy Temple court. The point is that the supposedly cultic hymns are actually designed for their own celebration, not the actual Temple, and therefore the cultic is read allegorically: it is what the table of shewbread *means* that is important. It is the cultic singing and dancing's *purpose* that is critical.

However, there is some kind of implication here that the Mareotic group understood that the real Temple was indeed to be understood as a sacred place. If their artefacts and rituals are in some way imitating things in the Temple, even if it was the symbolism which mattered, this indicates that the Temple was considered in some way holy. In *Migr*. Philo seems to be able to use the extreme allegorizers' acceptance of the holiness of the Temple as a means to shame them into consideration of their neglect of the law: if the laws of circumcising or the festivals are ignored, 'then we would be ignoring the holiness of the Temple and a thousand other things' (*Migr*. 92). You cannot have it both ways. If the physical Temple is truly a holy place, then you cannot throw out materiality altogether. The idea is that the extreme allegorizers would not wish to ignore completely the Temple's actual holiness.

Interestingly, in both *Migr*. 93 and *Contempl*. 78 there is a metaphor of Torah as a living being whose body is composed of literal, outward laws and its soul of the spiritual meaning of those laws; the only passages in the entire extant Philonic corpus where this image is to be found,[54] though the image probably derives from Plato (*Phaedrus* 264c). Philo exhorts the extreme allegorizers to draw the logical conclusions of this image, which they must accept for Philo to be able to use it as a piece of argumentation. Philo states that, 'we take care of the body because it is the dwelling-place of the soul' and therefore the outward, literal laws should also be regarded (*Migr*. 93).

However, the Mareotic group might have argued in defence to *Migr*. 93 that Philo's logical conclusion is anything but logical, given that the things of the outward body are almost inconsequential. In their very simple hut-like dwellings, they take 'no drink, no food, nothing necessary for the needs of the body' (*Contempl*. 25). They pray that 'the soul being *entirely relieved* from the disturbance of the senses . . . may follow the way of truth' (*Contempl*. 27). The needs of the body are associated with darkness:

They first lay down self-control as a certain foundation stone of the soul [and then] they build the other virtues [on it]. None of them would ever eat food or drink before sunset, since they have decided that

---

[54] See Hay, 'Philo's References', 50.

philosophizing is appropriate to the light [of day], but the needs of the body [are appropriate] for the darkness [of night]. They have allotted one to the day and a small part of the night for the others. (*Contempl.* 34)

Philo goes on to state that some of the people in this group do not think of food for three days, or six days. Only on the seventh day do they rest from the work of the soul and nurture the body (*Contempl.* 36). All this implies that for them the body should be very tightly controlled, and not regarded so much as the abode of the soul, but as a thing of darkness that must be kept in check as much as possible, and only indulged a little on the seventh day, when the mind and soul should rest somewhat. They then eat the necessary things without which life could not be sustained, but refuse to let hunger and thirst be 'mistresses' over them (*Contempl.* 37), avoiding complete satisfaction. Given all this, if the literal laws are like the body, then the Mareotic group might well have replied to Philo that they should be indulged as little as possible, belonging to the world of darkness rather than that of light. In *Migr.* 90, Philo writes that the extreme allegorizers try to live like 'souls without connection to the body'; this is exactly how the Mareotic group tried to live, according to Philo's description. Both groups are then ascetic.

Asceticism as a term need not necessarily imply a denial of all the body's desires. Stephen Fraade's helpful definition of the term as it applied in the Graeco-Roman world is a 'practice and exercise that leads to moral as well as physical excellence'. However, a more severe type of asceticism that would lead to a greater degree of fasting and regimes to dampen down desire appeared during the Hellenistic era.[55] This may be traced back in the Western tradition to Plato (*Timaeus* 90a–d; *Phaedo* 81c cf. Cicero, *De Deorum Nat.* 2: 140), who may in turn have derived these notions from Eastern philosophy, since extreme asceticism was practised in India much earlier, as we see in the Vedic *Aranyakas* (added to the Vedas *c.*700 BCE). Cynics championed the lifestyle of extreme asceticism, going about homeless in coarse clothing, and living on bread and water.[56] Musonius

[55] The word ἄσκησις literally means 'exercise' or 'training': Stephen Fraade, 'Ascetical Aspects of Ancient Judaism', in Green (ed.), *Jewish Spirituality*, 253–88, at 256. For instances of philosophical asceticism, see above, pp. 110–11.

[56] See Wimbush, *Ascetic Behaviour*, 129–33.

Rufus wrote a treatise, *On Training* (Discourse 4) which stressed the importance of asceticism to some degree.[57] But perhaps the most explicit description of the ascetic lifestyle of a Stoic allegorizing philosopher is Martial's poem describing Chaeremon:

> Because you, Stoic Chaeremon, praise death too much,
>   do you want me to admire and esteem your spirit?
> A jug with a broken handle creates this virtue for you,
>   and a sullen hearth warmed by no fire,
> and a mat, bugs, a framework of a bare cot,
>   and the same short toga for night and day alike.
> Oh, how great a man you are, who can do without
>   the dregs of cheap red wine and straw and black bread!
> Come, let your pillow swell with Leuconian wool,
>   and let woolly purple enwrap your couch,
> and let the boy sleep with you who, while he mixes
>   the Caecuban wine, tortures your guests with his rosy mouth!
> Oh, how you will long to live Nestor's life-span three times,
>   and want to lose nothing of any day!
> In poverty it is easy to despise life;
>   that man only shows a strong character who knows how to be
>   wretched.[58]

Martial is clearly cynical about such displays of asceticism and how philosophers such as Chaeremon could be so detached about little matters such as life and death given the austerity of their lives. It would have seemed strange too that Chaeremon was living this lifestyle in the imperial court. Philosophy and asceticism went together, however, to varying degrees.

Philo saw life as a battle between the rational side of human beings and that of an irrational side—the senses—which wanted pleasure. The body was just a corpse without the vivification of the soul (*Conf.* 177). We are weighted down by the body and need to detach ourselves from it in order to see the real, incorruptible things of the universe (*Deus* 150–1; *Gig.* 29, cf. *QG* 3: 10). 'The business of Wisdom is to become estranged from the body and its cravings' (*Leg.* 1: 103, cf. Plato, *Phaedo* 65a). Philo's comments about those who embrace a life of asceticism provide evidence that people from the allegorical school of exegesis (not the extreme allegorizers alone) chose to leave behind their work

---

[57] Lutz, *Roman Socrates*, 52–6.
[58] Martial, *Epigram* 11: 56, from Van der Horst, *Chaeremon*, 5.

and their possessions to live a lifestyle involving the hard toil of meditation and study. While it is quite probable that he had the Mareotic group in mind when he wrote some of these lines, his comments taken as a whole give a wider ascetic context for the group. As Philo tells us in *Contempl.* 21–2, the group who live next to Lake Mareotis in the most ideal location are 'the best' ones of all those around Alexandria (and other places) who have chosen to live the life of contemplation, 'attending' God.

In *Gig.* 31 Philo identifies that there are 'unfleshly and un-bodily souls who spend their days in the theatre of the All, which they enter with insatiable passion (*erōs*), beholding and hearing divine things'. He describes them as shutting their eyes, stop-ping their ears, and spending their days in solitude and darkness (*Migr.* 191). In *Her.* 48 Philo characterizes this God-regarding lifestyle as one which people in general hate: 'frugality, self-control, the life of austerity and knowledge, not sharing in laugh-ter or fun/sport, full of meditation and deep thought, friend of contemplation, enemy of ignorance, superior to money, glory and pleasure, yielding to self-restraint, respect and sight rather than blind wealth', a lifestyle followed by 'the children of virtue'. One is worthy of divine things when one disregards the body, its leanings and passions, so that the soul is released from the prison of the body (*Her.* 68, cf. 84–5). Then one can become ecstatically inspired (69–70). He has the soul, in first-person, tell the story of her journey: 'I emigrated from the body . . . when I took no heed of the flesh and sense-perception, when I denounced all things that have no true existence' (71). She 'sentences' speech to long speechlessness. Philo identifies that the one who 'goes away from us' and desires to be the 'attendant' (here ὀπαδός) of God is the divine heir (76) and can truly see (78).

In *Mut.* 32 Philo identifies those who live in this way as a sacred company (*thiasos*) who have stripped themselves of possessions and rejected what is liked by the flesh. They are por-trayed by Philo as pale, weak, and emaciated, and also few in number (33–6).

However, as in the case of the extreme allegorizers, whom Philo esteems in terms of their virtue but criticizes for their neg-lect of the usual customs of Judaism, Philo can be harsh on the ascetics he otherwise so admires. In *Dec.* 108–20 he notes that the people who have devoted their whole lives to the attendance/

service of God (θεραπεία θεοῦ) are indeed lovers of God (110) but they go only halfway in virtue because they do not share the joy of people at the common good or grief at the reverse (that is, they are too detached) and they do not show proper respect for those who brought them forth from non-existent to existent. Ultimately, piety and holiness do not dwell within souls who neglect parents (119). This is stinging criticism from someone who can otherwise esteem contemplative ascetics so highly.

Philo opted for a mixed life (*Somn.* 1: 151; *Her.* 45–6) in which he strove for philosophical excellence but still lived in the city, undertaking business and representing his community if necessary.[59] Therefore, he can criticize those who, especially while still young, embrace a life of contemplation, and suggest it is more appropriate to choose this lifestyle late in life, after people have proven themselves as virtuous in business and ordinary life. In *Fug.* 28–9 he justifies keeping money; the challenge is to use it well. One should not turn one's back on fame (30) or reject a luxurious dinner (31–2); one should simply be modest and moderate. Here he criticizes those who give up their businesses and possessions and say they have no regard for fame and pleasure. He is cynical about the 'dirt' and 'sullen look' of the ascetics, who are so rough and impoverished that they bait people into thinking that they love order, self-restraint, and endurance (33–4) when they should have proven this in the course of an ordinary, 'practical' life. It is better to run your business well, rather than to leave it all behind and risk being labelled 'lazy' for your choice of lifestyle (37). As in the case of the extreme allegorizers, Philo here too shows himself to be sensitive to public reputation. He would not wish to be called 'lazy'. Ideally, no one should choose a contemplative life until they have reached 50 years of age.

This is interesting criticism coming from someone who regretfully wrote in *Spec.* 3: 1–6 that he once spent his time in philosophy and contemplation of the universe, he had no base thoughts, nor cared about fame, wealth or bodily comforts, and travelled to the heights by inspiration, with the sun and moon, having escaped from 'mortal life' (1–2), but he was pulled down to earth by 'envy' and plunged into a sea of troubles in which he almost drowns (3), yearning always to return to the air, and

---

[59] See Hay, 'Veiled Thoughts', 170–2.

escape from his pitiless masters in the darkness. One might explain the various opinions expressed by Philo by identifying that he wrote these passages at different times of his life, or that the comments inhabit different rhetorical fields, or both. It seems, however, that despite any criticisms he may have had of the contemplative, ascetic lifestyle, he went along this path for a time and was called back from it by people who envied him. He yearned for it again. Furthermore, it was while he was so frustrated, in the 'sea of troubles' representing the Jewish community to successive emperors, that he wrote of the Mareotic group with such unreserved praise.

It is not necessary for every ascetic to leave the city and join a group outside, and perhaps Philo was solitary in his devotion to philosophy and contemplation, for all we know, within the city still. Nevertheless, Philo seems to know of cases in which people go off to a community such as the Mareotic group only to fail completely to bear the harsh lifestyle. In other words, among the juniors, not all would succeed in becoming seniors. Philo writes that if 'we' try the contemplative life, the life of attendance/ service to the only God (ἡ θεοῦ μόνου θεραπεία, *Fug.* 40), unready for it, 'we arrive at the court of divine service and turn away from this austere way of living more quickly than we came, for we are not able to bear the sleepless observance, and the unceasing and relentless toil' (41).

Returning now to his comments about the extreme allegorizers of *Migr.* who aim to live in the soul without connection to the body, we can see them within the context of Alexandrian Jewish allegorical philosophy. They are ascetics and people very supportive of ascetics who have gone too far, advocating the neglect of the 'body' of the law along with the physical body. It must have been possible to be an ascetic of another type, as Philo is the prime example of such a person, even though he was drawn back from his own contemplative lifestyle into the furore of civil strife.

Philo characterizes the extreme allegorizers as 'living alone by themselves as if they were in a wilderness' (*Migr.* 90). This does not mean they actually live alone by themselves in a wilderness. They live alone because they ignore the social life of the city where 'a good reputation' is important, and wantonly break through established customs decreed by divine men of great wisdom. This apparent social carelessness in itself produces censure from their co-religionists (*Migr.* 93). As we saw, Philo characterizes them in his description of activities they might do on the Sabbath as being situated in both town and country (*Migr.* 91), and they had children, but their attitude was isolationist. They went about things without regard to anyone else's opinion.

Hay resists identifying the Mareotic group with the extreme allegorizers for '[Philo] implies that these persons [of *Migr.*] do not actually live apart from society (in contrast to the Therapeutae, who do.)'.[60] Clearly, it would be wrong to make a simple equation between the Mareotic group and the extreme allegorizers of *Migr.* In *Migr.* the reference appears to be to a larger group than the Mareotic group alone: people who lived in the city and the countryside. However, if they derived from the exegetical tradition of extreme allegory, as an *ad hoc* group, then this would make sense of the correspondences between what Philo says about these groups in *Migr.* and *Contempl.* without the need for us to make a simple equation.[61]

There were not a huge number of extreme allegorizers. In *Migr.* we get the impression that the group he is discussing is fairly small, they are just τινες, 'some people',[62] not an identifiable school but rather those with wrong praxis who are nevertheless part of Philo's own school. As David Hay has pointed out, he uses 'we' in the passage,[63] and adopts a 'generally positive tone' which shows that he substantially agrees with them, at least in regard to their exegesis.[64] *Migr.* is a work addressed to other Jewish allegorical exegetes: an exegetical commentary on Genesis 12: 1–6 about the spiritual path, in which he can collectively refer to a 'we' and an 'us' that includes extreme allegorizers as well as those who follow the law literally.

I have already noted that consideration of practical matters in

[60] Hay, 'Extremism', 132., though cf. id., 'Veiled Thoughts', 172: '[i]t is not impossible that the Therapeutae ignored some Mosaic laws in their literal meaning and that *Migr.* 89–92 in some measure alludes to them.'

[61] The suggestion that the Therapeutae were 'extreme allegorizers' was first made by Alfred Gfrörer, *Philo und die Alexandrinische Theosophie* (Stuttgart: E. Schweizer, 1831), ii. 106.

[62] Ibid. 141.

[63] e.g. 'Why, *we* shall be ignoring the sanctity of the Temple and a thousand other things . . .' *Migr.* 92.

[64] Hay, 'Philo's References', 47–8; id. 'Extremism', 128, 130.

the community would suggest that there were benefactors within the city who helped support it. In *Contempl.* there is a clear allusion to a wider circle of people within Alexandria itself from which the members of the group derive. In *Contempl.* 67 Philo comments: 'They are those who from early youth have matured and grown up in the contemplative part of philosophy, which indeed is the most beautiful and godly.' Logically, the members of the Mareotic group could not have grown up within it in their location as described by Philo, since here there are only celibate adults who have chosen this lifestyle, having left families behind. The people of the Mareotic group have grown up then in a milieu supportive of the kind of contemplative philosophy the group espouses within Alexandria. They are the tip of the iceberg, not the whole thing. It would not be hard to think of reasons why this group chose to leave Alexandria to live a lifestyle of quiet asceticism in the countryside. Philo himself indicates this was because of the innumerable disturbances of the city (*Contempl.* 19–20). Given the terrible riots, persecutions, evictions, and murders of recent years, the reasons for a departure from the city were acute (*Flacc.* 55–6, 64; *Legat.* 128). It was not simply that any city was noisy and disturbing; Alexandria was the scene of horrors and commotions which would have been the very antithesis of everything philosophical people aspired to.[65] We do not know how long the group had been living their lifestyle prior to the time Philo wrote. Their traditions need not at all have entailed residence in the countryside forever. Their connections and origins are in the city. It is from here that they have come, and they have grown up in a particular social (exegetical, ideological, and intellectual) milieu. I have already identified that this milieu was elite.

To summarize, Judaism is conceptualized by Philo and by many others as the *philosophia* of God, communicated to Moses, who functions as the teacher of Israel. There are only a few in Israel who are truly the students of Moses. For Philo, these are most particularly those who adopt an allegorical type of exegesis. The use of allegorical interpretation is linked with inspiration, and a spiritual journey, and also to degrees of asceticism. The

---

[65] I am grateful to Russell Gmirkin, who noted this in the Orion electronic discussion group, though he in fact considers that the group were primarily political refugees.

members of the Mareotic group are included in the category of the students of Moses, since they adopt the allegorical exegesis of Philo himself, a type of exegesis that can be traced back to Aristobulus in the second century BCE. They are also extremely ascetic. However, their interpretations may not all have been approved of by Philo. We have looked at the indications that the philosophy of the Mareotic group may derive from that of the extreme allegorizers Philo defines in *Migr.* 86–93. In going away from the city they have isolated themselves from general discourse within Alexandrian Jewish philosophy, aiming to live a life dedicated to the principles of allegorical exegesis: they want to release the soul from the body in order to 'see' God. They are then a group who take the philosophy of extreme allegory to the utmost conclusion: they are *extreme* extreme allegorizers, living as if in the soul alone.

Philo can praise them in one treatise and criticize them in another because the two treatises are intended for different audiences. While *Contempl.* was for outsiders, *Migr.* was for insiders. *Contempl.* seems to be part of the rhetoric designed to prove the virtue of the Jews and the Jewish case in Alexandria, and it appears to be directed to the Romans (and against the 'Greek' opposition); *Migr.* is directed to a Jewish exegetical group in Alexandria in which subtle differences of exegetical opinion could lead to major differences in praxis which caused concern within the Jewish community as a whole.

The above evidence for a connection between the extreme allegorizers and the Mareotic group cannot be proven, but there is one feature that needs addressing that may make the argument more persuasive, and that is the issue of the calendar. As we saw, in *Migr.* 92 it is stated that the extreme allegorizers did not follow the usual festivals of Judaism. The Mareotic group likewise did not follow these festivals. The Mareotic group clearly followed the solar schema which had the new day beginning with sunrise, while Philo followed the normative Jewish luni-solar calendar in which the day begins at sunset. The use of a distinctive calendar is important, and we need to try to find out exactly what calendar was being used, and whether it had any relationship with calendars used by other Jewish groups.

7
A Solar Calendar

Hail to thee, beautiful god of every day!
Rising in the morning without ceasing,
[Not] wearied in labor.
When thy rays are visible,
Gold is not considered,
It is not like thy brilliance . . .
Thou traversest a journey of leagues,
Even millions and hundred-thousands of time.
Every day is under thee.
When thy setting comes,
The hours of the night hearken to thee likewise.
When thou hast traversed it
There comes no ending to thy labors.
All men, they see by means of thee.
Nor do they finish when thy majesty sets,
[For] thou wakest to rise in the morning,
And thy radiance, it opens the eyes [again].

> (Hymn in Praise of the Sun from the stela of
> Suti and Hor, c. 1400 BCE[1])

Egypt was a land of sun-worshippers, whose calendar was organized on the basis of the sun and the Nile River. Philo notes of the Mareotic group that every sunrise and sunset they pray (*Contempl.* 27) and that at the dawn of the fiftieth day they 'stand with eyes and their whole bodies tuned to the east. When they see the rising sun, they stretch out their hands up to heaven, and pray for a "bright day" and truth and clearness of vision' (*Contempl.* 89). Such a portrayal has deep ramifications. Chaeremon described Egyptian wisdom as emphasizing that the sun is 'the greatest god'.[2] In the cult of Isis, her son Horus/Harpocrates was identified with the sun and the Greek sun god

---

[1] Quoted from James Breasted, *Development of Religion and Thought in Ancient Egypt* (Philadelphia: University of Pennsylvania Press, 1940, repr. 1972), 315–16. British Museum stela no. 826.

[2] As mentioned by Michael Psellus, quoted in Van der Horst, *Chaeremon*, 13.

Apollo.[3] In the understanding of the Mareotic group, the physical sun is interpreted allegorically: it symbolizes the divine light
behind the sun (*Contempl.* 11), but in praying in the direction of
the sun, and seeing a new day beginning with its rising, the group
might appear to show some influence from the Egyptian culture
surrounding them.[4] While all kinds of elements of solar symbolism could be explored, I shall focus here on the issue of the solar
calendar. It was noted in the last chapter that both the extreme
allegorizers and the Mareotic group did not follow the usual
feasts of Judaism. A particular kind of solar calendar underpins
this praxis.

In the second century BCE the Jewish allegorizing philosopher
Aristobulus stated that the Passover is 'in the middle of the first
month' and should be fixed to the time of the spring equinox
(Eus. *Hist. Eccles.* 7: 32: 16–18), since this connects the festival
with an important natural (solar) occurrence. This shows that,
like Philo, Aristobulus believed you should celebrate Passover
at the spring equinox, but it also shows that Aristobulus was,
with the Mareotic group, a proponent of the solar calendar,
since Nisan is the first month not in the normative Jewish calendar but in the old solar calendar of Jubilees, 1 Enoch, and the
Temple Scroll.[5] Philo did not follow this calendar, but rather

---

[3] Witt, *Isis*, 212–14.

[4] Josephus states that the Essenes prayed towards the sun as if entreating it to
rise (*War* 2: 128, cf. 148), which reflects a slightly different petition than that
described in *Contempl.*

[5] Philo explains that Nisan is called the first month in scripture (Exod. 12:
6)—when it is really the seventh—because it is first 'in power' (*Spec.* 2. 152–5).
For Jubilees and the Temple Scroll, it was really the first month, in accordance
with a more ancient calendar (see below). In the usual Jewish calendar, the first
month is Tishri. In the Babylonian calendar, Nisanu (corresponding to Hebrew
Nisan) was the first month, and it began in the spring equinox, not the autumn:
see William M. O'Neil, *Time and the Calendars* (Sydney: Sydney University
Press, 1975), 92–3. Beckwith erroneously identifies that Aristobulus followed
the lunar calendar, *Calendar*, 100. He supposes that one could follow the system
of a new day beginning with sunrise or a new day beginning with sunset concur-
rently, and there was no problem (pp. 3–9). However, Beckwith seems to be
confused by the very thing he points out: that the Hebrew word for 'day', יום,
refers to both 'day' (as in a 24-hour unit) and 'daylight'. The apparent combina-
tions of two systems he identifies may all be explained by translating יום 'daylight' rather than 'day', or vice versa. It is a semantic issue. See for Philo's own
ambiguity here *Contempl.* 34, but it is clear from *Contempl.* 65 and 89 that the
new 50th day, following on from the 49th-day Sabbath meal, begins at dawn.

the normative luni-solar calendar operating in Jerusalem (*Spec.* 1: 177; 2: 140, 155, 210).

In addition to this, Aristobulus argued that Homer, Hesiod, and Linus borrowed the idea that the number seven is holy from the Jewish recognition that the seventh day is holy (*Praep. Evang.* 13: 12: 13–16). The number seven is a principle (*logos*) that is pervasive in nature, and through this Jews have knowledge of human and divine matters, for 'the cosmos of all living beings and growing things revolves in series of sevens' (*Praep. Evang.* 13: 12: 12–13). As we have seen, both Philo and the Mareotic group believed in the importance of the number 7; but Aristobulus and the Mareotic group agree in combining the veneration of 7 with the solar calendar. The Mareotic group sees the new day as beginning with the rising of the sun, at which point they return to their usual labours, with the Sabbath over. After praying for a 'bright day' at sunrise 'they go back into each their own reverence-place, again to ply their trade and cultivate the use of philosophy' (89). Philo describes these people returning to 'work' by using the language of trade and cultivation for their contemplative exercises. Philo reflects the solar sequencing of the group's regulation of time when he notes that 'twice every day, at sunrise and sunset' these members of the group are accustomed to pray (*Contempl.* 27). The connection between sunlight and goodness is also clear in this passage (cf. 34).

The combination of the reverence for the number 7 and the solar year resulted in a special calendar. The members of this community held the seventh day to be holy, and also the power of seven—7^2—to be so (*Contempl.* 65). Therefore, according to Philo, the community celebrated not only the seventh day—which he does not call the Sabbath—but also the forty-ninth day, which also happens to be the eve of the fiftieth day. Every seventh Sabbath was especially important, and the day after was considered significant for being the fiftieth day of this cycle though no feast proper seems to have been celebrated on this day. Philo does not indicate that the week-of-weeks—7^2—Sabbath was celebrated only once a year, or that the fiftieth day was Pentecost; rather it was a constantly recurring festival following on from a week of weeks. Conybeare's identification of the week-of-weeks festival eve as definitively only

Pentecost[6] rests on an association of the name 'Pentecost' with Philo's mention of 50 and a hypothetical assimilation of the Mareotic group's calendar to Jewish norms which is simply not indicated here. Philo does not link the fiftieth day with the *omer* sacrifice of Passover at all. The forty-ninth-day eve festival is held to be important because of some special significance of 50 which is the most holy and natural of numbers because it represents the power of the right-angled triangle (*Contempl.* 65): $(3 \times 3) + (4 \times 4) + (5 \times 5) = 50$. Via the Euclidean problem of the square of the hypotenuse, Philo tells us that the fiftieth-day festival is the greatest festival which the number 50 has been assigned (for its own sake) because of its special significance as a number, just as the seventh day is significant because of the number 7's purity and virginity. Philo himself fully supports the glory of the number 7, as we see in his extended eulogy to the number in *Opif.* 89–128, and uses the same Euclidean equation in this passage as an example of how 7 is the fountain of every figure and every quality (*Opif.* 97).[7] Fifty, of course, was a sacred number to the Pythagoraeans.

What is in fact celebrated by the Mareotic group is the forty-ninth day, that is, the week-of-weeks Sabbath. It rolls through the year, just as the Sabbath does, and is not counted from any particular festival. According to Philo, they greet the day when the sun comes up in communal prayer with outstretched hands (89), which indicates that the fiftieth sunrise is of special concern, but it closes the festival rather than opens it, now that the forty-ninth day has ended. What Philo seems to present us with is a sequential, cyclic calendar based on the number 7 and multiples of 7. That is the sequence they follow. Philo indicates this as baldly as possible. He does absolutely nothing to argue for or against it. The mathematical purity of the calendar may have made perfect sense to a Roman audience familiar with philosophy and may well have served to show the purity of the group's thinking.

Essentially, this seems to be a solar pentecontad calendar. The pentecontad calendar was not necessarily solar, but rather an

---

[6] Conybeare, *Philo*, 306, 313; Colson, *Philo ix* (Loeb), 152 n. *a*: 'I believe with Conybeare that this refers to the feast of Pentecost'. This identification is common: see Kraemer, 'Monastic Jewish Women', 345.

[7] See also *Spec.* 2: 58, 176, 211 and *Mos.* 2: 80.

agricultural calendar preserved in some parts of southern Palestine up until the beginning of this century. It originated in Western Mesopotamia (probably among the Amorites) in the third millennium BCE.[8] In this calendar, the year is divided into fifty-day intervals of seven weeks plus an additional day (the fiftieth) possibly being known as the *'atzeret* (cf. Joel 1: 14; 2 Kings 10: 20), and an additional period at the end.[9] The ethnographer Tawfiq Canaan found in 1913 that people in southern Palestine divided the year into seven periods of fifty days.[10] These Muslim agriculturists used Christian designations for the festivals on the fiftieth days which in turn overlaid far more ancient agricultural festivals: grape-watching, grape-pressing, sowing, etc.[11] At some point in the evolution of the Jewish calendar, which originated within the rubric of the pentecontad calendar, the fiftieth day ceased to become extra and was integrated into a continuous flow, while the importance of the number 50 was retained in regard to Pentecost but lost its rolling significance.[12]

The Mareotic group described by Philo are continuing to use the pentecontad calendar. Unlike in Mesopotamia, however, in this case the pentecontad calendar is accommodated to a solar year of 364 days, with the fiftieth day being also the first day of the new cycle. It is unlikely that this was purely some kind of sectarian development. Morgenstern noted that in 3 Maccabees 6: 38–40 there is mention of a fifty-day period during which time the Jews of Egypt were sentenced to be executed by Ptolemy IV

[8] Eviatar Zerubavel, *The Seven Day Circle: The History and Meaning of the Week* (Chicago and London: University of Chicago Press, 1985), 8; Julius Morgenstern, 'The Calendar of the Book of Jubilees, its Origin and its Character', *VT* 5 (1955), 37–61, basing himself on the analysis by Julius and Hildegard Lewy, 'The Origin of the Week and the Oldest West Asiatic Calendar', *HUCA* 17 (1942–3), 1–152.

[9] See J. van Goudoever, *Biblical Calendars* (Leiden: Brill, 1961), 26–9, 173–4.

[10] Tawfiq Canaan, 'Der Kalender des palästinischen Fellachen', *ZDPV* 36 (1913), 266–300, at 272.

[11] See also the description in Gustaf Dalman, *Arbeit und Sitte in Palästina*, 7 vols. (Gutersloh: C. Bertelsmann, 1928–39), i, 8–9, 48–50, 181, 461–3.

[12] Morgenstern notes the importance of elements of the pentecontad calendar in the Nestorian calendar also (*Calendar*, 46–8) which he traces to the oldest type of Christian calendar based on the Galilean agricultural year (49–50).

Philopator, who changed his mind and spared them; the Jews then celebrated for the last seven days of this period. He writes:

This passage suggests very strongly that not merely the Therapeutae but actually the entire Egyptian Jewish community were well acquainted with fifty-days periods which ended in festal celebration. This suggests further that certain practices of time-reckoning according to the principles of the pentecontad calendar lingered long among the Jews of Egypt in much the same manner as among their brethren in Palestine.[13]

The Falashas of Ethiopia likewise preserved a form of this calendar, with every seventh Sabbath given special sanctity as a Sabbath of Mercy. The year is divided into seven periods of seven weeks, with the luni-solar calendar of normative Judaism used alongside this pentecontad system.[14] According to the Slavonic version of Josephus, the Essenes celebrated each seventh day, week, month, and year.[15]

The calendar used in the definition of Jewish festivals in Jerusalem in the first century was the luni-solar calendar of 354 days (with an additional month inserted every three years). The solar calendar is particularly linked with Egypt. Civil rites of Egypt were based on twelve thirty-day months, which were divided into three ten-day weeks, with five epagomenal days at the end of each year, giving a year of 365 days.[16] The normative Jewish calendar divided up time into months, or moon-phases.[17] The Babylonians had months based on the sighting of the first visible crescent of the moon, with an intercalary month

---

[13] Morgenstern, *Calendar*, 50 n. 2; Goudoever notes that the reckoning of the year into blocks of 50 days is found in medieval sources, such as Saadia Gaon, quoting 'Judah the Alexandrian', possibly Philo but more likely another Alexandrian exegete, see Goudoever, *Biblical Calendars*, 27–8. Beckwith has noted that 'Judah the Alexandrian' refers to four first-fruits festivals, indicating an adaptation of the solar calendar, see Beckwith, 'The Solar Calendar of Joseph and Asenath: A Suggestion', *JSJ* 15 (1984), 90–111.

[14] Morgenstern, *Calendar*, 51.

[15] Goudoever, *Biblical Calendars*, 27.

[16] Zerubavel, *Seven Day Circle*, 10–11. The understanding was that each year was in fact 365.25 days, which is very close to the true length of the year: 365.2422 days, see K. G. Irwin, *The 365 Days* (London: George Harrap & Co., 1965), 36–7. The calendar of Thoth began at the autumn equinox (23 Sept.). The Persian calendar followed a similar programme, see Beckwith, *Calendar*, 97.

[17] In this calendar an intercalated month was inserted after every 36 lunar months to ensure its rough correspondence with solstices and equinoxes.

inserted every few years.[18] However, Jews had absorbed some influences from solar time-reckoning, and the calendar is properly described as 'luni-solar', with a phase of more solar time-reckoning preceding a more heavily lunar calendar.

There are different views on when the luni-solar calendar was adopted by Jews. Solomon Zeitlin believed that it was adopted soon after the restoration, in the sixth century BCE, and that by the first century there was widespread agreement about it.[19] It was partly for this reason that Zeitlin dated the Book of Jubilees very early, in order that the debate about the calendar would be pushed back to the fourth or fifth centuries BCE. According to VanderKam, the luni-solar calendar adopted by the Jerusalem priesthood may have been introduced into Judaism at the time of the Hasmoneans.[20] The normative Jewish calendar may finally have been fixed as a result of the influence of Greek or Syrian calendars which were more reliant on the moon than on the sun.[21] In Daniel 7: 25 the 'little horn on the fourth beast', possibly the Syrian ruler Antiochus IV, would attempt to change the times (or 'festivals') and the law. Zeitlin has questioned whether the reference is really to a calendar; it may rather be the festivals themselves that were changed, and this would certainly fit with what we know about the actions of Antiochus.[22] It would also be surprising that the Maccabees accepted this innovation, when they apparently rejected so many of the other coercive innovations brought about by the Seleucids.[23] But we clearly have a situation in which there were alternative calendars in use by different groups in the first centuries BCE, from the testimony of the Dead Scrolls and the pseudepigrapha.

[18] O'Neil, *Time*, 42.

[19] Solomon Zeitlin, 'Some Stages of the Jewish Calendar', in id., *Studies in the Early History of Judaism*, i (New York: Ktav, 1973), 183–93.

[20] Ibid. 188–9 and id., '2 Maccabees 6, 7A and Calendrical Change in Jerusalem', *JSJ* 12 (1981), 58–60. VanderKam links this also with 2 Macc. 6: 7a and 1 Macc. 1: 59.

[21] The Greeks used a lunar system of twelve or thirteen months for each year, see Irwin, *365 Days*, 52–4; O'Neil, *Time*, 42. Every three years in a cycle of eight an intercalary month was inserted. The Metonic cycle (5th cent. BCE) used seven intercalated months over nineteen years.

[22] Solomon Zeitlin, 'The Book of Jubilees and the Pentateuch', in id., *Studies in the Early History of Judaism*, ii (New York: Ktav, 1974), 147–64. He may have instituted the celebration of his birthday, accession, and other festivals.

[23] See the comments by Philip Davies in *CBQ* 44 (1983), 24–37.

Morgenstern's examination of the calendar of the Book of Jubilees traces its origins to the ancient pentecontad calendar, somewhat influenced by lunar time-reckoning but quite solar.[24] In the calendar of the Book of Jubilees, the Book of Enoch, and the Temple Scroll, along with other documents found in the corpus of the Dead Sea Scrolls, the solar year is divided into fifty-two weeks, so that the length of each year is 364 days.[25] The year is also divided into four sections of thirteen weeks each, probably most usually two months of thirty days and one month of thirty-one days. For those advocating these calendars, there is evidence of a deep resentment against those who have changed the days of the festivals in line with an even more lunar form of calendar. As is written in the Book of Jubilees:

And there will be those who will examine the moon diligently because it will corrupt the (appointed) times and it will advance from year to year ten days. Therefore, the years will come to them as they corrupt and make a day of testimony a reproach and a profane day a festival, and they will mix up everything, a holy day (as) profaned and a profane (one) for a holy day, because they will set awry the months and sabbaths and feasts and jubilees.[26] (Jub. 6: 36–7)

The year of Jubilees begins not on day 1 (Sunday) but on day 4 (Wednesday)—the day the sun and moon were created (Gen. 1: 14–19)—ending on day 3 (Tuesday), so the weeks are calculated mid-week to mid-week rather than Sabbath to Sabbath, though there would of course have been fifty-two Sabbaths in any year. The day begins at dawn. In *Contempl.* 89, we noted that, after the group's all-night vigil, the people greet the rising of the sun. Even when not praying all together at dawn, they would pray individually when the sun rises that they should have a 'fine' or 'bright' day (*Contempl.* 27). When evening comes there is no indication that a new day was beginning. The members of the Mareotic group seem to associate the darkness with the needs of the body (cf. 34); appropriately then at dusk they pray that the

---

[24] Morgenstern, *Calendar*, 54–65.

[25] See e.g. 1 Enoch 72: 8–32; 74: 10–12; 75: 1–2; 82: 4–6, 11–12, 15–20; 89: 7–8; Jubilees 6: 23–38. For a useful examination of the calendars in the Dead Sea Scrolls corpus, see James VanderKam, *Calendars in the Dead Sea Scrolls* (London and New York : Routledge, 1998).

[26] Tr. O. S. Wintermute in Charlesworth (ed.), *Old Testament Pseudepigrapha*, ii. 68.

soul should be 'relieved from the disturbance of the senses'. They therefore allegorize their own calendar, finding metaphors in the sun and the night.

In the Jubilees calendar there are twelve months of thirty days each, with an extra day added at the end of every third month (third, sixth, ninth, twelfth), so that each season of three months has ninety-one days and thirteen weeks. This means that the day of the week for the Passover, Shabuot, Day of Atonement, and so on will always be the same. Every jubilee year was forty-nine years (a week of a week of years), while in the Pentateuch it is the fiftieth year.[27] The year began with 1 Nisan, at the spring rather than the autumn equinox, as also in the writings of Aristobulus, noted above.

The Temple Scroll gives us further understanding of this type of calendar, and indicates the special significance of both 7 and 50 in the sequence of festivals.[28] The counting of the *omer* is counted as day 1 in terms of the calculation of the festival of shabuoth (Feast of Weeks), which occurs on day 50. Day 50 also becomes day 1 of the new period of fifty days leading up to the wine festival, and this day likewise becomes day 1 of the new period leading up to the oil (and wood) festival (cf. b.Bikk. 1: 10; 1 Chron. 31: 5–7), reflecting the pattern of the old pentecontad calendar. However, at this point the sequence of fifty days breaks down so that the Day of Atonement occurs on the nineteenth day of the next period and the Feast of Tabernacles occurs on the twenty-fourth. Already, the Passover had occurred on 14 Nisan, in the first month. Therefore, while sequences of fifty do occur in the Temple Scroll and the Book of Jubilees there is not the consistent repetition of the fifty- (or rather forty-nine-) day cycles. The calendar of Jubilees and the Temple Scroll do show the overlap between sequences of fifty days, that is, day 50 is day 1 of the next time period. However, this calendar is formulated within a sequence of Hebrew months in which festivals had to occur on certain days of this month (14 Nisan, 10 Ab, etc.). The calendars of Jubilees and the Temple Scroll fix the duration of months in order that they are not dependent on the lunar cycle, and are

[27] Zeitlin, 'Jubilees', 162–3.
[28] See Johann Meier, *The Temple Scroll* (Sheffield: Sheffield Academic Press, 1985), 70–6; Roger Beckwith, 'The Temple Scroll and its Calendar: Their Character and Purpose', *RQ* 69/18 (1997), 3–20.

somewhat tied into an alternative system based on the importance of 7 and its power, and 50. However, the Mareotic group
seems much more absolutist in terms of numerical patterning, if
we are to believe Philo's description.

In terms of the Dead Sea Scrolls overall, it is generally held
that the group(s) interested in preserving the Scrolls held to a
different calendar to that endorsed by the Temple establishment
in Jerusalem.[29] Not only do we have the Temple Scroll[30] and the
Book of Jubilees[31] in the Dead Sea Scrolls corpus, but 1 Enoch
72–82 indicates a belief in the 364-day calendar (cf. Jub. 4: 18; 6:
32, 38) and Enoch also was used by those who preserved the
scrolls found near Qumran.[32] 1QpHab XII: 4–8 indicates that
the 'Wicked Priest' confronted the Teacher of Righteousness
and his disciples on the Day of Atonement, the 'day of *their* rest'.
CD VI: 17–19 and 1QS I: 13–15 both appear to indicate the
keeping of a different calendar, and CD VI: 3–4 cites Jubilees
positively. 11QPsalms XXVII: 5–7 states that a year lasted
364 days (with fifty-two sabbaths), so also 4Q252 II: 3 and
4QMMT^{a}I: 2–3. The community should be in tune with 'the
laws of the great light of heaven' (1QH 12: 9).

The 364-day calendar cannot be linked exclusively with any
one sectarian group. The calendars of Book of Jubilees, Enoch,
the Testaments of the Twelve Patriarchs, or the Temple Scroll
were the type supported by the group(s) responsible for the
Dead Sea Scrolls corpus, but they are probably not so much
sectarian as archaic, or influenced by Egyptian norms.

Any group that followed a solar calendar cannot have accepted
the dates of the festivals celebrated at the Jerusalem Temple, and
would not have participated in these cultic festivals. The invective of Jubilees 6: 36–7 illustrates the bitter feelings involved.

---

[29] See for a concise and useful survey: James C. VanderKam, 'Calendrical
Texts and the Origins of the Dead Sea Scroll Community', in Michael Wise,
Norman Golb, John J. Collins, and Dennis Pardee (eds.), *Methods of
Investigation of the Dead Sea Scrolls and the Khirbet Qumran Site* (Annals of the
New York Academy of Sciences, 722; New York: Academy of Sciences, 1992),
371–88; Annie Jaubert, 'Le Calendrier des Jubilés et de la secte de Qumran: Ses
origines bibliques', *VT* 3 (1953), 250–64; VanderKam, *Calendars*, 71–90.

[30] The Temple Scroll exists in two versions: 11QTemple^a and 11QTemple^b.

[31] Fragments of the text have been found in five of the caves; e.g. 4QJub^{a-f};
11QJub; 3QJub, 2QJub^{a-b}, 1QJub, and 4QpsJub^c.

[32] Fragments of Enoch were found in Cave 4: 4QEn^{a-g}.

The fantasy of a perfect Temple operating according to a perfect calendar that we find in the Temple Scroll is surely produced in a context of deep resentment and frustration. For those who believed God should be worshipped according to the solar calendar there was, however, an alternative temple, appropriately in Egypt.

The Jewish temple in the nome of Heliopolis (*War* 7: 421–36, cf. *Ant.* 13: 62–73, *Ap.* 2: 49) was, as I have argued elsewhere, probably built by the high priest Onias III, *c*.160 BCE.[33] This site is to be identified with Tell el-Yehoudieh, in the lush Delta area (see Figure 10).[34] There is a rather curious mention by Josephus that the temple there survived 343 years (*War* 7: 436), that is a week of jubilee years (7 × 49 = 343).[35] Such a coincidence seems to indicate some kind of meditation on the significance of multiples of 7 in Josephus' source.[36] Also very interesting here is Josephus' note that in the Temple of Onias there was not the seven-branched lampstand, but rather a hanging lamp with one single flame which shed 'a brilliant light' (*War* 7: 428). Robert Hayward has perceptively noted that Philo understood the central light of the tabernacle menorah to be symbolic of the sun (*Mos.* 2: 102–3; *QE* 2: 75) and that cosmic symbolism concerning the menorah was widespread.[37] On the basis of this

---

[33] For a detailed discussion of this temple see Joan E. Taylor, 'A Second Temple in Egypt: A Reconsideration of the Evidence for the Zadokite Temple of Onias', *JSJ* 29 (1998), 1–25; Richardson and Heuchan, 'Jewish Voluntary Associations', 226–39; Erich S. Gruen, 'The Origins and Objectives of Onias' Temple', *Scripta Classica Israelica*, 16 (1997), 47–50; Paul Rainbow, 'The Last Oniad and the Teacher of Righteousness', *JJS* 48 (1997), 30–52; Gideon Bohak, *Joseph and Asenath and the Jewish Temple in Heliopolis* (Atlanta: Scholars, 1996); id., 'Theopolis: A Single-Temple Policy and its Singular Ramifications', *JSJ* 50 (1999), 3–20.

[34] The site was partially excavated and surveyed by Flinders Petrie a century ago, see W. M. F. Petrie, *Hyksos and Israelite Cities* (London: Egypt Exploration Society, 1906). I visited the site in Nov. 1999. One can see a huge quantity of surface sherds and burnt brick, which tallies with destruction by the Romans in 73 CE (*War* 7: 420). The site is, however, poorly maintained and swampy around the perimeter, and badly needs excavating. Fragments of small Ionic columns, probably from the Oniad temple, are on display at the Petrie Museum, London, with a few other items from the site.

[35] This number cannot be right, and is clearly 'spiritualized'.

[36] The significance of this for the provenance of the Temple Scroll may also need to be considered further.

[37] Robert Hayward, 'The Jewish Temple at Leontopolis: A Reconsider-

10. Tell el-Yehoudieh, probably called Leontopolis, site of Jewish fortress and temple built by Onias III, c. 164 BCE. High sand bank on which temple stood

understanding, Hayward suggests in regard to Onias' lamp that
'the overwhelming probability is that it represented the sun'.[38]
He speculates that this lampstand innovation may have derived
from an interpretation of Isaiah 30: 26. The Masoretic Hebrew
text reads: 'the moonlight will be bright as sunlight, and sunlight
itself be seven times brighter, like the seven days in one, on the
day that YHWH dresses his people's wound, and heals the scars
of the blows they have received'. The Targum of Isaiah refers
to $7 \times 7 \times 7$ ($= 343$) years that light will shine on the chosen
people of God.[39]

If this is so, then it may indicate an acceptance of a solar calendar, since the light of the sun would have been considered to be
in some way 'godly'.[40] It is here also that we can recall what was
stated above concerning Aristobulus, the 'teacher' of Ptolemy
VI Philometor in Egypt, under whose reign the Temple was
built. Aristobulus apparently supported the notion that the
Passover should be linked with the spring equinox: a solar astro-
nomical event. The equinoxes appear to be very important in the
architectural plan of the Temple in 11QT and also in 1 Enoch,
where the spring equinox occurs when the sun is at the 'great
gate' of the Temple (72: 6).[41] Whatever calendar Aristobulus
promoted, with its emphasis on the solar event of the spring
equinox, it was not the one that came to be normative in Judaea.

ation', *JJS* 33 (1982), 429–43, at 434–6. See Jos. *Ant.* 3: 145–6; 182; *Targ. Ps.
Jon.* Exod. 39: 37; 40: 4; *Num. Rab.* 15: 7.

[38] Ibid. 435.

[39] Ibid. 436, followed by Mélèze-Modrzejewski, *Jews of Egypt*, 128–9. The
section in the Temple Scroll which describes the menorah (column 9) is unfortunately very damaged, but it seems to relate fairly well to the description in
Exod. 25: 31 and 37: 17–21, though it weighs twice as much, a view that also
appears to be implied in the LXX Exod. 25: 39. For discussion of the menorah
of 11QT see Mathias Delcor, 'Is the Temple Scroll a Source of the Herodian
Temple?', in George Brooke (ed.), *Temple Scroll Studies* (Sheffield: JSOT
Press, 1989), 67–89 at pp. 82–3.

[40] Hayward, 'Jewish Temple', 435, notes that in Ps. 84: 11–12 YHWH 'is a
sun'.

[41] See Margaret Barker, 'The Temple Measurements and the Solar Calendar', in George Brooke (ed.), *Temple Scroll Studies: Papers Presented at the
International Symposium on the Temple Scroll, Dec. 1987* (Sheffield: JSOT,
1989), 62–6, at p. 65. The 'great gate' of 1 En. 72: 6 is, according to Barker, 'presumably the name for the central eastern gate through which the sun's light
could reach the Temple'.

Aristobulus himself would have been an Oniad, since he was 'one of the family of the anointed priests' (2 Macc. 1: 10). The siting of the Temple of Onias itself may be telling: Heliopolis means 'city of the sun'. According to Josephus, Onias found his mandate for the building of the temple in the region of Heliopolis in Isaiah 19: 18–19 which states that there will be an altar to YHWH in Egypt in—according to one reading (so 1QIs^a)—'the city of the sun'. The Egyptian word for Heliopolis, On, likewise means 'sun': when Philo refers to it he writes that 'On [is] the mind, which they called Heliopolis, because the mind, like the sun, holds power over the body, and extends its power over all like the rays of the sun' (*Her.* 77). Perhaps not entirely irrelevant also is the fact that the LXX 'translates' the reference to the city of Isaiah 19: 18 as *polis asedek*, that is, עִיר הַצֶּדֶק, 'the city of right-eousness'.[42]

In conclusion, the continuation of the old solar calendar appears to have been particularly endorsed by some of the Jews of Egypt, as Morgenstern suggested, our evidence coming from both Alexandria and Heliopolis. Not only did they live in a milieu in which a solar calendar was the one commonly accepted in their surrounding culture, as refugees and emigrants from Judaea they preserved an old pentecontad calendar. The usual feasts of Judaism were celebrated in accordance with this reckoning of time. Meanwhile, in Judaea, the calendar was changing according to different influences, and the pentecontad calendar and solar reckoning were passing away. Philo himself—with his clear acceptance of the norms of the Jerusalem Temple—accepted the Judaean calendar as it was used in the Temple, and rejected the calendar still used by some (many?) Egyptian Jews.

The acceptance of a pentecontad solar calendar is one thing, but can we be a little bit more specific about the group's organization of time? If the Mareotic group did not have the idea that the fiftieth day was an extra day in each cycle, then one could conjecture that their year would perhaps have been one of 343 days (7×49 days). A year of 343 days would have been neat, and

---

[42] There is evidence of considerable fascination with the site/area of Heliopolis. It was supposedly the home of Asenath, Joseph's wife (Gen. 41: 45, 50; 46: 20; Joseph and Asenath i–iii), and Joseph was believed to have settled his father and brothers there (Artapanus, Frag. 2, 23: 3; Jos. *Ant.* 2: 188). The LXX of Exod. 1: 11 lists Heliopolis as one of three cities the Israelites rebuilt.

would have allowed for easy repetitions of the cycle, but it is too short, and would actually disregard the cycle of the seasons. If the Mareotic group adopted the solar 364-day calendar of Jubilees, then it would have been able to make a simple division of the year to give fifty-two weeks, which they would then need to accommodate to the fiftieth-day festivals. There would be three weeks of the new first cycle carried forward into the next year, nine the following year, twelve the year after that, and so on. The sequence would not have returned to its starting point until seven years elapsed, at which point there would have been fifty-two weeks of weeks, just as there are fifty-two ordinary weeks in the 364-day year.[43] This is a fairly tidy system, though completely detached from the agricultural year.

In beginning the year on day 4, the groups responsible for both Jubilees and the Temple Scroll could ensure that the Feast of Weeks, and Festivals of First Fruits always fell on the day after a Sabbath, and that the Day of Atonement was always on the eve of a Sabbath, which may have seemed particularly appropriate, but it was only necessary if one were concerned to fix all Jewish festivals in line with these requirements, and it has a very cultic and agricultural focus. These festivals were to be celebrated *at the Temple* at these times.

We have no indication in Philo's text that the Mareotic group accepted lunar months at all, and the strong implication is that they did not. Philo defines their time-keeping as a constantly recurring pattern of 7 and 7^2 celebrations. The celebration for day 7 is because of the power of the unoriginated one, an entitlement to rest from the soul's labours, which harks back to an allegorical exegesis of the creation account of Genesis. The celebration of 7^2 is based on their exegesis of Exodus, not Passover exactly but rather the crossing of the Red Sea and the redemption of Israel. It occurred not at Passover but at *every* forty-ninth day eve. While the Temple Scroll ties the fiftieth-day festival to actual Temple observances, the allegorized mathematical calen-

[43] The 364-day calendar, however, is still too short since a true year is actually 365 days, 5 hours, 48 minutes, and some 48 seconds. According to Zeitlin, it was for this reason that the Jubilee year was introduced. This was not an actual year, but was the 49 days—a week of weeks—required to get the Jewish solar calendar back in sequence with the natural world again, Zeitlin, 'Some Stages', 183–93; E. R. Leach, 'A Possible Method of Intercalation for the Calendar of the Book of Jubilees', *VT* 7 (1957), 392–7 at p.393.

dar of the Mareotic group does not do so. In the Temple Scroll, when no actual festival can be associated with the fiftieth day, the system breaks down. Without the need to tie in the fiftieth day to actual Temple-based festivals, the calendar of the Mareotic group could continue uninterrupted year after (solar) year. Moreover, there would be no point in celebrating Passover separately from the forty-ninth-day celebrations. The redemption event of Passover was essentially celebrated by the Mareotic group seven times per year, rather than once, on days that connected redemption with the creative power of the universe.

While one of the key features of the Jubilees and Temple Scroll calendars is the attempt to regulate the days of the week in order to ensure that the festivals always fall on the same day every year,[44] the impression we get from Philo's description is that this group *only* celebrated Sabbaths and weeks of Sabbaths, the latter as the 'greatest festival which the number fifty has been assigned' for the fiftieth eve and dawn, when they celebrated the great feast of redemption from Egypt. They therefore neglect to celebrate the usual (Passover) Feast, or any other feast. They do not follow the calendar of the Temple Scroll and Jubilees, but rather one much more rarefied, in which numbers and symbols are celebrated, not the usual feasts. As Philo states in regard to the extreme allegorizers of *Migr.* 92: 'It is true that the feast is a symbol of the happiness of the soul and thankfulness to God, but we should not for this reason spurn the general gatherings of the year's seasons.' I have suggested that the extreme allegorizers were the exegetical group from which the Mareotic community came. This means that the calendar itself described by Philo in relation to the Mareotic community would be that of the extreme allegorizers in Alexandria.

We have seen here that a solar calendar was advocated by Alexandrian and other Egyptian Jews. In line with what we see in the case of other calendrical variants, it seems likely that this solar calendar was like that of the Temple Scroll and Jubilees, in which pentecontad calendrical elements also appear. The extreme allegorizers would have taken over this calendar, enforced the

---

[44] See discussion by Annie Jaubert, 'Le Calendrier des Jubilés', in *La date de la cène: Calendrier biblique et liturgie chrétienne* (Paris: Gabalda, 1957); ead., 'Le Calendrier des Jubilés et les jours liturgiques de la semaine', *VT* 7 (1957), 35–61, at pp. 38–40.

pentecontad elements more vigorously throughout the system, and dropped the celebration of the usual Jewish feasts, conforming all festivals to a regular pattern based on the power of 7, which, interpreted allegorically, indicated the generative power of the universe. It was this that Philo was reacting against in *Migr.* (without going into the details with which his audience was familiar), but in *Contempl.*—designed for a different audience— he describes the practice without any criticisms at all.

Even without calendrical considerations, the correlation between two groups who allegorize and neglect to follow the usual feasts of Judaism is striking. Extreme allegorizers neglect the usual feasts of Judaism and the Mareotic group neglects these feasts. The only others who did so were people who had fallen away from Judaism completely, but neither the extreme allegorizers nor the Mareotic group were apostates. The Mareotic group should therefore be included in the classification of extreme allegorizers, though these people living by the lake are to be considered only one community within that wider category.

Overall, the study of the calendar serves to situate the Mareotic group within the currents of Alexandrian scriptural exegesis, within a certain social milieu, and within Alexandrian Jewish philosophy. Much more could be stated about the philosophy of numbers in the Graeco-Roman world, especially in Pythagoraeanism and Platonism, but for the present purposes the connection between the Mareotic group and the extreme allegorizers is what is important. The extreme allegorizers are an exegetical group with which Philo himself is quite sympathetic. They shared very many of his own allegorical interpretations, and are 'good', even if not necessarily perceived as good by Jews who follow traditional Jewish praxis.

Having situated the Mareotic group within the allegorical school of exegesis, in the extreme sector of this school, and as part of Jewish philosophy in Alexandria, we can now turn to the issues of women and gender both in Philo's rhetorical construction of *Contempl.* and in the actual group that Philo describes. If the group represents a small offshoot from this sector, then we can read from the group something more about the school from which it has come. Ultimately, the women of this group point to many more women within first-century Alexandria, undescribed in our sources, who are engaged in Jewish philosophy.

II

Women and Gender in
De Vita Contemplativa

8
Paradigms of 'Women' in Discourses on *Philosophia*

Yes, but I assure you, some will say, that women who associate with philosophers are bound to be arrogant for the most part and presumptuous, in that abandoning their own households and turning to the company of men they practise speeches, talk like sophists, and analyze syllogisms, when they ought to be sitting at home spinning.

(Musonius Rufus[1])

Philo wished to present a group of extreme allegorizers as living the *bios theoretikos*: Jewish men and women living a philosophical lifestyle more excellent than any known in the Graeco-Roman world. How then would he deal with the women? For us, inclusion of women in a group of people considered virtuous would generally be considered a good thing. Was it for Philo? Was it necessarily a good thing in terms of his audience? In order to understand what Philo may have had to deal with, rhetorically, we need to consider how women appear in the discourse of Graeco-Roman philosophy. I shall make this survey brief, so as not to unbalance the discussion, but comprehensive.

In exploring the discourse, I am not concerned particularly with actual, historical, women philosophers but rather with how they are presented in extant texts and art (which I see as 'texts' within the discourse). There is no need to argue the point that real women were active in this field, and could live some kind of philosophical life. The extant evidence suggests overall that there were women philosophers and students of philosophers from the very origins of philosophy in Greece in the sixth century BCE to the late Roman period and beyond. However, writings about philosophers are fraught with historiographical problems. We cannot simply read off from various descriptions

[1] 'That Women Too Should Study Philosophy', in Cora E. Lutz, *Musonius Rufus: 'The Roman Socrates'* (New Haven: Yale University Press, 1947), 43.

of women in philosophical traditions an account of real women, as did Gilles Ménage in 1690, with his *Historia Mulierum Philosopharum*: a kind of catalogue which identified at least sixty-five actual women philosophers.[2] The accounts of women philosophers and students of philosophers reflect an awareness of real women active in philosophy without necessarily representing them. Our ancient authors—invariably men—had reasons for including women in certain accounts. The trope 'woman student/philosopher' could work to further the argument of the author, or function as tool of propaganda. The trope could be apologetic or satirical, commending or condemning. This is not to say that texts cannot contain material useful for the historian, but only that we should be careful to avoid superficial readings of such texts. It is not a case of simple 'information' from the ancient world about real women, as if the text is a window to reality.

Many of the attestations of women are much later than the time the women lived, even though they preserve much more ancient traditions. The most extensive evidence of philosophers in the ancient world, including much of what we have on women philosophers, is contained in the survey of ancient philosophy by Diogenes Laertius (third century CE), or in the work of Johannes Stobaeus, a fifth-century compiler, or in even later texts such as the Suidas (or Suda),[3] a biographical encyclopaedia from the tenth century utilizing then extant classical sources.[4]

Apart from a few surviving works of women philosophers themselves, the most reliable evidence of 'real' women who philosophized is anecdotal or quite cursory. For example, Diogenes Laertius points to the literary output of the philosopher Chrysippus and just happens to note that the old/senior woman (ἡ πρεσβῦτις) who sat next to him in the Stoic philosophical school of Cleanthes commented that he wrote 500 lines a day (Diogenes Laertius, *Lives* 7: 181). That this commentator was a woman seems to have had no significance in the story; the

---

[2] See Gilles Ménage, *Historia Mulierum Philosopharum (History of Women Philosophers)*, ed. and tr. Beatrice H. Zedler (Lanham, Md.: University Press of America, 1984), 3.

[3] For which see the *PG* 117 or Ada Adler (ed.), *Suidae*, i. 1–5.

[4] Ioannis Stobaeus, *Anthologius*, ed. Kurt Wachsmith and Otto Hense, i–iv (Berlin: Weidmannsche Verlagsbuchhandlung, 1958), henceforth abbreviated as WH.

observer could have been any fellow student. Therefore, in this aside, we may well have evidence—or rather some historical memory—of at least one woman in an early Stoic school. However, when women who study philosophy are explicitly described as a central concern, literary and rhetorical purposes come more forcefully into play.

In general, what we find is evidence of how certain men conceptualized women philosophers and students. These references appear to indicate paradigms of women philosophers and students which authors felt confident in utilizing and replicating. The paradigms within the discourse as a whole inform the rhetoric of individual texts, and this rhetoric in turn informs and reifies the paradigms.

In this chapter, we shall explore what is stated about women philosophers and students of philosophers in an attempt to consider how the women are presented in the texts, including epigraphy and art. The parameters of the survey will be set by the subject matter: the women who are represented, who allegedly lived from the sixth century BCE to the third century CE. I generally omit Christian women from the survey of subjects, since the question of whether they were conceptualized in philosophical terms deserves a large study in its own right. I also omit discussion of Julia Domna and later pagan philosophers such as Hypatia, since I think the material dealing with these falls into slightly different categories of discourse.[5]

This study owes much to the work of Gilles Ménage,[6] his

[5] Since the concern is with paradigms within a certain discourse, the usual historiographical issues of evidence revolving around the 'earliness' and 'lateness' of a source are not so important. We are not concerned with actual women here, but with the representations of women in a discourse in which Philo participated. This is not to say that views about women philosophers were the same throughout a thousand years, but only that certain paradigms of women philosophers and students could occur repeatedly over this span of time. This is the span of the discourse on Graeco-Roman *philosophia* that I think is relevant to this particular study.

[6] Ménage compiled his assemblage of classical sources, with commentary, as a 'feminine' appendage to Diogenes Laertius' *Lives of the Philosophers*, probably intending to impress and support the *femmes savantes* of 17th-cent. Europe. His work was written in Latin, and published in both 1690 and 1692. It was translated into English in 1702 and into French in 1758. The French title implicitly comments on the thinness of the material: *Abrégé de l'Histoire de la Vie des Femmes Philosophes de l'Antiquité*, see *Historia*, p. xvii.

modern contemporary Mary Ellen Waithe, and especially also to an article responding to Waithe by Richard Hawley.[7] In surveying the presentation of women, I follow the leads of Ménage and Waithe in dealing with these in roughly chronological order, but this should not confuse the reader into thinking I am giving a history of women philosophers in any way. It is simply a method for organizing the material. After this general survey, I will summarize the major paradigms of women to be found within the discourse on *philosophia*.

WOMEN PHILOSOPHERS AND STUDENTS

Prototypes

It was believed that wise women were adept at *philosophia* from its inception. According to Plutarch (*c*.46–119 CE), Thargelia of Miletus was known as a *hetaira*, 'companion' or 'courtesan', the lover of Antiochus king of Thessaly (*c*.520–510 BCE).[8] In Philostratus' *Letter to Julia Augusta*[9] he notes that Aeschines the Socratic (fl. *c*.400 BCE) wrote a discourse on her.[10] The sophist Hippias called her 'beautiful and wise'. Little more of her is said in extant texts, but it is interesting that there is the association of her wisdom with beauty and sexuality. She is clearly not the cloistered 'respectable' lady of the house in ancient Athens, but rather a courtesan; that is, she makes her living by being entertaining and engaging to a man who is not her legal husband. The Suidas, however, may indicate an alternate tradition that she was a queen of Thessaly, and therefore Antiochus' legal wife.[11]

Plutarch mentions Eumetis, nicknamed Cleobulina, daughter

---

[7] See Mary Ellen Waithe (ed.), *A History of Women Philosophers: Ancient Women Philosophers 600 B.C.–500 A.D.* (Dordrecht: Martinus Nijhoff, 1987); Richard Hawley, 'The Problem of Women Philosophers in Ancient Greece', in Leonie Archer, Susan Fischler, and Maria Wyke (eds.), *Women in Ancient Societies: 'An Illusion of the Night'* (Basingstoke: Macmillan, 1994), 70–87.

[8] Plutarch, *Pericles* 24: 2.

[9] Philostratus, *Letter* 73.

[10] This is not listed in the works of Aeschines given by Diogenes Laertius, *Lives* 2: 61.

[11] Θαργηλία, Ἀγησαγόπου θυγάτηρ, βασιλεύσασα Θεσσαλῶν λ' ἔτη, Μιλησία τὸ γένος, ἀναιρεθεῖσα δὲ ὑπό τινος Ἀργειου, δεθέντος ὑπ'αὐτῆς. See Adler (ed.), *Suidae*, ii. 684, ll. 19–21 (no. 51).

of the philosopher Cleobulus (fl. *c*.570 BCE), as being 'wise and famous'[12] mainly on account of her expertise in making up riddles, though he notes also that she was possessed of 'wonderful good sense and a statesman's mind'. In Plutarch's writing she is associated with the symposium of Seven Sages along with another woman named Melissa, who has 'prophetic' dreams.[13] Eumetis and Melissa participate modestly but positively in the first part of this symposium, before retiring. Diogenes Laertius mentions Cleobulina as Cleobulus' daughter, who wrote riddles in hexameter verse, and he states that Cratinus wrote a play entitled *Cleobulinae* (pl.) in which she appears.[14] Her fame for making up conundrums was known in the fourth century BCE, for Aristotle uses one of her riddles as an example.[15] That she actually wrote them down is indicated by the Suidas.[16] Perhaps to ensure that readers acknowledge her dutiful and submissive position at the dinner, Clement of Alexandria identifies that she washed the feet of her father's guests.[17] Cleobulina therefore appears not as a courtesan but as the dutiful virgin daughter, much influenced by her father.

---

[12] Plutarch, *Moralia* 148c–e, cf. 150e, 154a–c.

[13] Plutarch, *Moralia* 146d.

[14] Diogenes Laertius, *Lives* 1: 89; Athenaeus, *Deipnosophistae* 4: 171b; 10: 448b.

[15] He uses the riddle on two occasions: *Poetics* 1458a and *Rhetoric* 3: 2: 12, 1405b.

[16] Adler (ed.), *Suidae*, iii. 127 ll. 24–7 (no. 1718, cf. no. 1719 on Cleobulus).

[17] *Strom.* 4: 123: 19. According to Clement she was 'not ashamed to wash the feet of her father's guests'. That she was 'not ashamed' may indicate that Clement knew some women would have been ashamed to do so, i.e. that some women considered that the action indicated a demeaned position. Ménage (*Historia*, 6) comments that it was common in antiquity for women to wash men's feet (at banquets). Whether that conclusion can be drawn depends on the emphasis one places on certain sources, and how one interprets what may have been complex rituals of hospitality, e.g. Herodotus, *Hist.* 6: 19 or Plutarch, *Moralia* 249d, cf. 1 Sam. 25: 41 where Abigail puts herself in a position of a slave 'to wash the feet' of David's servants who have come to her (though in fact does not do this). In 1 Tim. 5: 9 a widow is to have 'washed the feet of the holy ones' as part of her exemplary service to the community (presumably imitating Jesus' example of humility, as in John 13: 2–20, cf. Luke 7: 36–50). Certainly here Clement seems to set the action as the proper one for the daughter of the house to administer to male guests. Foot-washing otherwise seems to be more associated with a slave's role than one done by women as a service to men.

The Pythagoraeans

A comparatively substantial body of literature relates to women in traditions of and about the Pythagoraeans.[18] Pythagoras was considered the first person to be called a *philosophos* as such,[19] and in the traditions about him certain conceptual precedents for philosophy are set in various elements of his life and work, especially in the idea that philosophy encompasses intellectual, moral, and spiritual aspects, and a distinctive way of life (so Plato, *Republic* 600b). The precedent for women's participation in the philosophical life is also found. In Iamblichus' *Life of Pythagoras* (third to fourth centuries CE) he lists seventeen famous women Pythagoraeans.[20] The speeches of Pythagoras are clearly directed to both men and women (and children).[21] Pythagoras himself is said to have learnt philosophy from the Delphic priestess Themistoclea, who acted as a spokesperson for Apollo.[22]

Pythagoras' student (μαθήτρια) and wife Theano was the subject of considerable interest, and could be seen as the model of virtue, modesty, and fidelity typifying the ideal 'philosophical' wife in the Pythagoraean system.[23] According to Theodoret

[18] Iamblichus, *Vita. Pyth.* 36: 267; Diogenes Laertius, *Lives* 8: 42–3; Porphyry, *Vita Pythag.* 4 and 19.

[19] Iamblichus, *Vita Pyth.* 12: 57.

[20] Ibid. This list seems to comprise the following: Timycha, the wife of Myllias the Crotonian; Philtys, the daughter of Theophris the Crotonian and sister of Byndakos; the sisters Okkelo and Ekkelo, Lucanians; Cheilonis, the daughter of Chilon the Lacedaemonian; Cratesiclea the Lacedaemonian, the wife of Cleanor the Lacedaemonian; Theano the wife of Brontinus of Metapontion; Myia the wife of Milon the Crotonian; Lasthenia the Arcadian; Habroteleia the daughter of Habroteles the Tarentine (or: of Taras); Echecratia the Philasian; Tyrsenis the Sybarite; Peisirrode the Tarentine; Nisleadusa (or: Thedousa/Nestheadusa) the Lacedaemonian; Bryo (or: Boio) the Argive; Babelyma (or: Babelyka) the Argive; Cleaechma the sister of Autochridas the Lacedaemonian. For Timycha see also Iamblichus, *Vita Pyth.* 106: 8, 116: 6, 146: 17, and Proclus, *Commentary on Plato's Republic* 8: 248: 25.

[21] See Nancy Demand, 'Plato, Aristophanes and the *Speeches of Pythagoras*', *Greek, Roman and Byzantine Studies*, 23 (1982), 179–84. Iamblichus, *Vita Pyth.* 9: 50, states that he taught men in the Temple of Apollo (Pythaion) and women in the Temple of Juno (Hera).

[22] Porphyry, *Vita Pythag.* 41; Diogenes Laertius, *Lives* 8: 8, 21, citing Aristonexus.

[23] See Clement of Alexandria, *Strom.* 1: 80: 4, where he quotes Didymos as stating that she was the first women to philosophize, and cf. 4: 121: 2;

(fifth century CE), however, Theano was an independent philosopher, since she ran the Pythagoraean school with her sons
Telauges and Mnesarchos after her husband's death.[24] If
Iamblichus knew of such a tradition, he explicitly rejected it, and
stated instead that Aristaeus succeeded Pythagoras, educated his
children, and married Theano because, all in all, 'he was pre-
eminently skilled in the Pythagoraean doctrines'.[25] However, the
Suidas describes Theano as 'Cretan, philosopher, daughter of
Pythonaktos, wife of the great Pythagoras, from whom she had
Telauges, Mnesarchos, Myia and Arignote'.[26] It should be noted
perhaps that the term used for a woman 'philosopher' is
φιλόσοφος, just as a woman teacher is a διδάσκαλος. Words like this
are worth noting in Greek because if an individual philosopher
or teacher is mentioned by a word found only as masculine, without any defining gendered description, a woman may be possible
as a subject. Diogenes Laertius uses the rare feminine form
μαθήτρια, '(female) student', to describe Theano. This implies
that Diogenes Laertius considered Theano to be of the same
status as other μαθηταί of Pythagoras, which would naturally lead
her to become a philosopher herself, since the aim of anyone
deemed a 'student' of a philosopher is to become like their
teacher.[27]

Theano is credited with several apophthegms indicating her
exemplary modesty.[28] In one story, when a man comments that
her forearm is beautiful, she retorts: 'but it is not (for the) public'
(ἀλλ' οὐ δημόσιος).[29] Such an example of a feminine paragon of

---

Paidagogos, 2: 114: 2; Plutarch, *Moralia* 142c, 145f; Theodoret, *Therapeutike*
12: 73; Diogenes Laertius, *Lives*, 8: 42–3. References to Theano are quite
diverse and some may result from a conflation of Theano, the wife of
Pythagoras, with one or two other women students of Pythagoras.

[24] Theodoret, *Therapeutike* 2: 23, cf. Eusebius, *Praep. Evang.* 10: 14: 14.
[25] *Vita Pyth.* 36: 265.   [26] Adler (ed.), *Suidae*, ii. 688, ll. 18–20 (no. 84).
[27] Cf. the Q logion of Jesus: 'A student is not superior to his teacher, but every
one who is fully qualified (κατηρτισμένος) is as his teacher' (Luke 6: 40, cf. Matt.
10: 24). An exemplary woman student (μαθήτρια) of Jesus like Tabitha,
described in Acts 9: 36–43, would therefore, to a Graeco-Roman audience,
naturally also be a teacher of Jesus' 'philosophy'.
[28] See Holger Thesleff, *Pythagoraean Texts of the Hellenistic Period* (Abo:
Abo Akademie, 1965), 125; Stobaeus, *Anth.* 1: 10: 13, and Waithe, *Women
Philosophers*, 12–14.
[29] Clement, *Strom.* 4: 121: 2, cf. Diogenes Laertius, *Lives* 8: 43; Theodoret,
Therapeutike 12: 73.

modesty is used by Plutarch to argue for even more modesty. He notes that her arm was glimpsed as she drew her *himation* around her, indicating that she was usually well-hidden, and that 'not just the arm of the virtuous woman but also her speech too should be not public' since for a woman to speak in public is ἀπογύμνωσις, an utter exposure (or 'stripping naked') of herself, for 'in her speaking her feelings and character and disposition may be seen'.[30] A virtuous woman should then, according to Plutarch, speak in public through her husband, 'and she should not feel vexed if—like a flute-player—she sounds more impressive by means of another tongue'.[31] The tradition that Theano ran the Pythagoraean school was presumably not known to Plutarch or, if known, was rejected.

Plutarch also cites Theano as replying to the question: 'What is the duty of a wife?' with the answer: 'To please her husband.'[32] In another tradition of Theano, when asked how soon after lying with her husband should a woman attend the Thesmophoria (or alternatively be pure to go to the temple) she replies: 'From her own, right away, from another, never': ἀπὸ δὲ τοῦ ἀλλοτρίου οὐδεπώποτε.[33] In other words, Theano as a woman advocates that other women refrain from sexual activity outside their marriages. Advice on sexual matters appears here as particularly the domain of women.[34] But even more so, the advice of a respected woman to other women might seem to be more authoritative to women than that of a man. Theano therefore gets used as a weapon in the battle to control women, as countless 'exemplary'

[30] Plutarch, *Moralia* 142d.

[31] Viewed historically, the instruction that women should not be vexed seems to indicate that some women were indeed feeling vexed in this situation. Whether Plutarch gained this 'ultra-modest' perspective for women from Pythagoraean women precedents is impossible to determine, but it would be hard for Plutarch to have argued for such extreme 'modesty' (i.e. the suppression of 'virtuous' women's public voices) if Pythagoraean women were themselves widely vocal publicly.

[32] *Moralia* 145.

[33] Clement, *Strom.* 4: 121: 3; Diogenes Laertius, *Lives* 8: 43; Theodoret, *Therapeutike* 12: 73. Iamblichus ascribes this saying to Pythagoras himself, speaking to the women of Croton (*Vita Pyth.* 11: 55), and then to Deino (Theano) the wife of Brontinus, 'a woman of wise and exceptional soul', though he acknowledges here that some attribute the remark to Theano (wife of Pythagoras), 27: 132.

[34] See Hawley, 'Women Philosophers', 78.

women have been used over the ages. She is the preferred model to use to indicate to women their proper behaviour with men, both their own husbands and men in general. According to Diogenes Laertius, Theano advises a woman going in to her own husband to take off her shame along with her clothes.[35] Modesty and chastity with other men go hand in hand with immodesty in regard to one's own husband.

Theano was one of several lauded Pythagoraean women.[36] Her daughters Myia and Arignote were well known, and the latter is stated in the Suidas to be 'student of Pythagoras the great and Theano, Samian, Pythagoraean philosopher' (μαθήτρια Πυθαγόρου τοῦ μεγάλου καὶ Θεανοῦς, Σαμία, φιλόσοφος Πυθαγορική).[37] Pythagoras' daughter Damo was said to have kept safe her father's writings, and passed these on to her daughter Bistala.[38] Myia was extolled as one of the most illustrious women Pythagoraeans.[39] Lucian, in his *Praise of a Fly* (11), mentions that he could say many things about Myia the Pythagoraean were it not for the fact that her history is known to everyone.[40] Ironically, today, her history is known to absolutely no one.[41] Still, according to Pythagoras, children and old people could also participate in philosophy, and there may be here an assumption that the mentally weak are still capable of something.[42]

Pythagoraean women could be ridiculed for doing philosophy at all. According to Diogenes Laertius, comic writers of the

---

[35] Diogenes Laertius, *Lives* 8: 43.

[36] See also Porphyry, *Vita Pythag.* 19 who refers to women as well as men Pythagoraeans, the most famous being Theano.

[37] Quoting Adler (ed.), *Suidae*, i. 350, ll. 18–19 (no. 3872). See the references to Myia by Clement of Alexandria, *Strom.* 4: 121: 4; Iamblichus, *Vita Pyth.* 30: 70, 36: 26; Adler (ed.), *Suidae*, iii. 421, l. 28 (no. 1363). For Arignote, see Clement of Alexandria, *Strom.* 4: 19; Porphyry, *Vita Pyth.* 4; Adler (ed.), *Suidae*, i. 350, ll. 18–21 (no. 3872) = *PG* 117: 1226, 1335, 1353.

[38] Diogenes Laertius, *Lives* 8: 42, quoting Lysis, but cf. Porphyry, *Vita Pythag.* 4 where the children of Pythagoras are given as Telauges, Myia, and Arignote, and these three preserve the writings.

[39] Iamblichus, *Vita Pyth.* 30: 170; Porphyry, *Vita Pythag.* 4; Jerome, *Against Jovinian* PL 23, 1: 42, col. 285.

[40] πολλὰ δ᾽ ἂν εἶχον εἰπεῖν καὶ περὶ Μυίας τῆς Πυθαγοπικῆς, εἰ μὴ γνώριμος ἦν ἅπασιν ἡ κατ᾽ αὐτὴν ἱστορία, p. 92 in the Loeb edn. tr. Austin M. Harmon, *Lucian* (Cambridge, Mass.: Harvard University Press, 1961), i. 92–3.

[41] A point made by Ménage, *Historia*, 52.

[42] Hawley, 'Women Philosophers', 71, who compares this also with Plato, *Protagoras* 325a; Clement, *Strom.* 4: 58: 3; Minucius Felix, *Octavius* 16: 5.

fourth century BCE, Cratinus the Younger and Alexis, wrote pieces with the title *Pythagorizousa*, the 'Female Pythagorizer'.[43] The traditions of the exemplary modesty of Theano the wife of Pythagoras may be juxtaposed with the presentation of women Pythagoraeans as objects of ridicule. Both images of 'ultra-modest woman' and 'funny woman' can exist in a society which views women in philosophy as engaging in an activity proper to men. The first image is apologetic in that it confirms that, while a woman is philosophical, she remains a model of feminine modesty; the second tradition is antagonistic in that it simply laughs off the idea of a woman philosopher as silly. In the breaking of gendered intellectual boundaries, Pythagoraean women could be considered anomalies: exemplary or ridiculous depending on one's perspective. The literature suggests that the early Pythagoraean women were talked about, but not necessarily in the most flattering ways. The stress on Theano's exemplary modesty and catchy, submissive apophthegms may well have been the defensive measure most helpful in creating the acceptable face of female Pythagoraeanism.[44]

Aspasia

There is a rich range of presentations found in regard to one single 'philosophical' woman of fifth-century BCE Athens: Pericles' famous partner, Aspasia of Miletus.[45] The philosophical character of Aspasia results from the fact that she was associated in some way with Socrates.[46] A student of Socrates, Aeschines of

[43]   Diogenes Laertius, *Lives* 8: 37, see Hawley, 'Women Philosophers', 71 and n. 5.
[44]   For texts supposedly written by Pythagoraean women, see Ch. 9.
[45]   For traditions about Aspasia from antiquity to the present, see Madeleine A. Henry, *Prisoner of History: Aspasia of Miletus and her Biographical Tradition* (New York: OUP, 1995) and also Susan C. Jarratt, 'The First Sophists and Feminism: Discourses of the "Other"', *Hypatia*, 5 (1990), 27–41; Cheryl Glenn, 'Sex, Lies and Manuscripts: Refiguring Aspasia in the History of Rhetoric', *College Composition and Communication*, 45 (May 1994), 180–99; Elena Duvergès Blair, 'Women: The Unrecognized Teachers of the Platonic Socrates', *Ancient Philosophy*, 16 (1996), 333–50.
[46]   Clement of Alexandria, *Strom.* 4: 122: 3; Xenophon, *Oec.* 3: 14–15; Adler (ed.), *Suidae*, i. 387, ll. 15–24 (no. 4202) = 'Aspasia', PG 117, 1230; scholiast on Aristophanes, *Acharnians* 526; Plato, *Menexenus* 235e; Theodoret, *Therapeutike* 1: 17; Plutarch, *Pericles* 24. See Waithe, *Women Philosophers*, 75–81.

Sphettus, wrote a dialogue named *Aspasia* in which he described a conversation between Aspasia, Xenophon, and Xenophon's wife. The assessment of Aspasia's character here may have been mixed, or at least eroticized.[47] Plutarch cites Aeschines' *Aspasia* in noting that, after the death of Pericles, she lived with a sheep-dealer, a man of low birth.[48] Another student of Socrates, Antisthenes, wrote a dialogue entitled *Aspasia* in which Pericles' passion for her is described.[49] In Xenophon's writings, Aspasia advises on match-making and marital relationships (*Mem.* 2: 6: 36; *Oec.* 3: 14), a role which is limited but reasonably positive, following Xenophon's own views that men and women are different in character and aptitude and women's character meant that their proper place was in the home.[50] Xenophon suggests that a husband should teach his wife anything she wants to know, citing here Aspasia as an example of such a well-trained and good wife.[51] A work entitled *Aspasia* by Hegesias (*c.*250 BCE) is listed in a second-century BCE library catalogue from Rhodes, though nothing is known of it.[52] Other works using Aspasia as an example may have existed but, whether positive or negative, descriptions of Aspasia have one thing in common, as Madeleine Henry notes: '[a]ll of the fragments relevant to Aspasia refer to her sexuality and/or relationship with Pericles'.[53]

According to Clement of Alexandria and Plutarch, she was the frequent subject of comic writing.[54] These plays tend to

[47] See also Diogenes Laertius, *Lives* 2: 61–2.

[48] Plutarch, *Pericles* 24: 4.

[49] So Athenaeus, *Deipnosophistae* 5: 220d, cf. Diogenes Laertius, *Lives* 6: 16.

[50] Xenophon, *Oec.* 3: 10–16; 7: 22–8. He quotes Socrates as indicating that women lack judgement (γνώμη) and physical strength (*Symp.* 2: 8–9). Theophrastus' view was much the same, see Stobaeus, *Anth.* 2: 31: 31.

[51] Xenophon, *Oec.* 3: 10–16.

[52] See Amedeo Maiuri, *Nuova silloge epigrafica di Rodi e Cos* (Le Monnier: Facolta filologica della R. Universita di Firenze, 1925), no. 11, l. 9 above another entitled 'Alcibiades' (l. 10). [53] Henry, *Prisoner of History*, 32.

[54] Clement of Alexandria, *Strom.* 4: 122: 3; Plutarch, *Pericles* 24: 6. Plutarch notes that she is laughingly dubbed 'the new Omphale' and 'the new Deianeira' or 'Hera' in these plays. Comic playwrights known to have included humorous references to Aspasia include Cratinus, who described her as a 'dog-eyed con-cubine', Eupolis, Hermippus and Aristophanes. The latter two indicated she was a whore who kept whores. Aristophanes blames a whore-stealing incident she was involved in as beginning the Peloponnesian war, which is probably a vicious joke rather than an actual charge. For references and discussion see Henry, *Prisoner of History*, 19–28.

configure her as a whore. On the basis of Aristophanes' *Acharnians*, Plutarch and Athenaeus both comment that she was a keeper of prostitutes, and somehow caused the Peloponnesian Wars.[55] Plutarch notes also that she emulated the legendary Thargelia, whom he identified as a courtesan.[56]

Aspasia is credited as the author of the *epitaphios*, which comprises most of Plato's *Menexenus*, set in 386 BCE. The way she is presented in this work is probably satirical.[57] In the *Menexenus* Socrates recites a funeral oration that Aspasia has taught him to young Menexenus. This speech is mostly a set pattern for such an oration, which can be modified and used anywhere. Socrates expresses the view that such orations—though expert—are a kind of bewitchment and not true to the 'real world'.[58] Moreover, to make a eulogizing speech is 'not difficult' (235d): to eulogize the Peloponnesians to the Athenians or vice versa would be taxing, but not to eulogize Athenians to Athenians; even a poor rhetor could win credit for this (236a). Aspasia is introduced as Socrates' διδάσκαλος (235e, cf. ἡ διδάσκαλος 236c) and here *she* is the one who has instructed Pericles in rhetoric, as well as many other fine orators. She is credited with writing the funeral oration given by Pericles recorded by Thucydides (*The Peloponnesian War* 2: 24–46). It is unclear whether Plato wished to undermine Pericles' speech in some ironic fashion. If so, he has done so by indicating that it was an example of oratory which is not very hard to write successfully, for Athenians would acclaim any eulogizing of Athenians. Moreover, in stating that Pericles took his speech from his wife's repertoire of orations, Plato may well be poking a little fun at Pericles.[59] As for Aspasia,

---

[55] Plutarch, *Pericles* 24: 3; Athenaeus, *Deipnosophistai* 5: 219, 13: 569 (alluding to Aristophanes, *Acharn.* 524–9); and see what is stated in the *Suidas*. She is there understood to have been notorious, and dubbed Pericleia, the female Pericles.

[56] Plutarch, *Pericles* 24: 2.

[57] The question of how satirical is the *Menexenus* is debated. Edmund F. Bloedow has pointed out that Plato may be trying to deflate the 'real' Aspasia, whom he saw as a principal exponent of the rhetoric he wished to argue against, 'Aspasia and the "Mystery" of the Menexenos', *Wiener Studien* (Zeitschrift für Klassiche Philologie und Patristic, Neu Folge), 9 (1975), 32–48.

[58] Plato, *Menexenus* 234b–235c.

[59] In the *Phaedrus*, Plato attributes Pericles' real brilliance to the influence of Anaxagoras, who taught him 'high thoughts' and the 'nature of mind', which makes him 'the most perfect rhetor of all', *Phaedrus* 269e–270a.

he both praises her highly as an expert in oratory, but then punctures the praise by indicating that expertise in oratory does not necessarily count for very much. That she, as a woman, could even be so expert may itself indicate the feebleness of the enterprise. At the end of the piece, Menexenus acclaims, 'By Zeus Socrates, from what you say Aspasia is to be congratulated if though a woman she can compose such a speech!' (249d), but Menexenus' judgement has been undermined at the very opening passage. Here Socrates indicates that, while Menexenus is young, he has *finished* his studies in philosophy and is now ready to go into the political world (234a). The idea that someone could have 'done' philosophy at a young age is clearly ironic. Moreover, the idea that oratory is generally not worthy of praise parallels one of the main themes of the *Gorgias* concerning the power and limits of language. Gorgias, Polus, and Callicles, defending rhetoric, argue with Socrates, defending philosophy. The latter argues that words, in philosophy, should be intended only for the furtherance of truth.[60] It seems likely then that in the *Menexenus* Plato intended to condemn the unprincipled politics of Athens and its rhetoric.[61] Plato can use Aspasia the way he does because she is both a foreigner and a whore, an 'interchangeable commodity', as Henry puts it, which highlights the theme of interchangeability in the Menexenus.[62]

Following Plato, Plutarch identifies her as a teacher of rhetoric and somewhat modifies the Platonic view that Aspasia instructed Socrates and Pericles in such study, by stating that Socrates sometimes came to see her with his students (γνώριμοι), who also brought their wives to hear her.[63] Clement of Alexandria notes that Socrates 'led her away into philosophy and Pericles into rhetoric' (*Strom.* 4: 122: 3), implying that she was student of both. Philostratus and Alciphron record that Aspasia taught rhetoric.[64] The Suidas calls her a Sophist and teacher of rhetorical speeches (σοφίστρια ἦν καὶ διδάσκαλος λόγων

---

[60] See the discussion by Paul Gooch, *Jesus and Socrates: Word and Silence* (New Haven and London: Yale University Press, 1996), 89–93, 99–106.

[61] See Lucinda J. Coventry, 'Philosophy and Rhetoric in the Menexenus', *Journal of Hellenic Studies* 109 (1989), 1–15, cf. Blair, 'Women', 336–8.

[62] Henry, *Prisoner of History*, 34, and her discussion as a whole, pp. 32–40.

[63] Plutarch, *Pericles* 24: 3–4. The assumption by Plutarch is that Socrates had only male students.

[64] Philostratus, *Letter* 73 to Julia Augusta; Alciphron, *Letter* 4: 7: 7.

ῥητορικῶν).[65] Lucian presents Aspasia as a teacher (*De saltatione* 25), but Maximus of Tyre (24: 4; 38: 4b–d) and Synesius of Cyrene (1: 18: 59a) specify she was a teacher of erotics. Herodicus of Babylon, a student of the Cynic Crates (fl. 125 BCE) wrote an anti-Platonic tract in which Aspasia was Socrates' *erotodidaskalos*, quoting a poem by Aspasia (Athenaeus, *Deip.* 5: 219b–e). Hermesianax, in his *Leontion*, apparently wrote of Socrates' passion for her (Athenaeus, *Deip.* 13: 597a–99c). The notion that she taught erotics may derive from Aeschines' *Aspasia* in which Socrates most likely cited Aspasia to demonstrate that *eros* can be an instrument of moral improvement.[66] This is interesting given the figure of Diotima in Plato's *Symposium*, to which we now turn.

Diotima

In Plato's *Symposium* (*c*.385 BCE) Socrates is taught the philosophy of love (*erōs*) by Diotima of Mantinea.[67] 'Love' being so critical in the Platonic system, it is perhaps significant that this knowledge is passed on to Socrates by a woman. Luce Irigaray notes that Diotima defines Eros as a mediator for '[a]ll love is seen as creation and potentially divine, a path between the condition of the mortal and that of the immortal',[68] though later on in the *Symposium*, '[l]ove becomes political wisdom, the wisdom of order in the city, not the intermediary state that inhabits lovers and transports them from the condition of mortals to that of immortals. Love becomes a kind of *raison d'état*.'[69] This slight dissonance may indicate that there is a real Diotima who taught

---

[65] Adler (ed.), *Suidae*, i. 387, ll. 23–4 (no. 4202).

[66] So Barbara Ehlers, *Eine vorplatonische Deutung des sokratischen Eros: Der Dialog Aspasia des sokratikers Aischines* (*Zetemata*, 41; Munich: Beck, 1966).

[67] Plato, *Symp.* 201d–212a, see also Lucian, *Eunuchus* 7; *Pro Imag.* 19, Aristides, *Orationes* 46; Maximus of Tyre, *Dissertation* 24: 4, 7 and 27: 4; Themistius calls her 'the teacher of Socrates', *Orationes* 165d; Proclus, *Commentary on Plato's Timaeus*, 2: 53, 59; 3: 295; 5: 281; *Commentary on Plato's Republic* 8: 248; 9: 255; 16: 337.

[68] Irigaray, 'Sorcerer Love', 25, and see also Catherine Osborne, *Eros Unveiled: Plato and the God of Love* (Oxford: Clarendon Press, 1994). See also Waithe, *Women Philosophers*, 83–91 who argues that Diotima's philosophy differs from Plato's in its conceptualization of 'the good', of immortality, and *eros* itself.

[69] Ibid. 30.

a philosophy of *erōs*. David Halperin has argued, however, that there are literary reasons why the teacher is a woman in this text. As Halperin notes: 'Gender enters the text of Plato's *Symposium* . . . as part of a larger figurative project whose aim is to represent the institutional and psychological conditions for the proper practice of (male) philosophizing'.[70] To what extent Diotima is historical, or simply a reconstituted Aspasia, may be impossible to say, but she appears as a type of 'wise woman', particularly adept at matters of *erōs*: a paradigm within the discourse of *philosophia*.[71]

The 'wise woman' type, who could instruct men, was by no means accepted by all. The fifth-century CE Christian writer Theodoret, clearly baffled by Socrates' apparent acceptance of tuition by Aspasia and Diotima as reported by Plato, notes that this shows how low he would stoop to pursue philosophy, for 'he was even proud of having learnt wisdom from women, like Diotima and Aspasia'.[72]

In the figure of Aspasia, we get a range of portrayals which present her in some way as the clever, sexy, 'other' woman who is somewhat 'philosophical' but not a philosopher, strictly speaking. She's either a good wife like Theano or a whore/courtesan like Thargelia. Her association with Socrates—who was in many ways the 'perfect' philosopher type—make her a powerful model in terms of the way women were configured in the discourse of *philosophia*. With Diotima, the portrayal is more unidimensional and mysterious, but in the case of both there is a link between the 'philosophical' woman and the erotic.

---

[70] David Halperin, 'Why is Diotima a Woman?', in his *One Hundred Years of Homosexuality and Other Essays on Greek Love* (New York: Routledge, 1989), 113–51, at 150.

[71] For an argument in favour of Diotima's historicity, see Waithe, *Women Philosophers*, 92–108. Diotima's speech is given an explicit tradition history in the text as being given orally to Socrates, who then passed it on to the participants of the symposium including Aristodemus, who passed it on to Apollodorus, Plato writing it down only at some stage much later on. The inconsistencies may indicate that Plato is modifying a received tradition, rather than creating a dialogue from scratch which would perhaps not have had these inconsistencies. The inconsistencies actually work in favour of the view that there was a historical figure (perhaps actually Aspasia?) who has been reshaped in accordance with the Platonic schema.

[72] Theodoret, *Therapeutike* 1: 17.

Aspasia and Diotima in Art

Aspasia is depicted on drawings of two gemstones from (late) antiquity which survived into the seventeenth century (see Figures 11 and 12). The drawings are found in the *Iconografia* of Giovanni Angelo Canini (Rome: Nella Stamparia d'Ignatio de 'Lazari, 1669) and in Giovanni Pietro Bellori's *Veterum Illustrium Philosophorum, Rhetorum, et Oratorum Imagines* (Rome, apud Io: Jacobum de Rubeis ad Templum Sta. Mariae de Pace suis sumptibus & cura, cum Privilegio Summi Pontificis, 1685).[73] The first gemstone (Figure 11) is number XCII in Canini's volume and is listed as 'Aspasia diaspro delli Sig. Rondanini'. Bellori's citation identifies it as a jasper gem belonging to Felicia Rondanina.[74] The inscription reads *ΑϹΠΑϹΟΥ*, reflecting a form of her name 'Aspaso' rather than 'Aspasia'. The second (Figure 12) is number XCIII in the same volume, and is listed as 'Aspasia Gemma del Sig. Cardinale Barberini'.[75] The inscription reads *ΑΠΟΛΛΟΔΟΤΟΥΛΙΘΟ*, 'stone given by Apollo'.

The helmeted figure in profile was used frequently of male military heroes, as is shown by numerous examples in Canini's collection, including images on gemstones of Alexander the Great and Philip of Macedon.[76] But Aspasia is clearly not a male military hero here: she is Athena. The image reflects Phidias' great statue of Athena which stood in the Parthenon. Pausanias (1: 24: 5–7) describes this as being of gold and ivory, having a sphinx in the middle and griffins on either side of the helmet, with a breastplate depicting Medusa, made of ivory. The Varvakeion Athena, now in the National Museum of Athens (a second-century CE copy of the Parthenon Athena), provides more details, and shows that Athena was depicted with long flowing hair and jewellery (Figure 13).[77] The iconographic correlation between the gemstone images of Aspasia and the Varvakeion Athena are: female, flowing hair, earrings, helmet, sphinx (gemstone 1 only, hidden in gemstone 2 but indicated by plumes), griffin, feathery

---

[73] Aspasia's picture here is the third plate of the section on rhetors (s. 3).

[74] It is marked with the Vatican library number 73.

[75] Pp. 122 and 123.

[76] See pls. XIII, XXIV, XXXIII, XXXV, LV, LXXXIV.

[77] This statue is made of marble and stands 1.10 m high. It was found in 1880 in the Varvakeion gymnasium.

11. Drawing of late antique (?) portrait gemstone of Aspasia with inscription *ΑΣΠΑΣΟΥ* (Houghton Library, Harvard University); Giovanni Angelo Canini, *Iconografia* (Rome: Nella stamperia d'Ignatio de'Lazari, 1669), number XCII; typ. 625.69.259F, Department of Printing and Graphic Arts, Houghton Library, Harvard College Library

12. Drawing of late antique (?) portrait gemstone of Aspasia with inscription *ΑΠΟΛΛΟΔΟΤΟΥΛΙΘΟ* (Houghton Library, Harvard University); Giovanni Angelo Canini, *Iconografia* (Rome: Nella stamperia d'Ignatio de'Lazari, 1669), number XCIII; typ. 625.69.259F, Department of Printing and Graphic Arts, Houghton Library, Harvard College Library

13. The Varvakeion Athena, now in the National Museum of Athens, 2nd-century Roman copy. Drawing from E. H. Blakeney, *A Smaller Classical Dictionary* (London: J. M. Dent, 1910), 612

plumes sticking out of the sphinx and griffin, and breastplate depicting Medusa, with snakes (gemstone 1).[78]

An image equating Aspasia with Athena can only be considered positive.[79] It may be from a Hellenistic context, since at this time there seems to have been a trend to view the *Menexenus* as a serious piece, a *politikos logos* that articulates Athens' self-image.[80] Henry notes that the *Menexenus* was repeatedly recited in antiquity, and that non-ironic readings began in the Hellenistic period.[81] Aspasia as author of the *epitaphios* becomes then Aspasia who is somehow representative of Athens.

A portrait herm of Aspasia was found in Italy in 1777. It is inscribed at the base with the name *ΑΣΠΑΣΙΑ*, and is now in the Vatican Museum (Salle della Muse, inv. 272). It depicts a woman with covered head, and is probably a Roman copy of a Greek original. It may be a simple grave portrait of the real Aspasia, as mentioned by Pausanias (1: 23: 1).[82] This image coheres with the more respectable presentation of Aspasia we find in Xenophon.

A Roman sarcophagus discovered in the eighteenth century, which is now in the Louvre, depicts in relief a woman and Socrates conversing near an archway (Figure 14). Since Socrates is in the sitting, 'teaching', position, with his hand raised expressively, it seems likely that this is a representation of Socrates instructing a woman student in philosophy. She leans against a

[78] Unfortunately, Henry, *Prisoner of History*, does not notice the iconography of Athena here and states: 'On the lady's helmet is painted a four-horse chariot, and above the chariot, Pegasus and the sphinx, a fantastic iconography that cannot possibly have come from classical antiquity' (p. 89). She therefore does not place the gemstones with the evidence from antiquity. The artist that drew gemstone 1 has rendered the griffin to look like a winged Pegasus, though in gemstone 2 it is easier to see that it is indeed a griffin: a beast that looked like a lion but with the beak of an eagle and wings. Gemstone 2 is otherwise a more simplified depiction.

[79] One wonders whether there was an idea that Aspasia was in fact the model for Phidias' statue.

[80] Cf. Cicero, *Orat.* 151.

[81] Henry, *Prisoner of History*, 34, 146 n. 17.

[82] See Gisela Richter, *The Portraits of the Greeks*, 3 vols. (London: Phaidon, 1943), i. 41, 154–5, pl. 875–6. Brunilde S. Ridgway, *The Severe Style in Greek Sculpture* (Princeton: Princeton University Press, 1970), 65–88, has argued that it is a type of portrait deriving from Calamis the Elder's 5th-cent. statue of Aphrodite Sosandra on the Acropolis. See also Henry, *Prisoner of History*, 17–18 and her fig. 1.1.

14. 'Sarcophage des Muses': Roman marble sarcophagus depicting Socrates and a woman (Louvre Museum, Paris, no. 93DE1149)

balustrade and listens intently.[83] Clement of Alexandria believed that Socrates taught Aspasia, and this may depict the instruction. If so, Aspasia can be seen as a type of woman student of philosophy. She is dressed modestly, with a *himation* over her head and well-wrapped around the body.

A pair of Alexandrian bone carvings, dated to the third–fourth centuries, now in the Boston Museum of Fine Arts, depict Socrates with a woman holding a wreath in her right hand (Figure 15).[84] As with the relief from the Louvre sarcophagus, the woman is dressed modestly with a *himation* over her head, but she is swaying in a way that suggested to Cornelius C. Vermeule III 'the animation of an accomplished courtesan or dancer'.[85] It seems a curious juxtaposition to have a woman covered up and yet swaying like a courtesan, while holding a wreath. She may be holding something in her left hand, positioned above her shoulder. I am not sure the sway itself is necessarily significant here, but may be simply an attempt by the artist to give the figure some movement.

A depiction of a woman teaching Socrates was found in 1882, in a bronze relief from Pompeii, now in the Museo Nazionale di Napoli (see Figure 16).[86] The same image is found on part of a handle attachment of two silvered terracotta pails, now also in Naples, and dated to the third to second centuries BCE, meaning

---

[83] See Richter, *Portraits*, i. 118(k), who identifies the woman as a 'muse'; ii. 19–20, fig. 21; Henry, *Prisoner of History*, 80; Reinhard Kekule von Stradonitz, 'Die Bildnisse des Sokrates', *Abhandlungen der preussischen Akademie der Wissenschaften philosophische-historische Klasse* (1908), 1–58, at 58.

[84] The image of the woman is found in two forms, inventoried as nos. 57.693 and 57.694. For discussion see Cornelius C. Vermeule III, 'Socrates and Aspasia: New Portraits of Late Antiquity', *Classical Journal*, 54 (1958), 49–55, at 52–4. The reliefs were set in caskets and used as a veneer for ceremonial furniture.

[85] Vermeule, 'Socrates and Aspasia', 52.

[86] See Richter, *Portraits*, i. 117(j) and discussion in Paolino Mingazzini, 'Su due oggetti in terracotta raffigurante Socrate', *La Parola del Passato: Rivista di Studi Antichi*, 134 (1970), 351–8, following the identification by Otto Jahn, 'Socrate et Diotime: Bas-relief de bronze', *Annales de l'Institut Archéologique*, 13 (1841), 1–24, and cf. Karl Schefold, *Die Bildnisse der antiken Dichter, Redner, under Denker* (Basle: Benno Schwabe, 1943), 162. See also Waithe, *Women Philosophers*, 102–5. The bronze plate was one of three covering a wooden box found in a fragmentary state. The other two bronzes depict funerary motifs, which gives us the heady mixture of love and death. Waithe (104–5) thinks the box contained a scroll of the *Symposium*.

15. Bone furniture pendant depicting woman with a wreath,
accompanying another pendant depicting Socrates (Museum of Fine
Arts, Boston, no. BFA 57.693: John Michael Rodocanachi Fund,
1957)

16. Bronze relief from Pompeii. Woman sitting down and addressing Socrates, with winged Eros behind (Museo Archeologico Nazionale di Napoli)

that this relief image was one which had quite a long history.[87] The woman teacher sits on the left on a cushioned stool. She leans forward earnestly and raises her right hand, gesturing as she speaks, though in it she holds some kind of cloth or wreath, offered to Socrates. Winged Eros stands behind reading a scroll (or carrying a box), while Socrates leans on a stick, with one hand on his hip, listening intently to her discourse. The woman is portrayed as serious and authoritative, while Socrates is depicted as pondering her words in silence. The woman, with her bare head and arms, easy pose, and crossed legs, is probably here depicted as a *hetaira*,[88] but she is also someone whom the viewer is forced to consider a worthy speaker. The candidates for the identity of

[87] Richter, *Portraits*, i. 117(i).
[88] According to Jahn, the crossing of the legs 'était considéré comme une posture indécente' in antiquity, p. 3.

the woman would be Aspasia or Diotima. Diotima is not in fact specifically identified as a *hetaira* in the *Symposium*, though this may have been assumed. There was another *hetaira* associated with Socrates: Theodote. In Xenophon's *Memorabilia* Socrates visits her and they talk about seduction (*Mem.* 3: 11, cf. 2: 6: 28–39) while she is posing in scant attire for a painter (cf. Athenaeus, *Deip.* 5: 220e–f; 12: 535c; 13: 588d). However, it seems most likely that the woman should be identified with Diotima. In Lucian's *Pro Imaginibus* 19, Diotima is described as a model of the qualities of 'general intelligence and power to give counsel'. Such a model may be shown here, perhaps with the implication that she is giving good counsel as regards *erōs*, erotic love. As such, there may be a kind of traditional motif here: the courtesan—or any 'knowing woman'—giving good counsel in matters of the heart to the man who is wise enough to listen.[89]

The Platonists

Given Plato's use of the character of Diotima in the *Symposium*, and his notions that men and women should both be educated (*Rep.* 5: 452a, *Leg.* 804c) and could rule an ideal world together with men (who shared a 'community of wives and children'),[90] it is not surprising to find that women are associated with Plato's Academy.[91] The Pythagoraean Perictione was considered to be

[89] For Diotima there may be another image worth noting, though not philosophical: a sculpted relief dated to *c*.400 BCE found in the agora of Mantinea, now in the National Museum of Athens. In this relief, the women holds a liver in her hands, identifying her as a kind of diviner adept at extispicy.

[90] For mention of the community of women/wives see: *Rep.* 423e, 457d, 458c–d, 460b–d, 540, 543.

[91] See Hawley, 'Women Philosophers', 73. The views of Plato about women are not our subject here, but see Giulia Sissa, 'The Sexual Philosophies of Plato and Aristotle', in Paula Schmitt Pantel (ed.), *A History of Women in the West*, i. *From Ancient Goddesses to Christian Saints*, tr. Arthur Goldhammer of *Storia delle Donne in Occidente*, i. *L'Antichità* (Rome and Bari: Gius. Laterza & Figli Spa, 1990, Cambridge, Mass.: Belknap of Harvard University Press, 1992), 46–81; Julia Annas, 'Plato's *Republic* and Feminism', *Philosophy* 51 (1976), 307–21; Sarah B. Pomeroy, 'Feminism in Book V of Plato's *Republic*', *Apeiron*, 8 (1974), 32–5; D. Wender, 'Plato: Misogynist, Paedophile and Feminist', *Arethusa*, 6 (1973), 75–90, and the articles in Bat-Ami Bar On (ed.), *Engendering Origins: Critical Feminist Readings in Plato and Aristotle* (Albany: State University of New York Press, 1994), 1–96.

Plato's mother.[92] Diogenes Laertius mentions two women, Axiothea of Philesia and Lasthenia of Mantinea, who were fourth-century BCE μαθήτριαι, 'students', of Plato and his successor Speusippus.[93] A papyrus fragment (P.Oxy 42: 3656) mentions a woman who studied under Plato, Speusippus, and Menedemus, who may be one of these women.[94] Axiothea is said by Themistius to have read Plato's *Republic*, and then travelled from Arcadia to Athens to be his student.[95] She is said by Dicaearchus to have dressed as a man in order to gain acceptance into Plato's Academy.[96] This cross-dressing may indicate that she fooled Plato into supposing she was a man, given how this functions as a frequent motif in Greek drama. It also could have a comic touch, as in the plays of Aristophanes.[97] As for Lasthenia, nothing is stated in extant sources about a similar masculine dress being worn by her but, quoting a letter of Dionysius to Speusippus, Diogenes Laertius uses Lasthenia negatively as illustrating Speusippus' avarice. He has Dionysius say, snidely, that 'we may apprehend your wisdom from the Arcadian woman who is your student'. He goes on to indicate that 'his wisdom' consists of levying payment on all people who come to hear philosophy (taught by her) and collecting this whether they are willing or not, when Plato provided his services gratis.[98] Lasthenia is also described as having an affair with Speusippus, in accounts which were designed to undermine him.[99] The use of a woman student—now teacher—of Speusippus as a means of undermining the male philosopher is interesting, and alerts us to a type of woman philosopher who is

---

[92] Waithe, *Women Philosophers*, 68–71, cf. Diogenes Laertius, *Lives* 3: 1; Plato, *Ep.*12.

[93] Diogenes Laertius, *Lives* 3: 46; 4: 2.

[94] See Hawley, 'Women Philosophers', 73–4.

[95] Themistius, *Orations* 23: 295c.

[96] Dicaearchus, in Diogenes Laertius, *Lives* 3: 46, cf. Clement of Alexandria, *Strom.* 4: 122: 2.

[97] Aristophanes certainly ridiculed notions like those found in Plato in e.g. the *Ecclesiazusae*, 'Council Women'. Hawley puts down the characterization of Axiothea as dressing like a man to '[t]he notoriety of the discussion of the equality of the sexes in Plato's *Republic*': Hawley, 'Women Philosophers', 73.

[98] Diogenes Laertius, *Lives* 4: 2.

[99] The accusation also came from Dionysus of Syracuse, so Diogenes Laertius, *Lives* 4: 2; Athenaeus, *Deipnosophistai* 7: 279e.

conceived as 'bad'. The accusations also underline the expectation that a student, whether μαθήτρια or μαθητής, graduated, as
it were, as an independent διδάσκαλος and θιλόσοφος capable of
teaching the philosophy that they had learnt and that the close
relationship expected between teacher and student meant that
people would assume sexual interaction could have taken place.

Hipparchia and the Cynics

In the early Cynic school the woman philosopher, Hipparchia, is
described by Diogenes Laertius as falling madly in love with
the Cynic Crates (fl. 328–325 BCE) along with his discourses.[100]
Her brother Metrocles was also a philosopher, a student of
Theophrastus at the Lyceum, and the implication may be that he
instructed her in philosophy prior to her marriage to Crates and
very public life.[101] She is the only woman philosopher to have her
own section in Laertius' account, and she is called a *philosophos*
of whom many stories were told: καὶ ταῦτα μὲν καὶ ἄλλα μυρία τῆς
φιλοσόφου.[102] But her motives for adopting the Cynic way of life
are in this description clearly mixed. Laertius indicates she
wanted to be just exactly like Crates and inseparable from him,
wearing the same clothing as him (as another cross-dresser),
doing everything with him, going to the same symposia even—a
kind of Yoko Ono to Crates' John Lennon. The union of Crates
and Hipparchia was the famous 'dog-marriage' looked on with
fascination and disgust. Crates and Hipparchia apparently had
two children, a son[103] and a daughter, whom Crates apparently

---

[100] Diogenes Laertius, *Lives* 96–8; see also Epictetus, *Discourses* 3: 22: 76,
Theodoret, *Therapeutike* 12: 49; Clement of Alexandria, *Strom.* 4: 121: 6,
Antipater of Sidon, *Anthology* 3: 12: 52; Adler (ed.), *Suidae*, ii. 657, ll. 13–19
(no. 517) = 'Hipparchia', *PG* 117: 1275.

[101] Diogenes Laertius, *Lives* 6: 94, 96–8.

[102] *Lives* 6: 98. Despite living on in memory and having many stories told
about her, her works have not survived. The *Suidas* lists three works:
Philosophical Hypotheses, *Epicheiremata*, and *Questions to Theodorus*. One
should probably not take from the example of Hipparchia an inference that
women were much in evidence in the Cynic school, given the blatant misogyny
of certain sayings in the tradition of Diogenes of Sinope: 'On seeing a woman in
a litter, he said, "the cage is not in keeping with what's inside!"' (Diogenes
Laertius, *Lives* 6: 51) or worse: 'On seeing women hanged from an olive tree, "If
only all trees bore such fruit"' (ibid. 52).   [103] Ibid. 88.

gave in a trial marriage.[104] The latter action was again an example of his complete outrageousness.

Hipparchia's presence at symposia already places her close to the 'courtesan', *hetaira*, category, since in Greece of the fourth century BCE the women who sat at the same table as men at symposia were not respectable wives of the household. Nakedness is a repeated motif in Laertius' story.[105] Crates confronts the lovesick Hipparchia by taking off all his clothes and stating: 'This is the bridegroom. Here are his possessions.'[106] Hipparchia does not run away in utter embarrassment, which would really be an appropriate action for a genteel woman, but takes him as her husband. In the next paragraph, Theodorus tries to strip her of her *himation* at a symposium, and, according to the rather disapproving Laertius, 'Hipparchia was not alarmed or disturbed as a woman.'[107] Her lifestyle with Crates in public (ἐν τῷ φανερῷ συνεγίνετο) is here linked with nakedness and lack of modesty unbecoming to the woman of wealth and high birth that she was.[108] This notion is found in other writers also. The couple allegedly lived in the stoa of Athens, according to Musonius Rufus.[109] Apuleius notes that the couple did not only live there, but had sex there publicly in broad daylight.[110] The Cynic ideal of shamelessness, *anaideia*, here in evidence, was at odds with the feminine ideal of modesty. If modesty was natural to good women, then presumably a Cynic woman who exhibited shamelessness was not a good woman, in any conventional sense.

[104] Ibid. 93.

[105] The nakedness image of 'liberated' women is found already in Plato's *Republic*, where he devotes considerable space to promoting the idea that women should exercise naked with men in the gymnasium and that one should not laugh at the notion (assuming that all men would laugh at it). Indeed the image of women exercising naked frames Plato's entire discussion of the (almost) equality of the sexes: *Rep.* 452a–457b.

[106] *Lives* 6: 96.

[107] Ibid. 97. It is possible that the dramatic encounter between Theodorus and Hipparchia in Diogenes Laertius' account actually comes from her work against Theodorus, or else is a *reductio ad absurdum* of a philosophical debate between the two, set appropriately in a symposium.

[108] *Lives* 6: 96–7.

[109] Musonius Rufus, 14: 4, answering the question: 'Is marriage a handicap for the pursuit of philosophy?' See Lutz, *Roman Socrates*, 91–3.

[110] Apuleius, *Florida* 2: 49.

Hipparchia appears to have come from a 'good' wealthy family. In one epigram attributed to Hipparchia preserved by Antipater of Sidon, and apparently to be found on her tomb in Boeotia, she identifies herself as leaving behind the garb of a wealthy woman in order to dress simply and sleep on the ground.[111] It reads:

I Hipparchia have not followed the customary practices of the female sex, but with a masculine heart I have followed the strong dogs. The brooch which fastens a garment, or the well-clad foot, or the headband scented with perfume have not given me pleasure, but rather a stick, and bare feet, whatever scrap cloth clings around my limbs, and the hard ground instead of a bed. Still my life is better than that of the Menalian girl, for hunting is not as good as seeking wisdom.

If this epigram was indeed on her tomb, it is curious that the most striking aspect of Hipparchia that was identified is that she did not look like an elite woman should look. The comic writer Menander (third century BCE) dismissively wrote that Hipparchia 'went around in an old cloak'.[112]

Moreover, she is presented as important only in her relationship with Crates. Her portrayal adds colour and sexiness to the already rather bizarre traditions about Crates. Men within the Cynic tradition were more likely to be unmarried. Epictetus notes that Crates was the exception to the rule, because his marriage arose out of erotic love (ἐξ ἔρωτος) and his wife was 'another Crates'.[113] Freelance unmarried wandering women Cynics are not evidenced in the discourse on *philosophia*.[114] Hipparchia is presented as one of a kind.

---

[111] *Anthologia Palatina* 7: 413.

[112] Didumi, frag. 117k in *Menandri Quae supersunt*, ed. Alfred Koerte (Leipzig: Teubner, 1959).

[113] *Disc.* 3: 22: 76.

[114] In Cynic literature, women are often associated with materialism. In the *Cynic Epistles* (ed. Malherbe), 'Crates' addresses *Ep.* 28 to Hipparchia to warn her against backsliding and is disapproving of her making him a nice cloak, which he sends back (*Ep.* 30), though the epistles do insist that women are 'not by nature worse than men' (*Ep.* 28–9) and see *Ep.* 31, 32, and 33: letters addressed to Hipparchia advising an austere life for her and her unborn child. Crates' marriage to Hipparchia is exceptional given that Cynics generally spurned marriage as troublesome (*Ep.* 47), though apparently Diogenes of Sinope advocated a 'community of wives' (6: 72). There seems to be an assumption that women did not independently take up a Cynic lifestyle.

The Epicureans

In the Epicurean 'Garden' (early fourth century BCE) women students are referred to directly. Epicurus may have had a student named Themista of Lampsacus, wife of Leontius,[115] and some others, including Leontium.[116] Cicero, in his tirade against Piso, damns Themista with faint praise by stating, 'though you may be *wiser* than Themiste' (that is, not very wise).[117] As regards Leontium, Athenaeus, in his *Deipnosophistai*, identifies her as someone who philosophized, but also one who was well-known as a courtesan, and Epicurus' mistress.[118] He goes on to say that she played up to 'all the Epicureans in their gardens (pl.) right in front of Epicurus', for which he cites a letter of Epicurus to Hermarchus (which may have been spurious). Elsewhere, Leontium is associated with Metrodorus (*c*.330–277 BCE), possibly as his wife,[119] though Theon refers to her as the 'courtesan Leontium who philosophized'.[120] She was the author of a work replying to Aristotle's pupil Theophrastus (fourth century BCE), which Cicero scorned as indicative of the licence of the Epicureans: a school that would permit this 'little whore' to write such a work was itself outrageous, despite the fact that she wrote, as he admitted, in 'fine Attic prose'.[121]

Leontium was presented as the courtesan lover as well as student of Epicurus in literature that smacks of sexual fantasy.[122] She appears sometimes also as the lover of Metrodorus, not his

[115] Diogenes Laertius, *Lives* 10: 5, 25, 26; Lactantius, *Divine Institutes* 3: 25: 15 (who states that she was the only woman to philosophize); Clement, *Strom.* 4: 121: 4; Cicero, *In Pisonem* 26: 63 and *De Finibus* 2: 21: 68.

[116] Diogenes Laertius, *Lives* 10: 4–7, 23. See discussion by Hawley, 'Women Philosophers', 79–81. Jane McIntosh Snyder points out that all the women associated with Epicurus have courtesan names, *The Woman and the Lyre: Women Writers in Classical Greece and Rome* (Carbondale and Edwardsville, Ill.: Southern Illinois University Press, 1989), 105.   [117] *Speeches* 26: 217.

[118] Athenaeus, *Deipnosophistai* 13: 588b, 593b, and see Plutarch, *Moralia: How a Pleasant Life is Impossible According to Epicurus* 1089c, 1098b; *Whether it is Rightly Said that One Should Live Alone* 1129b.

[119] Diogenes Laertius, *Lives* 10: 6, 23; cf. Jerome, *Against Jovinian* 1: 48; Clement of Alexandria, *Strom.* 2: 138: 6.

[120] Theon, *Progymnasmata* 8.

[121] Cicero, *Natura Deorum* 1: 93; cf. Pliny, *Nat. Hist.* Praefatio 29: 'I do not know how a woman has dared to write against Theophrastus!' See discussion by Hawley, 'Women Philosophers', 80, and McIntosh Snyder, *Woman and the Lyre*, 101–5.   [122] Summarized in Diogenes Laertius, *Lives*, 10: 5–6.

wife.[123] It should be remembered that most of our evidence of possible women students of Epicurus is likely drawn from Theodorus' *Against Epicurus* or from a denunciation of the philosopher by Diotimus the Stoic, who published fifty 'scandalous letters' apparently written by Epicurus, which appear also to have been used by other anti-Epicureans such as Posidonius the Stoic, Nicolaus, Sotion (in a work entitled *Dioclean Refutations*), and Dionysius of Halicarnassus,[124] so that it is quite difficult to know whether Epicurus' purported writing of (amorous) letters to these women may indicate he was their teacher, or just a philandering lecher, or whether the entire corpus of letters between Epicurus and women was an invention by people who wished to discredit him via a construction which defined all of his possible women students as no more than whores.

Another opponent of Epicurus criticized the philosopher for allowing Leontium to take the leadership, *prostasia*, of the community.[125] This is designed to undermine the credibility of Epicureanism. Here a woman leader points to the weakness of the entire philosophy.

Leontium was the subject of a work of art. According to Pliny the Elder, she was painted by Aristides Thebanus; among the works of the fourth-century BCE artist he lists 'Epicurus' Leontium thinking' (*Leontium Epicuri cogitantem*).[126] Hawley comments on this that the possessive distinguishes her from others bearing the same courtesan name, and that the 'verb used *cogito* . . . might imply that she was depicted in a normally masculine pose of philosophic contemplation'.[127] This is interesting in view of the evidence of the Boscoreale mural, from the Villa of Fannius Sinistor (*c*.40 BCE), now in the Museo Nazionale di Napoli, which shows a rather masculine woman with bare arms looking at a philosopher and thinking hard (see Figure 17). The

---

[123] Diogenes Laertius, *Lives* 10: 23, cf. Theon, *Progymnasmata* 8.

[124] So Diogenes Laertius, *Lives* 10: 3, 5.

[125] Christian Jensen, 'Ein neuer Brief Epikurs', *Abhandlungen der Gesellschaft der Wissenschaften zu Göttingen Philologisch-Historische Klasse*, 3/5 (Berlin: Weidmannsche Buchhandlung, 1933), 1–94. Jensen identifies a letter of Epicurus in Philodemus' Περὶ κακιῶν, see his manuscripts N and Dis. II Col. II, pp. 16–17. The criticisms may come from Timocrates.

[126] Pliny, *Nat. Hist.* 35: 99, cf. Ménage, *Historia*, 44.

[127] Hawley, 'Women Philosophers', 86 n. 42.

17. Boscoreale mural of philosopher, Macedonian and woman (Museo Archaeologico di Napoli)

mural is most likely a copy of a Hellenistic original, but quite what it depicts is uncertain. The figures have been identified as Menedemus of Eretria, a student of Phaedo's school,[128] and two members of the Macedonian royal family: King Antigonus Gonatas and his mother Queen Phila, wife of King Demetrius.[129] Alternatively, and more likely, the mural may depict a young Alexander (behind) fixing his long pike (sarissa) into the soil of Asia, with the philosopher Aristotle coming towards Asia, and a personification of Asia as a 'woman thinking' in the foreground. The figure behind is identified as Macedonian since he is depicted in Macedonian costume.[130] He carries the Macedonian shield with a star at its centre, and his youthfulness definitely suggests Alexander. The water may depict the Hellespont.[131] Whatever the case, the woman figure is clearly a type: an image of a student/philosopher, who gazes pensively at the philosopher approaching. It may be significant here that Phila is remembered as a magnanimous and intelligent queen.[132] However, this identification of the woman as a royal figure may be disputed. She has large features, a strong neck and muscled arms clearly exposed to view. Not only her arms, but her neck and under her arms are revealed by a rather loose-fitting garment. The exposure of her body does not seem quite appropriate for a queen, and may be better understood in terms of a personification of Asia, for which the artist has used a 'thinking courtesan'. The artistic representation of a thinking, philosophical woman is then eroticized. She is a *hetaira*. The model of Leontium thinking may well have influenced this depiction.

[128] Diogenes Laertius, *Lives* 2: 125–44.

[129] See Jean Charbonneaux, Roland Martin and François Villard, *Hellenistic Art (30–50 BC)*, tr. Peter Green of *Grèce hellenistique* (New York: G. Braziller, 1973), 134–6; Pomeroy, *Women in Hellenistic Egypt*, 66. Pomeroy notes that 'Phila' is depicted as 'showing much more interest than Antigonus' in the philosopher (assuming that the background figure is Antigonus). Indeed the background figure is showing no interest at all in the philosopher, and considerable interest in the foreground woman.

[130] Charbonneaux *et al.* comment that 'the royal personages' are 'in Macedonian costume', p. 135.

[131] Nicholas G. L. Hammond, *The Genius of Alexander the Great* (Chapel Hill, NC: University of North Carolina Press, 1997), 65, 207 n. 7.

[132] Diodorus Siculus, *Bibl. Hist.* 19: 59: 4, see Pomeroy, *Women in Hellenistic Egypt*, 15, 59, 66, 177 n. 53.

The Stoics

The Stoics accepted that *virtue* was attainable by both sexes,[133] though access to virtue does not necessarily lead to equality in practice. According to Diogenes Laertius, Zeno of Citium (333–261 BCE) advocated a 'community of wives' (7: 33), as did Chrysippus his student (7: 131).[134] Zeno is said to have advocated equal education for slaves and free, men and women.[135] This may have given rise to the tradition, cited as coming from his critic Cassius the Sceptic, that Zeno advocated men and women wearing the same dress, in which some of each part of the body should be exposed.[136] The idea that Stoic women went along with a dress code that resulted in exposure of the body immediately casts aspersions on their feminine modesty. As we saw, in the tradition of the student of Cleanthes, Chrysippus, there is a reference to an 'old/senior woman' (ἡ πρεσβῦτις) who sat next to him while he studied, an indication that she herself was a student of Cleanthes.[137] Nothing otherwise is said of early Stoic women.

Given that Stoicism was by far the leading philosophy in Rome, and its empire, the example of Stoicism is possibly the most important to consider. Named Stoic women are hard to find, but women learning (Stoic) philosophy are referred to in a number of places. Seneca (4 BCE–65 CE) accepted that women could learn philosophy as a healing refuge to offset sorrow.[138] In a letter to his unhappy mother, Seneca laments that his old-fashioned father would not allow his mother to acquire philosophy, since his father was reacting to women who used philosophy to display their learning in an unbecoming way. Such evidence

---

[133] Cleanthes, Zeno's successor, apparently wrote a piece titled: *On the Thesis that Virtue is the Same in Man and Woman* (Diogenes Laertius, *Lives* 7: 175).

[134] It is possible that the origin of this notion, though Platonic in its principal articulation, does indeed go back to Socrates, and is picked up by numerous philosophers in the succeeding centuries. See also Peter Simpson, 'Aristotle's Criticism of Socrates' Community of Wives and Children', *Apeiron*, 24 (1991), 99–114; Robert Mayhew, 'Aristotle's Criticism of Plato's Communism of Women and Children', *Apeiron*, 29 (1996), 231–48.

[135] Sextus Empiricus, *Hypotyp.* 3: 245; *Adversus Mathematicus* 9: 190, Diogenes Laertius, *Lives* 7: 12.

[136] Diogenes Laertius, *Lives* 7: 34, cf. 6: 65.

[137] Ibid. 181, citing Diocles.

[138] Seneca, *Ad Helviam Matrem* 17: 3.

suggests that women in the elite first-century Roman circles in which Seneca moved were acquiring philosophy, and that some men found their knowledge, exhibited publicly, rather offensive. The Stoics in particular were renowned for promoting 'plain language', which resulted in Stoic philosophers using obscene terms or language that 'polite' society thought offensive or disgusting.[139] Such language would have seemed perhaps particularly out of place on the lips of elite women.

However, along with the Stoic notions of the law of Nature, Seneca could characterize women as naturally wild and passionate unless they had some instruction, so that philosophy tamed them.[140] A philosophical woman was a woman controlled. Epictetus (fl. 89–92 CE) emphasized that women's honour lay in being modestly virtuous and of nice demeanour,[141] which may indicate a Stoic ideal of philosophizing women as unthreatening to men and homely, somewhat in line with Pythagoraean notions.

The good controlled philosophical woman could be contrasted with a woman who did not know her boundaries. Brutus' wife Porcia is said by Plutarch to have been a philosopher.[142] Women were certainly learning philosophy in a first-century Roman context, but in doing so they were clearly in danger of infringing male and general societal sensibilities about what was proper for a woman. The notion of an appropriate, more retiring, and modest, 'woman-appropriate philosophy' served to offset this danger. Those women who traversed the boundaries were likely to be thought offensive by men such as Seneca's father.

Epode 8 of Horace may tell us something about how a woman reading (Stoic) philosophy was somehow considered offputting. Amy Richlin translates the Latin as:

> And so what if Stoic booklets like to lie
>   between your silk pillows?
> Do unlettered cocks harden less for that?

Richlin states, '[t]he poem's last section belittles the woman's literary and philosophical pretensions, suggesting that all her

---

[139] See the letter of Cicero to Paetus (*Fam.* 9: 22) given in Latin and English translation in Richlin, *Garden of Priapus*, 18–21.
[140] Seneca, *Moral Essays* 2: 14: 1 (On Firmness).
[141] Epictetus, *Encheiridion* 40.
[142] Plutarch, *Life of Brutus* 13, 53.

lovers, literati and ordinary men alike, are impotent with her'.[143] However, it seems here to me that the woman herself has considered the possibility that her reading of Stoic books has caused a lack of male arousal, to which the (male) speaker—who has not been aroused—can respond 'so what?' The booklets are not responsible for his lack of interest: his 'unlettered cock' clearly is not interested in them at all. It is the woman's overall repulsiveness that is to blame for his lack of arousal.[144] Richlin goes on to note that *libelli* might be roll-shaped, and that the book roll occasionally represents the phallus (for example, in Juvenal, *Satires* 6: 337–8), which may suggest that the woman has lovers who talk philosophy with her in bed. Whatever the case, the woman here is characterized as getting on in years, wealthy enough to afford silk pillows and huge pearls ('may there not be a wife who walks laden with rounder pearls'). She is high-born, as she would have a funeral in which portraits of famous men would be exhibited ('may portraits of great men precede your funeral train'). Her reading of philosophy is therefore associated with an elite social status and wealth, but also with sexual promiscuity.

The contrasting chaste ideal of the woman philosopher may be explored by looking at the writing of Musonius Rufus (*c*.28–100 CE), especially his discourse III, 'That Women Too Should Study Philosophy' and IV, 'Should Daughters Receive the Same Education as Sons?'[145] Musonius argued that both men and women had the faculty of reason and an inclination towards virtue. It becomes clear that Musonius is directing his advice only to elite men and women, in that he acknowledges that the first job of a woman is to be a good housekeeper in regard to the welfare of her house, and capable of directing the household slaves. She should be chaste and controlled, just, loving her children, courageous, energetic, 'prepared to nurse her children

---

[143] Richlin, *Garden of Priapus*, 111.

[144] For English translation of the poem, see Richlin, *Garden of Priapus*, 109–10.

[145] See Hawley, 'Women Philosophers', 75. For Greek text of Musonius with English translations see Lutz, *Musonius Rufus*, 39–49. See also Anton C. Geytenbeek, *Musonius Rufus and Greek Diatribe* (Assen: Van Gorcum, 1965), 51–62. The discourses of Musonius are now extant mainly in the work of Stobaeus, though were most likely originally compiled by a certain Lucius, a student of Musonius, and circulated some time after his death, so Lutz, *Musonius*, 6–8.

at her own breast, to serve her husband with her own hands, and willing to do the work of slaves'. It seems here that Musonius is directing his description of the ideal philosophizing woman against a stereotype of a philosophizing woman who neglects house, husband, and children in the pursuit of philosophical goals. In fact, he explicitly addresses this stereotype at the end of his discourse. He notes that some will say that women who associate with philosophers are arrogant and presumptuous 'when they abandon their own households, turn to the company of men, exercise themselves in speeches, act like sophists and analyze syllogisms, when they should be sitting at home spinning'. Musonius calmly responds that if a woman truly learns philosophy this will in fact increase her virtue, modesty, self-restraint, and good household management in every way that such men should approve of. He notes that 'the teachings of the philosophers exhort the woman to be content (with her lot) and self-motivated'.

In his discourse IV, 'Should Daughters Receive the Same Education as Sons?' Musonius likewise replies in the affirmative. Virtue was shared by both sexes, and education towards virtue should then also be given to both sexes. When it comes to the suggestion that perhaps then men should learn spinning and women gymnastics, however, Musonius resorts to the Stoic belief in Nature. It is natural that, since man's constitution is stronger and women's weaker, men should have heavier tasks and women lighter, and therefore gymnastics and outdoor work are activities suitable for men, while spinning and indoor work are suitable for women. However, Musonius does allow for some flexibility, when men may be more suited to indoor work and women might do heavier work. Sheer observation of non-elite women doing decidedly heavy work may have accounted for this concession.[146] The final passage of this section is particularly interesting. He asserts the importance of women learning philosophy, but then adds: 'I do not wish to say that it is appropriate for women to be very clear at speeches or to be very clever, for

---

[146] See e.g. the evidence presented in Päivi Setälä, 'Brick Stamps and Women's Economic Opportunities in Imperial Rome', in Arina Angerman, Geerte Binnema, Annemieke Keunen, Vefie Poels, and Jacqueline Zirkee (eds.), *Current Issues in Women's History* (London and New York: Routledge, 1989), 61–74.

that would be unnecessary for women if they are indeed philosophizing *as women* (εἴπερ φιλοσοφήσουσιν ὡς γυναῖκες).' Musonius
affirms that philosophy is about goodness and nobility of character, and nothing else. In other words, it does not inexorably lead
to new roles for women, or the erosion of old gender boundaries.

In Musonius, we have evidence then of both positive and
negative paradigms of women in *philosophia*: the ideal homely
woman versus the non-homely 'arrogant' woman. A woman
studying philosophy could also give rise to gossip, if she engaged
in the close relationship of student–teacher which was considered acceptable male to male. Cicero the Academician, who
was so scornful of Leontium, wrote approvingly in a letter to
Atticus[147] of a woman named Caerellia who had a great love of
philosophy, so much so that she had carefully copied his entire
book, *De Finibus*. However, Fusius Calenus reproached Cicero
for loving Caerellia in his old age; for Calenus their relationship
was apprehended as being not philosophical but sexual.[148]

In the early second century CE Plutarch expresses the opinion
that a woman should learn philosophy, but only secondhand
from her husband. The husband should carry back the 'pollen'
of philosophy like a bee to his wife, waiting at home, so that he
becomes for her 'guide, philosopher and teacher of all that is
beautiful and divine'.[149] Such study of philosophy will keep a
woman from straying into unbecoming conduct (for example,
dancing or magic), for left to themselves women 'conceive many
absurd and worthless plans and emotions'.[150] But Plutarch does
not advise that a woman should seek to learn philosophy from
any man other than her husband. This also implies that ideally
women should not learn philosophy prior to marriage, so that
they would be ripe for tuition by the husband. The learning of
philosophy is part of the training that an ideal husband gives his
wife. Given the foregoing evidence, Plutarch's ideal seems to
have been constructed against a backdrop of two historical
circumstances: (1) in which women were indeed learning
philosophy from men other than their husbands and falling then
into social disrepute and (2) in which women were being banned

---

[147] Book 13, letter 21a to Atticus, cf. book 15, letter 26.
[148] Dio Cassius, *Rom. Hist.* 5: 45: 18.
[149] Plutarch, *Moralia* 145c.
[150] Ibid. 145e.

from learning philosophy at all by overprotective or controlling fathers/husbands. Plutarch therefore comes across, like Musonius, as a 'moderate' man, who is attempting to define an acceptable paradigm for women in philosophy.

Others

There is the story of a woman named Arete of Cyrene, daughter of the philosopher Aristippus (fourth century BCE), who allegedly wrote forty books, and taught 110 students in a school she established.[151] Her acquisition of learning appears to have come as a result of her father's instruction, since Diogenes Laertius lists Arete as one of the students of her father.[152] Having been so instructed in this learning, she was apparently considered competent to teach publicly. Her son Aristippus was nicknamed 'Mother-taught', $M\eta\tau\rho o\delta i\delta\alpha\kappa\tau o\nu$. Diodorus the Socratic Dialectician (fourth to third centuries BCE) was said to have had five daughters who were also Dialecticians.[153] An inscription from Apollonia in Mysia from the late second or early third century CE is dedicated to 'Magnilla the philosopher, daughter of Magnus the philosopher, wife of Menius the philosopher.'[154] The Suidas mentions a *grammatikē*, named Agallis, daughter of Agallias (third century BCE), who was a pupil of Aristophanes of Byzantium.[155] The Egyptian daughter of Soteridas the Epidauran, named Pamphile (first century CE), apparently wrote eight books on philosophy, some of which are used by Diogenes

[151] Diogenes Laertius, *Lives* 2: 72, 86; Aelian, *Nat. Anim.* 3: 40; Theodoret, *Therapeutike* 11: 1; Clement, *Strom.* 4: 122: 1; Boccacio, *De Laudibus Mulierum*; Strabo, *Geography* 17: 3: 22; Eusebius, *Praep. Evang.* 14: 18: 32 (764a); Themistius, *Orationes*, 21: 244. See for Arete and the Cyrenaic hedonistic philosophy, Waithe, *Women Philosophers*, 197–201.

[152] Diogenes Laertius, *Lives* 2: 72, 86.

[153] Clement of Alexandria, *Strom.* 4: 19 citing Philo the Dialectician's *Menexenus*, cf. also Jerome, *Against Jovinian*, PL 23, 42 (col. 285). The names of these daughters are given as: Menexene, Argia, Theognis, Artemesia, Pantaclea.

[154] Mary R. Lefkowitz and Maureen B. Fant, *Women's Life in Greece and Rome* (London: Duckworth, 1982), 160 (no. 168), from *IGR* iv. 125; *IG* ii². 3704: 9, 12.

[155] Athenaeus, *Deipnosophistai* 1: 14d, calls her Agallis, and identifies her as a $\gamma\rho\alpha\mu\mu\alpha\tau\iota\kappa\dot{\eta}$, and see also Pomeroy, *Women in Hellenistic Egypt*, 61 and Adler (ed.), *Suidae*, i. 162, ll. 26–7 (no. 1817).

Laertius, though they have otherwise perished.[156] All these women are 'acceptable' in the sense that Musonius defined, falling into the paradigm of the essentially homely father-taught women philosophers.

Other women remembered by their families in Greek epigraphic sources as 'philosophers' include a woman named Aurelia Oppia and her daughter Heracleia from second-century CE Sparta. On a fragment of a marble column, we find commemorated [*THN ΦΙΛ*]*ΟCΟΦΩΤΑΤΗΝ ΚΑΙ CΩΦΡΟ*[*ΝΕCΤΑΤΗ*]*Ν ΑΥΡΗΛΙΑΝ ΟΠΠΙΑΝ* [*ΤΟΥ*] *ΦΙΛΟCΟΦΩΤΑΤΟΥ ΚΑΛΛΙ-*[*ΚΡΑΤΟΥC*] *ΘΥΓΑΤΕΡΑ*, 'the most wisdom-loving and most moderate Aurelia Oppia, daughter of the most wisdom-loving Kallikratos'.[157] On a marble base found in 1840 near the theatre in Sparta is an inscription mentioning Heracleia who is *CEMNO-TATHN ΚΑΙ ΦΙΛΟCΟΦΩΤΑΤΗΝ ΚΑΙ ΕΥΓΕΝΕCΤΑΤΗΝ*, 'most majestic and most wisdom-loving and most generous (or: most well-born)'.[158] In another inscription from Paros, dated to 292 CE, a highly esteemed and wealthy woman named Aurelia Leita, wife of Marcus Aurelius Faustus, is described as φιλόσοφος, 'one loving wisdom'. This is included as one among other adjectives that point to feminine virtues: she is: φίλανδρος, 'one loving her husband', φιλόπαις, 'one loving her children', and φιλόπατρις, 'one loving her country'.[159]

A handful of women remain who are not stated in our extant sources as fitting into any school, or as being related to any men philosophers. Berenice is mentioned by Photius in his *Bibliotheca* as one of the philosophers Stobaeus used in his apophthegms.[160] A certain Myro, is mentioned by the Suidas as being a philosopher from Rhodes and is also referred to by Eustatius and Eunapius.[161]

Aristotle (fourth century) of course rejected the notion that

---

[156] Photius, *Bibliotheca* 2: 161, 175; Adler (ed.), *Suidae*, iv. 15, l. 30 to 16, l. 2 = 'Pamphila' *PG* 117: 1311, where it is stated that she wrote 33 books; see also iv. 410, ll. 9–10 (no. 876) = 'Soteridas' *PG* 117: 1349; Aulus Gellius, *Attic Nights* 15: 17, 23.

[157] *IG* xii. 5: 1, no. 598.

[158] Ibid., no. 599.

[159] Ibid., no. 292, pp. 76–7.

[160] Photius, *Bibliotheca* 2: 155.

[161] Adler (ed.), *Suidae*, iii. 429, ll. 4–5 = 'Myro' *PG* 117: 1300; Eustatius, *Comm. ad Homeri Iliadem* 1: 310; Eunapius, *Lives of the Sophists* 411.

women were capable of philosophy on account of a fundamentally inferior (cooler) constitution.[162] Possible Peripatetic women
do not appear in the extant tradition until the fifth century CE.[163]
Given Aristotle's weighty opinion, and the widespread influence
of the Peripatetic school founded on Aristotelian philosophy,
one may expect various defensive and offensive positions on the
part of authors treating women in philosophy. I shall now go on
to examine the discourse on *philosophia* to see how the tropes
'woman philosopher' and 'woman student' are formulated by
our various extant writers into certain paradigms.

PARADIGMS OF WOMEN IN PHILOSOPHY

In analysing the ways the women philosophers and students are
used paradigmatically, I have divided these into several fairly
broad categories. These categories are: (1) woman as sexual
partner; (2) woman as comic character; (3) woman as agent of
inclusivity; (4) woman as honorary male; (5) woman as bearer of
secret knowledge; (6) woman as model of virtue; (7) bad woman.
For ease of reference, and somewhat influenced by the light-
hearted asides of Diogenes Laertius, I have given these
categories stereotypical epithets.

'Sexy Babe': Woman as Sexual Partner

Much of the literature tends to blur being the female lover or
erotic adviser of a (male) philosopher and being a female student
of a philosopher into one, presenting a kind of pillow-talk
pedagogy. In this category fall all the instances in which a woman
student or philosopher is described as a courtesan or prostitute,
or keeper of prostitutes, talking about erotic love or sex, and/or
the lover of a philosopher: Thargelia, Aspasia, Diotima,
Leontium, Hipparchia, and so on.

They are beautiful, immodest, using their sexual powers over
men, and wise with it. Athenaeus' *Deipnosophistai* in particular
ensures that the philosophers have courtesans who might
philosophize, rather than serious female students. Lais is the

---

[162] Aristotle, *Politics* 1259b–c. See Hawley, 'Women Philosophers', 74.
[163] Ménage, *Historia*, 41–2.

lover of Aristippus, Demosthenes the Orator, and Diogenes the Cynic.[164] She is not so much a student as a woman with a sexual predilection for philosophers. According to Athenaeus, Nicarete of Megara is a courtesan who studied with Stilpo.[165] For Athenaeus, to be a female student of a philosopher appears equatable with sexual impropriety, whether it is Thargelia of Miletus, who he says was 'married' fourteen times,[166] or Aspasia who kept whores,[167] or Leontium.[168] Plutarch, like Athenaeus, tends to portray notable women philosophers as sexually improper. Thargelia of Miletus was a *hetaira* of Antiochus king of Thessaly.[169] Aspasia is identified by Plutarch as keeper of prostitutes.[170] Plutarch notes that she emulated the legendary Thargelia.[171] As Hawley notes, '[u]nattached women . . . could be called courtesans, whether rightly or wrongly, and used as tools of satire or invective.'[172]

The male teacher sleeping with the female student, or any woman, could be used as part of a literary type of humorous deflation of philosophers who might seem pompous or self-righteous.[173] This may have resulted in women students being remade as courtesans and lovers in some traditions. An early writer on Pythagoras, Hermesianax (third century BCE) mentions Pythagoras' 'madness' ($\mu\alpha\nu\acutei\alpha$) for Theano,[174] perhaps indicating that somewhere in the tradition history she was understood as a student for whom Pythagoras had a wild passion. By the third century CE there was some debate as to whether she was really his student or his wife, since authors appear to have wished to conflate different Theanos into one person.[175]

---

[164]   Athenaeus, *Deipnosophistai* 13: 588d–e.
[165]   Ibid. 13: 596e.
[166]   Citing Hippias, *The Collection*, in *Deipnosophistai* 13: 608f.
[167]   Ibid. 13: 569f–570a; 589d.
[168]   Ibid. 588b, cf. 593b. For discussion see Richard Hawley, ' "Pretty, Witty and Wise": Courtesans in Athenaeus' *Deipnosophistai* Book 13', *International Journal of Moral and Social Studies*, 8 (1993), 73–91, who argues that in this text the wise *hetairai* are constructed as opposites to women philosophers proper.
[169]   Plutarch, *Pericles* 24: 2.
[170]   Ibid. 3, cf. Cratinus, in his *Cheirons* 3: 3, who calls Aspasia a 'prostitute'.
[171]   Plutarch, *Pericles* 24: 2.
[172]   Hawley, 'Women Philosophers', 82.
[173]   So ibid. 79.
[174]   In Athenaeus, *Deipnosophistai* 13: 599a.
[175]   Diogenes Laertius, *Lives* 7: 42.

With such a paradigm, women who wished to be respectable and yet study philosophy might have well been cautious, though there was no protection from gossip, as the instance of the enthusiastic Caerellia and the older Cicero clearly demonstrates. Philosophers who wished to present their philosophy in a good public light might also be very careful about presenting women as students. Too close a relationship between female students and a male teacher might easily be misread as indicating sexual licence, which would invite opponents to charge them with lechery and pure hypocrisy. Philosophers, after all, usually advocated varying measures of self-control.

'Stupid Cow': Woman as Comic Character

The presence of women in a philosophical school could be used to portray the school as weak and hypocritical. In the essay by Cicero (first century BCE), *On the Nature of the Gods* (1: 93) he ridicules Leontium's reply to a work by Theophrastus, but the purpose is to undermine the Epicureans who would allow a 'little whore' to write such a piece.[176] As noted by numerous authors, Aspasia was the subject of many comic writers' attacks, or the very idea of a philosophical woman.[177] This motif is also found in Juvenal's *Satires*.[178]

In satiric comedies of the fourth century BCE by Cratinus the Elder and Alexis, a woman who practises the philosophical regimen of Pythagoras exemplifies the ridiculousness of the system.[179] Diogenes Laertius includes a humorous tradition of the 'origin' of women students of Pythagoras which at the same time undermines the possibility that women may have chosen the philosophy seriously or independently. He states that, according to a rather comic story by Hermippus, Pythagoras made a cave dwelling deep in the earth, setting his mother to guard the entrance and tell him of what happened above, and when he eventually came out he told everyone he had been down to Hades and read out a story of his experiences. The gullible men who heard this outside the cave were so affected they wailed and wept

---

[176] Hawley, 'Women Philosophers', 80.
[177] Clement of Alexandria, *Strom.* 4: 122: 3; Plutarch, *Pericles* 24: 6.
[178] *Satires* 6: 434–6.
[179] Diogenes Laertius, *Lives* 8: 37; Kock, ii, 290, 370.

and considered him divine. In awe, they gave their wives to him (sexual implication present) in the hope that they might learn something from him, and 'so they were called Pythagoraeans (fem.)' (*Lives* 8: 41). This story makes the women completely passive, sexual objects for Pythagoras to use, and describes Pythagoras as a charlatan and sexual opportunist. It depicts the men as utter idiots and the original female Pythagoraeans as no better than prostitutes, in terms of the standards of the day.

The notion of a woman's leadership of a philosophical school for a period may also have originated in comedy or pastiche. Here the accusation that Leontium led the Epicurean circle is relevant, and this throws into question whether the tradition that Theano led the Pythagoraean school, or even that Aristippus' epithet 'Mother-taught', was really always a compliment. If a woman leader of a school was just plain laughable, even if women did exercise leadership roles, then would a school itself advertise the fact? Opponents of the school seem to have made use of the notion that leadership by a woman spelt nothing but fundamental weakness.

This paradigm may have been fed especially by those who followed the Aristotelian idea that women were incapable of philosophy. The women themselves could be laughed at then for aspiring to achieve a goal that was for them impossible. A woman would constantly fall short of being anything like a true philosopher, like an ape trying to play the piano. A woman would always be a woman, and therefore inferior, laughable in that she was taking on airs and graces, getting 'too big for her boots', and thereby seeming just plain silly. Such a characterization would inhibit women from appearing knowledgeable in philosophy, or confident. A woman might fear appearing amusing to men by articulating philosophical ideas. A writer depicting women philosophers would have to be careful to depict them in a way that could not raise a smile.

'Even a Woman can do it': Woman as Agent of Inclusivity

Women are used at times also, positively, to prove a thesis that since even a woman can do philosophy, every man certainly can. Women (as an essential category) are given as examples of the weakest members of society, who may yet do philosophy of a kind. For example, in Lucian of Samosata's *Eunuchus*, probably written around 180 CE, he tells the story of a debate between Diocles and Bagoas who are in competition for a lucrative chair in philosophy that had been established in Athens by Marcus Aurelius. The chair available is Peripatetic, and the two philosophers attempt to win the judges' approval as the appropriate person for the job. The entire dialogue is presented as if reported by a man named Lycinus, who cannot stop laughing about its absurdity, and the aim of the piece is clearly comic. The highlight of this comedy is when Diocles argues that Bagoas cannot be a philosopher on account of being a eunuch (*Eunuchus* 6). Pamphilus, Lycinus' audience, bursts out laughing at 'this incredible accusation' but Lycinus goes on to present a caricature of Bagoas' 'feminine' features which itself is supposed to be laughable. He states:

At the beginning, out of shame and cowardice—the kind of behaviour that is natural to them [eunuchs]—he stayed silent for quite a while and blushed and was visibly sweating. Then at last with a small (λεπτόν) and effeminate voice he said that Diocles acted unjustly in excluding a eunuch from philosophy when women could also pursue it. And so he brought in Aspasia and Diotima and Thargelia to support him. (*Eunuchus* 7)

Women here are used to indicate the inclusivity of philosophy, which would take no account of physical 'weakness', but rather the strength of the soul and mind and knowledge of doctrines (*Eunuchus* 9). Implicitly, however, women are in more or less the same category as eunuchs. They lack the physical attributes of manhood, and therefore participate in philosophy as exceptions, when somehow the mind is sufficiently strong despite the impediment of the female body. One of the judges of Lucian's story says that well-endowed physical features (as befitting a man) should be a mark of a philosopher, including a long beard which would inspire confidence in prospective students (*Eunuchus* 8). After an accusation then that Bagoas was not actually a eunuch at all but used this identity as a ruse to get out of a charge of adultery, Lycinus reports that the judges were divided on the matter, and some advocated stripping Bagoas 'to determine whether he was able to philosophize' (that is, had all his male genitals), others thought they should take him to a brothel, and someone could then 'see whether he could philosophize', that is, perform penetrative sex with a woman (*Eunuchus* 12). The piece ends jokingly with Lycinus saying he hoped his young son would have the suitable requirement for practising philosophy apart from brain or tongue (*Eunuchus* 13)! Lucian is parodying the absurd notion that a man should be fully 'intact' and able to perform sexually in order to practise philosophy, but still lets the characterization of the eunuch as 'effeminate' and therefore overly flustered and sensitive stand. Even if Bagoas is not a eunuch, he is still an effeminate man, with a small womanly voice and hardly any beard, which counts against him in popular appraisal of his abilities. The 'woman philosopher' motif is used to bolster his case: if even a woman can philosophize, then surely he could, since he is at least basically male. However, it still undermines women philosophers as being at the lowest rung of the ladder.[180]

In a second-century Christian context also, Clement of Alexandria could point to the examples of women philosophers of the past to argue that women should participate in (Christian) philosophy. Combining his assertions with Galatians 3: 28 he summarizes his thesis as: 'both slave and free alike should philosophize, whether one happens to be man or woman in sex' (*Strom.* 4: 1: 1). Clement makes it clear, however, that women are in a 'weaker' category when he stresses that Christian philosophy is for everyone, 'whether Barbarian, Greek, slave, old man, boy or woman', with the woman coming last in the list behind two examples of weaker types of males: old man and boy (*Strom.* 4: 58: 3). If a woman could philosophize, then everyone—at least, all men—could. The usual catalogue of female philosophers is by Clement given with this thesis in mind: Theano the Pythagoraean, Themisto of Lampsacus the Epicurean, Myia the daughter of Theano the Pythagoraean, Hipparchia of Maronitis the Cynic—'for whom the "dog-marriage" was celebrated in the Poecile'—Arete of Cyrene, Lasthenia of Arcadia, Axiothea of Philasia, and Aspasia of Miletus whom Σωκράτης . . . ἀπέλαυσεν εἰς φιλοσοφίαν, 'Socrates led away into philosophy' (*Strom.* 4: 121: 2–122: 3). Other women of accomplishment are given

---

[180] It is interesting that this argument is reported in the context of a debate between men who wished to follow Aristotle, in whose philosophy women are indeed to be excluded on the basis of physical (qua mental) inferiority.

alongside the women philosophers to show that perfection is possible for a woman as well as a man (*Strom.* 4: 118: 1).

The trouble is that including women as people who practise philosophy can lower the value of the philosophy, or whatever other enterprise is under scrutiny. The citing of Aspasia as an expert in rhetoric in Plato's *Menexenus* both praises her as a principal expert in the art of rhetoric, and yet subtly undermines her expertise, as well as that of the entire discipline. In other words, this inclusion of women can easily backfire. If a woman can do it, then it is not worth doing.

'One of the Guys': Woman as Honorary Male

Those writers who accepted women as philosophers might see these women as being different from other women, so that the women are not so much exemplary as exceptional. The women who philosophize are seen as taking on a function that would normatively be that of men, and are themselves therefore masculinized. In Lucian's *The Eunuch*, a male eunuch and a masculine woman therefore belong in rather similar categories. Both are capable of philosophy, even though the ideal or normative philosopher and student of philosophers is a virile, hirsute male who has not been 'feminized' by castration. If not comic, then Axiothea's male clothing in the Platonic Academy may also fall into the stereotype of the woman who has become—for all intents and purposes—a male. The same dress for men and women advocated by Zeno of Citium, in negative appraisals of the philosopher (Diogenes Laertius, *Lives* 7: 33), likewise could fall in this paradigm, as might the portrayal of Hipparchia (*Lives* 6: 96–8) as a kind of female Crates. This idea that a woman could become an 'honorary male' in thought and appearance by doing what men do is found also later on in the Christian Apocryphal Acts, where Thecla cuts her hair and dons male clothing before going off to teach (the Christian philosophy).[181] In the heretical Christian tradition of Eustathius of Sebaste (*c*.300–77) women cut their hair short and dressed like men, a practice that provoked the Synod of Gangra (*c*.345) to legislate against it.[182]

---

[181] *Acts of Paul and Thecla* 5: 25.

[182] See Susanna Elm, *'Virgins of God': The Making of Asceticism in Late Antiquity* (Oxford: Clarendon Press, 1994), 108–9.

Women who are taught philosophy by their husbands may also be mentally masculinized. Pythagoras' wife Theano, if taught by her husband, is clever and astute, but also very modest and homely. In Plutarch's way of thinking, a philosophical training is actually a benefit to wives, for otherwise women could stray off into a kind of untamed feminine silliness and get involved in magic or dancing. We find this also in his presentation of Eumetis as having 'wonderful good sense and a statesman's mind'. The women who are trained in philosophy by their fathers have become, in some way, feminine replicas of their fathers. At the same time, wives and daughters of male philosophers, instructed in a home context, still maintain the appropriate gender boundaries of women during their instruction. They are not in the dangerous liminal situation of women who have gone out to study in a school, like Axiothea or Lasthenia, or those who practise a philosophical life out in public like Hipparchia. Daughters who lead philosophical lives have respect because of the dignity bestowed upon them via their fathers; they become the 'little Cleobulus' as in the case of Cleobulina, as with Magnilla daughter of Magnus, or Agallis, daughter of Agallias. However, Clement ensures that Cleobulina does an action—foot-washing—that defines her as unthreatening and humble. In the extant stories about her, she does not go out from the home, but engages in philosophy with her father's guests there. Despite Plutarch's compliment, he does not at all propose that, since Eumetis/Cleobulina possessed a statesman's mind, she should actually become a statesman.

If such women trained in philosophy by husbands or fathers do engage in semi-public or homely instruction of men, it is more as replicas of the father, that is, they transmit teaching that originates with a male philosopher, rather than their own original thought, apart from a few witty or clever riddles or apophthegms. They have become preservers of the philosophical tradition established by their fathers or husbands. In this case the notion that Theano ran the Pythagoraean school (at home) after Pythagoras or that Arete did so after the death of Aristippus fits into the tradition of *diadochoi* essential in the passing down of the oral traditions of each philosopher. The mechanisms of a philosophical school required that the tradition of teaching is accurately passed orally from teacher to student. These women are official transmitters because of their exceptionally close association with the philosopher. They are then considered in some way 'honorary males' because it is perceived that they were the closest students of the philosopher. Given their honorary maleness, they can at times traverse social boundaries and become accepted in a male sphere, as *didaskaloi*, in a society which normally would define gender boundaries very carefully.

'Woman's Stuff': Woman as Bearer of Secret Knowledge

The centrality of women in passing on certain key elements of the teaching of the philosophical group comes through in the strand of tradition which has Theano's daughter Damo con- serving in secrecy the central tenets of Pythagoraeanism. When Diogenes Laertius wrote of this tradition, however, he appears to credit her with a noble determination and strength of charac- ter, ending his description of her refusal to show Pythagoras' memoirs to anyone 'outside the house' or sell them for a large sum of money with the comment, 'and these things (by) a woman', καὶ ταῦτα γυνά (*Lives* 8: 42). This betrays Diogenes Laertius' own rather low opinion of the capabilities of women since this comment is not found in other quotations of the tradi- tion from Laertius' source Lysis.[183] The origins of the tradition, however, may play as much into the notion of women's secrecy. A great deal of mystery revolved around Pythagoraeanism in terms of many of its key ideas and practices. Here in this tradi- tion it is a mystery associated with the secretive associations of women. In a society where many things may be closeted away from men as 'women's business', not least of all sexual lore, menstruation, childbirth, breastfeeding, and babycare, the idea that women keep things hidden away (from men) might not be hard for men to believe. Specific 'women's cults' and 'mysteries' in the Graeco-Roman world appear also to have played into these stereotypical notions.[184] As such, this paradigm is not so much one which is central to philosophical women, but rather to women in general. That women might have a tendency to magic, as Plutarch noted, relates to this paradigm also.

---

[183] Porphyry, *Vita Pyth.* 4; Iamblichus, *Vita Pyth.* 28: 146. See Hawley, 'Women Philosophers', 79.

[184] For discussion of these, see Kraemer, *Her Share of the Blessings*, 3–92.

With Pythagoras learning doctrines from the Delphic priestess Themistoclea, and Socrates being initiated into the mysteries
of sexual love by Diotima—who is also a priestess—we also find
similar motifs. The secrets known to women are passed on to the
initiated man, who becomes more powerful by his awareness of
things only women might otherwise know. Women may be the
vehicles of divine knowledge. As Hawley writes, 'As poets could
speak with the divine authority of the Muses, so the priestess of
Delphi could act as the mouthpiece of Apollo. By having her as
his teacher (whether in reality or in legend), Pythagoras could
partake of her authority.'[185]

This links too with the idea of the *hetaira* as being particularly
wise. Since *hetairai* based their livelihood on being pleasing to
men, they cultivated 'arts' which men would find seductive,
sexually and intellectually. The mysterious fascination and
power of the beautiful woman whom a man can simply not resist
despite his better judgement is then linked with an idea of her
being particularly wise, and wise in ways which a man could
not completely comprehend by mere rational thought, for his
rational thought seems unable to stop him from succumbing to
her powers.

Even the otherwise pure Cleobulina is an expert in making up
riddles that completely baffle her (male) audience. This skill
seems to reflect a notion that women's 'lateral' thinking was more
advanced than the more linear, rational way of male thinking.

'Just a Housewife': Woman as Model of Virtue

The truly good and noble women philosophers in the extant traditions do not traverse social boundaries or challenge accepted
understandings of gender. Here the paradigm is overt and
prescriptive. Foremost as examples of these women are the
Pythagoraeans: the two Theanos, Phintys, Perictione, and
others. The first Theano in particular is considered a model of
virtue. She is an exemplary, modest woman whom all women
should emulate. Implicitly, she is one who learns from her husband, stays faithful to him, keeps herself well hidden, and
remains truly 'feminine' in all respects. Pythagoraean women

---

[185] Hawley, 'Women Philosophers', 72.

remain domestic and married: good wives and good daughters, despite their 'masculine' minds.

The Stoic 'good woman' model, which was so powerful in the first century CE, is similar to the Pythagoraean, and clearly resulted in severe criticism of women who did not behave in the acceptable way. Xenophon, Seneca, Musonius Rufus, and Plutarch are among those who advocate that women's learning should be domestic, ideally guided by a woman's husband, and women should at all times be modest about this learning. Philosophy should not lead to unfeminine social behaviour. The characterization of a true philosophical woman by Musonius Rufus is the strongest indication of the ideal type. A woman who learns philosophy does not do so in order to engage in debates at dinner parties, or make speeches, or even think deeply about life's greatest questions, but rather in order to learn *virtue*, so that ultimately she can serve her house, husband, and family better than ever. Philosophy will make her self-sacrificing and tireless in her duties. Women are naturally suited to the indoor life, and philosophy should be consistent with Nature. Through philosophy a woman becomes a better woman, content with her womanly lot. She should absorb philosophy as a woman, and not fall into the traps of being a 'sexy babe', 'stupid cow', or 'one of the guys'. Certainly, if a woman behaves like an honorary male without the males themselves deeming her worthy, she is considered outrageous by them.

A more subtle literary pattern found in writings about philosophical schools is the tendency to classify model virtuous women students and philosophers in neat bunches, which underscores their marginality and rarity, while yet holding them up as exemplary figures. This is not a self-consciously negative rhetorical device used by authors, but a positive one, which still may go awry in terms of women's empowerment. We get lists of 'women philosophers' in Iamblichus, *Vita Pyth.* 36: 267; Sopater, *Photius*, 161 and in Clement of Alexandria, *Strom.* 4: 121: 1–123: 1.[186] Philochorus the Grammarian (third century BCE) wrote an entire work on Pythagoraean women, thereby defining them as a separate category of Pythagoraeans.[187]

---

[186] See Hawley, 'Women Philosophers', 87 n. 55. Cf. also Tatian, *To the Greeks* 32: 2–3; Lactantius, *Divine Institutes* 3: 25.

[187] Adler (ed.), *Suidae*, iv, 736, ll. 6–21 (no. 441) = 'Philochorus' PG 117:

Apollonius the Stoic (second century CE) apparently wrote a book on women philosophers, thereby also defining them by sex rather than by school.[188] They become models for women to emulate, or are used for flattery, as in Lucian's *Pro Imaginibus* 18–19 where a woman is compared with Theano, Diotima, and other exemplary women, or in Plutarch's *Moralia* (145–6) where he lists Theano and Cleobulina among six exemplary women 'and other women of shining fame'. The sex of the subject is what is fundamentally important in the creation of the list, rather than any other factor, for the aim is the careful moral modelling of the women readers.

Essentially, these ancient studies and lists were prescriptive. Certain women are given as models which women should follow. They are defined by male authors with this specific intention, and no whiff of any unsavory element is to be found in these constructions. The model women are constructed in ways that would be considered exemplary for the women of the author's circle. A woman in a story could function as a model of womanhood, though men in stories did not so often function as models of manhood particularly, but rather of what was normatively 'human'. This is where this strategy is ultimately marginalizing.

'Stuck-up Bitch': Bad Woman

This paradigm accommodates the arrogant type of philosophical woman of whom Musonius disapproved. Seneca indicates that his father would not allow his mother to study philosophy for fear she would show off her learning. A strong or powerful woman in philosophy could easily be understood as bad or damaging. The invective against Leontium taking over the leadership of the Epicurean garden illustrates the unease some men felt about women in power: these were not good women, and their leadership was a sign of the weakness of the philosophy they espoused. The 'strong, educated woman' type seems to have

1319, where the work is called a 'collection of heroic women'. Ménage (*Historia*, 47) comments that 'it could seem remarkable that there were so many Pythagorean women philosophers when the Pythagoreans had to observe silence for five years and had many secrets which they were not allowed to divulge, as women are very talkative and can scarcely keep a secret' (!).

[188] So Photius, *Bibliotheca* 2: 161.

caused some anxiety to Roman men, who feared loss of virility.
We see this fear indicated in Horace's epode 8.

Juvenal sums up how Roman men might have felt considerable distaste faced with any outspoken, educated woman:

Still more exasperating is the woman who begs as soon as she sits down
to dinner, to discourse on poets and poetry, comparing Virgil with
Homer: professors, critics, lawyers, auctioneers—even another
woman—can't get a word in. She rattles on at such a rate that you'd
think all the pots and pans in the kitchen were crashing to the floor or
that every bell in town was clanging. All by herself she makes as much
noise as some primitive tribe chasing away an eclipse. She should learn
the philosophers' lesson: 'moderation is necessary even for intellectuals.' And, if she still wants to appear educated and eloquent, let her
dress as a man, sacrifice to men's gods, and bathe in the men's baths.
Wives shouldn't try to be public speakers; they shouldn't use rhetorical
devices; they shouldn't read all the classics—there ought to be some
things women don't understand.[189]

The fear of women immodestly displaying their learning, being
overly talkative and rather vain about their knowledge, seems a
particularly Roman, Stoic, concern. The 'just a housewife' paradigm is used frequently to offset the 'stuck-up bitch', who does
not know the importance of moderation, despite education.
A woman who behaves like a man, in seeming educated and
eloquent, might as well go all the way and 'be' a man.

Noisy arrogance is one thing, but a wise woman could also be
devious. Aspasia is depicted at times as a dangerous woman, who
was responsible for beginning the disastrous Peloponnesian
Wars. The bad women of philosophy seduce the male philosophers, like the Epicurean women, or charge too much money, like
the Platonist Lasthenia, or generally cause trouble. Overtly sexy
or available women are never quite as virtuous as they should be,
unlike the 'just a housewife' type, whose sexuality is hidden and
reserved for her husband alone. Ultimately, the bad women of
philosophy are those who are not safely subservient to husband or
father. Their mental masculinization is not mitigated by male
power. They do not strike the right balance between male mental
excellence and female modesty. They reject usual gender roles.

---

[189] Juvenal, *Satires* 6: 434–56, quoted from Sarah Pomeroy, *Goddesses,
Whores, Wives, and Slaves: Women in Classical Antiquity* (London: Pimlico,
1975 and 1994), 172.

It is a fine balance between becoming an honorary male in a good sense and getting to be a masculinized woman on the other. A manly woman was considered dangerous, weakening the men with whom she was involved. Plutarch describes Mark Antony's wife Fulvia as masculinized, rejecting usual female jobs like spinning and housekeeping. She weakened Mark Antony's Roman (manly) character and ultimately prepared him for his domination by the non-Roman (womanly) wiles of Cleopatra (Plutarch, *Ant.* 10). Plutarch has Porcia, the wife of Brutus, gash her thigh to prove she can endure pain like a man, and can therefore bear to hear his private troubles. Being the daughter of Cato and wife of Brutus, she has gone beyond her female nature, for 'good rearing and excellent companionship do much to strengthen character' (*Brut.* 13). Porcia is also defined as a philosopher (13, cf. 53), but this characterization serves to make Brutus look weak.

CONCLUSIONS

I have reached widely to get a sense of the paradigms employed in the discourse on *philosophia*. Clearly, there may be more subtle and complex factors at work than can be analysed here, in a study which must necessarily be concise and purposive in terms of what exactly is looked for. Nevertheless, the results of this study may help comparative analysis. Texts are not written in a cultural vacuum. It is axiomatic to this analysis that the writers of all texts operated with cognizance of cultural paradigms, inasmuch as all participants in culture would find such paradigms part of the cognitive technology in which they formulated ideas. As we have explored, Philo used this cognitive technology in terms of Judaism, and was deeply indebted to Graeco-Roman philosophy for his concepts and terms. He understood not only Judaism to be philosophy, but also different groups within that philosophy to be 'schools'. How then would he explain the 'school' he describes in *Contempl.*? How would he deal with the women of the group, in describing them to an audience familiar with the above paradigms?

9
Women and Sex in *De Vita Contemplativa*

Philo reports that women were an integral part of the monastic, contemplative, mystical Jewish association called the Therapeutae. Like their male counterparts, the Therapeutrides were highly educated, mostly older women, who had severed their familial and social ties to pursue the contemplative life. In contrast to the situation with the Pharisees, Sadducees, and Essenes, there is no doubt in Philo's representation that the women were full members of the society, dedicated to the philosophical life, and fully trained to engage in it.[1]

In describing the women specifically in the Mareotic group, Philo's chief rhetorical aim was to present them as 'the good', along with all other elements. At every stage, the women have to be completely virtuous. For this, he needed to fit his description of the women of this group with wider notions of 'good' philosophical women, and avoid any association of his women with the negative paradigms identified in the previous chapter. However, Philo himself had constructed a theory of woman and the feminine which would dictate not only how he modelled his allegorical universe of interpretation, but how he saw real women. The feminine element was not, in his interpretation, necessarily very good.

As we have seen, there was nothing intrinsically positive about a 'woman philosopher' in extant Graeco-Roman literature. The motif of women as philosophers *per se* could be used to undermine a presentation of a philosophical group as much as to enhance it, depending on the paradigms which were utilized. In Philo's other idealizing description of a Jewish group—of the Essenes—there are no women (*Prob.* 75–91), and nothing is lost

---

[1] Ross Shepard Kraemer, 'Women's Judaisms at the Beginning of Christianity', in ead. and Mary Rose D'Angelo (eds.), *Women and Christian Origins* (New York and Oxford: OUP, 1999), 50–79, at 70.

by that rhetorically in terms of arguing for the sect's exemplary character. Likewise, Chaeremon did not include women in his description of Egyptian priests as ideal contemplative philosophers. If anything, the lack of women among the Essenes perfectly coheres with Philo's notions about the dangers of women in the household, which he indicates were Essene views also (cf. *Hypoth.* 11: 14–18). In fact, Philo tends to forget, conveniently, that women are there in the Mareotic group at all in several places. He writes, regarding the *therapeutai* in general, of the 'superlative virtue of the men (τῶν ανδρῶν)' (1, cf. 78). These men leave behind their property (13) and 'brothers/sisters (ἀδελφούς), children, *wives*, parents, numerous relatives' (18). The community also uses the writings of 'the men of old' (παλαιῶν ἀνδρῶν) (29). But sooner or later it seems he must address the women.

We might expect, then, that Philo's tone in regard to the inclusion of women as students of Moses in this ideal Mareotic group outside Alexandria might be a little apologetic. He may have his own rhetorical reasons for including women, as we shall explore in the final chapter, but he still has to deal with the negative paradigms in the minds of his audience. If he is going to use women positively and constructively, he has to tread carefully through a minefield.[2]

Most critically, Philo had to deal with the 'Sexy Babe' paradigm. The sexual association of female philosophers or students with male teachers was a common trope. How could a woman be philosophical and yet good in terms of what was expected of a respectable, well-born, 'free' lady of high social standing? The question was answered in terms of the results of her instruction: if she remained modest, domestic, and dutiful, she was good: 'Just a Housewife', practising female philosophy. If she became immodest and neglectful of her duties, she was bad—a 'Stuck-up Bitch'—or comic—a 'Stupid Cow'.

The truly good women philosophers in the extant traditions of philosophy do not traverse social boundaries or challenge accepted societal understandings of gender. Pythagoraean women are the leading examples of this type of model: the two Theanos, Phintys, Perictione, Myia, and others. In extant literature, they are fully μαθήτριαι, 'students' or 'disciples', of

---

[2] Hay, 'Things Philo Said', 674; Sly, 'Philo's Alexandria', 145; Szesnat, 'Virgins', 196.

Pythagoras, but this does not mean they behave in identical ways to the male disciples. The women disciples are contained within the domestic sphere as wives and mothers, even when they teach. Pleasing the husband was thought to be a special part of the correct way of life for a Pythagoraean woman.[3] Modesty was a critical feature which indicated her philosophical correctness.[4] The same situation applied in Stoic philosophy. While first-century men in a Roman context knew of Stoic women who were indeed behaving in a way that was deemed not socially appropriate for women—or even offensive—the ideal Stoic woman was modest and domestic, instructed by her husband. Such is the rhetoric of Musonius Rufus, when he addresses the question of the philosophical woman.[5]

Philo seems to have had in mind that the portrayal of the Mareotic group would eclipse any description of an ideal philosophical group of the Graeco-Roman world. He alludes to philosophical 'heroes' of the Greek tradition (cf. *Contempl.* 14–17, 53–63), who turn out to be not very heroic at all, and seems in particular to wish to outdo the Pythagoraeans and the Platonists. After all, God is 'better than a "Good" and purer than a "one" and older than a "Monad"' (*Contempl.* 2).[6] How then would the women serve this purpose? They too had to eclipse any good precedents in Graeco-Roman philosophy. Perhaps Philo's fundamental problem may be expressed as: how could the *therapeutrides*, the female attendants of God, be presented in a way that would not only surpass the paradigms of good women philosophers but also conform to his own gender theory?

PHILO'S THEORY OF 'WOMAN'

This was possibly not so easy for Philo to resolve, for 'woman' as a category both actual and metaphorical, tends to be configured somewhat negatively in his works.[7] Philo constructs 'woman' by

---

[3] e.g. Plutarch, *Moralia* 145.

[4] Clement, *Strom.* 4: 121: 2; Diogenes Laertius, *Lives* 8: 43; Theodoret, *Therapeutike* 12: 73; Plutarch, *Moralia* 142d.

[5] See Hawley, 'Women Philosophers', 75.

[6] Hay, 'Things Philo Said', 678.

[7] Philo's construction has been explored in depth by both Dorothy Sly and

mainly focusing on elite women. Women—inferentially, of the upper class—should remain modestly at home (*Spec*. 3: 169–71; 4: 225; *QG* 1: 26). They should be seen only fleetingly in public, always accompanied by escorts (*Sacr*. 26–7), or else they were in danger of appearing morally lax. Lower class women can be described by Philo as being out in the market-place; the immodest women who fight and use bad language (*Spec*. 3: 172–5). The 'public' woman is, for Philo, stereotypically, the whore (*Spec*. 3: 51; *Sacr*. 21–5). Philo seems highly influenced by notions of Aristotle in regard to gender,[8] for women are inferior to men *by nature* (*Spec*. 2: 124; 4: 223; *QE* 1: 7), more prone to be deceived (*QG* 1: 33) and to deceive (*Hypoth*. 11: 14–17; cf. *Opif*. 165). A male is more related to domination and the 'efficient cause', while a female is imperfect, subject, the passive rather than active (*Spec*. 1: 200), an image derived from classical notions of sexual power relations,[9] as well as common beliefs about the determinative active power or movement of the male seed to form a new human being in passive, formless female material in the womb.[10] Given this 'natural' situation, husbands should be in control of their wives (*Hypoth*. 7: 3). However, Philo's *therapeutrides* are clearly not in the domestic sphere. They are living outside it, even outside the city, with men who are apparently not their husbands, brothers, or fathers. How could they be 'good', and conform to his theory of gender?

Richard Baer and only the most salient issues will be discussed here. See: Dorothy Sly, *Philo's Perception of Women* (Brown Judaic Studies, 209; Atlanta: Scholars, 1990); Richard A. Baer, *Philo's Use of the Categories Male and Female* (Arbeiten zur Literatur und Geschichte des hellenistischen Judentums, 3; Leiden: Brill, 1970).

[8] See e.g. Aristotle, *De Generatione Animalium* 4: 4, 775a. Discussions of Aristotle's views on women may be found in S. Clark, 'Aristotle's Woman', *History of Political Thought*, 3 (1982), 177–91; Sissa, 'Sexual Philosophies'; N. Smith, 'Plato and Aristotle on the Nature of Women', *Journal of the History of Philosophy*, 21 (1983), 467–78. For other Hellenistic influences on Philo's construction of gender see Judith Romney Wegner, 'Philo's Portrayal of Women—Hebraic or Hellenic?', in Amy-Jill Levine (ed.), *'Women Like This': New Perspectives on Jewish Women in the Greco-Roman World* (Atlanta: Scholars, 1991), 41–66.

[9] See Bernadette J. Brooten, *Love between Women: Early Christian Responses to Female Homoeroticism* (Chicago and London: University of Chicago Press, 1996), 1–2.

[10] *Opif*. 67, 132; *QG* 3: 47; Aristotle, *Metaphysics* 1: 6: 998a.

Much can be learnt of Philo's perception of gender relations by an exploration of his metaphorical, allegorical psychic universe. Philo writes that νοῦς, mind, corresponds to man and αἴσθησις, sense-perception, to woman (*Spec.* 1: 202; *Leg.* 2: 38). Mind is active and sense-perception passive. In the same way that male is superior to female, mind is superior to sense-perception; men should rule over women as the mind should rule over sense-perception and vice versa (*Leg.* 3: 222).[11] There seems no question that Philo considered maleness and men superior to femaleness and women in every way that he determined to be important. In Philo's exegesis of the creation of humankind, ἄνθρωπος is created which is 'neither male nor female' that is, it is genderless. Despite this, for Philo, the supposedly genderless state is still somehow essentially masculine.[12] This is quite different from later rabbinic exegesis which would have Adam as androgynous, or rather hermaphroditic, containing both male and female.[13] This ἄνθρωπος is both νοῦς and λόγος (*Det.* 83–4): masculine entities in Philo's symbolic schema. Only with the creation of woman does the feminine appear. Materiality, namely the human body (σῶμα), enters the pure, masculine, and spiritual construction of 'humanity', bringing with it/her bodily pleasure which issues forth sin and violation of God's law (*Opif.* 151–2, 165–6), and ultimately death (*QG* 1: 37, cf. 43, 45).[14] The creation of woman, therefore, opens the pathways to sin and death (cf. Sirach 25: 24).

Women naturally reflect the essential characteristics of the first woman, in the same way that men naturally reflect those of the first man. For Philo, the masculinity of the soul manifests itself as self-control, asceticism, reason, and activity, and the femininity of the soul as passion, materiality, irrationality, and passivity.[15] Theoretically, perhaps, one need not connect these

[11] See Sharon Lea Mattila, 'Wisdom, Sense Perception, Nature and Philo's Gender Gradient', *HTR* 89 (1996), 103–29, esp. 112–20.

[12] The group ἄνθρωποι, 'human beings', tends also to be masculine in Philo's usage, see Sly, *Perception*, 59–70.

[13] Romney Wegner, 'Portrayal', 47, citing b.Ketub. 8a, b; b.Ber. 61a, b; b. Erub. 18a.

[14] Ibid. 48–9.

[15] See Baer, *Use*, 38–44; Sly, *Perception*, 96–7. For specific passages illustrating such a conceptualization, see *Leg.* 2: 38, 49–50; 3: 49–50, 222–4; *Spec.* 1: 200; *Opif.* 165–7; *QG* 1: 43; 4: 15–18; *Fug.* 51.

gendered characteristics of the soul with the physical body. However, indeed, the body's sex does determine the innate sexual characteristics of the soul. A man therefore thinks in a more 'masculine' way, and a woman in a more 'feminine' way, because the sex of the body is duplicated in one's essential nature (cf. *Prob.* 117). In general, it is natural and good that women should be women and men should be men, and therefore that the former should be in a subordinate position to the latter. Ordinarily, Philo does not think women should try to become like men, a view he shares with many of his contemporaries. Philo can use the notion of masculinized women negatively when talking about women in the market taking on masculine actions or attending gymnastic contests (*Spec.* 3: 172–7).[16] What then should he do with the women of the Mareotic group, who, in living a spiritual and intellectual lifestyle (focusing on the νοῦς) together with men in a small extra-domestic group, may have been construed as being rather 'manly'?

We may consider Philo's description of Livia, wife of Augustus, who adorned the Jerusalem Temple with libation bowls and golden vials. Philo comments:

The judgments of women are usually weaker [than those of men] and do not apprehend any mental conception apart from what their senses perceive. But she [Livia] excelled all her sex in this as in everything, for the purity of the training she received[17] supplemented [her female] nature and practice provided maleness to her faculty of reason. (*Legat.* 319)[18]

In this Philo makes Livia follow the paradigm of the philosophical woman as 'One of the Guys' by her exemplary training by a related man.[19] Livia is trained in reason, as a disciple of her husband, in the same way that a philosophical student is trained

---

[16]   See also his negative use of the word γυνάνδρος (*Sacr.* 100; *Her.* 274; *Virt.* 21), noted by Szesnat, 'Pretty Boys', 98 n. 45; id., 'Homoeroticism'.

[17]   Her instructor in this training is understood to be Augustus.

[18]   See on this passage particularly Sly, *Perception*, 179–209 and ead., *Philo's Alexandria*, 72. It is interesting that this appears in the *Legatio*, which is the first part of *On Virtues*, so that the imperial family is given great credit for philosophical virtue.

[19]   The notion that a woman could reflect the virtues and abilities of a male relative, particularly of her father, is a motif in the literature, see e.g. Judith M. Hallett, 'Women's Lives in the Ancient Mediterranean', in Kraemer and D'Angelo (eds.), *Women and Christian Origins*, 13–34, at 24–5.

by the teacher. Augustus is, in this text, a virtuous philosopher (*Legat.* 143, 309, 318). Livia excels her sex and therefore becomes an honorary male in certain respects. Like Hipparchia, whose tombstone apparently designated her as having a 'masculine heart', so too did Livia have a masculinity in her faculty of reason. Livia is here being characterized similarly to Theano, who was taught philosophy by her husband Pythagoras, or the daughters of philosophers Eumetis/Cleobulina, Magnilla, and Agallis. Ideally, however, despite having 'a statesman's mind' or in other respects thinking like men, the perfect philosophical woman should still refrain from engaging in traditionally masculine pursuits, save—in certain circumstances—the actual teaching of philosophy to students. Such women are safe to use as paradigms of virtue because they are in a subordinate position to the men who have trained them. The husband or father educates the woman, who remains modest and feminine, keeping to usual patterns of acceptable female behaviour. This kind of training improves the woman's mind appropriately. To excel one's female sex in a good way is not the same as simple 'manliness', because manliness in a woman is configured as bad if a woman becomes overt about her education and fails to recognize her subordinate position in relation to men.

Philo can clearly play the card of the 'One of the Guys' woman if it suits him. He accounts for the historical virtue of Sarah—as well as providing a rationale for his symbolism of the matriarch as virtue—by masculinizing her. Like the Greek goddess Artemis, she has left a women's world and is motherless, having kinship only with her father's side (*Ebr.* 59–61).[20] Szesnat also points out Philo's description of the Dardanian women who killed their children rather than having them brought up as slaves (*Prob.* 115) as another example of the heroic woman with male faculties.[21] Philo clearly had the option, in terms of describing his *therapeutrides* as good, of arguing that they were women with masculinized minds, resulting from an excellent training by fathers or husbands. However, the paradigm relies upon establishing the women's subordinate and quite close relationship to a male teacher. Without that, the women would become freelance 'manly' women who immediately could be classified according

---

[20] See Romney Wegner, 'Portrayal', 55–6.
[21] Szesnat, 'Virgins', 198 n. 16.

to the negative paradigm of the 'Stuck-up Bitch'. Philo would need to tread carefully here.

It should be noted also that, while women could accrue maleness, men could also accrue femaleness. The male mind could be feminized by sense-perception. This is considered damaging. A man, for example, 'emasculates' himself (his soul) when exhibiting the desire which results in having sex with his wife (*Cher.* 40–1), for this involves a high degree of (feminine) sense-perception. Only by having sex purely for procreation (by rational decision for a specific purpose) could men escape to some degree such emasculation (*Spec.* 3: 9, 32–4; *QG* 4: 154).[22] Szesnat has explored also how slave boys are described as having 'female disease' (*Contempl.* 60) since the effeminacy of their appearance and the passive submission of these boys in sex changes their bodies and essential natures into a more feminine form (cf. *Spec.* 3: 37).[23] Such a boy becomes an ἀνδρόγυνος, a 'womanly' man. This kind of gender blending was not positive.

The perfect woman is, for Philo, perfect in her femininity as well as in her virtue. In *Spec.* 3: 171 she does not venture beyond the realm of *oeconomia* in her interests and concerns. She cultivates solitude—a home-bound lifestyle—and shuns the busy streets, tiptoeing out of her house at the least busy time of the day, for the sole purpose of attending the temple. This model is stereotypical in the Graeco-Roman world. Ideally, no one should have any cause to mention a good woman; even her virtue should not be a reason for anyone to discuss her. This ideal is already found in Thucydides (*Hist.* 2: 45: 2): 'Your reputation is glorious if . . . there is the least possible talk about you among men, whether it may be in praise or blame.' For example, in an inscription from Rome, a son's funeral oration for his mother

---

[22] According to Kathy L. Gaca, the view that only purposive sex for procreation is justified is to be traced to Pythagoraean thought, see her 'Philo's Principles of Sexual Conduct and their Influence on Christian Platonist Sexual Principles', *SPA* 8 (1996), 21–39.

[23] Szesnat, 'Pretty Boys', 94–101. Szesnat points out, interestingly, that despite Philo's characterization of same-sex intercourse as the most extreme form of sexual desire (cf. *Anim.* 49; *Abr.* 135; *Spec.* 2: 50) the 'mad love' for boys robs the boys (not the men who penetrate them) of ἀνδρεία, manliness, and that Philo's concern here is not even with citizen boys but slaves (p. 99). Presumably the transgression of nature is so vile to Philo that the slave boys' low social status is irrelevant.

sums up the ideal: 'My dearest mother deserved all the greater praise, because in modesty, uprightness, purity, obedience, wool-working, diligence and faithfulness she was equal and similar to other good women.'[24] One might expect that her son would have said she was outstanding, but that would have made her too exceptional, and her virtue was better protected by being one of many. He notes that 'praise for all good women is customarily simple and similar, because . . . sufficient is the fact that they have all done the same good deeds worthy of reputation'.[25] A good woman has a good reputation, but does not seem exceptional. Even when praising her in a funeral oration, one should not discuss her specifically too much. While men may be praised by distinctive features and actions, this kind of focus on individuality is not appropriate in regard to good women. A good woman leads a quiet and modest life of virtue, focusing on her home and family, and nothing much should ever be said about her. Philo's good woman conforms to the pattern perfectly.

Despite the ideal presented by Philo, a point to note is that, when Philo looked around him to what was going on in regard to the psychic dimensions of humanity, the feminine element appeared dominant. There is something strangely powerful about the feminine in Philo's construction.[26] For while ostensibly the masculine element of the soul is superior to the feminine and ideally should be in control, the feminine element of the soul frequently prevails over the masculine. In Philo's construction of the soul, it is almost impossibly difficult to throw off domination by sense-perception. Likewise, women are, in Philo's construction, physically weaker than men (cf. *Her.* 164), but women exercise a curious control over men socially. In *Legat.* 39 Philo states: 'A woman has an incredible ability to paralyse and seduce her husband, especially if she is lustful, for her guilty conscience increases her fawning.' He notes how women's customs prevail over men and 'we are not yet able to wash them away, or to run over to the hearth of the men's

---

[24] *CIL* vi. 10230, ll. 27–9, quoted from Robert K. Sherk, *The Roman Empire: Augustus to Hadrian* (Cambridge: CUP, 1988), 241–3, at p. 242. I am grateful to Christopher Ehrhardt for this reference.

[25] Ibid., ll. 20–5.

[26] This is recognized by Romney Wegner, when she quotes *Cher.* 59–60 and points out that Philo's true attitude to women may have have been ambivalance 'perhaps even cognitive dissonance', 50–1.

chamber' (*Ebr.* 59). In Philo's description of Essene views, men's 'better' natures are easily overcome by women in the household (*Hypoth.* 11: 14–17).

Philo appears to situate male domination by women in women's power to manipulate men on account of male desire. The mind becomes the slave of sense-perception through its quest for pleasure, and therefore becomes trapped in an inferior realm (*Leg.* 2: 50). Sense-perception deceives the mind by sly means (*Opif.* 165). A wife deceives her husband by the same sly means in Philo's (or the Essenes') construction of a marriage in which a man is completely at the mercy of his wife's wicked wiles and is indeed understood to be a slave (*Hypoth.* 11: 14–17).

Sense-perception is, however, not completely to be cast off, since it is a creation of God, and somehow also an important power of the soul, designed by God so that the mind can contemplate both material and immaterial things (*Cher.* 59–60; *Cong.* 21). It should simply be kept in its right place, in the same way that women should be. Men and women were created as equal by God in respect to their role as parents; despite women lacking strength they are biologically both necessary and equal in their contribution to forming progeny (*Her.* 164). Ideally, then, both men and women should participate in the government of the world, the men controlling the more important public institutions, and the women controlling the less important private ones, as Philo states in *Spec.* 3: 169–71. This is the correct balance in society. In the soul, the male, rational element should drive the mind. The female element is necessary but not the driving force.

Philo's metaphorical constructions of female and male in the soul owe a great deal to his perceptions of gender relations in the world around about him, though I do not want to push the correspondences too far, because Philo's symbolism could easily break free entirely from any correspondence to the observed world if necessary. It is only in basic essentializing of categories such as 'male' and 'female' that the analogies are obvious.

How then would Philo achieve the presentation of the female philosophers of *Contempl.* as 'good' in a way that would be consistent with his gender theory, and in a way that would appeal to his audiences? How could male and female be balanced here?

WOMEN AS STUDENTS OF MOSES

As noted above, Philo could have stressed that all the women of the group had masculinized minds, since they were taught perfect philosophy from their fathers, husbands, or other male close kin. They would then have been like the exceptional Livia and other women engaged in philosophy who kept to the social rules of acceptable behaviour. He does imply that they are themselves disciples in a certain philosophical school, but he never uses the term specifically in regard to the women. Rather, Philo describes *all* the members of the group as being 'pupils' or 'disciples' of Moses, Μωυσέως γνώριμοι (*Contempl.* 63 cf. 64). In Philo's terms, this designation is extremely flattering and significant. They are nothing like 'Stupid Cows'. This term does not refer only to the small group of people living outside Alexandria that Philo focuses upon in the text, but is much more general. As we have seen, for Philo this term was linked with those who practised an allegorical interpretation of scripture, which was thought to be passed down from Moses to the present day.[27]

This identifies the group as one which forms part of the wider philosophical school of thought to which Philo himself belonged in Alexandria. Implicitly then, the term indicates that women were part of this wider school, for if women were included in the group and the Mareotic group collectively were among the 'disciples of Moses' (= allegorical interpreters) found in Alexandrian society, then women could be involved in allegorical interpretation in Alexandrian Jewish society. They did not come to this isolated community in order to study allegorical Jewish philosophy, but rather they chose the contemplative lifestyle as a result of their excellence in allegorical Jewish philosophy. In order for the women to make the choice to embrace a life of special devotion to God in this extreme form, they would have needed to have been studying the Jewish philosophy of the allegorical school for some time within the city of Alexandria. In other words, Philo's text indicates not only that there were a few women *therapeutrides* in one particular exegetical group, but that some of Jewish women in Alexandria were in fact studying a

[27] *Det.* 86; *Post.* 12; *Conf.* 39; *Mos.* 2: 205; *Spec.* 1: 319, 345; 2: 88, 256; *Hypoth.* 11: 1; *Heres* 81; *QG* 3: 8. See Hay, 'Philo's References', 45.

sophisticated allegorical form of biblical interpretation, the highest type of philosophy, as Philo defined it.

In seeing Judaism as a whole as philosophy, Philo cannot really help indicating that women (and children) were involved in some way in this philosophy too.[28] It must have been widely understood that there was a clear place for women within this system, even though Hellenistic Jewish male authors, from Ben Sira to Josephus, tend to give the impression that it is men's business. Josephus, for example, states that, in regard to the law, 'the woman is in all things inferior to the man' (*Apion* 2: 201, cf. Philo, *Spec.* 2: 32), a statement he cites as scriptural,[29] though he notes too that even Jewish women and slaves knew Torah (*Apion* 2: 181). Luke 13: 10–17 tells the story of Jesus healing a woman in a synagogue, and she could easily come to the front to be healed. Women's knowledge of Torah is exemplified in a number of stories in rabbinic literature.[30] There is evidence that women were more involved with synagogues (the schools of the sacred philosophy, in Philo's understanding) than Philo overtly indicates.[31] In Alexandria it would have been quite natural for women to be involved in a deeper allegorical/philosophical exploration of Judaism, given that women were Jews as much as the men, following the instructions of Moses.

Certain rabbinic statements should not be taken on face value to mean Jewish women everywhere were somehow prevented from learning Torah. Rabbi Eliezar (end of second century CE) allegedly stated: 'Anyone who teaches his daughter Torah, it is as though he has taught her lechery' (m.Sota 3: 4). In terms of the paradigms from the discourse on *philosophia*, this is interesting, for here Rabbi Eliezar seems to be rejecting the 'safe' method for the education of girls/women in philosophy by their male relatives, linking the acquiring of philosophy specifically with the

---

[28] It is clear from texts such as 2 Macc. 6: 10 (cf. 1 Macc. 1: 20–2) that women were responsible for keeping the law as much as men were.

[29] See Leonie J. Archer, 'Notions of Community and the Exclusion of the Female in Jewish History and Historiography', in Leonie J. Archer, Susan Fischler, and Maria A. Wyke (eds.), *Women in Ancient Societies: An Illusion of the Night* (London: Macmillan, 1994), 53–69.

[30] Ilan, *Jewish Women*, 196–7.

[31] See Bernadette J. Brooten, *Women Leaders in the Ancient Synagogue: Inscriptional Evidence and Background Issues* (BJS, 36; Chico, Calif.: Scholars, 1982).

sexual licentiousness of the *hetairai*: there was no such thing as a
'One of the Guys' or 'Just a Housewife' woman philosopher, only
a 'Sexy Babe'. In the literary context of the statement, Rabbi
Eliezer's pronouncement is a reaction against the view of Rabbi
Ben Azzai who states: 'A man must give his daughter knowledge
of Torah' (m.Sota 3: 4). Tal Ilan has explored how Rabbi Eliezer
is portrayed as being fiercely opposed to women studying Torah.
He states: 'They shall burn the teachings of Torah rather than
convey them to women' (y.Sota 3: 4, cf. b.Yoma 66b),[32] but the
individual reality of one rabbi cannot be used to represent the
reality of all Jewish women, both in Palestine and throughout the
Diaspora, from the Hellenistic period to the late Roman. Ilan
goes on to note that other rabbinic evidence suggests that women
were studying Torah, and could even teach their husbands
Torah.[33] The characterization of such women is essentially
domestic, the most famous exemplar being Beruriah, wife of
Rabbi Meir and daughter or Rabbi Hananiah ben Teradion,
though she was vilified in a later tradition for improper conduct
with a student (who was set up to proposition her by her husband), a story that shows fear of the 'Stuck-up Bitch' and 'Sexy
Babe' paradigms.[34] The reason for certain authors downplaying
the role of women in the philosophical life of Judaism as a whole
may be put down to deep-seated worries about the threat posed
by philosophical women in society and the negative paradigms
which were much in currency, despite the activity of women
in the field both within and outside Judaism. At the very
least, women were understood to 'hear' by their attendance at

[32] Ilan, *Jewish Women*, 190–1.

[33] For these examples, see Ilan, *Jewish Women*, 192–4.

[34] See Ilan, *Jewish Women*, 197–200 cf. Daniel Boyarin, *Carnal Israel:
Reading Sex in Talmudic Culture* (Berkeley: University of Califormia Press,
1993), 181–93; David Goodblatt, 'The Beruriah Traditions', *JJS* 26 (1975),
68–85; Rachel Adler, 'The Virgin in the Brothel and Other Anomalies:
Character and Context in the Legend of Beruriah', *Tikkun*, 3/6 (1988), 28–32,
102–5. She is unusual in being named, for, as Judith Hauptman states: 'Since
most of the women who appear in Talmudic anecdotes are close relatives of
rabbis, they are identified as the daughter of Rabbi X, the sister of Rabbi X, the
wife of Rabbi X, and sometimes even the mother of Rabbi X. Only on rare
occasions are they identified by their own name', *Rereading the Rabbis: A
Woman's Voice* (Boulder, Colo.: Westview Press, 1998), 12. This, in fact, should
probably be understood as a strategy to protect their virtue, rather than a
misogynistic oversight.

synagogue, even if in general men were understood to be under-taking the serious study (t.Sota 7: 9). There is a specific ruling in the Tosephta that even men and women who were ritually unclean may still read the Tanakh, learn mishnah, midrash, halakhah, and aggadah (t.Ber. 2: 12).[35] If they could do so ritual-ly unclean, then they could also do so clean.

Early Christian tradition depicts the Jewish women around Jesus as being in a student–teacher relationship with him. Acts 9: 36 specifically names Tabitha/Dorcas as a *mathetria*, 'student', of Jesus. In the Akhmim Fragment of the otherwise lost Gospel of Peter (12: 50), Mary Magdalene is described as a *mathetria tou kuriou*. She calls him her 'teacher' in John 20: 15–16. In Luke 10: 38–42 Mary of Bethany is portrayed as a disciple of Jesus, sitting at his feet and listening to his discourse.[36]

If Jewish women students are attested elsewhere, then we would expect to find them in Alexandria also. In *Fug.* 55 and 58 Philo says he went for instruction to a wise woman (φοιτήσας οὖν παρὰ γυναῖκα σοφήν) named Skepsis, 'consideration'. It is com-mon in translations to see Skepsis as only a personification and not a real woman.[37] However, while Philo is being purposely ambiguous on this point, the model of a wise woman instructing Philo in allegorical interpretation must be based on existing real models for it not to appear ridiculous to the audience Philo addresses. While 'Skepsis' herself as an individual may not be real, the characterization points to the real. It was not absurd as an image for Philo to use.

WOMEN PHILOSOPHERS IN ALEXANDRIA

At this point we should pause to think of the evidential aspects of Chapter 8. Rhetoric aside, there is considerable evidence of women philosophers in the Graeco-Roman world. Female

[35] Boyarin, *Carnal Israel*, 180–1.

[36] There is a huge literature on women and Jesus, often with a feminist theo-logical thrust, though no one to my knowledge has as yet explored in detail the dimensions of the student–teacher relationship between women and Jesus in terms of contemporaneous *philosophia* specifically.

[37] See the translation by Colson in Francis H. Colson and George H. Whitaker, *Philo v* (Loeb Classical Library; Cambridge, Mass.: Heinemann, 1934), 39. In the Greek text here the name is not capitalized.

philosophers are attested in Alexandria from pagan circles: Agallis, daughter of Agallias, Ptolemais, and a number of Pythagoraeans.[38] It should not be at all surprising, given this context, that there were Jewish female philosopher-teachers as well. Jewish women were participating in a milieu in which women were acquiring philosophy in various traditions, and could also teach it.

The best evidence comes from the philosophical school of the Pythagoraeans. Pythagoraean works allegedly written by women circulated in the Hellenistic and Roman periods, and examples of such works have been found in Egypt.[39] Several Pythagoraean works attributed to women are still extant, thanks to Stobaeus, though the question of whether they are really works by women has at times been raised.[40] Even if these are not all genuine, the attribution of works to Pythagoraean women seems to suggest that Pythagoraean women were known to have authored philosophical works and engaged in teaching. This is quite noteworthy in itself, given the paucity of women's philosophical treatises surviving from antiquity; the Pythagoraean tracts outnumber the other scraps by far. In the tracts ostensibly written by the Pythagoraean female philosophers Theano (not the wife of Pythagoras but another), Perictione, Phintys, and Melissa, there is concentration on the virtues of trust, temperance, frugality, marital fidelity, and harmony within the domestic sphere.[41]

The domestic character of the extant texts may of course be the result of the selection process, which determined which works would be most suitable to copy. Theano the philosophical writer—as opposed to Theano the wife of Pythagoras who said apophthegms—is said in the Suidas to have written numerous poems and treatises: *Concerning Pythagoras, Concerning*

---

[38] See Pomeroy, *Women in Hellenistic Egypt*, 61–72.

[39] *P. Haun.* ii. 13, dated to the 3rd cent. CE, which is a version of letters by Melissa and Theano, see Rowlandson (ed.), *Women and Society*, 327–8; Pomeroy, *Women in Hellenistic Egypt*, 64.

[40] For the texts see Mario Meunier, *Femmes pythagoriciennes: Fragments et lettres de Théano, Périctioné, Phintys, Mélissa et Myia* (Paris: Guy Trédaniel, 1932; repr. 1980).

[41] Voula Lambropoulou, 'Some Pythagoraean Female Virtues', in Richard Hawley and Barbara Levick (eds.), *Women in Antiquity: New Assessments* (London: Routledge, 1995), 129. Lambropoulou argues that this is a later modification of a radically egalitarian Pythagoraeanism of an earlier time.

Excellence, *Advice for Women*, and *Sayings of the Pythagoraeans*, though only one work, her *Concerning Piety* (which may be that referred to as 'Advice for Women') has survived.[42] One may wonder whether the selective processes of the centuries whittled down the corpus of works by Pythagoraean women to their texts which mainly address women and women's place, rather than wider concerns. Selective processes may also be responsible for the survival of works which stress the usual feminine expectations of women. Aesara of Lucania apparently wrote a book on human nature, of which only fragments survive.[43] A woman named Ptolemais—usually identified as a Pythagoraean—wrote a text on musical theory.[44] Works such as the variety of texts written by Arignote on the mysteries of Bacchus/Dionysus[45] have simply disappeared.

Nevertheless, it seems clear from Phintys' *On Women's Modesty* that the author here considered that virtues were gendered, at least by the third to second centuries BCE when this tract was most likely written.[46] She notes that what makes a horse excellent is not what makes a human being excellent, so too with men and women. The excellence for women is moderation, and while men should exercise authority in public, women should stay at home, even though courage, justice, and intelligence are shared equally by men and women.[47] Pythagoras' daughter Myia

[42] Adler (ed.), *Suidae*, ii. 688, ll. 14–17 (no. 83) = *PG* 117: 1356. She is probably also to be credited with *writing*: 'Life would be a feast to the wicked who, having done evil, then die [except that the soul is immortal]. If the soul was not immortal, death would be a windfall.' Clement of Alexandria, *Strom.* 4: 44: 2.

[43] See Thesleff, *Pythagoraean Texts*, 48–50; Stobaeus, *Anth.* 1: 49: 27 (WH 355–7); Waithe, *Women Philosophers*.

[44] She apparently came from Cyrene to Alexandria *c*.250 BCE. Her Pythagoraean identity is not entirely sure, since apparently in a dispute between the Pythagoraeans and the Peripatetics she supported the latter, see Pomeroy, *Women in Hellenistic Egypt*, 61; Thesleff, *Pythagoraean Texts*, 7 n. 2 and 242–3.

[45] See Adler (ed.), *Suidae*, i. 350, ll. 19–21 (no. 3872). We do not even know whether these texts were positive or negative about the cult, though most probably the latter.

[46] See Stobaeus, *Anth.* 4: 23: 61 (WH 588–93) and Thesleff, *Pythagoraean Texts*, 151–2, Waithe, *Women Philosophers*, 26–8. For Perictione's 'On the Harmony of Women' and 'On Wisdom' see Stobaeus, *Anth.* 4: 25: 50 (WH 631–2), cf. 3: 1: 120 (WH 85–7); Waithe, *Women Philosophers*, 32–9; Thesleff, *Pythagoraean Texts*, 142–5.

[47] Thesleff, *Pythagoraean Texts*, 152.

is credited with a text which applies the Pythagoraean principles of moderation to caring for a newborn baby.[48] The letters of yet another Theano to fellow women philosophers likewise indicate domesticity, and also a lively mind full of philosophical enquiry and endearing frustration which points to the tension experienced by these women.[49] In ancient philosophy, the school was itself often found in domestic space anyway, and therefore not strictly 'public', a matter I will return to in the following chapter. Therefore, early Pythagoraeans might well have accepted that it was within the bounds of women's modesty to teach and learn in this context. Domestic space in antiquity itself should not be configured on the basis of modern parallels. The home in antiquity could be a centre of education and work.[50] It was here that an elite woman would receive her education, including philosophy. Aristophanes has Lysistrata say she was taught by listening to her father and older men in her family, an activity which took place in the home.[51]

If Pythagoraean women really did accept domesticity as appropriate to women and public life as not appropriate, they do not need to be judged by the standards of a later time as being 'unliberated'. As Gillian Clark has noted, 'we need not dismiss these works as attempts, by men or collusive women, to keep women in their place. They set out to show that traditional female concern for a well-run household, healthy upbringing of children, tactful handling of husbands, personal modesty and frugality, are important manifestations of the harmony of the cosmos.'[52] If these texts are indeed genuine, the point is not that Pythagoraean women either broke gendered social boundaries or felt entirely satisfied, but that they incorporated philosophy into

---

[48] Ibid. 123–4; Waithe, *Women Philosophers*, 15–16. See Clement of Alexandria, *Strom.* 4: 121: 4.

[49] See Waithe, *Women Philosophers*, 41–55.

[50] See the discussion by Carolyn Osiek, 'The Family in Early Christianity: "Family Values" Revisited', *CBQ* 58 (1996), 1–24, at 9–14.

[51] Aristophanes, *Lysistrata* 1126–7.

[52] Gillian Clark in her commentary, *Iamblichus: On the Pythagorean Life* (Liverpool: Liverpool University Press, 1989), p. xvii. Iamblichus reflects this in Pythagoras' speech to the women of Croton, in which the philosopher is concerned with morality within the women's usual lives. Women are obliged to be faithful to their husbands (132), but husbands are advised that a man's neglect of his wife may drive her to adultery (48), see Clark, pp. xvii–xviii.

the world of women, thereby breaking gendered intellectual boundaries, and were open to acknowledging the frustrations of gendered space and roles. In fact, the texts by the women show that the *logos* could be at home in the home.

Intellectual achievement still perhaps did not redefine woman's place in society. When considering how to *live*, given the authenticity of these texts, it seems to have been a case of working out how to live within the kinds of societal structures that were already in existence. The rhetoric of Pythagoraean texts themselves therefore presents us with a situation in which women do not traverse boundaries of what is acceptable in terms of 'virtuous' elite women's social sphere, though they do indicate that women's intellectual skills were appreciated by Pythagoraeans in general and that women's philosophizing was not curbed by gendered roles, or even an acceptance of a specifically feminine intrinsic nature different from the masculine. The tradition of apophthegms of Theano the wife of Pythagoras in the literary tradition about Pythagoraeans (rather than the Pythagoraean texts themselves) would suggest at first sight that Pythagoraean women were perceived as being rather more modestly confined and under the domination of their husbands than they were in practice. The Pythagoraean texts point to a literacy among such women and intellectual searching which is not generally indicated by descriptions of them. If anything, the texts by women Pythagoraeans, if genuine, hold the domestic sphere as equally worthy of serious philosophical reflection as that of the public world of the *polis* and therefore give increased value to the normative social world of women. Myia's text on the Pythagoraean way of caring for an infant may be viewed then as radical to an extreme, in that it takes to women what might have been considered beyond what women were capable of apprehending.

When Philo came to present the women members of the Mareotic group as 'students of Moses', he might have considered not only the positive paradigm of the 'Just a Housewife' in the discourse of *philosophia* but also actual women who studied Jewish or Pythagoraean philosophy in Alexandria, in the domestic context. Pythagoraeans were, according to Philo, a 'holy company' who teach well (*Prob.* 2). He writes positively of Pythagoraean ideas on several occasions (*Opif.* 100; *Leg.* 1: 15;

QG 1: 17, 99; 2: 12; 3: 39; 4: 8; 4: 27). Had he addressed the issue of Jewish women philosophers within Alexandria, in the context of allegorical interpretation of scripture that was being undertaken there, it is very likely that he would have constructed them very much along the lines of the ideal Pythagoraean women: ultra-modest, household-minded, and very feminine apart from their 'masculine' mental powers. The problem he had, however, was that the Mareotic group could not be configured in terms of the normal domestic context. The Mareotic group was a community of non-related adult philosophers living outside the city, outside a domestic situation.

The women of the Mareotic group appear to have abandoned the world of domesticity and procreation. They have no fathers, husbands, brothers, or uncles to be obedient to. Philo cannot present the women of this community as the Jewish equivalent of Pythagoraean women philosophers, whose locus was very much within the household, or an ideal that would be recognized as instantly good by Stoics, or anyone else. In leaving the household to live an ascetic life of few possessions, away from normal society, the women of the Mareotic group may seem closer to the model of Hipparchia the Cynic, wife of Crates.[53] However, Hipparchia was considered an exceptional woman, a female Crates, and a very ambiguous figure for a role model, even with a husband who instructed her. Despite her asceticism, she too was sexualized in traditions concerning her. She was the epitome of an immodest woman: outrageous and unique. It is highly unlikely that Philo would have commended his *therapeutrides* to anyone by arguing that they were in any way like Hipparchia. Rather, he seems to be very aware that the women he describes would face the criticism of being undomestic 'Stuck-up Bitches' or even 'Sexy Babes' if he was not very careful. He wants to use them and be positive about them, but they are a rhetorical problem.

The fairly strong tradition of describing women positively within both the Pythagoraean school and the Platonic Academy[54] may have given him a precedent, but we do indeed

[53] Diogenes Laertius, *Lives* 96–8; see also Epictetus, *Discourses* 3: 22: 76; Theodoret, *Therapeutike* 12: 49; Clement of Alexandria, *Strom.* 4: 19: 121: 6; Antipater of Sidon, *Anthology* 3: 12: 52; *Suidas*, 'Hipparchia', *PG* 117: 1275.

[54] Waithe, *Women Philosophers*, 68–71; Hawley, 'Women Philosophers', 73–4, cf. Diogenes Laertius, *Lives* 3: 1; 4: 2; Plato, *Ep.* 12.

feel his discomfort, and apologetic tone, when he introduces the Mareotic women in the text. He immediately stresses that they have 'the same zeal and purpose as the men' (32), so they are 'One of the Guys' types of women, and not 'Stupid Cows' or just engaged in 'Women's Stuff'; that they are very modest (33), so they are not 'Stuck-up Bitches' or 'Sexy Babes' and are more like 'Just a Housewife' models; that they are in fact 'mostly elderly virgins' (68), so they are not 'Sexy Babes'. They are completely proper, modest, and chaste: models of femininity, 'Just a Housewife' types in many important respects. His solution to the problem of how to make the apparently non-domestic masculinized *therapeutrides* safe is to make them conceptually domestic: virgin matrons in the household of perfect philosophy.

'MOTHERS' OF THE CONGREGATION

In terms of the domestic ideal, a woman should be a good mother. Perfect women philosophers should also be good mothers, even a Pythagoraean philosopher like Theano, and so it is not surprising to find that in *De Vita Contemplativa* the senior women are described by Philo as being precisely that: mothers. The junior members who manage the day-to-day running of the community consider the 'seniors' of the congregation to be 'their parents in common, more closely connected with them than by blood' (*Contempl.* 72).[55] This is the basis of the extremely loving relations Philo notes, and the lack of subservience among the junior members who wait at table as *diakonoi*. He writes: 'They are just like real children who are affectionately glad to be of service to fathers *and mothers*' (72) and 'they fulfil the requirements of servants not by compulsion or by enduring orders, but, with voluntary, free will they anticipate quickly and willingly any requests' (71).[56]

---

[55] As we have seen, Philo notes that the 'children' of this group may not in fact be young—someone old may still be understood as a 'child' if s/he had only recently come to the community (*Contempl.* 67).

[56] As already noted, this image of children helping out at a symposium may have struck chords with the Emperor Claudius, who, according to Suetonius, insisted on children being present at his *convivia* (*Div. Claud.* 32), as in old Roman custom.

The identification of the senior women as mothers is important not only because it enables these women to fulfil the role of a
good woman in normatively gendered society, but because in
much of the ancient world, as in the world today, a woman's
status in a given social group was connected with her being a
mother. This was the case also in the Jewish community in
antiquity, in which the status of a mother in family and community appears to have been quite high. The status of a mother
along with a father in the ancient Israelite household is affirmed
in Deuteronomy 5: 16; Exodus 20: 12, cf. Leviticus 19: 3. A child
who strikes either father or mother is liable to punishment
(Exod. 21: 15, 17). Proverbs 1: 8 and 6: 20 exhorts children to
listen and adhere to the teaching of both father and mother.[57] In
the household, children would have expected to learn from both
parents and obey them. Deborah is called 'Mother in Israel', a
designation of her divinely ordained leadership of the nation
(Judges 5: 7).[58] In a non-Jewish context we have Tata of
Aphrodisias (second century CE) described as being a 'mother' of
the city.[59] In Jewish contexts, a woman of high status or donor
who may have played an important leadership role in the life of
the community and synagogue might be deemed 'mother of the
synagogue' in inscriptions (*CIJ* 523, 496, 166, 639).[60] The
'mothers' of the congregation are referred to also in a fragmentary text within the Dead Sea Scrolls corpus (4Q270: 7: i: 14),
probably indicating senior women of high status as here.
Therefore, Philo indicating that the senior women of the
Mareotic group were mothers was a way not only of making them
safe in terms of the paradigms of philosophical women, but also
of enhancing their honour within the community.

[57] See for discussion of mothers in Israel, Carol Meyers, *Discovering Eve:
Ancient Israelite Women in Context* (New York and Oxford: OUP, 1988), 150–2.

[58] Meyers, *Eve*, 159–60. Meyers also notes that the northern Israelite city of
Abel is called 'a mother in Israel' (2 Sam. 20: 19) and conjectures that it may
have been an oracular centre. It was where a wise woman resolves a crisis concerning David's general Joab (2 Sam. 14: 1–24). See also Rachel Adler, ' "A
Mother in Israel": Aspects of the Mother-Role in Jewish Myth', in Rita M.
Gross (ed.), *Beyond Androcentrism* (Missoula, Mont.: Scholars, 1977), 237–55
at pp. 246–9; Cheryl Exum, 'Mother in Israel: A Familiar Story Reconsidered',
in Letty M. Russell (ed.), *Feminist Interpretation of the Bible* (Oxford:
Blackwell, 1985), 73–85.

[59] Kraemer, *Her Share*, 86, 120–1; see also *CIJ* 100, 738.

[60] See Brooten, *Women Leaders*, 63–70.

This works on the level of history as much as within Philo's rhetoric. If the women were understood to be 'mothers'—as Philo states—then they were held in a position of respect within the Mareotic group. The Dead Sea Scrolls fragment 4Q270: 7: i: 14 indicates that the configuration of senior women as mothers in a congregation was known in at least one contemporary Jewish group. It is in fact part of a version of the famous Damascus Document. In 1QH 7: 20–2 the author acknowledges that God has made him 'a father to the children of grace, and a foster-father to the people of wonder'. The earliest Christians likewise clearly saw themselves as a family. They were all brothers and sisters with God as divine Father: an ἀδελφότης, group of siblings (1 Pet. 2: 17; 5: 9). This self-conceptualization was known outside their circle and laughed at. In Lucian's *The Passing of Peregrinus*, he notes that the 'wretches' (κακοδαίμονες) 'believe that their first lawgiver (Jesus) convinced them they are all brothers and sisters (ἀδελφοὶ πάντες) once they deny the Greek gods, worship that impaled sophist, and live according to his laws' (13). The Christians were strikingly different from the Mareotic group in that they were all siblings together, not stratified into parents and children. 'Call no one on earth "father"', said their founding philosopher, Jesus of Nazareth (Matt. 23: 9). The Mareotic group appears quite different, divided between mothers and fathers on the one hand, and children (who presumably saw themselves as siblings) on the other. But the familial language is still significant.

CELIBACY

The issue of women's maternal role in society is obviously a concern to Philo, and it is linked with issues of sexuality in general. A housewife in normative domestic contexts was also engaged in sex: she may be modest, but she had sex with her husband. In the case of the *therapeutrides*, this was not so. Philo then needs to make a case for the celibacy of the women while yet affirming their quasi-maternal role. Not only do the senior women ('mothers') of the congregation have the junior members as children, Philo theorizes that their souls also bring forth spiritual children (*Contempl.* 68). Elsewhere he notes that the soul becomes 'mother of a large family' when it returns to a virginal state, receives the divine seed, and then produces the perfect children: prudence, courage, temperance, justice, holiness, piety, and other virtues and dispositions (*Praem.* 159–60).[61] Holger Szesnat points out that this definition of spiritual children is particularly important in regard to the women, since Philo has already stated that *men* leave children behind (*Contempl.* 13, 18) and therefore they, and not the women, have fulfilled their proper duties of procreation.[62] This was perfectly proper, for it was generally held by Jews that it was men who were obligated to multiply, not women (m.Yeb. 6: 6), and Philo insists that men have fulfilled the law. While this point would have been lost on a Roman audience, it was important for Philo, and points to elements in the rhetoric of *Contempl.* which show Philo's unease about having to present the group as completely 'good'.

In *Contempl.* 68, Philo defines the women of the Mareotic group as celibate, and engages in numerous extraordinary rhetorical strategies to explain this. Philo's assertion that the women of this group were 'mostly aged virgins' (πλεῖσται γηραιαὶ παρθένοι) is clearly made at this point in order to insist on the women's lack of sexual licentiousness when he introduces them in a meal setting, to avoid the 'Sexy Babe' at dinner image, but women here also become a signifier for sexuality.

There is also a kind of rhetorical dissonance, for Philo presents their perpetual virginity in this instance as positive, when Philo believed that men at least were obligated to 'multiply', in order to fulfil the command of God, as Szesnat notes.[63] We find this view of Philo indicated in his comments on the obligation to divorce a barren woman, where he kindly takes pity on men who continue to be married to their barren wives from force of familiarity, but has no sympathy—rather, outright condemnation—for men who married women who have previously been shown to be barren (*Spec.* 3: 32–4). Because it is important to procreate—even if women are not actually obligated to do so—Philo stresses that the women of the Mareotic group are mothers not only to the adopted juniors but to spirit children within their virginal souls. The women have the immortal offspring which Philo defines elsewhere as virtues and dispositions (*Fug.* 51–2).

[61] See Baer, *Use*, 51–3.   [62] Szesnat, 'Virgins', 197.
[63] Ibid. 193 (cf. *Praem.* 108–9; *Det.* 147–8).

A lifelong-celibate may have been problematic, but a 'virgin' itself was good as a motif. Philo uses the different categories of 'virgin' and 'woman' symbolically, ascribing a positive value to the former and a negative to the latter. In terms of Philo's society, there was a fundamental status shift that affected females: up until marriage they were παρθένοι, 'virgins'. With sex/marriage, they became γύναι, 'women'. What Philo has observed in the world, he uses in his symbolism. For example, Philo writes in his description of Sarah that with ordinary sexual relations (upon marriage) virgins are turned into women but when God begins to consort with the soul he makes what was before a woman into a virgin again (*Cher.* 50 cf. *QE.* 2: 3; *Somn.* 2: 185). The soul itself should be virginal in order to ascend towards union with God. The soul, ostensibly female in Greek (ψυχή), needs to rid itself of the encumbrance of materialistic feminization in order to become a virgin: a higher spiritual state (*Cher.* 50; *Praem.* 159–60).[64] Using the number symbolism of the Pythagoraeans, Philo asserts that the number 7 is itself a 'virgin', motherless, begotten by the Father, as an ideal male form without the female (*Leg.* 1: 15 cf. *Her.* 170, 216; *Mos.* 2: 210; *QG* 2: 12; *QE* 2:46). In *Contempl.* 65 this *number* is considered to have the qualities of 'purity and perpetual virginity'. It is interesting to remember that, when Philo addresses the significance of Miriam singing in the story of Exodus, he describes her as representing sense-perception that has been made 'pure and clean' (*Agr.* 80), perhaps then also virginal.

Is it possible then for real women to become like Sarah or Miriam, renewed virgins?[65] By denying their sexual physiology could women ascend to a higher (more masculine) spiritual status, 'female in form only', as Ross Kraemer put it?[66] Was Philo here recommending a lifestyle which would have women who were once married choosing celibacy and therefore renewed 'virginity'?

Nowhere does Philo indicate that real women could become virgins again in terms of their actual social or physical status or even that celibacy in itself was a condition for spiritual excellence

---

[64] Baer, *Use*, 45–53.

[65] See Sly, *Perception*, p. xx; cf. *Cherubim* 50.

[66] Kraemer, 'Monastic Jewish Women', 353, and also ead., *Her Share*, 114; Mattila, 'Wisdom', 107.

or the bearing of soul-children. His description of Sarah seems designed to surprise the reader, to provoke an awareness of how spiritual things can work so very differently from material ones. Celibacy itself does not make women virgins again in body, and even less honorary males.[67] Philo's comments about the maternal capacity of the pure, virginal soul is one thing, but he does not link it with celibacy of the body *per se* as a prerequisite. Livia develops masculinity in her faculty of reason as a (presumably sexually active) wife, married to the exemplary Augustus (*Legat.* 319). However, in so far as celibacy is a condition resulting from control of sense-perception, then it perhaps indicates virginity and purity of the *soul* which has been uncorrupted by (feminine) sense-perception. But this is the case for both males and females, not for the latter alone.

Let us explore this further. There is a division between what was possible for the soul and what was possible for the body. Philo could throw away the constraints of earth-bound gendered language if it suited him to explain spiritual realities in a way that is designed to bamboozle his readers into awareness of the conundrums of spiritual truth, exactly *because* the world of spirit simply does not behave like the world of material things. Philo in fact scoffs at people who confuse material with physical realities; they are ridiculous and naïve (*Her.* 81). Philo's imagery is therefore inconsistent and at times contradictory on purpose. As we have seen, in Philo's symbolic construction, the female state is passive, material, bodily, sense-perceptible, while the male is active, rational, incorporeal, and more like mind and thought (*QG* 1: 8). The virgin soul really indicates a kind of masculinized soul, whether this soul is in a male or female body. As partially or fully masculinized, the soul can unite with a feminized God: Sophia, or Wisdom.[68] In *Fug.* 52, Sophia, the daughter of God, is also masculine, and is herself 'father' who can sow and beget in souls aptness to learn, education, knowledge, wisdom, good and praiseworthy actions. This is precisely what is taking place here in Philo's description of *Contempl.* 68: God and Wisdom are essentially the same, but Philo initially stays with

[67] See Szesnat, 'Virgins', 195; cf. Kraemer, 'Monastic Jewish Women', 352–7.

[68] For an exploration of the motif see Richard A. Horsley, 'Spiritual Marriage with Sophia', *VC* 33 (1979), 30–54.

the terminology of the male 'God' rather than the female 'Sophia' in order to tie the language to the sex of the (physical) women he discusses in regard to *spiritual* reproduction. They are, he states, mostly elderly virgins. He then jumps to consider the fruits of a virgin *soul*; the soul here remains feminine, passive, and gives birth to 'immortal offspring', or more particularly a male perceptive faculty—intelligence—which enables her (the soul, the woman) to see, by its lights, the doctrines of Sophia/Wisdom. The feminine soul of the woman remains and God 'sows seed' as a masculine subject in order to create a masculine faculty. This model has parallels in various other passages among Philo's writings, and Philo could have said the same about the males.[69] But then, having replicated bodily gender in the soul, he suddenly switches the gender of the divine by stating that the women want to live with Sophia/Wisdom.[70] Had the subjects been male, the sexual metaphor would have been more obvious.[71] As Richard Horsley states:

The metaphors are mixed, or rather the 'persons' in the spiritual intercourse are mixed . . . (b)ut more is involved that mere metaphor. The abstention from normal sexual relations . . . is connected with and occurs because of a higher spiritual marriage with Sophia. The intense and exclusive contemplation of the divine mate leaves no time, energy or interest for any of the normal social or marital relations.[72]

What do we make of all these gymnastics? Philo has in fact side-tracked the reader from seeing the real women of the group. 'Woman' leads to 'virgin', which leads to 'virgin soul', which

[69] In *Spec.* 2: 30 the *logos* impregnates the soul with excellent thoughts; in *Post.* 135 God impregnates 'Leah' with the seed of Wisdom and she brings forth beautiful ideas. In *Cher.* 42–9 God's seed is 'the seed of happiness'; see Horsley, 'Spiritual Marriage', 35–7.

[70] Because spiritual realities are not bound by physical constraints the sex of the divine can switch around. God incorporates both male and female elements. There is absolutely nothing static here in terms of divine sexual realities, see Winston, 'Philo', 202–3, 206–8.

[71] Philo could look to Plato for the precedent. Plato used the language of pregnancy and birth for men in *Symp.* 206b–e, 207a, 208a–e, 209a–e, etc., though this language is placed in the mouth of Diotima whose gender is, as Halperin states, 'a condition of her discourse . . . it is inscribed in what she says'. Halperin, 'Why is Diotima a Woman?', 117.

[72] Horsley, 'Spiritual Marriage', 43. Kraemer reads this differently, as indicating that 'they had purged their souls of their feminine elements and become male and/or virgin', see Kraemer, 'Monastic Jewish Women', 353.

leads to 'children of the virgin soul', and we are led out of the door. Suddenly the actual women are almost living incarnations of the pure and ever-virginal number 7. He has changed course. What he states about the soul's productivity by its intercourse with the divine could have been said about all the members of the group, but he has gone there only in relation to the women.

If we turn to consider the real women here, it is actually unclear whether Philo means to refer to 'mostly elderly' virgins (that is, they are all virgins, most of whom are aged), or 'mostly virgins' who are elderly (that is, they are mostly virgins, who all happen to be elderly), or both (that is, they are mostly virgins, most of whom are also elderly). It may be best to read the word πλεῖσται as governing both adjective and noun, so that we leave open the possibility that there were women in the group who were (*a*) not virgins and (*b*) not old.[73] As Szesnat points out, Philo elsewhere uses the word γύναι to refer to the women, not παρθένοι.[74] The 'mostly' of Philo's text becomes more and more interesting. Philo's sudden insistence that his audience visualize the women as virgins is not simply a way of insisting on the women's lack of sexuality, but is also a smoke screen to avoid direct discussion of the tricky issue of celibacy, which seems in fact the real situation for *all* members of the group, men and women. Philo wrote that *therapeutai* leave their wives behind (*Contempl.* 17) in their quest for the contemplative life. In other words, it is a condition of all (male) *therapeutai* that they be celibate, but it is implied that they do the right thing and reproduce prior to this celibate lifestyle. Ross Kraemer wonders if the lack of any mention of husbands being left indicates that the women of the community had never married.[75] But Philo could not have written that the women left their husbands and children behind and still have them considered 'good'.[76] What is acceptable for men is not acceptable for women. When he comes to discuss the women in the symposium, however, the issue of reproduction

---

[73] Kraemer notes here that Philo may have thought some younger women were capable of the philosophical life, 'Monastic Jewish Women', 354.

[74] Szesnat, 'Aged Virgins', 196.

[75] Kraemer, 'Monastic Jewish Women', 352–3.

[76] Consider the trauma evidenced in the Christian apocryphal acts when a woman like Maximilla chooses to embrace a celibate lifestyle away from her husband, *Acts of Andrew* 2: 414. See Virginia Burrus, 'Chastity as Autonomy: Women in the Stories of the Apocryphal Acts', *Semeia*, 38 (1986), 101–35.

and celibacy immediately presents itself, because 'woman' is a signifier for the body and sexuality. He discusses virginity rather than celibacy, and side-tracks the focus even further by stressing that this is self-chosen virginity rather than anything inflicted upon the women by others, thereafter jumping into a discussion of the fruitful virginal soul. The conclusion is that these *virgins* are superior. But Philo actually avoids discussing the issue of the non-virgin celibate women and, moreover, celibate men. His rhetoric blinds us just as he gives us a glimpse.

If the whole community were in fact celibate, what did these people really think? How did they rationalize this form of asceticism? It is certainly probable that the notion of being spiritually fruitful was itself one that the community understood and accepted, and was not Philo's own invention. The origins of the 'spiritually fruitful celibate' ideal are to be found both in the Septuagint and in Plato.[77] In Wisdom 3: 13 it is stated that a 'barren' woman who has remained sexually chaste 'will have fruit at the visitation of souls'. The parallel passage dealing with the good 'barren' man—a righteous eunuch—gives his reward as 'a most desirable portion in the temple of the Lord' (3: 14). This latter promise goes back to Isaiah 56: 3–5, where it is stated that no eunuch should say: 'Behold, I am a dried-up tree', that is, one who cannot bear any fruit, for YHWH states that the righteous eunuchs will be given 'in my house and in my walls a memorial and a name better than sons and daughters. I shall give them an eternal name that will never be erased'. The spiritual 'child' here is imagined as a kind of stone monument with their name inscribed indelibly forever.[78] In terms of its construction, Wisdom adds to Isaiah's promise another specifically addressed to women who can have no children, promising similar spiritual 'fruit' in the end.

The Mareotic group may very well have accepted Wisdom's promise, and—reading allegorically—may have brought this

[77] Verna E. F. Harrison, 'The Allegorization of Gender: Plato and Philo on Spiritual Childbearing', in Vincent L. Wimbush and Richard Valentasis (eds.), *Asceticism* (New York: OUP, 1995), 520–34. The similar notion that 'bearing good fruit' indicates righteousness is found also in the New Testament (cf. Luke 3: 8–9 and rabbinic literature, cf. Gen. Rab. 16: 3).

[78] Cf. Matt. 19: 12 where Jesus talks of 'eunuchs for the Kingdom of Heaven', possibly implying that those men who live celibate lives give up the hope of mortal offspring for anticipated spiritual rewards in the Kingdom.

promise of future fruit forward in time, so that now those who participate in the community do not desire mortal but immortal offspring in their present experience. However, Philo elsewhere accepts without question the Septuagint's exclusion of eunuchs from the assembly of Israel (Deut. 23: 11 in *Spec.* 1: 325)[79] and insists on the divine rule that one must produce physical children (*Det.* 147–8). In fact, Philo even states outright in *Praem.* 108–9 that 'all genuine attendants (θεραπευταί) of God will fulfil the law of Nature for the procreation of children'. If it were not Philo's own view that the celibacy as such could be wholly justified on the basis of spiritual fruit, he is using someone else's point of view, namely the arguments of the Mareotic group itself.

As a justification for their celibacy, it would have been reasonable for them to claim that total abstinence from engagement in sense-perception and the rejection of all bodily pleasures (σῶμα ἡδονῶν) rendered their souls free to unify with God and thereby bear spiritual fruit. We have already explored how asceticism and extreme allegory go together, and how this group appears to have engaged in both. Philo can only go so far along this track. For the sake of his rhetoric, Philo applied the imagery of the fruitful celibate to the case of the elderly virgin women in order to avoid making overt prescriptions for sexual abstinence for the entire group, males included. The way we read it, then, it is these virginal women who bear spiritual fruit. Philo's employment of their theory of the fruitful celibate is used strategically in regard to gender issues—since it is there to show the women in a positive (maternal) light—and in regard to side-tracking the focus from the group's celibacy as a whole, for Philo himself saw the soul as able to be fruitful even if one still did engage in procreative sex. Procreative sex is commanded by God for the purpose of procreation. It is not a necessary condition for the soul's fruitfulness that one is celibate in body, or that women remain virgins.

As we saw, the women's own choice of a virgin lifestyle is also used to score points in Philo's rhetorical schema. Philo mentions that continued virginity is found among 'the Greeks' but disparagingly puts down that of Greek priestesses as being done 'out of necessity' (*Contempl.* 68). Interestingly, Philo does not

---

[79] See Szesnat, 'Pretty Boys', 100.

refer to the Romans here, though one of the most striking examples of women who were virgins out of necessity were of
course the Vestal Virgins. Still, Philo can appeal to a positive
view of certain virgin lifestyles for women in wider Hellenistic
and Roman culture.[80] Cultic virginity appears to have been
esteemed as a means to achieve a greater access to the world of the
spirit and the divine, and was part of a rubric which Judith
Gundry-Volf defines as 'inspiration asceticism'.[81] The Pythia at
Delphi had to be a virgin in order to prophesy.[82] According to
Diodorus, *Bibl. Hist.* (16: 26: 6) this is because virgins had their
natural innocence intact and were like the virgin goddess
Artemis (who is a kind of warrior or guardian), and could then
also guard the secrecy of the disclosures.[83] A woman who proph-
esies at the temple of Apollo in Corinth in the second century is
celibate (Pausanias, *Descr. Graec.* 2: 24: 1), and other Apollo
prophetesses are virgins (Euripides, *Troad.* 41–2; Lycophron,
Alex. 348–64; Herodotus, *Hist.* 1: 182). Certain sibyls are called
virgins (Virgil, *Aen.* 3: 443–5; 6: 42–5; Ovid, *Metam.* 14: 129–53;
Lycophron, *Alex.* 1278–9; Pausanias, *Descr. Graec.* 10: 12: 6).[84]

The link between prophecy and virginity or celibacy appears
to have influenced Jewish praxis and belief by at least the first
century BCE. In terms of virginity, the Testament of Job (46–53),
probably dated to the first century BCE, contains the interesting

[80] It should be remembered that virginity focused on cultic/prophetic service
was sanctioned, but in general, among 'ordinary' girls in the household, prolonged virginity was not considered a particularly good thing, and could lead to
various disorders, see Aline Rouselle, *Porneia: On Desire and the Body in
Antiquity*, tr. of *Porneia* (Paris: Presses Universitaire de France, 1983; Oxford:
Basil Blackwell, 1988), 63–77.

[81] Judith Gundry-Volf, 'Celibate Pneumatics and Social Power: On the
Motivations for Sexual Asceticism in Corinth', *USQR* 48 (1994), 105–26.

[82] So Plutarch, *Def. Or.* 51, cf. id., *Pyth. Or.* 22; Lucian, *Astr.* 23. See
Gundry-Volf, 'Celibate Pneumatics', 110–11, basing herself on E. Fehrle, *Die
kultische Keuschheit im Altertum* (Giessen: Alfred Töbelmann, 1910), 76–97.

[83] See Gundry-Volf, 'Celibate Pneumatics', 122 n. 30.

[84] Two inscriptions from Lebanon refer to prophetesses at the shrines of the
Syrian goddess and a local god, and we may expect that resident prophetesses at
such shrines were frequently virgins or celibate, on the basis of the foregoing
evidence, though this is not stated explicitly, see M. T. Milik, *Dédicaces faites par
des Dieux (Palmyrie, Hatra, Tyr) et des thiases sémitiques à l'époque romaine*
(Institut Français de Beyrouth: Bibliothèque Archéologique et Historique, 2;
Paris: Guethner, 1972), 371–5.

story of Job's three virgin daughters—Jemimah, Keziah, and
Keren-happuch—who have ecstatic visions upon donning parts
of his special spark-shooting girdle which enables prophetic
power to come upon the wearer (47: 9). This prophetic power is
manifested in 'sending up a hymn to God in accord with the way
angels sing hymns' (48: 2–3).[85] The emphasis on celibacy as a
factor which enhances spiritual achievement is found in 4 Ezra
(5: 13, 20, 31; 6: 29–35; 9: 23–4; 12: 50–13: 20) and 2 Baruch
(9–10: 3; 12: 5–13: 3; 20: 5–21: 3; 47: 2–48: 1).[86] According to
both Philo and rabbinic sources, Moses became celibate after his
call from God (*Mos.* 2: 68–9; b.Shab. 67a), even though there is
a later critique of his marital celibacy in the midrash (Siphre on
Num. 12: 1).[87] In the midrash, when a youth shouts 'Eldad and
Medad are prophesying in the camp!' (Num. 11: 28) Tzipporah
says, 'Woe to the wives of these!' The assumption is that they will
no longer have sex with their wives.[88] Daniel Boyarin suggests
that the model of Moses' celibacy was a powerful received tradition by rabbinic times, and the rabbis needed to explain it as an
exception rather than the rule for people of exemplary holiness,
in order to discourage the practice. The midrash uses God's
statement that with Moses he spoke 'mouth to mouth' as indicating his unique position in regard to sexuality that should not be
copied. In this state he is either like the angels, or only slightly
below them.[89] Christian women in Pauline churches adopted

[85] See Randall D. Chesnut, 'Revelatory Experiences Attributed to Biblical
Women in Early Jewish Literature', in Lewvine (ed.), '*Women Like This*',
107–26.

[86] In Exod. 19: 10, 15 the people of Israel are to be celibate for three days prior
to YHWH's descent on Mount Sinai. Enoch had visions before he was married
(1 En. 83: 2; 85: 3).

[87] See for discussion Vermes, *Jesus the Jew*, 99–102. For discussion of the
midrash, see Boyarin, *Carnal Israel*, 160–5. The passage is interpreted here as
indicating that Miriam spoke on behalf of the Ethiopian woman (= Tzipporah)
whom Moses was sexually neglecting. See for a different interpretation,
Bernard P. Robinson, 'The Jealousy of Miriam: A Note on Num. 12', *ZAW*
101/3 (1989), 428–32. For further references see Louis Ginzberg, *The Legends
of the Jews* (Philadelphia: Jewish Publication Society, 1937–66), ii. 316; iii. 107,
258; vi. 60.

[88] See Boyarin, *Carnal Israel*, 162. Boyarin contrasts this attitude with a certain Babylonian school which advocated extended periods of celibacy for men to
study Torah.

[89] Ibid. 163–4.

celibacy to enhance prophetic power and communion with angels (1 Cor. 7: 1–40).[90] Acts 21: 9 tells of Philip's four virgin daughters with the gift of prophecy. There seems to have been an assumption that celibacy improved both prayer and prophecy: that is, the lines of communication between heaven and earth. Paul suggests periodic celibacy for devotion to prayer (1 Cor. 7: 5), probably towards a specific purpose. Still, in terms of the Mareotic group, Philo prefers to focus on the virginity of some, or most, of the women, alone (*Contempl.* 68).

Celibacy of course is a wider category than virginity and, as noted above, this seems to have been more the focus of the group itself than (women's) virginity. Given the use of the term θεραπευταί for the group of *Contempl.* and the term's linkage with the cultic attendants of Serapis and Isis, which were noted in Chapter 3, it is interesting that in the cult of Isis abstinence from carnal pleasure is essential (temporarily) for the reception of the sacred word (Plutarch, *Is. et Os.* 351f–352c, Apuleius, *Met.* 6: 19–21).[91] Chaeremon stated that the Egyptian priests abstain from sexual intercourse during their times of purification (Porphyry, *Abstin.* 4: 7). Sexual abstinence for certain reasons was known widely in the ancient world. The problem was possibly more that lifelong celibacy for males was not quite as acceptable as extended virginity for women, especially if conceptualized cultically.

For example, there is some evidence of the value of sexual abstinence in the writings of Musonius Rufus, the Stoic philosopher, who in *On Training* (discourse 6) does not recommend marriage or the bearing of children, a notion found also in the Cynic epistles,[92] and Epicurus, *De Natura*. This strand of philosophical thought may be traced back to Plato's later work (*Laws* 838a, 841b–c). Despite the sanctioning of marriage and the domestic world, Pythagoras himself in one tradition considered

[90] Gundry-Volf, 'Celibate Pneumatics'; ead., 'Controlling the Bodies: A Theological Profile of the Corinthian Sexual Ascetics', in R. Bieringer (ed.), *The Corinthian Correspondence* (BETL 125; Leuven: Leuven University Press and Peeters, 1996), 499–521; Schüssler Fiorenza, *In Memory of Her*, 220–30; Antoinette Clark Wire, *The Corinthian Women Prophets: A Reconstruction through Paul's Rhetoric* (Minneapolis: Fortress Press, 1990), 116–34.

[91] And see Richardson and Heuchen, 'Jewish Voluntary Associations', 243–5.

[92] Epistle 47 in Malherbe (ed.), *The Cynic Epistles*.

sexual pleasures harmful to a man and not conducive to health (Diogenes Laertius, *Lives* 8: 9), since they sap a man of strength. One should ideally have sex only in winter. Medical writing could also warn of damage caused by sexual activity.[93] Michel Foucault has pointed out that the model of the hero who could renounce sex was an exemplum of virtue: Xenophon's Agesilaus or even the Socrates in Plato's *Symposium*.[94] In due course, one would find Apollonius of Tyana vowing celibacy for a lifetime. Had Philo wanted to, he could then have found celibate male models of virtue in the literature, or configured the men of the Mareotic group as athletes, who were also known for periodic sexual abstinence.[95] But one senses that Philo resisted extolling prolonged male celibacy on any grounds. Even in regard to the Essenes, Philo makes no claim for the intrinsic benefits of life-long sexual abstinence, but rather configures their lifestyle as owing to the troublesome nature of women and the household life, as we saw above. Only then, in this case, may it be justified. In *Prob.*, when Philo describes the Essenes, he simply omits any mention of this issue.

Moreover, there may have been a possible rhetorical problem if he turned to consider the celibacy of the men. Philo has noted that the members of the Mareotic group are called *therapeutai* and *therapeutrides*, meaning 'attendants' in a cultic setting. In defining the women as virgins they may be compared with virgin priestesses. But the cultic celibacy of males was of a different order to that of females. In terms of the Roman way of thinking, the very Roman cult of the Vestal Virgins was counterbalanced by the very un-Roman *galli* of the cult of Magna Mater, who were celibate as a result of castration.[96] This conceptual dichotomy did not at all fit with the nature of the community Philo

---

[93] Oribasius, 3: 181; Aristotle, *Gen. Anim.*, 5: 3, 783b; Hippocrates, *Diseases* 2: 51; *Epidemics* 3: 17, 18, see Michel Foucault, *The Use of Pleasure: The History of Sexuality*, ii, tr. of *L'Usage des plaisirs* (Paris: Editions Gallimard, 1984, Harmondsworth: Penguin, 1992), 118–19.

[94] Ibid. 20.

[95] Ibid. 119–20.

[96] See Mary Beard, 'Re-Reading (Vestal) Virginity', in Richard Hawley and Barbara Levick (eds.), *Women in Antiquity: New Assessments* (London and New York: Routledge, 1995), 166–77 at p. 171: 'Roman literature and culture put the Vestals and the *galli* together in order to parade their difference'. See also ead., 'The Sexual Status of Vestal Virgins', *JRS* 70 (1980), 12–27; ead., 'The Roman

was describing. Moreover, while most of his audience may have accepted the need for a certain amount of moderation or even periodic sexual abstinence on the part of men, they may well have considered lifelong celibacy as unnecessary as Philo apparently thought it was. It was simply not a strong card to play.

So now we may look at the women of the Mareotic group with a more expansive vision. Some of these women may, historically, have had both husbands and children. We do not know whether non-virgin women in the community were still married or not, and may—in the absence of evidence—suggest all kinds of possible circumstances. They may have joined the community along with their husbands and chosen to live a celibate lifestyle. Or they may have decided unilaterally to leave their husbands for the sake of the philosophical life, a matter Philo would have kept well hidden from his readers, since what was acceptable for a male philosopher (leaving wife and children) was not so acceptable for a female. As for the virgins, Philo indicates that they themselves made the decision not to marry. It would be hard to imagine that such a decision could possibly have been made unless the girls grew up in households supportive of the philosophical lifestyle the Mareotic group espoused, those who endorsed the philosophy of 'extreme allegory'. We get an allusion to this wider context of people in *Contempl.* 67, where, regarding the distinction between 'seniors' and 'juniors', Philo states: 'The seniors are those who from early youth have matured and grown up in the contemplative part of philosophy, which indeed is the most beautiful and godly.' A girl growing up with such (allegorical, contemplative) instruction might well have made the decision to join a group such as Philo describes.

Some suggestion that there was indeed a tendency among high-class women to delay or even eschew marriage may be read from the fact that in places under Roman jurisdiction there were laws which were designed to encourage marriage by making the economic position of (wealthy) unmarried women much

and the Foreign: The Cult of the "Great Mother" in Imperial Rome', in Nicholas Thomas and Caroline Humphrey (eds.), *Shamanism, History and the State* (Ann Arbor: University of Michigan Press, 1994), 164–90 and Deborah Sawyer, *Women and Religion in the First Christian Centuries* (London: Routledge, 1996), 119–29.

harder.[97] However, overall, lifelong virginity was extremely rare.[98] Roman census returns from Egypt show that girls could be married around the ages of 12 or 13, even though these did not in general produce children till 15, but marriage normatively took place in a girl's late teens.[99] By the age of 20, three out of five girls were married and by the late twenties virtually all free women appear to have married at least once.[100] Eighty per cent of all women were still married (or remarried) at age 30, though only 40 per cent by their late 40s,[101] which indicates that there existed a sizeable group of widows or divorcees (from which some of the 'non-virgin' or 'non-elderly' Mareotic group women may have derived). Numerous divorce documents have been found from Ptolemaic and Roman times in Egypt.[102] The statistical identification of the rarity of lifelong celibacy, however, still indicates that such a state could exist in antiquity: 'maiden aunts' of the household were known. Philo notes that virgin girls/women had decided *themselves* to enter this community and take on a lifetime of celibacy. It was not a decision imposed upon them. This itself implies that girls in such households were

[97] Jane F. Gardner, *Women in Roman Law and Society* (London: Routledge, 1986 and 1990), 77–8. She notes, 'the laws of 18 B.C. and A.D. 9 (*lex Julia et Papia*) did not so much reward marriage as penalize celibacy' (p. 77). Unmarried women were unable to receive legacies from wills from relatives up to the sixth degree. Marriage entitled one to half the legacy, and if a child was born and survived, one could then get it all. The *Gnomon of the Idios Logos* in Egypt said that citizen women could not receive inheritances (from outside the immediate family) unless they were under 50 years of age and had three children; they could not inherit more than a quarter of their husband's wealth unless they had children, and Roman women who had 50,000 sestertii and were unmarried and childless could not inherit. The *Gnomon* also placed a 1% tax on unmarried reasonably well-off women, see Gardner, *Women in Roman Law*, 78; Rowlandson (ed.), *Women and Society*, 176–7.

[98] Susan Treggiari, *Roman Marriage: 'Iusti Coniuges' from the Time of Cicero to the Time of Ulpian* (Oxford: Clarendon Press, 1991), 83.

[99] Roger S. Bagnall and Bruce W. Frier, *The Demography of Roman Egypt* (Cambridge: CUP, 1994), 112–15, and see B. D. Shaw, 'The Age of Roman Girls at Marriage: Some Reconsiderations', *JRS* 77 (1987), 30–46, cf. D. W. Amundsen and C. J. Diers, 'The Age of Menarche in Classical Greece and Rome', *Human Biology*, 41 (1969), 125–32. The median age for girls at the time of marriage is 17.5 years.

[100] Bagnall and Frier, *Demography*, 113.

[101] Ibid., 115.

[102] See Montserrat, *Sex and Society*, 97–101.

brought up with the expectation that they could make decisions about their own futures. It is worth bearing in mind that the Christian apostle Paul may imagine that it is the norm for the Christian father to decide whether his daughter will remain a virgin or not, rather than the girl herself (1 Cor. 7: 36–8),[103] and Paul himself can quite unselfconsciously describe himself metaphorically as a father who has arranged a desirable marriage for his virgin daughter (2 Cor. 11: 2), and expect his hearers to know exactly what he means. This is not to say that all Christians accepted the father's authority here, especially if the father was pagan. Early Christian texts about ascetic women can play on the opposition from pagan family when the young woman *herself* rejects (pagan) marriage in favour of being a disciple of an apostle: the assumption is that discipleship requires celibacy, and also that society was deeply hostile to any independent decision on the part of the young woman which would overturn her expected social role. There is a sense that she brings shame on the family by choosing a celibate lifestyle.[104] There is no implication of this in *Contempl.*; quite the opposite. This in turn endorses the view that the Mareotic group derives from an Alexandrian philosophical milieu supportive of its approach.[105]

Overall then, this analysis points back to the historical Alexandrian context of the Mareotic group as a whole, and a Jewish allegorical interpretative philosophy in Alexandria in which girls are educated in scripture and in exegesis, encouraged along the

[103] This passage is sometimes translated so that the issue is between two people who are engaged rather than between a father and a virgin daughter. However, the fact that the man is giving in marriage (*gamizôn*) the virgin (1 Cor. 7: 38) must surely mean that the reference is to a father. A fiancé does not give his fiancée in marriage; he is given her.

[104] Kraemer, 'Monastic Jewish Women', 358, stresses the importance of childbearing in both Jewish and pagan contexts.

[105] Conybeare, *Philo*, 317, very rightly notes: 'It is true that Philo does not in his other writings anywhere tell us point-blank that there were around him women vowed to virginity; but where in any of his works, except in about three treatises . . . does he condescend to tell us at all of what was going on around him? From his clouds of impalpable allegory it requires the most careful alchemy of inference to distil, perhaps once in a hundred pages, a single historical fact. Still, of all the metaphors which he employs in order to enforce and convey to the minds of his readers moral and metaphysical truths, those drawn from female virginity are the most common.'

path of philosophy, and expected to decide for themselves what their future might be in terms of engagement in lifestyles consistent with this philosophy. The Mareotic group, as I have argued, is the tip of the iceberg in terms of a certain type of philosophy in Alexandria; the women of the Mareotic group are the tip of the women's iceberg here. Their existence points to many more, still living in the city, who have chosen to be actual rather than spiritual mothers, despite a basic agreement with many of the tenets of the philosophy. Philo himself is a male example of a moderate allegorizer. One thinks of the wives and children the males of the group have apparently left behind with an advance inheritance; if the family was one which supported allegorical philosophy, we have a situation of 'solo-mothers' managing the household (and business?) while the husband is living this ascetic existence outside the city. The support structure of people in Alexandria is critical to the survival of this group. Alternatively, women could have chosen a celibate lifestyle but not have moved out to live the harsh ascetic life of the Mareotic group, concentrating on expounding scripture and teaching, like the woman model for 'Skepsis', along with other allegorizers Philo knew in the city. Finally, we should remember that Philo says absolutely nothing at all about the celibacy or age of the junior members of the group who serve the seniors in the symposium. As noted previously, he forces us constantly to consider only the seniors, and it is only the senior women he determines to be 'mostly aged virgins', thereby defining the image of the safe 'old maid' on the minds of his audience. How would he have described the junior women? He preferred not to.

Philo states that the senior women of the Mareotic group were 'mostly elderly virgins' though we do not know the ratio exactly or precisely what he means here. Whatever their sexual histories, in fact, all the members of the group were celibate, not just the women. Their goal may have been to overcome the snares of sense-perception and bear spiritual fruit, which they believed was only possible through complete renunciation of all the body's desires. Unlike Philo, it seems likely that their own perspective did not allow for procreative sex. Philo makes his group acceptable by indicating that the men already had wives and children, thereby fulfilling the divine command to multiply. He cannot or does not indicate that the women left husbands or

children. This would have been a socially unacceptable comment (they would no longer be perceived as 'that which is good'').
Therefore, Philo focuses on the virgins. In order to satisfy
society's expectation of the maternal role of women, and also in
order to justify their celibate lifestyle, Philo uses the image of the
fruitful soul (which does not in fact require celibacy, in his opinion). As well as this, he stresses that all the senior members of the
community are fathers and mothers to the junior members, a
matter that is particularly relevant in terms of characterizing the
women as maternal. This may indeed be an understanding of the
community itself, since the notion of motherhood as indicating
status within a community is well-known in Hellenistic and
Jewish culture and not distinctively Philonic.

When we become aware of how Philo addressed potential
criticisms of the women of the group by reference to the paradigms of women in *philosophia*, we become better aware of how
he has attempted to describe the women in a way that would take
account of any criticism. Certainly, one cannot assume that Philo
was trying to impress anyone by noting the inclusion of women
in the group, but rather was seeking to describe their existence
apologetically. The women of the community have not become
male, but retain the identification of being women, displaying
modesty (*Contempl.* 33, 69) and maternity. We do not know
precisely how this congregation would have understood the progression of their souls towards the divine, but in terms of Philo's
presentation, gender remains and has not been blurred by spiritual achievement or by celibacy. Importantly for Jewish women
in Alexandria, here we find them engaged in learning and con-
tributing to the very heart of philosophy. However Philo may
account for this, this engagement is surely critical in how we see
Jewish women in this time and place.

10

Gendered Space

One is not justified in saying that the woman is locked up in
the house unless one also observes that the man is kept out
of it, at least during the day. As soon as the sun has risen he
must, during the summer, be in the fields or at the assembly
house; in the winter, if he is not in the field, he has to be at
the place of assembly or upon the benches set in the shelter
of the pent-roof over the entrance to the courtyard . . . The
man who stays too long in the house during the day is either
suspect or ridiculous; he is 'the man of the home' . . . A man
who has respect for himself should let himself be seen,
should continuously place himself under the gaze of others
and face them . . . He is a man amongst men.[1]

Philo was, as we have seen, concerned to locate his group very
carefully on a certain hill between the Mediterranean Sea and
Lake Mareotis. He indicates the surrounding villages and buildings, and the little houses in which senior members of the
Mareotic group live. He also shows us two meeting places: a
semneion where the seventh-day assemblies take place, and a
sumposion where the forty-ninth-day dinner is held. In fact, a
further dimension of Philo's rhetoric of gender in *Contempl.* concerns space. In terms of the ideal gender balance, the division of
space is a significant factor. In creating a vision of what is good,
in his presentation of the Mareotic group, Philo sought at times
to create an ideal spatial arrangement which would vouchsafe the
virtue of the group members. Along with this Philo gives details
about the personal space of the group members as signified by
clothing. Clothing is a primary indicator of gender, and can be
the first step towards the gendering of space in general. In this
chapter I will consider the spaces Philo constructs, communal,
personal, and sacred, within the context of what we know about
spatial arrangements in Hellenistic and Roman Egypt.

[1] Pierre Bourdieu, 'The Berber House', in Mary Douglas (ed.), *Rules and
Meanings: The Anthropology of Everyday Knowledge* (Harmondsworth:
Penguin, 1973), 98–110, at 103.

GENDERED SPACE IN URBAN CONTEXTS

In his *Specialibus legibus*, a treatise in which Philo explains the significance of the special laws of Judaism, Philo divides up the governing of the city between the places where many people gather (council chambers, market-places) and the smaller divisions where people live in households. He states that men are in charge of the πολιτεία, the public institutions of the city, and women exercise government of the οἰκονομία, the world of the household. This is presented as a kind of given fact that no one would dispute (*Spec.* 3: 169–71). Men are in charge of the former and women of the latter.

How do we interpret this comment? There seems no place for the Roman-style *paterfamilias* in Philo's domestic world, or even the Greek *kurios*. Did this division of authority reflect Philo's ideal notions of the perfect Jewish world, or an idea current in Alexandria, or Egypt as a whole? It does not seem a very Greek division. Aristotle had seen the *polis* as being comprised of *oikoi*, households, governed by a single male ruler, who controlled the females, the children, and slaves (*Pol.* 1254b; 1259a-b; 1260a). Roman census documents from Egypt seem to impose this kind of order in households for the purpose of taxation, but Sarah Pomeroy has noted that, on the basis of surviving personal records, this order does not necessarily obtain: '[e]xamination of the private documents suggests that in many cases the androcentric hierarchical *oikos* model based on the nuclear family was imposed by the authorities and reflected only in official documents'.[2] The situation in Alexandria, or Egypt as a whole, may not have been the way that the Roman census documents present it.

Plutarch stated in his *Moralia* (142c), that 'the women of Egypt traditionally are not allowed to wear shoes, so that they stay indoors'. How much weight should be placed on such a comment? Prior to the Roman administration of the area, 'Egypt' had become the signifier for anything strange and different from what was current in Greece or Rome. This paradigm of Egypt as 'other' than normal was established by Herodotus (*Hist.* 2: 35), when he noted, for example, that in Egypt 'the women manage

---

[2] Sarah B. Pomeroy, *Families in Classical and Hellenistic Greece: Representations and Realities* (Oxford: Clarendon Press, 1998), 208.

the market and the shops while the men weave indoors' and 'the women urinate standing but the men squat'.[3] In the first century BCE Diodorus Siculus (*Bibl. Hist.* 1: 27: 1–2) could comment that in Egypt the women ruled the men, and the men agreed in the dowry contract to obey their wives in everything, which seems just an example of a simple reversal of normality.[4] Surviving Demotic marriage settlement contracts from Egypt do not indicate that men made such an agreement; the concern is with property rights.[5] But Diodorus seems to be exaggerating on the basis of some truth: women themselves consented to a marriage (cohabitation); married women in Egypt retained full rights to their own property and could engage independently in business transactions; both partners could initiate a divorce.[6] If such women stayed indoors, or thought it preferable to do so, as Plutarch indicated (on the basis of an unknown source), then this was not construed as an impediment to a measure of autonomy higher than in classical Athens. In fact, the issue in the ultra-domesticity of women as presented by Philo in *Flacc.* 89 and in *Spec.* 3: 169–71 is modesty. It is we who, from our own perspective, tend to see women in antiquity as being confined to the home rather than in control of it.

Alexandria was an intellectually thriving cosmopolitan Hellenistic city and a mercantile hub well connected with the outside world, not rural 'Egypt'. Its official title in Roman times was 'Alexandria-by-Egypt', as we have seen. Studies of women in Hellenistic cities like Alexandria, on the basis of Greek papyri and extant literature, indicate how active women were economically, which seems to show some influence from Egyptian norms of female financial independence.[7] However, the Hellenistic

---

[3] See Rowlandson (ed.), *Women and Society*, 3.
[4] Ibid. 50–1.   [5] Ibid. 156–60.   [6] Ibid. 156.
[7] Pomeroy, *Women in Hellenistic Egypt*, and ead. 'Women in Roman Egypt'. See also Deborah Hobson, 'Women as Property Owners in Roman Egypt', *Transactions of the American Philological Association*, 113 (1983), 311–21; ead., 'The Role of Women in the Economic Life of Roman Egypt: A Case Study from First-Century Tebtunis', *Echos du Monde Classique/Classical Views*, 28 (1984), 373–90; Jane Rowlandson, 'Beyond the Polis: Women and Economic Opportunity in Early Ptolemaic Egypt', in Anton Powell (ed.), *The Greek World* (London and New York : Routledge, 1995); Peter van Minnen, 'Berenice, a Businesswoman from Oxyrhynchus: Appearance and Reality', in Arthur M. F. W. Verhoogt and Sven P. Vleeming (eds.), *The Two Faces of Graeco-Roman Egypt* (Leiden: Brill, 1998), and also Rowlandson (ed.), *Women and Society*.

milieu of Alexandria and the other Greek cities of Naukratis and Ptolemais imposed different legal and institutional requirements and held up different ideals of female behaviour to local Egyptian ones. In the Greek garrison town of Elephantine, immigrants set their laws on the basis of classical prototypes: as Jane Rowlandson has noted, '[t]he earliest Greek marriage contract [*P.Eleph.* 1] . . . surviving from Ptolemaic Egypt is full of legal language redolent of fourth-century Athenian usage and embodies the normal family-controlled, male-operated marriage system known for the classical period'.[8] Still, Greek documents from Egypt show, for example, a woman acting as guardian for a child (*SB* 16: 12720: 1–20), giving herself in marriage (*P.Giss.* 2), and a no-fault divorce (*BGU* 4: 1103),[9] indicating that in the peculiar Hellenism of Egypt a woman could act legally in ways quite different from the classical era or (apparently) in the Greek milieu elsewhere. In a marriage contract of 92 BCE (*P.Tebt.* 1: 104) a woman Apollonia is identified as having management in common with her husband Philiscus over all their possessions.[10]

How did all this affect the organization of domestic space? Andrew Wallace-Hadrill has noted: '[i]n the Greek house the most important single contrast is that between male and female space'.[11] In this he follows ancient authors such as Cornelius Nepos (first century BCE), who noted that a striking difference between Roman and Greeks was that the Roman matrons were not separated from the men (*Praef.* 6–8). Vitruvius (*Arch.* 6: 7: 2–4) saw Greek male space as an attempt to protect the men from the women! To what extent did Greek concepts about gendered space in the household inform the layouts of Hellenistic Jewish houses in Alexandria? While the archaeology of domestic space in first-century Alexandria has not yet provided answers, the spatial arrangement of Alexandrian Jewish houses may be fairly easily determined on the basis of Philo's comments.[12]

---

[8] Rowlandson (ed), *Women and Society*, 163.

[9] Ibid. 167–70.

[10] Pomeroy, *Women in Hellenistic Egypt*, 87–9.

[11] Andrew Wallace-Hadrill, *Houses and Society in Pompeii and Herculaneum* (Princeton: Princeton University Press, 1994), 8. See also Susan Walker, 'Women and Housing in Classical Greece: The Archaeological Evidence', in Averil Cameron and Amelie Kuhrt (eds.), *Images of Women in Antiquity*, rev. edn. (London: Routledge, 1993), 81–91, 304–5.

[12] There are few domestic houses excavated and published from Hellenistic

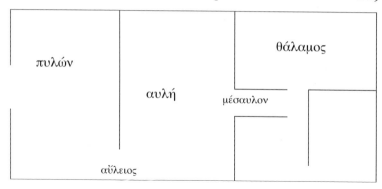

18. Schematic drawing of Philo's 'ideal' home

According to Philo's descriptions of the domestic Alexandrian house with which he was familiar (see Figure 18), there was an outer door to the home from the street inside which was the πυλών, or 'gatehouse'. Beyond this was an αὔλειος, 'entrance to the courtyard'; an αυλή, 'courtyard', and, lastly, the θάλαμος region: the private quarters and sleeping rooms. In the θάλαμος there was an αὐλών, a passage (*Leg.* 3: 40), the doorway to that part being the μέσαυλον (*Spec.* 3: 169).

The πυλών area is a feature of Egyptian architecture; tradition-ally, it was the entry vestibule for Egyptian temples.[13] In the Hellenistic Egyptian house, it was the entry area, and appears to be used by males, as Philo indicates (*Leg.* 3: 40). Richard Alston comments: '[a]s the gates of the temple frequently dominated the public space of the village and city so the gates of houses may have imposed themselves on the public space of the street'.[14] The conceptualization of the πυλών as liminal or in some way public explains why nearly all contracts and legal documents are

and Roman Alexandria. Comparative data may be found, however, in Karanis, see Rowlandson (ed.), *Women and Society*, 133–7; Richard Alston, 'Houses and Households in Roman Egypt', in Ray Laurence and Andrew Wallace-Hadrill (eds.), *Domestic Space in the Roman World: Pompeii and Beyond* (Portsmouth, RI: Journal of Roman Archaeology, 1997), 25–39. For Philo's understandings of space see: Richard Alston, 'Philo's *In Flaccum*: Ethnicity and Social Space in Roman Alexandria', *Greece and Rome*, 44 (1997), 165–75, esp. 171.

[13] For discussion see Husson, *Oikia*, 243–6.
[14] Alston, 'Houses and Households', 31.

witnessed in the 'street' rather than in a house, temple, or in the market-place; the πυλών was conceptualized as being in 'the street'.[15] Like the rest of the house, the πυλών could be comprised of two levels, with an *andrōn* (men's dining room), *sumposion*, or other room at the top.[16] For merchants and businesspeople, the ground floor of the *pulōn* was also the area of the shop or artisan industry.[17]

In Philo's ideal Jewish home unmarried girls stayed inside the areas of the θάλαμος and were allowed only to the μέσαυλον (*Spec.* 3: 169), which marked the border between the θάλαμος and the αυλή. They are θαλαμευόμεναι (*Flacc.* 89), and appear then (ideally) not even in the αὐλή, or courtyard.[18] It is unsurprising that in an urban context elite Jews living in areas of Hellenistic culture adopted the Greek ideal of elite unmarried girls' domestic containment. 2 Maccabees 3: 19, describing events of the second century BCE, incidentally comments that young women, who were normally inside the house, ran to the gates, walls, and windows of their homes to see what was happening (cf. 4 Macc. 18: 7).[19] In a classical Greek house, reasonably affluent citizen women would often live upstairs, in the ὑπερῷον and/or be confined to the γυναικών or the γυναικωνῖτις, which could be located in the dark, back part of the house. However, according to Philo, it appears that women (apart from the 'virgins') had the full run of the house, though their ideal limit was the αὔλειος, the door to the αὐλη from the πυλών. Philo indicates that the modesty of Jewish women was such that they did not even approach this entrance, beyond which was the (semi-)public male area and then the public street. Philo's over-statement is designed to show the ultra-modesty of a certain type of Jewish women, and is used rhetorically to increase the impact of Philo's description of the domestic violation which follows. Philo writes that soldiers

---

[15] Cf. ibid. 36

[16] *P.Lond.* iii. 978 mentions an *andreion* which is on the floor above the *pulōn*; *SB* vi. 8988: 57–8; *P.Lond.* 1724.

[17] *P.Lond.* iii. 131; *P.Mich.* v. 295, where a (first floor?) *triklinos* is also mentioned.

[18] The economic value of virginity is reflected here. The dowry for virgins could be as much as double that of the previously married, see Mordecai Friedman, 'Babata's Ketubba: Some Preliminary Observations', *IEJ* 46 (1996), 55–76, at 57.

[19] Kraemer, 'Women's Judaisms', 60.

looking for arms went into every secret recess of every Jewish house. Jewish men were glad to be vindicated when the soldiers found nothing, but were indignant because

their women, who were kept in seclusion and did not even approach the courtyard entrances, and their unmarried girls, who stayed in the θάλαμος and who shunned the eyes of men out of modesty, *even their nearest relations*, were now appalled at being shown to the public gaze, not only to men who were not relatives, but to common soldiers! (*Flacc.* 89)

Philo is not giving an accurate description of the lives of *all* Jewish women here, but rather is concentrating his rhetoric on what a good, elite Jewish household should be like, probably on the basis of elite households in Alexandria with which he was familiar. As Kraemer points out, 'true seclusion is likely to have been restricted to families with sufficient economic resources, for whom the seclusion of women functions as a sign of prestige'.[20] In both cases where he mentions the reclusive character of Jewish women, he undermines his description by slippages reflecting a different reality for less elite women than those he is considering. In *Spec.*, following on from his recommendation that all good Jewish women should stay at home, he notes the existence of other (Jewish) women who are out and about in the market-place, even fighting and using foul language (*Spec.* 3: 171–2). In *Flacc.*, a few paragraphs along from where he describes all Jewish women in Alexandria as cloistered in the home, he notes that Jewish women were 'seized like captives not only in the market-place but also in the middle of the theatre' (*Flacc.* 95). The point is then not that Philo describes a situation in which all Jewish women stay at home, but that it was an ideal placed on the free-born, high-status, wealthy women Philo is particularly concerned about, the kind of women we find in the Mareotic group itself.

The αὐλή, 'courtyard', was the centre of the house. It was usually closed off from public entry, and could be covered or uncovered. In the papyri it varies hugely in dimensions, between 11 m² and 112 m² (for a large villa). It was a place of cooking, household activity, and work, and in archaeological excavations many kinds of installations have been found in courtyards, particularly those

---

[20] Ibid. 61.

for cooking.[21] The μέσαυλον should probably be understood as an area between the αὐλή the θάλαμος, though in later papyri it designated what would correspond to the Roman *atrium* or *compluvium*: a porticoed court.[22] In Karanis, documentation belonging to a woman named Taesion was found in the more secluded part of a house,[23] which may correspond to a part of the θάλαμος.

An interesting parallel to the spatial arrangement Philo presents in his writings is found in a papyrus from Oxyrhynchus (*P.Oxy.* 24: 2406). The papyrus is quite damaged, but one can clearly see the first two letters of the word πυλών on the left (see Figure 19). From this room, there is a door leading to an L-shaped courtyard, the back part of which is designated as αἴτρειον, and the front part or else a small room or entrance behind the πυλών possibly as θυραυλεῖος,[24] though this word is hard to read. At the back part of the house is a large room designated by two words which are illegible, though the second word may have the readable letters: θ.μι..τ.. This back room would correspond with the θάλαμος Philo refers to. The structure differs from a Jewish house in that there is a cultic centre known as the ὀβολίσκος[25] next to stairs leading to an upper storey.[26]

The αὔλειος was actually the doorway to the house proper. Richard Alston has noted that 'there was a powerful ideological division between the front and back areas of the house' and that Philo uses the division as a metaphor for the separation of rational and irrational parts of the soul (*QG* 4: 15).[27] This is possible to do metaphorically on the basis of a spatial division that would have the front, partly public, area of the house (the gateway) as being where men conducted business and had dinner parties (upstairs). It is not even clear that men slept in the back part of

---

[21] Husson, *Oikia*, 45–54.

[22] Ibid. 55.

[23] Room C in House B1. See Rowlandson (ed.), *Women and Society*, 135.

[24] A θύρα or θύρωμα would designate a doorway. For the plan see E. Lobel, C. H. Roberts, E. G. Turner, and J. W. B. Barns, *The Oxyrhynchus Papyri Part XXIV* (London: Egypt Exploration Society, 1957), no. 2406, 142–5. The plan is dated to the 2nd cent. CE.

[25] So Alston, 'Houses and Households', 29–30.

[26] Rooms around the stairway may have been especially significant for Egyptian women as it seems they were supposed to keep to a small space here when they had menstrual periods, see Montserrat, *Sex and Society*, 48, cf. Husson, *Oikia*, 126.

[27] Ibid. 171–2.

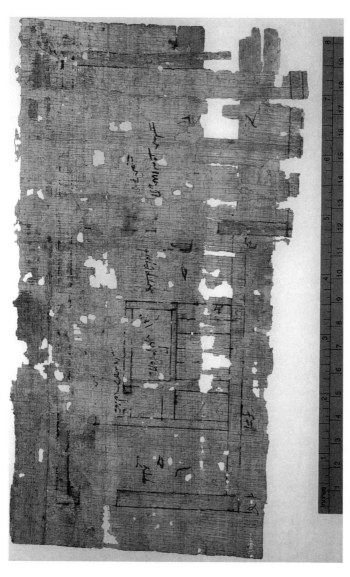

19. Late Roman papyrus from Oxyrhynchus (*P.Oxy.* 2406) showing house plan (Papyrology Rooms, Ashmolean Museum/Egypt Exploration Society, London)

the house, given that this is the locus of unmarried girls who are not seen by their own male relatives,[28] though one would probably have to assume that in the θάλαμος there were 'married quarters' as well as separate areas for women. It should be remembered too that we may have situations in which we have extended families rather than nuclear ones, and there would also need to be sleeping areas for slaves.

Despite the rhetoric and the idealization, which suggests a universality of practice that should not be read as existing throughout society, the kind of gendered division of space found in Philo's writings is of course extremely common in many societies to this day. In the Greek world, modesty was a sign of a woman's high standing in society; a well-born woman sought to do what was proper and, as Xenophon stated: '[so] it is proper for a woman to stay at home and not be outside; but for a man to stay inside it—rather than devoting himself to outside pursuits—is shameful' (*Oec.* 7: 30). This attitude is replicated in what the sociologist Pierre Bourdieu wrote regarding the Berber household, quoted at the head of this chapter, or what Fatima Mernissi describes in terms of her Moroccan childhood, where extended families occupy salons off an open courtyard, in a two-storied house, and observe carefully rules of space.[29] Countless other anthropological and sociological studies of gendered space in contemporary societies could be used comparatively to elucidate Philo's descriptions. The key is to recognize how gender balance is sought by such spatial divisions. Philo had a clear sense of where 'good' women should be. How would he deal with this in terms of the Mareotic group?

THE *SEMNEION*

As we have seen, Philo alerts his audience at the beginning of his treatise to the fact that he recognizes the women in the philosophical group he is going to describe. These people 'are called *therapeutai* and *therapeutrides*' (*Contempl.* 2) he states. In terms

[28] It is paralleled in Lysias, *Or.* 3: 6–7 where it is stated that virgins lived so modestly they were ashamed to be seen even by male relatives.

[29] Fatima Mernissi, *The Harem Within: Tales of a Moroccan Girlhood* (Toronto: Bantam, 1995), 3–8, 16.

of the spaces he refers to in his narrative, he moves from consideration of contemplative philosophers everywhere, to the one exemplary group he is discussing on this particular hill near Lake Mareotis and the sea, to the individual huts in which these contemplative philosophers live, to the reverence-place—*semneion*—where they meet together on seventh days. It is only when he gets to the *semneion* that women are specifically mentioned, because it is here that gender relations become critical. When the members of the group are considered individually, alone in their little houses, the sex of the individual is irrelevant. It becomes relevant only when the two sexes are brought together, and proper gender relations need to be established.

Philo creates an acceptable space for his specific reference to women *before* he mentions them. The first thing we learn is that there is a room which is divided, and only then do we get the reason for this division:

And this common reverence-place (σεμνεῖον) into which they come together on seventh days is a double enclosure (διπλοῦς ἐστι περίβολος): one part is set apart for men, and the other is [set apart] for women. For indeed also women customarily participate in listening [like the men], having the same zeal and purpose. And the wall between the areas rises upwards from the ground up to three or four cubits in the form of breastwork, but the upper section going up to the roof is wide open. [This arrangement is] for two reasons: so that the modesty which is becoming to the female nature be preserved, and so that, by their sitting in earshot, everything is easily audible, for nothing obstructs the voice of the speaker. (*Contempl.* 32–3)

Philo states here that the main purpose of the dividing wall in the double enclosure[30] is to divide men and women, in order to ensure women's modesty. It is plainly not necessary to Philo to preserve the modesty of men. Since a cubit was the length between the elbow and the tip of the longest finger, variously estimated (approximately 47 cm), the maximum height of the wall would have been around 188 cm, indeed high enough to keep the women from the eyes of the men, even when everyone was standing. When listening or speaking, everyone would have

[30] Richardson, 'Philo and Eusebius', 351 (following Conybeare, *Philo*, 215) notes rightly that the περίβολος often refers to a temple enclosure. However, here the *semneion* itself consitutes this double enclosure; there is not another one besides.

been seated, as was customary in the ancient world. Here, the women are perceived very much as women and the men as men. Normal gender norms are in operation. Women's bodies need to be kept away from men's gazes.

The word Philo uses for the room in which the group meets for instruction on the Sabbath—σεμνεῖον—is not used for a synagogue (normally called a προσευχή or συναγωγή), and is unique to this treatise. It is derived from σεμνός, 'august' or 'revered', a word applied to gods or greatly esteemed heroes. Was it understood to be a kind of synagogue, as Conybeare suggested?[31]

Elsewhere Philo characterizes Jewish women in Alexandria as *not* attending instruction in the synagogue. Philo states that a man returns home to the household in the evening and explains what he has heard of the laws to his wife, children, and servants (*Hypoth.* 7: 14). It is impossible to reconcile what Philo states here in the *Hypothetica* with evidence from the Diaspora that women appear to have held leadership positions in synagogues, and evidence cited in the previous chapter that women could 'hear' in this forum, and possibly also participate in various functions. Here Philo's apparent evidence for women's non-attendance in synagogue seems to be again a kind of upper-class ideal. He uses this ideal in order to make a case for ideal, modest women within Judaism. For Philo, the problem was that, in the city, the synagogue is part of the 'public' world. In insisting that Jewish women in Alexandria do not attend synagogue he is in fact protecting their modesty in the same way that he does by his configurations of gendered space in the household. The husband brings the synagogue back to his wife, and educates her, as Plutarch recommended husbands do in regard to philosophy, and she remains a virtuous, modest ideal. In *Spec.* 3: 171 Philo indicates that women should not be concerned with matters outside the household. She should cultivate solitude, and not be seen in front of men (unlike *some* women!), going to the temple (synagogue or Temple?) only at the least busy time of the day (again, unlike some women). Philo's comments do not indicate that women could not attend synagogue, but they do indicate that he was uncomfortable with the fact. However, in *Contempl.*, in presenting what he truly perceives to be the case in the

---

[31] Conybeare, *Philo*, 310. Conybeare tended to fit Philo's description with what he considered normative for Jews of 1st-cent. Alexandria.

Mareotic community, he has to show women together with men in the meeting space.

In Arlene Saxonhouse's discussion of classical notions of public and private, she notes that *philosophia* was not an enterprise constructed as a public activity. It did not as a rule involve the institutions of a *polis*: the agora, the temples, the gymnasia, and so on. *Philosophia* was more often in the preserve of the private. She points out that '[t]he philosophic activity of a Socrates removes him from the city, as the family removes the female involved in reproduction from the city',[32] an interesting analogy. Socrates introduced a community among his students, which created a new private social group. As Saxonhouse comments: '[t]he private for him now means a new family, which comes from philosophic discourse engaged in by his companions and followers. Within the new family Socrates often takes the woman's role and that which is traditionally most private (birth) comes to dominate (in the form of birth of ideas) over the male role of warrior and citizen in the public realm.'[33]

However, synagogues were considered public, since they were not only where Jewish philosophy was taught but also where sacred activities such as prayer took place,[34] and part of the sacred architectural space of the city.[35] However, if the community of *Contempl.* was one big family then the meeting hall of the community in the 'reverence-place' may not have been configured as a normal synagogue, but rather as a private room in the house. Practically speaking, this group was not in the city, where the distinctions between public and private applied; they were most likely living in and around some kind of modified country

---

[32] Arlene Saxonhouse, 'Classical Greek Conceptions of Public and Private', in Stanley I. Benn and Gerald F. Gaus (eds.), *Public and Private in Social Life* (London and Canberra: Croom Helm, 1983), 363–84.

[33] Ibid. 375.

[34] Hence the common designation προσευχή, 'prayer-place'.

[35] The designation of a synagogue as a ἱερόν is found in a number of authors (e.g. Josephus, *Apion* 2: 10). Allen Kerkeslager notes the similar ways that synagogues and temples were configured in Egypt, 'Jewish Pilgrimage and Jewish Identity', 115–17, and see also Ariyer Kasher, 'Synagogues as "Houses of Prayer" and "Holy Places" in the Jewish Communities of Hellenistic and Roman Egypt', in Dan Urman and Paul V. M. Flesher (eds.), *Ancient Synagogues: Historical Analysis and Archaeological Discovery* (Leiden: Brill, 1995), i. 205–25.

villa. Of course this place is private rather than part of the public realm of the polis. In using the term σεμνεῖον both Philo and the Mareotic group avoid using the normal terms for synagogue and ensure it is not put in quite the same spatial category.

Philo's division of space in terms of the Mareotic group should not then be read as normative for synagogues at this time. It is a specific reference to a room that he—and the group itself—sees as a private meeting space for instruction. His comment on the wall may even be read as indicating how unusual it was. None of the archaeological excavations of early synagogues have shown evidence of women's areas, in the form of clearly demarcated sections with walls or balconies. No literary sources indicate a division, even though it is clear that women attended synagogue and held leadership positions in them.[36]

If the Mareotic group are a kind of family, and they inhabit a kind of private space, then the modesty that is promoted in the reverence-place where they come together to hear discourses on the seventh days is the kind of private modesty that Philo promotes for ideal Jewish households, in which the ultra-modest virgins are not seen by their nearest male relatives. As noted above, Philo immediately associates women with the need for modesty in *Contempl.* 32–3. Philo prepares a room for the women even before mentioning them. The reverence-place is described as being a double enclosure prior to the introduction of the women. It is as if Philo is stating: there are women here, but they are modest, good women, nothing like the sexually licentious *hetairai* of philosophical discourse. From his discussion of the modesty of the women, connected with a description of the wall which divides them from the men, he then launches into a discussion of self-control, ἐγκράτεια, which is the foundation stone of the soul on which the Mareotic group builds all the other virtues (34). The flow of discussion moves from women, to modesty, to self-control, in one fell swoop. We are then blocked from the image of the 'Sexy Babe' by a wall of quick associations.

The σεμνεῖον in which the group come together is not the only

---

[36] For women's inclusion in synagogues and the absence of partitions see Brooten, *Women Leaders*; Kraemer, *Her Share*, 106–7; ead., 'Monastic Jewish Women', 367–9; ead. 'Women's Judaisms', 64–5, also S. Zabin, ' "Iudeae Benemerenti": Towards a Study of Jewish Women in the Western Roman Empire', *Phoenix*, 50 (1996), 262–82.

one Philo mentions in *Contempl*. In fact he can refer to it without comment in terms of the general meeting place because he has already introduced the word earlier in the text. The small houses in which the senior members of the group spend most of their time also contain this space, which 'is called' by this name. Philo writes:

In each there is a sacred room (οἴκημα ἱερόν), which is called a reverence-place (σεμνεῖον) and place-for-one (μοναστήριον) in which they solitarily perform the mysteries of the holy life. They take nothing [into it]—no drink, no food, nothing necessary for the needs of the body—but [only] laws, oracles declared through prophets, hymns and other [writings] which increase and perfect understanding and piety. (*Contempl*. 25)

There is then a general σεμνεῖον where everyone meets together (*Contempl*. 32) and also this 'place-for-one' type of σεμνεῖον where each person undertakes spiritual exercises alone (*Contempl*. 25, cf. 89). If the room described as a σεμνεῖον in the individual huts is a οἴκημα ἱερόν then so too is the general assembly room a 'holy room'. This brings the language of cult back into place: the θεραπευταί naturally inhabit an οἴκημα ἱερόν.

How was this reverence-place configured? Peter Richardson has made a very interesting and useful comparison between what is stated by Philo in regard to the group of *Contempl*. and the archaeological evidence of a widely dispersed Byzantine Christian monastery called the Kellia, centred 55 km south of Alexandria, occupied from the end of the fourth century onwards. The evidence of the fifth century shows clusters of small houses of mud brick, spaced a few metres apart. In each house there is first an outer courtyard, surrounded by a low wall, and then a small room for prayer and meditation entered by a vestibule. Off this vestibule there is also a small room for sleeping and storage areas. In all the earliest houses the prayer room is in the north-west corner of the structure with a niche on the east wall.[37] Essentially, these are mini versions of the standard houses of the city, without a *pulōn* entrance area: one walks straight into the courtyard.

[37] Richardson, 'Philo and Eusebius', 341–2, cf. Rodolfe Kasser, *Les Kellia, ermitages coptes en Basse-Egypte* (Geneva: Éditions de Tricorne, 1989), figs. 12–29. The Kellia were discovered in 1964 and over successive seasons five clusters of 1,500 'cells' in all have been found over a distance of 18 km between Nitria and Wadi Natroun.

It is a large jump chronologically between the Jewish Mareotic group of the first century and the Christian group of the fifth century, but the similarity of the structures described by Philo to the monastic structures of the Kellia are extraordinary, especially given that these single dwellings appear to have been called *monasteria*. The word *monasterion* is first found in a Christian context in Athanasius' *Life of Antony* to describe a single, solitary dwelling for a Christian ascetic. A Christian *monasterion* is decribed in the *Historia Monachorum* (*c*.400 CE), where there is reference to an incident that took place at the beginning of the fourth century. A thief (Patermouthios) came to rob the *monasterion* of a Christian woman ascetic in the Thebaid region. He climbed up on the roof of her dwelling but could not manage to enter the 'inner chamber', here τὸ ταμιεῖον, the 'closet' or 'prayer room'.[38] The word ταμιεῖον is referred to as being a feature of a first-century Palestinian Jewish house in Matthew 6: 6 (and Matt. 24: 26; Luke 12: 3): the inner room(s). Here, since the whole structure is called a *monasterion* and the inner room a *tamieion*, the nomenclature does not match exactly what we have in Philo, but there is still a correlation in terms of the organization of space.

In Athanasius' *Life of Antony* there is some indication that this type of *monasterion* for solitary ascetic practices was in use in the late third century prior to the interest of Antony. Athanasius writes that there were, prior to Antony, 'not so many *monasteria* in Egypt, and no monk at all gave heed to the distant desert, but all who wished to give heed to themselves practised the discipline in solitude near their own village' (*Vita Ant.* 3).[39] If there were not so many, there were still some. Eusebius did not recognize the structures of *Contempl.* as anything he knew, and insists that Philo is talking about churches when he talks about their frugal houses (*Hist. Eccles.* 2: 17: 19): 'He describes the character of their dwellings, and has this to say about the churches in the area: "In each there is a sacred room, which is called a reverence-place

---

[38] See Elm, *'Virgins of God'*, 318–19.

[39] Quoted from Philip Schaff and Henry Wace (eds.), *Library of Nicene and Post-Nicene Fathers Series III*, *Athanasius: Select Works and Letters*, iv (New York, 1924; repr. Peabody, Mass.: Henrickson, 1994), 196. For further see Derwas J. Chitty, *The Desert a City: An Introduction to the Study of Egyptian and Palestinian Monasticism under the Christian Empire* (London and Oxford: Mowbrays, 1966), 2–5.

and place-for-one in which they solitarily perform the mysteries of the holy life" '. Eusebius then peculiarly appears to indicate to his readers that the Therapeutae (= first-century Christians) go into a special reverence-place in a house-church for their ascetic and sacred practices.

It remains a possibility that Alexandrian Christians—who conserved and used Philo's works[40]—read from existing copies of *Contempl.* a pattern of asceticism that they decided to emulate. If this were the case, we would not necessarily have to find direct lines of continuity between Jewish asceticism and Christian asceticism over 250 years, one would see the influence coming directly from the primary literary source: the model that Philo established in *Contempl.*, which we know made a deep impact on one of the most illustrious Christian writers of the fourth century.

In terms of the domestic space of the usual *oikos*, the σεμνεῖον in the mini houses of both the Mareotic group and the Christian monastic structures of Kellia corresponds with the back 'inner' part of the house, known to Philo as the θάλαμος. Ruth Padel has pointed out that, in terms of the house in classical Athens, the μυχός—the dark, back part where women were sometimes supposed to be located—corresponds in some way to the ἄδυτον of the temple, which was also supposed to be the dark, innermost place, and writes: 'Perhaps there was an unconscious parallel between a sacred centre or sacred precinct and the female interior.'[41] In Greek papyri from Egypt, the association is actually made quite explicit. The word θάλαμος designated not only the interior room of the domestic house, but the place where one put precious objects, and could indeed designate an interior chapel or sanctuary.[42] This is curious, because one wonders if the

---

[40] For the use of Philo in early Alexandrian Christianity and elsewhere see: Runia, *Philo in Early Christian Literature*, esp. 119–211; Van den Hoek, *Clement of Alexandria*; ead., 'The Catechetical School'; ead., 'Philo and Origen'.

[41] Ruth Padel, 'Women: Model for Possession by Greek Daemons', in Averil Cameron and Amelie Kuhrt (eds.), *Images of Women in Antiquity* (London: Routledge, 1983), 8. In fact, in Athanasius' *Life of Antony* 14 the parallel between the *monasterion* of Antony and an *aduton* of a temple is made, see Chitty, *Desert a City*, 4, who notes that Athanasius is writing with a view to the pagan world, describing Antony as an initiate of the mysteries.

[42] As in *P.Oxy.* 8: 1144: 2, from the 1st–2nd cents. CE, see Husson, *Oikia*, 87–8.

Mareotic group consciously chose not to refer to the back room of the simple house as a θάλαμος precisely because of the associations between this area and Egyptian private cult, renaming the space as 'reverence-place' and 'place-for-one': apparently invented words.

The πυλών in Egyptian temple architecture acts as a buffer zone to separate out the areas of non-sacred (outside) and sacred (inside) space, just as it acts as a buffer zone in the city between public and private space. It is interesting also that the absence of the πυλών in the mini houses of both the Mareotic group and the Kellia removes the male space of the usual domestic dwelling within the city. This suggests too that the division between public and private space is not applicable in these environments. There is no public 'street' that requires a buffer zone—the πυλών—between the 'female' private interior of the houses.

There is a curious Philonic parallel regarding women in the back room, and the people of *Contempl.*: in *Flacc.* 89 Philo states that the women do not even approach the main (courtyard entrance) door (μηδὲ τὴν αὔλειον προερχόμενα); in *Contempl.*, the members of the Mareotic group were not coming near the outer door (τὴν αὔλειον οὐχ ὑπερβαίνοντες) of their small houses.[43] Interestingly then, all members of the group—both men and women—are therefore in the position of women, or even virgins, in the *oikos* of the city, except for when they come to the general meeting place(s).

THE *SUMPOSION*

The next locus for a specific mention of women in *Contempl.* is dining hall, συμπόσιον (83). The group assembles in an orderly fashion, and then prays. Philo notes (68): 'Women eat together [here] also. They are mostly elderly virgins.' He moves immediately from mention of women eating together ('also') with men to the fact that the women are mostly elderly virgins, in order to ensure that his audience has an image of a woman who is sexually chaste and non-erotic. As we have seen, Philo knows that 'philosophical woman' may be a signifier for the salacious, especially if

---

[43] This is not to say that Philo himself consciously made the connection.

they are represented as eating together with men in a Greek context. I have argued that Philo's primary audience is likely to be a Roman one, and in a Roman situation it was common for men and women to eat together at a *convivium*, but his audience would also have known this was not usual Greek practice. He could appeal to their sense of it being a good thing, but he had to counter the image of the licentious symposium.

The question may be asked as to whether the dining room is the same as the room where the seventh-day assembly takes place (*semneion*). Still, some kind of different room would probably be most likely, not only because Philo gives the room a different name altogether, but because in the *semneion* there was a wall dividing the men and women, but in the dining hall there is apparently no wall; 'the middle of the room' (*Contempl.* 83) is open. In the Hellenistic world, a dining room was often a large oblong room, which would have had movable *klinai* (couches), with individual small tables, around the outside.[44] In the Egyptian context, specially designed *sumposia* (dining rooms) are usually on the first floor, as with bedrooms, so if we are to imagine the main building of the Mareotic group as a kind of villa, maybe we should see the *semneion* on the ground floor and the *sumposion* above it. Large villas could have two *sumposia* (*P.Ryl.* ii. 233, *c.*118 CE).[45] A *sumposion* was not usually used for personal dining in a household but for festive dinners and could be hired out or sold separately; they could also be located in temples. *Sumposia* were also designated at times as *androues*,[46] which indicates a common assumption that it was men who participated in these.

If the festive dinner of the Mareotic group is conceptualized as taking place in the private space of a villa and participated in by members of one big family, then it becomes acceptable in terms of a Hellenistic social context, both to the members of the group and to Philo, if men and women eat together. But, as in the case of the meeting for instruction on seventh days, there is gender

---

[44] For an example, see Joseph Chamonard, *Délos VIII: Le Quartier du Théâtre* (Paris: E. de Boccard and École française d'Athenes, 1922) 1, pl. XIII, depicting the House of Trident. On the left side off the courtyard is a long room measuring 5.7 x 8.5 m, probably used as a *sumposion*. See Katherine M. D. Dunbabin, 'Triclinium and Stibadium', in Slater (ed.), *Dining*, 121–48, at 122.

[45] Husson, *Oikia*, 267–71.

[46] Alston, 'Houses and Households', 36.

separation. During the dinner, Philo tells us that there is a left (female) and right (male) side: 'The order of reclining is divided, with men by themselves (χωρίς) on the right, and women by themselves (χωρίς) on the left' (*Contempl.* 69). The word used, χωρίς, 'without, apart, separately',[47] governs the description of the seating arrangement and is important to remember when we read Philo's account: men are apart from the women and vice versa. The women are apart on the left. The notion of left and right derives from one's position at the entry point, since 'left' and 'right' change depending on where one stands. There is therefore from the point of entry a way in to the left and a way in to the right and women and men would have divided to go their separate ways, with each their own hierarchy of status. They are on either side of a centrally divided space. 'Left' in antiquity tended to be seen as inferior to 'right'. In a fifth-century letter of Sidonius (*Ep.* 1: 11) there is a description of a dinner in which the Emperor Marjoran is seated at the extreme right-hand end, with guests seated in descending order of importance along the semi-circular couch to poor Sidonius at the extreme left-hand end.[48]

Interestingly, at Qumran, by the Dead Sea, there is a dining hall which may have been divided in a similar way. Locus 77 is a very long room (22 m × 4.5 m) which has off to one side an area (Locus 86) in which a large store of pottery was discovered.[49] In Period Ib, when it was constructed, it had two doors: one near the north-western corner and the other near the south-eastern one (see Figure 20). The latter door was used for sloughing out water, after cleaning the floor, since the floor sloped towards this point to facilitate run off. The entrance door was the one in the north-western corner. The room has stone pilasters in its eastern part only, which may suggest that at this point there was some division of space, since these square pilasters would have enabled screens to be fitted more smoothly than the usual palm log pillars

---

[47] LSJ 2016.

[48] See Simon Ellis, 'Late-Antique Dining: Architecture, Furnishings, Behaviour', in Ray Laurence and Andrew Wallace-Hadrill (eds.), *Domestic Space in the Roman World: Pompeii and Beyond* (Portsmouth, RI: Journal of Roman Archaeology, 1997), 41–51, at 50.

[49] See Roland de Vaux, *Archaeology and the Dead Sea Scrolls* (London: British Academy and OUP, 1973), 11; Joan Taylor and Thomas Higham, 'Problems of Qumran's Chronology and the Radiocarbon Dating of Palm Log Samples in Locus 86', *Qumran Chronicle*, 8/1–2 (Aug. 1998), 83–96.

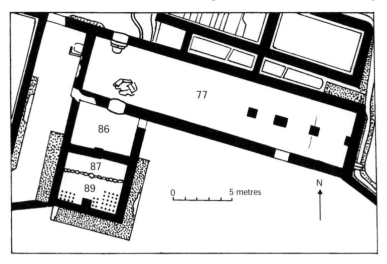

20. Locus 77 at Qumran

would have done. In addition, there is a stone marker on the floor of the room designed for positioning some important piece of furniture near the entrance to the store-room. It is positioned only in relation to the southern part of the room (the 'right' side, from the entrance), not centrally located. This off-centre positioning of an item at the 'front' of the room suggests it was a divided space. Given the need for men and women to be divided from each other in Hellenistic meal contexts, from the entrance men would go to the right and women to the left in order to sit at the table; the stone marker, for the leader's chair (or for entertainment?), was positioned in line with the right side of the room.[50] Unlike in the case of the Mareotic group, where everyone reclined, the long dining hall at Qumran would have

---

[50] In *Contempl.* 80, the president appears to be positioned at the front, and stands up after speaking in order to sing a hymn (*Contempl.* 80). If a male, this chair would presumably have been located on the right side of the room. If the stone circle in Locus 77 indicates the positioning of the leader's chair at Qumran, this may indicate that the leader here was normatively a male. The division of space and off-centre stone marker would nevertheless indicate that women could be present in the community, if we read the archaeology as indicating that a religious group occupied the site.

accommodated simple tables and benches, not couches. Sitting up to eat was the usual practice for children, for poorer people, and was standard in inns and taverns.[51] The very wealthy, both in Israel and in other parts of the Hellenized world, invested in separate dining halls for men and women rather than divided spaces, as we find in Herod's palace in Machaerus.[52]

Kathleen Corley's examination of meal customs in the Graeco-Roman world indicates that in the Greek and Hellenistic contexts men and women eating together was uncommon in the household, though in a relatives-only situation this was acceptable.[53] Cornelius Nepos (*Praef.* 6–7) noted that in Greece a woman was not allowed at a dinner party unless relatives only were present. In the case of the Mareotic group the senior women are in the dinner party, but still separate from the men. How would this reflect the actual ideology of the group? The women may have emulated the highest standards of extreme privacy and modesty of virgins in the context of certain elite Jewish households in Alexandria, as Philo would wish us to think, or they may have had other ideas. While remaining physically hidden from the men in group meetings, this does not mean the women could not speak or sing or command respect. If this space was 'private', there should have been no barrier to the leadership and full participation of women, because Philo himself has determined the private space of the household to be governed by women (*Spec.* 3: 169–71). This confirms that leadership in this community is not necessarily configured in terms of 'public' male norms.

So far so good. Philo has apparently preserved the modesty of his women in *Contempl.* while allowing for their full participation in philosophical meetings and enterprises. What happens next, however, in the festive dinner of the Mareotic group, requires that men and women move out of the separate gendered spaces. With this movement comes a new rhetorical problem for Philo, and the whole structure he has built which would preserve

---

[51] See Martial, *Ep.* 5: 70; Plutarch, *Cato* 56; James Packer, 'Inns at Pompeii', *Cronache Pompeiane*, 4 (1978), 12–24.

[52] Two dining rooms lie alongside one another: see Benedikt Schwank, 'Neue Funde in Nabatäerstädten und ihre Bedeutung für die neutestamentliche Exegese', *NTS* 19 (1983), 429–35.

[53] Kathleen Corley, *Private Women, Public Meals: Social Conflict in the Synoptic Tradition* (Peabody, Mass.: Hendrickson, 1993), 25–8.

female modesty via separations is in danger of breaking down as he pursues a different rhetorical purpose.

In *Contempl.* 83, Philo writes:

After the dinner they celebrate the sacred [eve] all night. And the night festival is celebrated in this way. They all stand up together and first place themselves in the middle of the dining room (κατὰ μέσον τὸ συμπόσιον) in two choirs, one of men and the other of women. The leader and chief is selected for each one as being the most honoured and also most musical.

Here Philo makes a division between the dinner itself and the night festival, in which everyone joins together in singing. The men and women leave their separate places where they have reclined for the meal, and go into the middle of the *sumposion*, where they form two choirs. There is still a separation, into these two choirs, but there is no indication that there is a dividing wall, or screen, or any other kind of structure to shield the modesty of the women. They are no longer apart by themselves.

At this stage we may wonder about how the group organized their close personal space through clothing. In antiquity, as in many contexts in the world today, women's modesty could be preserved by clothing, not only by separations of building spaces. We shall now turn to consider what Philo states in regard to the clothing of this group.

PERSONAL SPACE: THE CLOTHING OF THE MAREOTIC GROUP

In Graeco-Roman societies there were far stronger social norms that affected what people wore than is currently the case in modern Western societies. Much could be known about a person on the basis of his or her clothing. Therefore, what Philo tells us about the clothing worn by the members of the group he describes in *Contempl.* should not be passed over lightly. We need to consider it from the perspective of gender, and also more widely.

First, in *Contempl.* 38, we are told something quite strange. Each member of the group wore: χλαῖνα μὲν ἀπὸ λασίου δορᾶς παχεῖα χειμῶνος, ἐξωμὶς δὲ θέρους ἢ ὀθόνη, ('a thick mantle of woolly skin in winter, and an *exomis* or a linen cloth in summer').

An *exomis* was a garment worn by men engaged in physical labour. It was named such because it was an 'off-the-shoulder' *chiton*, or tunic: one side of the short tunic was unsewn to allow more freedom of movement.[54] Women could wear a longish *exomis* in Greek iconography: the Amazons,[55] or Artemis, for example. However, these were exceptional women engaged in hunting or warfare. The famous model of the Spartan girl running[56] depicts the girl in an *exomis*, which she would have worn in order to engage in athletic pursuits. The girl athletes at the female Olympic games wore the *exomis* also (Pausanias, *Hist. Graec.* 5: 16). But in Hellenistic Alexandria one could say categorically that rich girls did not wear the *exomis*: they did not engage in hunting, war, physical labour, or athletic contests. Philo is simply referring to male attire at this point.[57]

The word *othonē* is actually a large piece of linen cloth rather than a proper garment as such. In Homer, the word is used in the plural to refer to fine linen cloths (e.g. *Od.* 7: 107), mainly sheets. In singular form it is used as an individual linen cloth in Acts 10: 11, cf. 11: 5: the sheet—or rather table-cloth—seen by Peter in his vision. Such a large sheet of linen cloth could be wrapped around the body, but it would advertise the fact that the user did not care about using properly made items of attire. For Conybeare, the fact that an *othonē* was not a 'particular habiliment' indicated that the Greek manuscripts of Philo must be wrong;[58] but that it was not a proper garment seems to have been exactly Philo's point. When he used the term, his audience would immediately have recognized the oddness of the item. They dressed in sheets, as opposed to proper linen mantles,

[54] Conybeare, *Philo*, 221, suggests ἡ here, so that he has only an *exomis* made of linen, but ὀθόνη does not mean 'made of linen', only 'linen sheet' as an item.

[55] See Ethel B. Abrahams, *Greek Dress* (London: J. Murray, 1908), 52–3.

[56] e.g. see Pomeroy, *Goddesses, Whores, Wives, and Slaves*, fig. 1, a Roman copy of a Greek work of 440–40 BCE from the New York Metropolitan Museum of Art.

[57] British Museum, sculpture 208, illustrated in Sue Blundell, *Women in Ancient Greece* (Cambridge, Mass.: Harvard University Press, 1995), fig. 27. In the early Christian work, *The Shepherd of Hermas*, the author is given a vision of twelve virgins clad in *exomeis* 'as if they intended to carry some load'. He is perplexed because though they looked like delicate girls 'they stood like men, as if they intended to carry the entire Heavens'. They then engage in men's manual labour, carrying stones for building (*Similitudes* 9: 2: 4 [79]).

[58] Conybeare, *Philo*, 221.

himatia. While the distinction may seem difficult for us to grasp, it would not have been hard for those of Philo's world.

It was not just a case of wearing linen garments. Plutarch writes that Isis priests wore linen garments—which he calls λίνοστολίαι—and had shaved heads (*Is. et Os.* 352c, cf. Herodotus, *Hist.* 2: 37, 81). The wearing of linen cloths continued an ancient Egyptian style of clothing—the *kalaseris*—worn by men and women tied around the chest (for women) or waist. In fact, that is exactly what is depicted in a fresco from Herculaneum which shows priests and priestesses of Isis performing a water purification ritual. The priests are shown as men with shaved heads who wear creamy or white linen cloths tied at chest level, with their upper chest and shoulders bare. The priestesses—one in the left foreground and the other in the left background—wear white tunics with *himatia* (mantles). The priestess at the back has her head covered with a *himation*, and the one in the foreground has a cloth scarf around her head, like the other women in the picture (cf. Apuleius, *Metamorphoses* 11: 10). The illustration is designed to show a ritual in Egypt, as is indicated by the palm trees and ibises.[59] In another image of an Isiac ritual, a relief carving in the Museo Gregoriano Egizio in Rome, a priestess in the procession carrying a sistrum and ladle is dressed in a simple cloth tied around her chest (like the priests in the Herculaneum fresco), with her *himation* tied around her waist, and one of the priests is wearing only a piece of cloth tied around his waist.[60] A predilection for wearing simple linen cloths which expose much of the upper body is clearly shown here, and the cloths are worn by both men and women. I doubt that the Jewish group would have copied the style of clothing worn by Egyptian priests and priestesses because the term *othonē* (a linen sheet) appears elsewhere as a much larger piece of material than a *kalaseris*. Furthermore, a *kalaseris* was known in the Greek world as an item of attire for religious purposes outside the Egyptian cult. It appears on a list of dress for initiates in the cult of Demeter in the Andania mysteries inscription (*IG* 5: 1: 1390).

The other clothing of the Mareotic group is the thick woolly skin cloak worn in cold weather. A *chlaina* (cf. Lat. *laena*) is a

[59] This fresco is now in the Museo Archeologico Nazionale di Napoli (inv. no. 8924); see Beard *et al.*, *Religions of Rome*, ii. 303.

[60] Ibid. 136.

large, square cloak usually worn loose over a *chiton*. It was generally made of wool and fastened with a clasp. The word *chlaina*
is generally a male's cloak, but could be any cloak worn by the
poor that did not conform to the standard of a proper *himation*.
'A thick cloak of woolly skin' is clearly not a nice woollen *himation*, which we would expect on an educated, wealthy woman for
winter apparel. The image is of a shaggy goatskin or sheepskin.
In the Pythagoraean letter from Perictione, the perfect woman
Pythagoraean should 'satisfy only her hunger and thirst, and—if
she is of the poorer class and has a cloak made of goat-skin—her
need for warmth'.⁶¹ This kind of cloak would perhaps have made
the members of the Mareotic group look poor. Well-dressed
people of cities simply did not wear sheep or goatskin. They
would have looked very like poor Pythagoraeans aimed to look.

The image of an *exomis* combined with a sheepskin is also suggestive of the way shepherds can be depicted in Graeco-Roman
iconography.⁶² In the first-century Christian work, *The Shepherd
of Hermas*, there is a vision of 'a man who looked glorious in the
garb of a shepherd, with a white (sheep/goat-)skin wrapped
around him' (*Visions* 5: 2: 1 [25]) and another of 'a great shepherd
like a wild man in appearance with a white goatskin around him'
(*Similitudes* 2: 2: 5 [62]). The image of the shepherd was powerful in Second Temple Judaism, including nascent Christianity.
It connected with the imagery of religious leadership. Broadly,
the nation of Israel were sheep and the leaders of the nation—or
God and his messengers—were the shepherds. For example in
Isaiah 63: 11 people remember YHWH who 'brought them up
out of the sea with the shepherds of his flock'. The image was
used by Jeremiah: 'Then I will give you shepherds after my own
heart who will feed you on knowledge and understanding' (3: 15,
cf. 23: 1, 4; 31: 10; 50:19, Ezek. 34: 33). Philo himself wrote:

For just as goats and oxen and sheep are led by goatherds and ox-herds
and shepherds, and flocks and herds cannot possibly give orders to
herdsmen, so too the multitude, who are like cattle, require a master
and a ruler and have for their leaders men of virtue, appointed to the
office of governing the herd. Homer often calls kings 'shepherds of
the people' (*Iliad* 2: 243) but nature more accurately applies the title to

---

⁶¹ Stobaeus, *Anth.* 4: 28: 10, quoted in Pomeroy, *Women in Hellenistic Egypt*,
69.
⁶² I am grateful to Hero Granger-Taylor for this observation.

the good, since kings are often in the position of the sheep than of the shepherd. They are led by strong drink and good looks and by baked meats and savoury dishes and the dainties produced by cooks and confectioners, to say nothing of their craving for silver and gold and grander ambitions. But the good nothing can ensnare, and it is theirs also to admonish those whom they see caught in the toils of pleasure. (*Prob.* 30–1)[63]

'Nature more accurately applies the title to the good', states Philo. Here he seems to be drawing on a common assumption. In the New Testament, we find numerous references to the people of Israel as sheep (some of whom have gone astray) and Jesus as the 'good shepherd' (cf. Matt. 9: 36; 10: 16; 15: 24; 25: 32; 26: 31 and parallels; John 10: 7–16; Heb. 13: 20). In 1 Peter 5: 1–4 the community elders are the shepherds of the flock. The language was central to the idea of Christian community, as Paul's speech to the elders of Ephesus indicates: 'Be on guard for yourselves and all the flock, among which the Holy Spirit had made you overseers in order to shepherd the community of God that he purchased with his own blood. I know that savage wolves will come in among you, not sparing the flock, after my departure' (Acts 20: 28–9).

Elijah covers himself with a 'sheepskin' when he hears the voice of YHWH in the cave in the LXX 3 Kingdoms 19: 13 (=1 Kings 19: 13). It is this cloak that he throws on top of Elisha to commission him as his successor (1 Kings 19: 19; 2 Kings 2: 8, 13, 14). In Hebrews 11: 32–8 the author gives a vivid description of how some Jews imagined the prophets of old:

What more shall I say? There is no time for me to provide an account of Gideon, Barak, Samson, Jephthah, or of David, Samuel and the prophets. . . . They were stoned, or sawn in half, or killed by the sword. They were homeless, *and went about in sheepskins, in skins of goats* (περιῆλθον ἐν μηλωταῖς, ἐν αἰγείοις δέρμασιν). They were in want and hardship, and maltreated. They were too good for the world and they wandered in deserts and mountains and in caves and ravines.

In other words, prophets could therefore dress something like shepherds or very poor people. They were also the religious leaders of the nation.

Philo gives another indication of the clothing of the group in reference to the junior members. He writes that when they serve

---

[63] Quoted from Colson, *Philo*, ix (Loeb), 27–9.

the seniors at the festive meal they do so with their 'tunics ungirt and hanging down' (*Contempl.* 72). It was apparently customary for slaves to gird their loins—tuck their tunics into a belt (cf. Luke 17: 8)—when serving tables. In this case Philo uses the word χιτωνίσκος, which I translate simply as 'tunic' since it is a diminutive form of the word χιτών, equivalent to χιτώνιον, implying a basic type of tunic worn by men and women, some-times short (on men), sometimes an under-tunic (on women).[64]

Additionally, Philo gives some further clues to the clothing of this group in *Contempl.* 30, when he states that they sit εἴσω τὰς χεῖρας ἔχοντες, literally 'having the hands inside'. In Colson's translation, this phrase is given as 'with their hands inside the robe' which leads to the conclusion that they were in fact wearing robes of some kind. However, if they were wearing only *exomeis* or tunics it would be impossible to sit with the hands tucked inside these items of clothing in the manner Philo describes. Porphyry indicates that Chaeremon said something similar about the Egyptian priests: ἀεὶ δὲ ἐντὸς τοῦ σχήματος αἱ χεῖρες (*Abstin.* 4: 6): 'Always the hands [were] *inside of the figure*', liter-ally, which does not mean that the hands were always inside *clothing*—a fact not confirmed at all by the iconography of Egyptian cult[65]—so much as the hands were in some kind of proper positioning. From comparison with what Chaeremon says it is clear that Philo is contracting a phrase and if one were to supply a genitive noun it would be τοῦ σχήματος. Philo does not put the word in here because he has just used it: when listening to an address they sit μετὰ τοῦ πρέποντος σχήματος 'with the proper figure', literally, or perhaps we could say 'in the proper position'. This proper position when sitting is then defined as 'having the hands inside [the figure], the right hand in between chest and chin, and the left lowered along the thighs'. Philo uses similar

---

[64] LSJ 1993, and see Andrew Dalby, 'Levels of Concealment: The Dress of the *hetairai* and *pornai* in Greek Texts', in Lloyd Llewellyn-Jones (ed.), *Women's Dress in the Ancient Greek World* (London: Duckworth and Classical Press of Wales, 2002), 111–24, at 115–16.

[65] In all the rituals of the cult of Isis, the only person to hide hands was the 'Prophet' who carried the sacred Nile water in such a way that his hands did not come into direct contact with the container, see Beard *et al.*, *Religions of Rome*, ii. 303 and relief sculpture from Rome shown on p. 136. This is not a parallel to the position described by Philo or Chaeremon.

language in *Somn*. 2: 126 when he describes the bad ruler (Flaccus?) saying to the Jews: 'Will you go out and assemble according to the customary figure (μετὰ τοῦ συνήθους σχήματος), with the right hand inside (τὴν . . . δεξιὰν εἴσω) and the other one from under the outerwear (ὑπὸ τῆς ἀμπεχόνης) fixed along the thighs?' This position is identified by the bad ruler as being one in which at least the right arm is restricted, making the Jews unable to act or gesture in some way.

This positioning is found in dedicatory monuments showing standing Isis worshippers. It is usual to depict figures with their right arm tucked close to the chest in the fold of the *himation* (hand uncovered), with the left hand by the body hanging down.[66] It is also a common way of depicting figures in the funerary art of Palmyra, and may be seen also in the much-used 'large Herculaneum woman' figure type for statuary, among numerous other examples.[67] The pose is commonly known as a *pudicitia*, meaning 'modesty', and required the outer garment (*himation* or *pallium*) to be wrapped over the left arm and shoulder, around the back, under the right arm and over the left shoulder, forming a kind of sling for the right arm. In identifying the proper figure for the arms/hands, Philo is presenting his audience with an image of people sitting in a pose considered modest.

For the record, it should be noted that Philo states only that the clothing is, in winter, a cloak of woolly skin and, in summer, an *exomis* or *othonē*. I am assuming that there was something under the woolly skin in winter, namely, the *exomis*, *othonē*, or *chitoniskos*. But this may well be wrong, since the classic image of a philosopher in Graeco-Roman art has him clad only in a very large type of *himation* known as a περιβόλαιον, with no tunic underneath.[68] This group, according to Philo, go one step

[66] See Johannes Eingartner, *Isis und ihre Dienerinnen in der Kunst der Römischen Kaiserzeit* (Leiden: Brill, 1991), pls. lxii–lxvi, lxviii–lxxi, lxxiii–lxxvi.

[67] Glenys Davies, 'Clothes as Sign: The Case of the Large and Small Herculaneum Women', in Llewellyn-Jones (ed.), *Women's Dress*, 227–41, esp. 237; William H. Stephens, *The New Testament World in Pictures* (Nashville, Tenn.: Broadman, 1987), 70–1, shows two Palmyrene reliefs with the pose.

[68] For representations of this see Richter, *Portraits*, i. 108–20 and figs. 523–4, 544–5, 556–64, 571–3. Poets and artists were also depicted with this attire, e.g. Sophocles (figs. 680, 682, 705–7, 711–12), Euripides (figs. 760–1, 767), Aeschylus (figs. 597, 607).

further: their philosophical *peribolaion* is merely an *othonē* (in summer) or a shaggy sheep or goatskin cloak (in winter). But they can also discard even such vaguely philosophical attire in summer, donning the simplest clothing of working people.[69]

We should probably not look for any kind of uniform here. Philo wanted to stress that their clothing was extremely simple, and adopted purely for protection against cold and heat (*Contempl.* 38), and he described the simplest, most basic type of human attire possible, both for the seniors and for the juniors, though in both cases it is easier to imagine this clothing on men than on women: an impression Philo himself may have wished. Androcentrism in terms of the description of the clothing ensured that women were bracketed out until Philo wished to draw the audience's attention to them. In an interesting passage in his *Special Laws*, Philo states that some wealthy (male) rulers of cities adopt such simple clothing as part of a kind of 'retreat': 'and in the summer they wear a loin-cloth (*perizoma*) and a thin *othonē* and in winter any tough and stout *chlaina*' (*Spec.* 2: 20). Here the *chlaina* is not a woolly skin, however, and there is no mention of an *exomis,* but it is interesting to see this model of (male) ascetic clothing. A large linen sheet was ascetic attire for others than those in the Mareotic group. It would clearly have made the wearer look distinctive.

The other type of perfect Jewish philosophers Philo selects for his rhetoric in *On Virtues* were of course the Judaean Essenes. While we do not have this third treatise in the work, we do have Philo's description of their dress elsewhere. In terms of the dress of the Essenes, Philo indicates also that it is extremely simple. They wear *chlainai* in winter and *exomeis* in summer (*Hypothetica* 11: 12). The *chlaina* is not, however, identified as sheepskin and the implication would be that it is a normal type made of wool. Actually, in the case of the Essenes the 'working man's attire' of the *exomis* would be appropriate because they are busy labourers, craftsmen, and agricultural workers (11: 6–10). The Essenes clearly do not wear *othonai* (*a*) because they are not resident in Egypt, and it seems to be associated with ascetics of this region and (*b*) because they actually are male manual

---

[69] In the mosaic of Palestrina (*c.*100 BCE), the labourers and hunters of the Egyptian countryside are dressed in *exomeis* or loin-cloths while certain priests (playing music in the right foreground) wear the *kalaseris*.

workers, for which the *exomis* was the standard attire. The Essenes do not then look like philosophers, in Philo's presentation: they look like ordinary working men. In terms of Philo's descriptions it is only the Therapeutae that adopt a thick cloak of woolly skin, specifically.

Since in both other cases the descriptions only apply to men—male rulers of the cities who have undertaken ascetic 'retreats' and Essenes (for Philo they are all older men)—can we extrapolate from what Philo writes to 'see' what ascetic women wore, or more specifically what the Jewish women philosophers of *Contempl.* wore? On the basis of what Perictione writes, we know that poor women Pythagoraeans could also wear a simple skin *chlaina*. According to the epitaph of the ascetic Cynic woman philosopher Hipparchia, she spurned the philosopher's mantle and wore 'whatever scrap cloth she found'.[70] The overall 'look' of the group would have been of people who used clothing not for personal adornment, but only to keep warm, or to provide the most basic type of covering in summer. It would have been rough and threadbare. Plutarch notes that philosophers are τριβωνοφορίαι, 'wearing worn-out clothing' (*Is. et Os.* 352c).

What the women wore does, however, affect the issue of gendered space. If the women wore *himatia* and always properly covered themselves up by their clothing there would have been less reason for the wall that separated the men and the women in the *semneion*. It is significant that Philo insists that the women's modesty—that is, a view of their bodies—is protected by the wall rather than by their clothing, when normally a woman could easily hide her body by wrapping her *himation* around herself. If all the space was essentially private in the community, as argued above, public clothing was not necessary, but we saw how Philo wanted to characterize Jewish women in Alexandria as being more modest than any of their contemporaries. Given the fact that he presents the women in the group as a 'good' feature, it is striking that he does not insist on their modest *clothing*. While a linen sheet could supply that modesty, Philo instead insists that it is the wall in the *semneion*, and initial separation in the *sumposion*, that does so.

In *Contempl.* 66, it is said that the group assembles for the

[70] Didumi, frag. 117k.

forty-ninth-day dinner λευχειμονοῦντες, 'wearing white'. The sheep or goatskin cloak could be whitish, brown, or black. A *exomis* would normally be made of simple undyed wool or undyed linen. Undyed and unbleached white wool or linen was not considered to be properly white, and had a naturally creamy (wool) or beige (linen) hue. The *othonē* would—unless specially bleached—be beige. The members of the group don white garments for their most holy 'feast'. This contrasts the group with the Essenes, as described by Josephus, who apparently 'always wear white garments' (*War* 2: 123, 137), though interestingly Philo does not mention that they wore white in any extant text.

That the Mareotic group were wearing white clothing for their festive meal means that it was probably freshly laundered, bleached linen. In antiquity, it was not so easy to get clothing white. Wool and linen would be treated differently to make them white, and the former was much harder to bleach than the latter, since linen was whitened by laying it out in the strong sun and sprinkling it with water, as in parts of the world today. Wool was washed to remove the animal oils and dirt by fullers (launderers) prior to spinning or subsequent to weaving or wear. This would entail stamping on the cloth in tubs in which an alkaline detergent had been dissolved, specifically natron (cf. Prov. 25: 20; Jer. 2: 22) or soap (Mal. 3: 2), but also a mixture of urine, potash, carbonate of soda, and fuller's earth (Pliny, *Nat. Hist.* 38: 6, 8; Martial, *Ep.* 9: 93; Plautus, *Asin.* 5: 2), or bean-meal mixed with water (m.Shabb. 9: 5; m.Nidd. 9: 6).[71] Pliny notes that the poor used chalk or earth (including marl) to rub into their (woollen) clothes to make them white for festivals (*Hist. Nat.* 35: 17). Fullers were expensive and few people could afford regular treatments for their clothing.

While it seems likely then that the Mareotic group's white clothing was made of linen—perhaps their *othonai* were laun-

---

[71] There was a particular 'Fullers' Field' outside Jerusalem, cf. 2 Kings 18: 17. In Pompeii the fullery was located within the city on the Via Mercurio. Excavation of this building has greatly improved our knowledge of the ancient fulling process since not only have the tubs, vats, frames, and presses been found, but also a wall fresco illustrating stages in the fulling process. In this case the clothes requiring bleaching were hung on a conical frame over a pot of burning sulphur, see Walter Moeller, *The Wool Trade of Ancient Pompeii* (Leiden: Brill, 1976).

dered and bleached in the sun by the juniors for this occasion—it would not be essential for their white clothing to have been linen. In Mark 9: 3, in the story of the transfiguration of Jesus, the disciples see Jesus' (woollen) *himation* become 'shining white, extremely', and the author comments: 'which a fuller on earth would not be able to make so white'. Famously, Isaiah 1: 18 has:

> Though your sins are as scarlet,
> they will be white as snow;
> though they are red as crimson,
> they will be like wool.

The parallelism suggests that 'white as snow' and 'wool' are equatable in terms of an image for whiteness (cf. Dan. 7: 9), indicating cleanness and purity. The same image is found in Psalm 51: 7:

> Purify me with hyssop[72] and I shall be clean;
> wash me and I shall be whiter than snow.

In Malachi 3: 2 God's coming will purify the sons of Levi 'like fullers' soap'. In Revelation 7: 9–14 there is a vision of a huge crowd from all nations 'clothed in white *stolai*' and holding palm branches'. These people clothed in white are those who have, paradoxically, 'washed their *stolai* and made them white in the blood of the Lamb' (cf. 6: 11). Likewise, in Revelation 3: 4 white garments are those that have not been dirtied: 'You have a few people in Sardis who have not made their *himatia* (mantles) dirty. They will walk with me in white, for they are worthy. He who overcomes [temptation] will thus be clothed in white *himatia*' (cf. 3: 18; 4: 4). In all these cases, the usually woollen *himatia* and *stolai* (shorter outer tunics) are undirtied or washed clean by fullers and are therefore white.

While linen was widely used in Egypt, it had many different grades, and one should also distinguish between the fine forms and the rougher ones. Specially bleached fine linen was particularly valued for important occasions. One form of very special linen garment, as opposed to a piece of linen cloth, was called a

---

[72] In this first element of the imagery, the purifying with hyssop refers to the ritual sprinkling that would occur when a priest dipped hyssop in blood and sprinkled it over the person to be cleansed, cf. Lev. 14: 4, in the case of leprosy.

βύσσινον, identified as a kind of nuptial robe in Revelation 19: 8.[73] In this case it is 'clean bright'. The armies of heaven are 'clothed in fine linen (*bussinon*): clean white' (Rev. 19: 14). Likewise in the Dead Sea Scrolls text 1QM 7: 9–10 the warrior priests are dressed in fine *white* linen, *shesh laban*, not just the usual *shesh* or *bad* (linen) used by priests in the Temple (Exod. 39: 27–9; Lev. 16: 4), which is not described as being white unless there is a special occasion for it to be so. The Mareotic group are clearly not wearing fine types of linen, according to Philo.

Such examples also show that white is the colour of purity because it usually indicates that clothing was indeed newly laundered as well as bleached. In a Pythagoraean letter from a third-century CE papyrus (*P.Haun.* ii. 13), Melissa writes to Klearete that she should wear no adornment and be 'pure white and clean with her clothing'.[74] This is not simply metaphorical. While undyed wool and linen were very common as clothing in antiquity, they were not generally considered 'white' unless they were specially treated and clean. It would mean also that you smelt good. In Ecclesiastes 9: 8 the writer recommends: 'always wear white clothing and keep your head well-scented' as a good hygiene measure.

Philo himself writes of the benefits of linen and associates it, 'when carefully cleaned', with a 'very bright and luminous colour' (*Somn.* 217). This would indicate that Philo had cleanness in mind also when he wrote of the Mareotic group wearing white.

The special wearing of white for a festive occasion was common in antiquity (cf. Ovid, *Fast.* 1: 79; Statius, *Silv.* 1: 2), and was associated with putting on clean clothing. In Zechariah 3: 3 the prophet sees the High Priest Joshua standing before the angel of the Lord dressed in dirty clothes. The angel says: 'Remove the dirty clothing from him!' and people take his clothes off and clothe him with clean festal garments (3: 4–5). According to Josephus, when David heard that Bathsheba's child had died he changed from black to white (clean) clothing (*Ant.* 7: 156). After Archelaus has mourned for his father Herod he also changed into white (clean) clothing and went to the

---

[73] Donald A. McIlraith, ' "For the Fine Linen is the Righteous Deeds of the Saints": Words and Wife in Revelation 19: 8', *CBQ* 19/8 (1999), 512–27.

[74] Rowlandson (ed.), *Women and Society*, 327.

Temple (*War* 2: 1). According to the Mishnah, the daughters of Jerusalem wore white (clean, borrowed clothing) for the ninth and fifteenth days of Ab (m.Taan. 4: 8).[75]

In Apuleius' *Metamorphosis* (11: 9–10) the priests and the participants of the Isis cult wear dazzling white linen robes. However, it still remains essential to remember that there is no necessary equation between linen and the colour white, as E. P. Sanders has demonstrated from literary sources. For example, in m.Yoma (3: 6; 7: 1, 4) *buts* (= *bussos*, linen) garments are distinguished from white garments in regard to the clothing of the High Priest, here also apparently clean garments. In m.Parah 4: 1 a priest who burns the red heifer is singled out as being dressed in white, as if ordinarily the linen clothing priests wore was not white. In *Ant.* 2: 327 the people of Jerusalem wear white and the priests wear the linen garments prescribed by law.[76] It is wrong to think of an equation white = linen as if a particular kind of material has the sole monopoly on the colour. Linen may itself have seemed a good cloth to wear, an ancient type of fabric that was light, strong (cf. *Somn.* 217), and permitted air to circulate, but it was only white when it was specially bleached and clean. We may say that if someone was wearing white for a special purpose it was quite likely to be linen, but not necessarily. In the case of the Mareotic group, linen garments would have been easily sun-bleached, and therefore they were more likely to have been worn than white woollen clothing, for which whiteness required treatment by fullers.

The whiteness of the clothing worn by the Mareotic group on the occasion of the festive meal should not be a reason to connect the group with the Essenes. The fact that the Essenes 'always' wore white clothing (according to Josephus) would tie in with their fastidious habits in regard to purity and cleanliness. White clothing is mentioned in line with this: 'They consider that oil is defiling, and anyone who accidentally comes into contact with it scours himself, because they make a point of keeping a dry skin and of always being dressed in white' (*War* 1: 123). In *War* 1: 137 a new candidate to the sect is given 'white clothing' as part of his

---

[75] For these references see Sanders, *Judaism*, 97.

[76] Ibid. Examples of ancient textiles using bleached and unbleached linen thread to form a pattern can also be found. I am grateful to Hero Granger-Taylor for noting this.

equipment, which he presumably has then to put on and keep clean until he is fully a member of the Essene school, at which point his purity is affirmed. Daily purificatory baths are part of the Essene lifestyle according to Josephus, and the baths affect the clothing worn by the immerser. The Essenes work until the fifth hour in their various labours and then assemble in one place, where they 'gird their loins with linen cloths (λίνοι)' and 'bathe their bodies in cold water'. Josephus does not say they put on any new outer clothing, but it appears that they go off directly to a pure meal wearing these λίνοι. After this pure meal, 'they lay aside the clothing like holy vestments' and again return to work (*War* 2: 131), though obviously they are not naked when they work and Josephus has omitted to tell us of their work attire. Later on, when Josephus acknowledges the order of Essenes that marry, he notes that in the bath 'the women wear a wrap (ἀμπεχομένη)[77] as the men wear a loin-cloth (περίζωμα)' (*War* 2: 161). The way Josephus describes it, Essenes could only eat the pure meal in such purified clothing, which they would lay aside at the end like 'holy vestments' until they were required to bath and eat again.

Josephus also indicates elsewhere that the Essenes wore mantles (*himatia*),[78] which they wrapped around themselves when digging a hole to go to the toilet (*War* 2: 148). This was usual Hellenistic attire, worn by everyone who could afford one. *Himatia* were usually made of wool in this period, or sometimes of linen.[79] It is interesting that the site of Qumran is located in an area renowned for soap-production and that a soap-making installation has been found nearby.[80] A laundry area has been

[77] This word is difficult to translate and rare. It is possibly the same as an ἀμπέχονη which in classical Greece was sometimes a fine outer veil, but also could be any outer wrap, see Dalby, 'Levels of Concealment', 116–20. The verb ἀμπέχω means 'put around'.

[78] As we saw, Philo states that the Essenes wore a *chlaina* rather than a *himation*. As with the Mareotic group, however, we should not think of an Essene uniform as such, only an attempt at wearing a uniform colour. Warmth could have been provided by different sorts of outer wear.

[79] A very good example of a undyed white-wool mantle for a woman (evidenced by the gamma motifs in the corners) was found in the Cave of Letters (no. 43). It measures 270 x 140 cm: Yigael Yadin, *Finds from the Bar Kokhba Period in the Cave of Letters* (Jerusalem: Israel Exploration Society, 1963), 238.

[80] Recently Zohar Amar has identified the installations and materials found by Vendyl Jones in the so-called 'Cave of the Column' as being connected with

identified at the site.[81] Essene clothing was shared, according to Philo (*Prob.* 86; *Hypoth.* 11: 12; and implied by Josephus *War* 2: 7; *Ant.* 18: 20), and the purity and cleanliness of such shared clothing would presumably have been considered important. While I do not wish to go further into how ritual purity differs from straightforward cleanness here,[82] and it should be noted that the two are distinct (something can be physically very dirty but ritually pure), it seems from what Josephus writes that the Essenes placed the two conditions in quite close proximity, hence the avoidance of oil and the whiteness (bleached state and cleanness) of their undyed clothing. Josephus states that they would hang on to their clothing even when it was extremely threadbare (*War* 2: 126, cf. 1QS 7: 13–14). In fact, frequent washing of clothes would have greatly reduced the longevity of the textiles, though again there is a stereotype of the ascetic ideal of philosophers' clothing at work here.

Philo does not associate white with the clothing of the Mareotic group until they gather together for a festive meal. The most interesting piece of evidence is found in Diogenes Laertius' *Lives of the Eminent Philosophers*, where it is stated that the Pythagoraeans will not eat white cocks because they are wearing the clothing of suppliants (8: 34), from which we can conclude that suppliants generally wore white when entreating the deity for special favours. If the members of the Mareotic group considered themselves to be suppliants during the festive meal, then white was the right colour to wear to identify themselves in this role at this particular time.

What garments did they change into? Shaggy skin cloaks would not have been classed as white, and neither would *exomeis* as a rule. The best clue to what they wore may be in what Philo states regarding the junior members of the group not girding their *chitoniskoi*, so there is nothing about them that indicates

the production of soap from potassium-rich plants (from the family of *Chenopodiacae*) which grow wild in the vicinity. Zohar Amar, 'The Ash and the Red Material from Qumran', *DSD* 5 (1998), 1–15. An ostracon with the word *borit* (soap) has recently been found on the site, as reported by Yulav Peleg in the conference 'Qumran: The Site of the Dead Sea Scrolls' at Brown University, Nov. 2002.

[81] At locus 52 in Periods Ib and II (1st cent. BCE to 68 CE). See de Vaux, *Archaeology and the Dead Sea Scrolls*, 7, 10, 16.

[82] Though see my *Immerser*, 58–64.

that they are slaves (72). This seems to mean that their clothing was no different from those that they served, namely, all members of the group were wearing *chitoniskoi*. We noted already that Philo's mention of their hands being 'clean of income and not defiled by any gain' (66) may reflect Philo's consciousness that the group were not practising purity regulations. In mentioning white clothing in the same passage he implies physical cleanness of the clothing. It therefore links in rhetorically with the purity concerns he shows in this passage. It should be remembered also in regard to the activities of the junior members of the group that they were undoubtedly the ones to ensure that the contemplative seniors had clean, white clothing to put on for the sacred meal.

In conclusion, the clearest thing we could say is that both men and women in the Mareotic group wore freshly laundered white linen tunics (of the most basic kind) for the sacred meal, and otherwise mainly non-white *exomeis* (for men), linen sheets, and perhaps basic tunics (for both) in summer, with a shaggy sheepskin or goatskin cloak added for warmth in winter. While women's bodies could have been effectively hidden beneath the linen sheets, if women had hidden their bodies it would have been sensible of Philo to report the fact, since it would have endorsed his rhetoric of women's modesty perfectly. His silence is therefore telling, given his rhetoric. Moreover, since he defined the women's modesty by the wall in the *semneion*, and by separating out the men and the women by themselves at the beginning of the feast for the forty-ninth-day dinner in the *sumposion*, he provides us with indications that the women may have been more neglectful in their clothing than Philo may have wished. Had the women covered up their bodies in a modest fashion, it would not have been so necessary for Philo to emphasize these spatial separations which serve to protect their modesty.

SACRED SPACE

We have already touched on the definition of sacred space in the buildings of the Mareotic group: the *semneion*, 'reverence-place', is a 'holy room', whether in the mini houses or in the communal meeting place (*Contempl.* 25, 32, 89). Sacred language appears at various points in the text to underscore the cultic dimensions of activities. The meal is a 'sacred symposium' (71) in which they are dressed in white like suppliants in a temple, or people celebrating a holy feast. This kind of cultic language is not used metaphorically by Philo. The philosophers Philo describes '*are called* [cultic] attendants (m. and f.)' (2) and in their mini houses there is a 'holy room' that '*is called* a reverence-place and place-for-one'[83] (25). There is an indication here that Philo is reflecting cultic language, while yet wanting to present the group in terms of philosophical prototypes.

The cultic language is most powerful in relation to the forty-ninth-day feast. After they have come into the *sumposion* and prayed, the seniors recline in hierarchical order while the juniors stand attentive; the president gives a discourse, and then stands up to sing a hymn. Philo writes:

Then the [president] stands up and sings a hymn composed to God, either a new one of his own composition or some old one [composed] by the poets of old, for they have left behind many [songs] in many metres and melodies: hexameters, trimeters, hymns of processions, [hymns] relating to libations, [hymns] relating to the altar, for standing [in a chorus] and for [choral] dancing well measured out for turning and twisting. After him, in fact, the others according to order have a turn at singing. Everyone else listens in total silence, except when they need [to sing] closing lines and themes. For then all men and all women sing aloud. (*Contempl.* 80)

Philo here refers to their musical compositions as relating to cultic activities (processions, libations, altar-actions), as if the music in some way ushers in a cultic reality. The group joins in with the president in closing lines and themes, participating too in this powerful music. They (the seniors?) are each to sing a hymn of their own, individually, as if this includes them in the sacred activity. After this, when all is done, the juniors bring in a table which is configured as representing the table of the shew-bread in the Temple.[84]

When each person has finished a hymn, the juniors bring in the above-mentioned table, upon which the most all-pure food is [set out]: [loaves] of leavened bread, along with a seasoning of salt mingled with hyssop.

---

[83] Cf. Conybeare, *Philo*, 211.
[84] See Exod. 25: 23–30; 35: 13; 37: 10–16; 39: 36; Lev. 24: 5–9; cf. Num. 4: 7; 1 Kings 7: 48; 2 Chron. 3: 19; 13: 11; 29: 18. The loaves on the table are a permanent offering to God, and were made by Levites (1 Chron. 9: 31; 23: 28–9).

This [arrangement] is in deference to the sacred table in the vestibule of the holy temple court. For upon this [table] are loaves and salt, without flavouring, and the bread is unleavened, and the salt is not mixed [into the bread]. (*Contempl.* 81)

This is very powerful language. One is reminded of how the earliest Christians could make bread and wine represent, in various ways, the body and blood of the crucified and risen Jesus. Here, the bread and salt represents the holy food in the Temple.[85] In fact, the book of Leviticus (24: 8) itself states that the twelve loaves (the number indicating the twelve tribes of Israel) placed on the table are an 'everlasting covenant'. These people eat the bread of the covenant. In eating the holy food of the Temple, the group members hold themselves to be specially chosen priests, for only 'Aaron and his sons' are permitted to eat the loaves. Moreover, 'they will eat them inside the holy place since for him they are a very holy portion of the food baked/burnt for YHWH' (Lev. 24: 9). Philo states: 'For it was appropriate that the simplest and purest food be allotted to the most excellent portion of the priests, as a reward for services, while others would zealously seek the same [kind of food], but hold off from the [Temple loaves], in order that their betters might have precedence' (*Contempl.* 82). This identification of the members of the group as the most excellent portion of the priests, who have the right to eat the bread, fits with what Philo states a little earlier on, that 'just as right reason dictates abstinence from wine for the priests when sacrificing, so also for these people for a lifetime' (*Contempl.* 74), for these people are more excellent. The members of the Mareotic group provide their services, λειτουργία, continually in this holy Temple. The eating of the bread from the table is a reward for the services, which they offer all the time by means of their contemplative lifestyle.

In the *sumposion*, this space is transformed into the holy Sanctuary itself, where the chosen priests eat the bread offered to YHWH, which represents an everlasting covenant between God and Israel.[86] After eating, they then go into the middle of the

[85] In the Masoretic text there is only bread on the table, but the LXX adds salt. See also *Mos.* 2: 104.

[86] Even the celibacy of the group is relevant here, for in 1 Sam. 21: 2–7 Ahimelech the priest gives David the loaves to eat, 'as long as the men have kept themselves from women'.

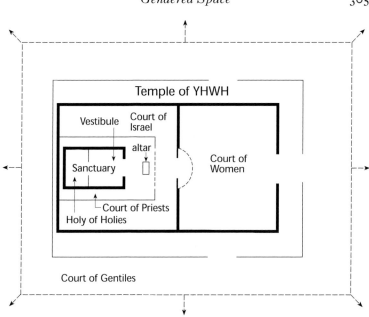

21. Schematic plan of the areas of holiness in the Jerusalem Temple

room, standing ready to sing praises to God in two choirs of
perfect attendants of the divine.

In terms of gendered space, this transformation is fascinating
given that in the real Temple in Jerusalem, no woman was permitted to be in the area of the Sanctuary vestibule. The Temple
in Jerusalem had different zones of holiness, from the lesser holiness of the outer court, in which even Gentiles were allowed, to
the Holy of Holies where only the High Priest was permitted on
the Day of Atonement (see Figure 21). Any woman, Jew or
Gentile could come into the Court of the Gentiles; any Jewish
woman could enter the Court of the Women (Josephus, *War* 5:
199), but at the entry to the Court of the Israelites, she could go
no further. In Exodus 38: 8 a woman could minister at the door
of the Tent of Meeting (corresponding to the Sanctuary), but by
the time of Herod's Temple in Jerusalem women's proximity to
the highest degree of holiness had been pushed back. Only
Jewish men could go into the Court of Israel. Beyond this zone
was the area where the priests undertook sacred duties and

sacrifices and no non-priest or priest who was not serving was permitted there.[87] Women could not be priests. The women could see into this area from a gallery in the Court of the Women (m.Midd. 2: 5).

The Temple proper, or Sanctuary, was divided into two areas: the outer vestibule and the Holy of Holies. As Philo notes, the table of shewbread was located in the outer vestibule, along with the tabernacle menorah and incense altar. The entrance to the vestibule was draped with a gigantic vine made of gold (*Ant.* 15: 395; m.Midd. 3: 8). The interior chamber, the Holy of Holies, was separated by a large curtain (Exod. 26: 33; cf. m. Yoma 5: 1; Shek. 8: 5), and was completely empty. E. P. Sanders points out that in a Greek temple 'the interior was usually the residence of the statue of the deity, and usually only priests, suppliants and people seeking refuge entered'.[88] The Sanctuary in Jerusalem was also accessible only to priests, though they performed only a few rites there. On the basis of Greek parallels, it may have been accessible also to suppliants. Again, this resonates with Philo's description of the group as 'suppliants' in his subtitle to the *Contempl.*, but in *Contempl.* 82 the group members are described as the most excellent portion of the priests themselves: those who have been allotted duties in the Sanctuary vestibule. There is a mixing of concepts in terms of cultic functions: 'attendants', 'suppliants', 'priests'. In terms of physical constraints, at the Temple in Jerusalem anyone not a priest—even a Levite—who approached the artefacts of the Sanctuary would die (Num. 18: 3).

The members of the Mareotic group, therefore, appear to have identified themselves as the perfect devotees of God, the true cultic attendants, an elite group who could be identified as the descendants of Aaron who were permitted to partake of the bread from the table of shewbread. In line with their extreme allegorizing and denial of physicality, the gendered body (and physical descent) counted little. One thinks again of *Migr.* 92, where Philo notes that the extreme allegorizers, thinking that circumcision symbolized the removal of the bodily passions, no longer circumcised baby boys in the flesh. Extreme allegory

---

[87] For a detailed discussion of the Temple layout and its operations, see Sanders, *Judaism*, 47–76.

[88] Ibid. 62.

22. The Table of Shewbread, seen through the entrance doorway of the Temple Sanctuary. Second Temple Model made by Alec Garrard, Harleston, Norfolk, UK (Photo: © Alec Garrard)

devalued the body, in favour of matters of the soul. It follows that sexual differences inscribed in the body are also devalued. Both males and females could be circumcised in the soul, or serve as 'priests' and 'attendants' in the 'Temple', because ultimately cultic service was dependent on the soul rather than the body. The eating of the sacred meal appears to usher in a reality in which the body is truly transcended and they participate fully in cultic service, a reality which can only be sustained once every forty-nine days, the sabbath of sabbaths night.

In identifying that the extreme allegorizers in fact were part of the allegorical school to which Philo himself belonged, we can to some extent quarry his writings to understand more about what they may have thought of the Sanctuary and the table of shew-bread. However, much of what Philo writes about the Sanctuary (Tent/Tabernacle) and the items it contains is illustrative of a particular kind of Platonizing exegesis that is not peculiar to Philo, or even to Alexandria, as Gregory Sterling has convincingly shown.[89] In this type of exegesis there is an understanding that the Sanctuary, both actual and in terms of the scriptural descriptions of the Tabernacle, reflects a noetic reality already established which underpins the whole cosmos.[90] For example, Philo links the organization of space in the Sanctuary with the four elements out of which the universe is constructed: earth, water, air, and fire/heaven (cf. *Plant.* 120; *Somn.* 16; *QE* 2: 83). The table on which the bread and salt are laid was placed on the northern side of the vestibule of the Sanctuary, because the north produces the most wind (*Mos.* 101). Certainly, in Alexandria, this is true. Philo explains that the menorah is located in the south, because it symbolizes the heavens (*Mos.* 102–3), the seven branches corresponding to the sun, moon, and five planets (cf. *QE* 2: 78, 83; Jos. *Ant.* 3: 146, 182). The altar of incense is located in the middle 'between earth and water' (*Mos.* 101), or just the earth (*Mos.* 105). Therefore the menorah stands

[89] Craig R. Koester, *The Dwelling of God: The Tabernacle in the Old Testament, Intertestamental Jewish Literature and the New Testament* (Washington DC: Catholic Biblical Association of America, 1989), 58–67; Gregory Sterling, 'Ontology versus Eschatology: Tensions between Author and Community in Hebrews', *SPA* 13 (2001), 190–211, esp. 199–204.

[90] For the definitive examination of this see Ursula Früchtel, *Die Kosmologischen Vorstellungen bei Philo von Alexandrien: Ein Beitrag zur Geschichte der Genesisexegese* (Leiden: Brill, 1968), 69–115.

for heaven/fire, the altar of incense for earth and water, and the table of shewbread for air/wind. In *QE* 2: 83 further specific representations are indicated, and the table of shewbread refers to the 'substance of the sense-perceptible world'.

This cosmological significance of the Sanctuary actually reifies the significance of the actual Sanctuary in Jerusalem, since it acts as a reminder of the noetic realities. In line with this reading, Philo notes that the twelve loaves of the table of shewbread represent seed-bearing plants required to sustain life (*QE* 2: 72; *Mos.* 2: 104). They are placed in the Temple in stacks of six each, each stack corresponding to the equinoxes (spring and autumn) (*Spec.* 1: 172, Jos. *Ant.* 3: 182, 217; cf. m.Men. 11: 1–9). For the twelve months of the year, Jews who followed different calendars could be in agreement, even though not about which was the first month of the year, but we have identified that the Mareotic group followed an extreme form of the solar calendar in which months were basically disregarded in their organization of time. In addition, it seems more likely that the twelve loaves stood for something more philosophically meaningful to the aims of the Mareotic group than the months of the year.

Philo's allegorical exegesis seems more helpful in explicating what the group believed when he notes that the loaves represent ἐγκράτεια (*Spec.* 1: 173) since 'bread to a lover of Wisdom is enough food, because it makes the body resilient against disease and the reason healthy and sober'. In *Contempl.* the entire presentation of the Mareotic group is built on championing their success in keeping to this great Stoic virtue. Philo's identification of the Tent of Exodus 33: 7 as Wisdom itself in which a wise person lives and dwells (*Leg.* 3: 46, cf. *Congr.* 116) likewise fits well with what he has stated about the group of *Contempl.* In *Her.* 112 the Tabernacle is a 'symbol of truth' and its contents are 'a representation and copy of Wisdom' in which we need to 'scrub and wash away everything that defiles our life'. But perhaps the most relevant piece of exegesis in Philo concerns Moses and the Tabernacle. In *Det.* 160 (cf. *Ebr.* 100), for example, Philo writes that when a person has ascended to become a soul free of the encumbrance of the body they can approach God, and that the Tabernacle is placed by Moses 'far away from the bodily encampment', because 'only by this might he hope to be a perfect suppliant (ἱκέτης) and attendant (θεραπευτής) of God'. We are clearly in the same world of exegesis here. Moses is the prototype for all who make supplication to God, because of his quest for Wisdom (*Spec.* 1: 41–50). For a suppliant/attendant, entering the Tabernacle means moving away from the body in the direction of God.

The Sanctuary is not then material space, in this sacred symposium, and the suppliants and attendants of God Philo describes in *Contempl.* are no longer entirely configuring themselves in terms of bodily materiality. The modest separations between male and female begin to break down. The holy attendants have eaten the holy food (virtue) and are now ready to sing together, and the singing itself ushers in a new stage in their journey toward the divine. Ultimately, they aim to become souls singing in the place of God's dwelling, entirely released from the 'Egypt' of bodily passions.

For greater appreciation of the dynamics of what takes place, we need to consider the spirituality of the Mareotic group in more detail.

I I
Gender Blenders: Moses, Miriam, and Music

[The mind] is seized by a sober intoxication, like those people filled with Corybantic frenzy, full of a different long-ing from theirs and a better kind of desire. Swept by this to the highest vault of things perceptible to the mind, it seems to be on its way to the great King. Striving to see, masses of pure and clear rays of concentrated light stream out like a swollen river, so that the eye of understanding is dazzled by such sparkling things. (Philo, *Opif.* 71)

In terms of gender roles, both men and women in the Mareotic group share a meal symbolic of God's everlasting covenant with Israel, which they then interpret as the triumph of *enkrateia*, self-control. They act together as priests in the holy Temple, in which they have somehow left the body behind. From the sep-aration of men and women we find in the seventh-day meetings, now in the Sanctuary context there is no need for separation. The material world is no longer important.

Previously, we saw how extreme allegory was linked with asceticism in Jewish exegetical circles of Alexandria. Extreme allegorizing is a method of interpretation which cuts loose from many of the traditional and distinctive aspects of Judaism such as the usual festival observances and circumcision, as Philo indi-cated (*Migr.* 91–2). If the whole of the Law could be interpreted allegorically, it was very easy to jump into the camp in which these things were no longer important. What was important were deep philosophical realities. As Philo stated regarding the extreme allegorizers in *Migr.* 93 and the Mareotic group in *Contempl.* 78, the Law is a living being whose body was com-prised of the literal words and whose soul was the invisible mind which lay behind the wording. The literal laws were symbolic of deeper realities (*Migr.* 89) which they explored in their naked absoluteness (*Migr.* 90). If gendered categories such as 'male' and 'female' were considered part of the literal words, 'the body' of the Law, then the Mareotic group could do what the Christian apostle Paul did exegetically and arrive at the same kind of conclusions of Galatians 3: 28. In Wisdom, there is no male and female. Men and women could both be attendants of God in the Sanctuary, participating in the holy meal of the covenant, for the sex of the body, and the gendered categories of scripture, no longer counted for anything

INSPIRATION

The Mareotic group appear to have understood that their contemplation of scripture and musical compositions, mortification of the body, and quiet solitariness involved some kind of training for a vision of God. Philo writes that 'the attending type of people who are beforehand taught always to see, desire the vision of the [Divine] Being, and would pass over the sun perceived [by sense] and never leave this [heavenly] company leading to perfect happiness' (11). 'Seeing', in Philo's thought, is fundamental to the contemplative life, the βίος θεωρητικός. The word θεωρέω means 'behold, see, look at'.[1] The whole purpose of the ascetic lifestyle is to enable such sight. In the Sanctuary that the group configures for the Sabbath of Sabbaths, the most excellent priests/attendants/suppliants are fit to see God. All their training here pays off. At the beginning of the treatise, Philo explains that the members of the Mareotic group go about their divine attendance (*therapeia*) 'because they are seized by a heavenly passion [and]—just like the Bacchic revellers and Corybants—they are inspired until they see the object of desire' (12).

He returns to the language of ecstasy when he comes to discuss the coming together of men and women in two choirs, in the middle of the *sumposion*, after the 'cultic' meal. The two choirs of men and women become unified into one blended choir.

When each of the choirs has sated itself by itself, as in the Bacchic rites they drink the liquor of the god's love, they blend together and become one choir from out of two. (*Contempl.* 85)

---

[1] LSJ 796–7.

So they are drunk [in this way] until dawn, with this beautiful drunkenness, with no heavy head or dozing, but [rather] they are roused more awake than when they came into the dining room. (*Contempl.* 89)

In using Bacchic language, Philo not only points to the idea that these people are 'beside themselves' as Bacchic revellers appear to be, but also points to the fact that they have developed a superior form of being 'beside themselves' than is ever possible via wine (cf. his grotesque parodies of a drinking party in *Contempl.* 40–7). They become the opposite of what wine-intoxicated people become: more awake rather than dozy. Interestingly, Colson adds to the translation of *Contempl.* 89 the idea that in this inspired, divinely intoxicated state, shame is abandoned. He renders the words μεθυσθέντες οὖν ἄχρι πρωΐας τὴν καλὴν ταύτην μέθην: 'Thus they continue till dawn, drunk with this drunkenness *in which there is no shame*'.[2] Certainly, the normal concerns of shame appear to have vanished, as they often do when people are very intoxicated, possessed, or inspired. Women's modesty is suddenly not on the agenda.

One cannot help but consider the parallel of the inspired people[3] in the church of Corinth, some of whose lack of modesty during prayer and prophecy (that is, when 'beside-themselves') so exercised the apostle Paul (1 Cor. 11: 1–16).[4] For Paul, despite the condition of being inspired, it was simply not right for women's head coverings to be thrown aside (or their *himatia* to slip). It is precisely at Corinth that we find a Christian connection with Alexandria, through the missionizing of Apollos. In Acts 18: 25 he is described as 'an Alexandrian by birth (and) a learned man, powerful in the Scriptures'. He goes on to Corinth, and appears in the Corinthian correspondence as a major leader of the church (1 Cor. 1: 10–12; 3: 4–10, 22; 4: 6; 16: 12, cf. Tit. 3: 13), a man with whom Paul did not necessarily agree.[5]

[2] Colson, *Philo ix* (Loeb), 167.
[3] By 'inspired people' I mean to refer to those who believed they were possessed by angels/Holy Spirit (cf. Philo, *Gig.* 6) and exhibited various forms of behaviour that they consider indicative of such possession. In the Corinthian congregation this included speaking in tongues, prophesying, etc., cf. 1 Cor. 12: 4–11; 14: 1–10.
[4] The literature on this question is vast. For an insightful analysis, see Antionette Clark Wire, *The Corinthian Women Prophets: A Reconstruction through Paul's Rhetoric* (Minneapolis: Fortress, 1990).
[5] Ibid. 209–11.

Unlike Paul (who was addressing a community directly), Philo avoids focusing on any forms of immodest behaviour during the Mareotic group's possessed state, and rather builds an impression of both men and women that ensures that we somehow imagine them as deeply serious and restrained even while singing and dancing together all night long. Philo emphasizes that there is an order about the community, and this order is reflected by intense concentration and quietness at appropriate times: the president who gives the seventh-day discourse speaks 'with a composed appearance and quiet voice, and with reason and thoughtfulness' (31); music is governed by dignified rhythms (29); self-control is laid down as the foundation stone of the soul (34); their common meal on the forty-ninth day is governed by 'the utmost seriousness' (66) and there is silence during any time apart from when there is the appropriate moment for the singing and dancing (75–7). Above all, there is *in general* a segregation of the sexes in common assemblies designed to ensure that the modesty appropriate to women be maintained, though the separation is only by a wall high enough to prevent men seeing the women, but low enough to ensure sound carries easily (32–3, 69). By the time we get to the dangerous issue of the group's inspired singing and dancing, we are weighted down with the impression of the whole group being stultifyingly decent, quiet, ascetic, and virtuous. Philo's rhetoric is designed to ensure that his readers do not mistake his inspired group with others who may be considered inspired in the Graeco-Roman world but who are in fact just gratifying the body's desires. The attendants of God are indeed 'intoxicated' like the Corybants and Bacchic revellers, but with *true* divine intoxication, and they are restrained at the proper times. Philo notes that they are 'drunk . . . with this beautiful drunkenness' (89). In this heavenly state they are truly 'citizens of heaven and also world' (90). Philo uses the notion of a kind of 'sober drunkenness' as one of his conundrums intended to bamboozle the reader into a recognition of a spiritual, rather than a material, truth; it is used as a way of indicating true heavenly inspiration, or elevation, and implicitly denounces the actual drunkenness of a Bacchanalia.[6]

---

[6] See Hans Lewy, *Sobria Ebrietas: Untersuchungen zur Geschichte der antiken Mystik* (Giessen: Töpelmann, 1929), who examined in detail every instance of the concept in Philo's works.

The members of the Mareotic group are nevertheless cast in the mould of Graeco-Roman mantics or divinely inspired people. Philo explicitly compares them to intoxicated Bacchic revellers or Corybants, the wild attendants of the goddess Cybele. This kind of divine madness was a well-known condition, explicable by reference to Platonic understandings (*Ion.* 533d–534e; *Timaeus* 71e; *Phaedrus* 244b) of inspired mantics and oracle singers, and divine mania in general.[7] Plutarch notes that the displacement of rationality comes with such inspiration (*Amatorius* 758d–e).[8]

If Ruth Padel is correct, women were considered especially susceptible to possession.[9] The evidence for mystical seizure in Jewish sources is late, and harder to interpret, but an interesting reference to what happens to Aseneth in the novel *Joseph and Aseneth* may reflect a notion that angelic or heavenly inspiration involved lack of control, as Judith Gundry-Volf has noted. The angel puts his right hand, shooting sparks, on Aseneth's head and shakes it (*Joseph and Aseneth* 16: 12–13).[10] The image of the Bacchic revellers brings to mind images such as we find in the House of the Mysteries in Pompeii, with women in various states of undress, engaged in curious (and erotic) activities. The association between women and the cult of Dionysus/Bacchus was well-known, and the problem of impropriety may have been a key reason for the cult being banned in Rome. Livy points out that men and women were mingling in 'the freedom of darkness' and that women were actually the culprits (Livy, *Annales* 39: 13).[11] Such a cult in a classical Greek context would have given

---

[7] See Plato, *Apol.* 22c; *Meno* 99c; *Ion.* 534c.

[8] For discussion, see John Levison, 'Prophetic Inspiration in Pseudo-Philo's Liber Antiquitatum Biblicarum', *JQR* 85 (1995), 310–11. Levison explores how such a notion is found also in the portrayal of Kenaz in Pseudo-Philo.

[9] Padel, 'Model for Possession', 13. In Greek, to be 'possessed' or 'inspired' is expressed by the word ἔνθεος which seems to reflect a pun on 'god inside' though the word is in fact derived from ἐντίθημι. Perhaps women may have seemed fitting receptacles of the divine spirit by virtue of their capacity to be receptacles of growing human life inside their bodies; a woman may be ἔντεκνος, 'having children', from the male seed which is ἔνθετος, 'implanted' within.

[10] Gundry-Volf considers it then explicable why Paul might speak about a woman needing to control her head, 'for the experience of inspiration could be so dramatic as to make one lose control over one's body and speech': 'Paul on Women and Gender', 206.

[11] I am grateful to Shelly Matthews for sending me the paper she read at the

women some release from the constraints of the *oikos*, as Ross Kraemer has argued,[12] but was not always approved of, especially not in a Roman context (Livy, *Annales* 39: 8–19).[13] In literature concerning Bacchic rites, women in particular are seized with frenzy, and in the foundational mythology of these rites women leave the household, neglecting the world of domesticity and childcare to run into the context of untamed nature, where they suckle wild animals rather than their own children. In the story of the maenads as described by Euripides, they are wild, immensely strong, and very dangerous. They lose control, and let their hair fall loose, down over their shoulders (Euripides, *The Bacchae* 695).[14] The festivals of Dionysus were celebrated in many Greek cities every other year and appear to have been participated in mainly by women (Diodorus Siculus, *Lib.* 4: 3: 3).[15] In Alexandria, the Dionysiac cult was one of the most popular. Dionysus was closely associated with Serapis and the Ptolemaic dynasty,[16] and Philo himself can consider worship of Dionysus positively (*Legat.* 82–3). Philo can use the image of the possessed maenad as a kind of archetypal model for one who is inspired, linking the term 'maenad' with the word 'mania' (*Plant.* 148).

SBL in Nov. 1998 which discussed the issue of 'honourable drunkenness' in this text, and for discussing with me the question of whether there was a dividing wall during the choral singing.

[12] Ross Kraemer, 'Ecstasy and Possession: Women of Ancient Greece and the Cult of Dionysus', in Nancy Auer Falk and Rita Gross (eds.), *Unspoken Worlds: Women's Religious Lives* (Belmont, Calif.: Wadsworth, 1989), 45–55; ead., *Her Share of the Blessings*, 36–49. See also Richard and Catherine Kroeger, 'An Inquiry into the Evidence of Maenadism in the Corinthian Congregation', in Paul J. Achtemeier (ed.), *Society of Biblical Literature Seminar Papers 1978*, ii (Missoula: Scholars, 1979), 331–8.

[13] Notwithstanding Livy, the Bacchic cult was not banned in Rome, despite fears of its un-Roman excesses. The inscribed bronze tablet found in south Italy which preserves the text of the senatorial decree indicates rather that the Senate wished to regulate its activities in 186 BCE, see Beard *et al.*, *Religions of Rome*, i. 93–5, ii. 290–1.

[14] See English translation of *The Bacchae* in Philip Vellacott (ed.), *Euripides, The Bacchae and Other Plays*, rev. edn. (Harmondsworth: Penguin, 1973), 191–244. For other possession-cult instances of loosing of the hair, including in the Isiac mysteries, see Elisabeth Schüssler Fiorenza, *In Memory of Her: A Feminist Theological Reconstruction of Christian Origins*, 2nd edn. (London: SCM, 1995), 227.

[15] Quoted in Kraemer, 'Ecstasy and Possession', 49.

[16] See Fraser, *Ptolemaic Alexandria*, i. 198–202.

The only difference is in the nature of the inspiration. Inspiration is not, in itself, dangerous. The right kind of inspiration should not lead to licentiousness. One should simply be careful to fix one's sights on the true God (cf. *Her.* 69). When Philo uses the motif of the sober intoxication of true divine inspiration, he is in fact contrasting it with the inebriated intoxication that was so common in drinking parties and the cult of Dionysus.

In Philo's presentation in *Contempl.*, the people of the Mareotic group retain a residual 'possessed' state at all times, so that 'they keep the memory of God' constantly and 'in dreams nothing else is dreamt of apart from the beauty of the divine attributes and powers'. In fact, 'many [of them] call out the famous decrees of the sacred philosophy in [their] sleep while dreaming' (26). God is clearly at work here, and this is what we might expect, given Plato's linkage of sleep with the inspired state in *Timaeus* 71e:

> And clear enough evidence that god gave this power to human being's irrational part is to be found in our inability for inspired and true prophecy when in our right minds; we only achieve it when the power of our understanding is inhibited in sleep, or when we are in an abnormal condition owing to disease or divine inspiration.

As Cicero noted, sleep releases people from the body, and therefore they can see things which they cannot see when connected with the body (*Div.* 1: 129).[17] That the Mareotic group should utter statements from the divine philosophy therefore would indicate that Philo believed they experienced a kind of inspired state whilst dreaming, a state which is attained by those who have rid themselves of any connection with cloying bodily desires.

The 'decrees of the sacred philosophy' are, of course, words of scripture. They ask in the sunrise prayers that 'their minds will be filled with a heavenly light' (27). They are inspired until they *see* the object of desire. The emphasis is on vision, of seeing the true light of God that is higher up in heaven than the sun. According to Philo, the 'sun' in scripture is itself symbolic of

---

[17] And see Plutarch, *De Defectu Oraculorum* 432c. Levison, 'Prophetic Inspiration', notes (at p. 313) the popularity of sleep being a condition of inspiration by noting Plutarch's disapproving quotation of Simmias in *De Genio Socratis* 589c–d that it is only in sleep that people receive inspiration from on high. Levison also relates this notion to the presentation of Kenaz in Pseudo-Philo's *Biblical Antiquities*.

God (*Somn.* 72–87), for there is 'the most brilliant and radiant light' emanating from God which, when it shines upon the mind, makes mere words set (*Somn.* 72). This idea that God may be seen as a stream of light has been most thoroughly explored by Erwin Goodenough,[18] and is found in various places in Philo's writings (e.g. *Opif.* 71; *Praem.* 38–40). The image links the group both with Philo's own distinctive philosophical Judaism, and with the traditions of contemporaneous apocalyptic literature, later Merkabah (throne-chariot) mysticism, and the Hekhalot texts. In this latter type of literature, the visionary ascends to the seven sacred halls (*hekhalot*) of God's heavenly palace, where s/he hopes to see God's glory enthroned.[19] The heavenly ascent and vision of the divine form is central to apocalyptic writings (e.g. Daniel 7).[20] The 'glory' is perceived as something shining more brightly than the sun (1 Enoch 14: 19–25; 2 Enoch 39: 1–6).

In Philo's writings overall, there is a clear theme involving the quest to 'see' God, which is the height of human joy.[21] The experience of seeing God is, as Ellen Birnbaum puts it, 'unmediated' by other human beings, and the God that is experienced

---

[18] Erwin Goodenough, *By Light, Light: The Mystic Gospel of Hellenistic Judaism* (New Haven: Yale University Press, 1935), esp. 11–47. God or what flows from God may sometimes also be identified with Wisdom (cf. *Leg.* 1: 64, 65).

[19] For discussions of early Jewish mysticism, see Gershom G. Scholem, *Major Trends in Jewish Mysticism* (New York: Schocken, 1941), 1–79 and Peter Schäfer, *The Hidden and Manifest God: Some Major Themes in Early Jewish Mysticism*, tr. Aubrey Pomerance (Albany: State University of New York Press, 1992); Elliot R. Wolfson, *Through a Speculum that Shines: Vision and Imagination in Medieval Jewish Mysticism* (Princeton: Princeton University Press, 1994), 13–124. For a bibliography, see Peter Schäfer, 'Research on the Hekhalot Literature: Where do we Stand Now?' in Gabrielle Sed-Ranja (ed.), *Rashi, 1040–1990: Hommage à Ephraim E. Urbach* (Paris: Cerf, 1993). Scholem (pp. 46–7) notes that after 500 CE texts appear, paradoxically, to refer to a descent to the Merkabah (throne). In terms of a spiritual journey, whether one goes in, out, up, or down may be understood differently, though often the result is the same.

[20] So Wolfson, *Speculum,* 29.

[21] See C. T. Robert Hayward, 'Philo, the Septuagint of Genesis 32: 24–32 and the Name "Israel": Fighting the Passions, Inspiration and the Vision of God', *JJS* 51 (2000), 209–26; Gerhard Delling, 'The "One who sees God" in Philo', in Frederick E. Greenspahn, Earle Hilgert, and Burton L. Mack (eds.), *Nourished with Peace: Studies in Hellenistic Judaism in Memory of Samuel Sandmel* (Chico, Calif.: Scholars, 1984), 28–33.

is 'transcendent and immaterial'.[22] 'Israel' itself is frequently described by Philo as having an etymology meaning ὁρῶν θεόν, 'one who sees God' (cf. *Leg.* 2: 34).[23] This etymology is unlikely to have been Philo's individual invention, since it is found in works as diverse as the *Prayer of Joseph*, a Midrashic collection known as the *Seder 'Eliyahu Rabbah* (27) and the Christian Gnostic *On the Origin of the World* (105: 24–5) found at Nag Hammadi.[24] Philo uses the etymology in *Praem.* 44–5 to describe (true) Israel as being comprised of suppliants who see God's light.

Philo himself sometimes hints at having had an experience of seeing a light he identified as divine (*Opif.* 71),[25] though frequently he means to utilize the language of spiritual ascent and the divine vision of light for intellectual insight into the truths of scripture and God's nature he discerns intellectually (e.g. *Migr.* 35). It seems that Philo could be purposely obscure, and refer to a personal experience of consciousness in one place and use the language metaphorically in another place, so that we cannot create a single coherent rubric out of this language. Overall, though, despite the deliberate obscurity, there is no reason to doubt that he had an 'ecstatic experience with . . . an experience of light', as Peder Borgen observes.[26] To what extent he believed

---

[22] Ellen Birnbaum, *The Place of Judaism in Philo's Thought: Israel, Jews and Proselytes* (Atlanta: Scholars, 1996), 5.

[23] For a full list of these passages, and wider discussion, see Birnbaum, *Place of Judaism*, 61–127. The false etymology may be arrived at by dividing up ישראל, with some additions, into איש, a person, a man; ראה, he sees/saw; אל, God. For other suggestions of possible Hebrew and discussion see ibid. 70–7.

[24] See discussion by Wolfson, *Speculum*, 50. See Jonathan Z. Smith, 'The Prayer of Joseph', in Jacob Neusner (ed.), *Religions in Antiquity: Essays in Memory of Erwin J. Goodenough* (Leiden: Brill, 1970), at pp. 265–8; Meir Friedmann (ed.), *Seder 'Eliyahu Rabbah we-Seder* (Vienna: Achiasaf, 1902), 138–9; *On the Origin of the World* in James M. Robinson (ed.), *The Nag Hammadi Library in English* (Harper: San Francisco, 1988), 170–89, at p. 176.

[25] For the type of 'mysticism' (variously defined) embraced by Philo, see David Winston, *Logos and Mystical Theology in Philo of Alexandria* (Cincinnati: Hebrew Union College Press, 1985), id., 'Was Philo a Mystic?', in Joseph Dan and Frank Talmage (eds.), *Studies in Jewish Mysticism* (Cambridge, Mass.: Association for Jewish Studies, 1982); id., 'Philo's Mysticism', *SPA* 8 (1996), 74–82; Wolfson, *Speculum*, 50–1; cf. Walter Völker, *Fortschritt und Vollendung bei Philo von Alexandrien: Eine Studie zur Geschichte der Frömmigkeit* (Leipzig: J. C. Hinrichs, 1938), who considered Philo's mystical language purely metaphorical, not experiential.   [26] Borgen, *Philo*, 18.

he 'saw God' in this experience may be debated, however, since—as in the passage quoted at the head of this chapter—the light emanates from God in such a way that the seer is dazzled before getting that close. So, for example, Moses sees the light around God, though not strictly speaking God himself (*Post.* 169, *Fug.* 141, 164–5, *Mut.* 8–10), because one would be blinded by the intensity of light (*Fug.* 165). Still the desire is for the mind, or soul, to see God, and to see some of the light that shines from him is reward enough. In *Somn.* 1: 232 Philo writes that to incorporeal souls occupied in his service (as *therapeutrides*) God appears as he is, as a friend to friends, but to souls still in the body he appears in the form of angels.

In *Contempl.*, the mystical ouranography of heaven begins with the physical sun. The sun is a mask in front of the true light which lies beyond it. In flying past the perceived sun in spirit the divine attendants find themselves in the dazzling true spiritual light of God (cf. *Opif.* 70–1). The sun nevertheless has some kind of divine purpose, for the prayers of the Mareotic group are to be directed towards where it is positioned in the sky, as if God sits behind it. The physical light of the sun orders the procedures of the group on earth, as we saw in regard to the group's calendar, but the object of its enterprise is to go beyond the sun to the abode of God, a place that can be reached only in spirit. The ouranography evidenced here is therefore quite close to what we find in later Jewish Merkabah or Hekhalot texts.[27]

The ascetic practices of the Mareotic group are paralleled in preparations taken for heavenly ascent in the Jewish mystical literature, particularly fasting.[28] Such preparations are found already in the Book of Daniel (9: 3; 10: 2–3), 4 Ezra (5: 13, 20; 6: 31, 35), 2 Baruch (9: 2; 20: 5), 1 Enoch (108: 8–9), and elsewhere.[29] In *Mos.* 2: 67, Moses purifies his soul and body by abstaining from sex, meat, and drink (wine), prior to his ascent of Sinai.

[27] Such as in *The Vision of Ezekiel*, see Wolfson, *Speculum*, 74–124. See also the Hekhalot Rabbati, *Synopse*, 105, where God is described as having a diadem which radiates the sun and moon and garment from which flows the stars and planets, but he sends a great light from between his eyes, *Speculum*, p. 93.

[28] See Scholem, *Jewish Mysticism*, 49. The significance of 7 in the Hekhalot Rabbati is interesting in view of its significance for the Mareotic group.

[29] See Dale C. Allison, *Jesus of Nazareth: Millenarian Prophet* (Minneapolis: Fortress, 1998), 193–4.

It is from the vision of the prophet Ezekiel (Ezek. 1: 4–2: 15) that Merkabah mysticism of course takes its name. With Ezekiel and Daniel, we get a clear indication that it was not just a case of God's spirit descending on someone which made them a prophet, but also a case of an ascent of the human spirit to the realm of God. To what extent the spiritual experience of divine light and prophetic inspiration might be conceptually distinct in Philo's thought is difficult to determine, and may be blurred. Philo models his presentation of Jewish prophecy with reference to Platonic ideas of inspiration (*Phaedrus* 244b–249e, 265b), which ultimately explained 'prophecy' within the Graeco-Roman world.[30] Plato considered four types of 'inspired madness' (*mania*): (1) an inspiration used for divination; (2) inspiration which enables priests to heal people; (3) poetic inspiration; and (4) the inspiration of a philosopher who can recall ideas unable to be perceived by bodily senses (*anamnesis*). Most interesting in terms of the Mareotic group is the fourth category, for this identifies an essential part of philosophy as incorporating inspiration. David Aune notes that Philo accepted that the highest knowledge, as for Plato, was the knowledge of ideas, but Philo substitutes the term 'prophecy' for the Platonic term 'recollection'.[31] The ideas of Plato are understood to be heavenly realities and attributes.

There were significant female models for this inspiration-based spirituality. The Babylonian Talmud lists seven prophetesses in scripture: Sarah, Miriam, Deborah, Hannah, Abigail, Huldah, and Esther (b.Meg. 14a). If God could choose women as vehicles for the divine word, then it would follow naturally that women could live a life which was designed to increase their chances of being permitted to see the light of the divine splendour. That both men and women were accounted to be inspired prophets in Israel's past might well be a reason why both men and women could be counted as priests in the spiritual Temple. While Temple service in the form of the priesthood was a male preserve—and permissible only for a minority of males—a cultic

---

[30] Wolfson, *Philo,* ii. 11–14; Robert M. Berchman, 'Arcana Mundi: Prophecy and Divination in the *Vita Mosis* of Philo of Alexandria', *SBL Seminar Papers* (1988), 406–7.

[31] David E. Aune, *Prophecy in Early Christianity and the Ancient Mediterranean World* (Grand Rapids, Mich.: Eerdmans, 1983), 147.

service based on *inspiration* was in principle gender-inclusive and not based on hereditary rights. Moses was the ultimate prophet, and those who imitated Moses' own prophetic journey out of Egypt to God were truly disciples of Moses. In Philo's *Life of Moses*, Moses is three things: king, lawgiver, and priest, indeed the chief priest (*Mos.* 1: 334; 2: 2–7, 66–71, 75; *Praem.* 53, 56; *Sacr.* 130; *Her.* 182). We also have seen that he is defined by Philo, importantly, as the prime suppliant and attendant of God (*Det.* 160). He is an attendant of God because he is a priest, and this is what priests do: 'It is an honour well-fitting the wise person to attend to the True Being, for the service/attendance of God is the business of the priesthood' (*Mos.* 2: 67). In being disciples of Moses, the Mareotic group aimed to follow in his path.

MUSICAL PROPHECY: MOSES, MIRIAM, AND THE 'SONG OF THE SEA'

As we have noted, in the case of the Mareotic group, one of the means by which the group ascends towards seeing the divine light of God is music. Music forms a key part of their contemplative life, their life devoted to seeing God. Various passages indicate how important the composition and singing of music was to the group.

Therefore, they do not contemplate [scripture] only, but also compose psalms and hymns to God in all kinds of metres and melodies which they have to write down in dignified rhythms. (29)

They are accustomed to live on air, just like the race of grasshoppers are said [to do], their song, I guess, makes the lack tolerable. (35)[32]

Then the [president] stands up and sings a hymn composed to God, either a new one of his own composition or some old one [composed] by the poets of old, for they have left behind many [songs] in many metres and melodies: hexameters, trimeters, hymns of processions, [hymns] relating to libations, [hymns] relating to the altar, for standing [in a chorus] and for [choral] dancing well measured out for turning and twisting. After him, in fact, the others according to order have a turn at singing. Everyone else listens in total silence, except when they need

---

[32] There is a double meaning here. Both grasshoppers and the members of the Mareotic group sing songs.

[to sing] closing lines and themes. For then all men and all women sing aloud. (80)

Then they sing hymns to God composed of many metres and melodies, singing all together, then again antiphonically and harmonically, tapping time with hands and feet, engaging in procession, then continuous song, and in the turns and counter-turns of choral dancing. (84)

When each of the choirs (of men and women separately) has sated itself by itself, as in the Bacchic rites they drink the liquor of a god's love, they blend together and become one choir from out of the two, a memory of the one established of old by the Red Sea, by reason of the wonderful works there . . . (when) both men and women were filled with inspiration and became a choir singing hymns of thanksgiving to God the Saviour. The men were led by Moses the prophet, and the women by Miriam the prophetess. (85, 87)

On this [model] (of the inspired singing of Moses and Miriam leading the people of Israel) most of all, the choir of the [devoted] attendants [male and female] is based. They sing with [canonic] echoes and re-echoes, with men having the bass parts and women the treble, combined together, and resulting in a really musical harmonious concord. The thoughts are lovely, the words are lovely, the choral singers are majestic, and the purpose of the thoughts and the words and the choral singers is piety. (88)

The composition of music was linked to heavenly inspiration. In the *Testament of Job*, Job's three daughters who have special spiritual powers also write hymns (*Test. Job.* 46–50).[33] The singing of songs could also be done with an awareness of the role of angels in singing continual praises to God. In the *Hekhalot Rabbati* (*Synopse* 94), one must sing songs continually upon entering the divine chariot.[34] Philo too believed that God was surrounded by a divine choir (e.g. *Fug.* 62), and the singing of songs would perhaps enable people to enter this illustrious company of angelic singers.

Philo's mention of hymns among the Mareotic group also relates to Graeco-Roman sung oracles. The reference to the metres of the songs they compose itself cleverly alludes to the metrical patterns of oracles in the Graeco-Roman world. Philo's

[33] For discussion of these women see Pieter van der Horst, 'The Role of Women in the Testament of Job', *Nederlands Theologisch Tijdschrift*, 40 (1986), 273–89.

[34] See the passage quoted by Wolfson, *Speculum*, 100.

repeated mention of metrical patterns is not simply an incidental detail but central to identification of the character of the music, since the gods took care to deliver their oracles in such patterns.[35] The surviving oracles are written in verse, usually dactylic hexameter, though other metres were also used, such as iambic trimeter, iambic tetrameter, trochaic tetrameter, and anapestic tetrameter.[36] As David Aune comments, '[t]he poetic form of oracles was regarded as an indication of their divine origin in the Hellenistic and Roman periods, since the Greeks widely accepted the divine inspiration of poetry. The beautiful form in which the oracles were cast revealed their divine origin.'[37] In the same way, the beautiful form of the songs sung and studied by Philo's *therapeutai* and *therapeutrides* would indicate the divine inspiration of their music. Aune notes that a borrowing of this sort occurred in the case of the Jewish Sibylline Oracles, which 'were written in dactylic hexameter in an attempt to clothe Jewish religious ideas in Greco-Roman oracular dress'.[38] The Delphic Pythia and Sibyls, prophetesses inspired by the god Apollo, always delivered their oracles in hexameters.[39] Not surprisingly then, perhaps, we find a belief that Moses, according to Josephus (*Ant.* 2: 346), composed the Song of the Sea in hexameter form.[40]

In fact, it is the Song of the Sea which is the most important basis for the singing of the Mareotic group after their special meal. With the men and women coming together into the middle of the room and singing, they are, according to Philo, imitating the choirs of men and women Israelites after the crossing of the

---

[35] At times these might not be recorded correctly in proper metrical rhythm, see Ps.-Justinus, *Cohortio ad Graecos* 37: 3.

[36] See Aune, *Prophecy*, 50–1. Robin Lane Fox, *Pagans and Christians* (Harmondsworth: Penguin, 1987), 205.

[37] Aune, *Prophecy*, 51, who notes also (p. 362) that in Plutarch's *De Pyth. Orc.* 396c–d the participants in Plutarch's dialogue express the view that the beauty of oracles in verse indicates their divine origin.   [38] Ibid.

[39] Ibid. 37.

[40] See Louis Feldman, 'Josephus' Portrait of Moses. Part Three', *JQR* 83 (1993), 301–30, at p. 321, a matter Feldman attributes to Hellenization. Aune notes (p.362) that this is not found in the Hebrew or in the LXX versions of the Song of the Sea. According to Josephus, Moses composes again in hexameter verse after he gives the law (*Ant.* 4: 303). Interestingly, there was an Egyptian Jewish poet (prophet?) named Philo who sang the praises of the city of Jerusalem in archaic (Greek) hexameters, see Modrzejewski, *Jews of Egypt*, 66.

Red Sea (cf. *Mos.* 1: 180). The crossing of the Red Sea is the key event in terms of the redemption of Israel from Egypt (Exod. 14: 15–31; Isa. 51: 9–10 cf. Josh. 2: 10; Isa. 43: 16–17). In Philo's thought, the redemption from 'Egypt' is understood as being redemption from bodily passions (see e.g. *Migr.* 151, 154; *Post.* 155–7; *Congr.* 105). Pharaoh is the 'leader of the company devoted to the passions' (*Somn.* 277). The virtuous people who are devoted to seeing (God) are opposed by the 'people of Pharaoh', and the passions of 'Egypt' are destroyed in the sea (*Somn.* 278–82). With the destruction of bodily desires of all kinds, people are truly liberated. This analysis coheres with the ascetic notions of the Mareotic group itself. On the forty-ninth day, they celebrate their redemption from Egypt, the destruction of the body's passions, and their triumph over the body.

The prototypes of Moses and Miriam as prophets are especially important here. In the inspired choral singing (and dancing) the members of the group are basing themselves on the text of Exodus 15, but in the Masoretic text of this passage Moses' song, 'the Song of the Sea', is lengthy while the Song of Miriam is hardly present at all. It is possible that the few words said by Miriam in Exodus 15: 20–1 are meant to indicate that she sang the same song; she becomes therefore an echo.[41] The variation in the Hebrew wording is very minor, and in fact the variation disappears completely in the LXX version.[42] Indeed, Philo interprets the passage as indicating that 'the same hymn is sung by both the choirs' (*Agr.* 82). Interestingly, Josephus does not mention Miriam and the women at all but states that the Hebrews (presumably men and women together) sang hymns, though Moses 'also composed a song to God containing his praises and thanksgiving for his kindness in hexameter verse' (*Ant.* 2: 346).

Later Jewish liturgy preserves a strong emphasis on the Song of the Sea in the Third Blessing of the Shema', and indicates also

[41] That the entire song is implied by the opening lines of the Song of the Sea is very likely; in the *qedusha* of the Sabbath *musaf* in the liturgy the whole Shema' is implied by citing the opening line of the first paragraph (Deut. 6: 4) and the closing line of the third (Num. 15: 41), see Kimelman, 'Shema'', 130.

[42] The Masoretic Text of Exod. 15: 21 has 'sing' שִׁירוּ for 'I will sing' אָשִׁירָה (Exod. 15: 1). אָשִׁירָה emphasizes the singular concentration on Moses as the composer of the song, and therefore may be an amendation of the tradition. In the LXX both versions have: Ἄισωμεν. The Samaritan Pentatuech has אשׁירו, which also conflates the readings.

why it was considered so important in the group of devotees Philo describes, if not also to Philo himself.[43] In terms of the liturgy, as Rueven Kimelman puts it, the redemption from Egypt is 'a foreshadowing, if not actual paradigm, of future redemption. Since the memory of redemption sustains the hope of redemption, past divine conduct serves as a warranty for future divine action.'[44] Therefore, '[j]oining in the chorus of past redemption . . . the worshiper finds him/herself praying for, if not actually announcing, the future redemption'.[45] This redemption is shown also in the Christian apocalypse, in Revelation 15: 2–6, in which there is an image of all those who had fought against the Beast and were playing harps: 'and they were singing the Song of Moses the servant of God and the song of the Lamb'. In the case of Philo's attendants of God, they were in fact celebrating their actualized redemption. They had triumphed over the body, and their reward was the sight of God.

In the liturgy, 'Moses and Israel' sing the song antiphonally 'to You' (God) and then join in unison to sing: 'Who is like You O Lord among the celestials? Who is like You glorious in holiness' (Exod. 15: 11).[46] This presumes the singers are Moses and Israel, in which both men and women are included. Miriam's separate song has then become elided with the Song of Moses. Instead of Moses leading the men and Miriam leading the women, Moses leads all Israel antiphonally.

In the Masoretic Hebrew text, Moses composes the song by means of heavenly inspiration, and the women, led by Miriam, echo the song, though also by means of heavenly inspiration. The text may indicate that the song and its echo took place more or less at the same time, rather than sequentially with men singing their song first and the women singing their song second. As Gerald Jantzen has argued, the summary of Exodus 15: 19 pushes the action back to the start of the story. Also, in Hebrew, Miriam and the women sing 'to them (masc.)' not separately to

[43] For a detailed investigation of the Song of the Sea in the form of the Aramaic *shirta* found in the Commentary on Exodus, or Mekilta, which represents the views of the 1st–2nd cent. Palestinian rabbis (the Tannaim), see Judah Goldin, *The Song of the Sea: Being a Commentary on a Commentary in Two Parts* (New Haven and London: Yale University Press, 1971). Miriam is discussed pp. 243–9. [44] Kimelman, 'Shema'', 128.

[45] Ibid. 129.

[46] Quoted from ibid. 129.

each other.[47] There is an indication that they are replying to the
men by their echoing song. Dancing is part of this activity also:
the women follow Miriam with timbrels and dance.

Study of the Hebrew text has led some scholars to suggest that
the 'Song of the Sea' was originally that of Miriam and the
women, and later redactors, who wished to place Moses in
the supreme position, reassigned the song so that Moses would
be the 'composer'. There would have been no reason to have the
women appear at all in the story, even as an afterthought, unless
they originally played a much greater part in the narrative.[48] In
order to glue the two parts together, the redactors recapitulated
the story of the crossing of the sea (Exod. 15: 19) which is redundant in terms of the sense of the present narrative but useful in
introducing Miriam and the women. However, if the recapitula-
tion actually serves the purpose of returning the story of Miriam
and the women to the beginning of the account, and asks us to see
the action as simultaneous, then it is not redundant any longer.
Still, this device relegates Miriam and the women to a secondary
position, and one might argue that in the narrative Miriam and
Moses could have sung the song together in a way that was not so
subordinating to females. A desire to promote Moses seems
manifest in the text we have.[49]

Another clue to the important place of Miriam in earlier traditions than those preserved in the Masoretic biblical text comes
with the comment attributed to her at Numbers 12: 1–2. Miriam
and Aaron are angry with Moses about his marriage to a Cushite

[47] Gerald J. Jantzen, 'Song of Moses, Song of Miriam: Who is Seconding
Whom?', *CBQ* 54 (1992), 210–20, though Jantzen's attempt to make Miriam
and the women prior seems strained.

[48] This theory was propounded over thirty years ago by Frank Cross and
David Noel Freedman, 'The Song of Miriam', *JNES* 14 (1955), 237–50. Cross
and Freedman argue that the song is archaic and its composition can be dated no
later than the 12th cent. BCE. See also Bernhard W. Anderson, 'The Song of
Miriam Poetically and Theologically Considered', in Elaine R. Follis (ed.),
Directions in Biblical Hebrew Poetry (Sheffield: JSOT, 1987), 285–96.

[49] However, Stephen Weitzman points out that, since it was apparently customary in ancient Israel for women to sing songs of victory to men as they
returned from battle (Judg. 11: 34; 1 Sam. 18: 6–7), the fact that Moses and the
sons of Israel join in the singing is intended to 'feminize' the men in their relationship to God, see Stephen Weitzman, *Song and Story in Biblical Narrative:
The History of a Literary Convention in Ancient Israel* (Bloomington: Indiana
University Press, 1997), 29.

woman, a relationship which is otherwise completely passed over in the narrative. Miriam and Aaron say: 'Has YHWH spoken only through Moses? Hasn't he spoken through us too?' The narrative consistently disconnects Miriam from Moses. Miriam is called 'the sister of Aaron', not of Moses, in Exod. 15: 20. She is identified as Moses' sister only once, at Exodus 2: 4, if indeed the young woman is to be identified as Miriam at all. The question of Numbers 12: 2 appears to reflect an acknowledgement that YHWH had indeed spoken through Miriam, though all we have in the written text of scripture is a single verse in which she and the women of Israel echo Moses' song. It is also significant that in the pro-Moses scriptural text, Miriam is severely punished for the challenge she makes to Moses. YHWH says to Aaron and Miriam that

if there is a prophet among you, I YHWH make myself known to him/her in a vision, I speak with him/her in a dream. But not so with my servant Moses. He is entrusted with all my house. With him I speak face to face, clearly, and not in riddles, and he sees the form of YHWH. Why then were you not afraid to speak against my servant Moses? (Num. 12: 6–8)

Ironically, YHWH appears to be speaking directly to Aaron and Miriam at this point, even if he failed to do so earlier. The story does imply, however, that Miriam and Aaron had experienced inspired dreams and visions, and had been respected among the people for this and hailed as prophets. Then, as a stinging rebuff of Miriam, YHWH inflicts her with 'leprosy' and she is flung out of the camp for seven days, while Aaron goes unpunished (Num. 12: 9–10). Later on, her death is reported, and her burial at Kadesh (Num. 20: 1–2), which indicates an interest in preserving the memory of the site of her tomb.[50]

---

[50]   For a thorough study of the biblical traditions about Miriam see Rita J. Burns, *Has the Lord Spoken Only through Moses? A Study of the Biblical Portrait of Miriam* (SBL Diss. Series, 84; Atlanta: Scholars, 1987). See also Phyllis Trible, 'Subversive Justice: Tracing the Miriamic Traditions', in Douglas A. Knight and Peter J. Paris (eds.), *Justice and the Holy: Essays in Honor of Walter Harrelson* (Atlanta: Scholars 1989), 99–109; ead., 'Bringing Miriam out of the Shadows', *Bible Review*, 5/1 (Feb. 1989), 14–25, 34. Interestingly, Miriam appears unmarried in the Bible, but in Jos. *Ant.* 3: 54 she has a husband. Josephus also identifies the place of her burial at Sin (*Ant.* 4: 78). Both these statements indicate that there were extra-biblical traditions about Miriam in currency in the 1st cent.

Even with the anti-Miriam rhetoric and the editing down of traditions concerning her, Miriam remains a prophet, and a leader. It would not have been surprising if 'inspired' Jews of the first century who looked to prophetic prototypes in the scriptures found her an exciting figure and a role model. In fact, some evidence for an attempt to restore Miriam to a higher status than in the Masoretic text has now been found in two fragments from the Dead Sea Scrolls corpus: 4Q365 Fr. 6a. ii and c. It remains open to debate as to whether these fragments are themselves part of an ancient tradition edited out of the textual standard (as preserved in the later Masoretic text).

4Q365 belongs in a group of fragments known as the 4Q Pentateuchal Paraphrases or 4QPP:[51] 4Q364, 365, 366, 367, and 4Q158.[52] Palaeographic analysis of the texts has led to a dating of *c.*75–50 BCE, though the calibrated Carbon 14 dating of the 4Q365 was 209–117 BCE.[53] There is some debate about whether these fragments come from one, two, or as many as four different manuscripts of the same work. This text has a number of interesting characteristics. It appears to be an alternative version of the Pentateuch. All the fragments testify to a work in which there is an interlacing of biblical text and exegetical comments. Sections of the biblical text are presented in an order different from other texts. Elements of the Masoretic text are omitted, and new sections are added. There is some possible overlap with material of the Temple Scroll (11QT). Some fragments may belong to either 11QT or 4QPP.[54] There are

---

[51] They are also known as the 'Reworked Pentateuch', see Harold Attridge, Torleif Elgvin, Jozef Milik *et al.* (eds.), *Discoveries in the Judaean Desert XIII: Qumran Cave 4.VIII: Parabiblical Texts, Part I* (Oxford: Clarendon Press, 1994), 187–351.

[52] For a textual analysis of these fragments see Emanuel Tov, 'The Textual Status of 4Q364–367 (4QPP)', in Julio Trebolle Barrera and Luis Vegas Montaner (eds.), *The Madrid Qumran Congress: Proceedings of the International Congress on the Dead Sea Scrolls, Madrid 18–21 March 1991*, i (Leiden and Madrid: Brill and Editorial Complutense, 1992), 43–82. 4Q158 was published by John Allegro in *DJD* v (Oxford: Clarendon Press, 1968).

[53] Sidnie White, '4Q364 & 365: A Preliminary Report', in Barrera and Montaner, *Madrid Congress*, 217–228 at p. 217.

[54] Tov, '4Q364–367' (p. 49), considers that 365 frag. 1* to 5* must belong to the Temple Scroll because the addition to the text of Leviticus would otherwise be too big for 4QPP, though we do not know enough about the contents of 4QPP to be sure that a sizeable addition would be out of place.

also some interesting parallels with the Samaritan version of the Pentateuch,[55] and the Book of Jubilees.[56] The language is archaic, and apparently has no characteristics of Mishnaic Hebrew.[57]

4Q365 a–c contains fragments of two columns covering Exodus 14: 12–15: 21; it is the material of column ii which is of interest here. Following on from Exodus 16: 21 there are seven lines which appear to preserve an alternative Song of Miriam. Unfortunately, only a few words from the beginning of each line are preserved, and some of the letters are unsure. With the additional material of 4Q365 Fr. 6b, lines 5 and 6, the entire preserved section on Miriam reads as follows:

ותקח   4Q365 Fr. 6b 5 (Exod. 15: 20)

תצינה   ל הנשימ אחריה ב   4Q365 Fr. 6b 6 (Exod. 15: 20[–1])

This seems to more or less follow the tradition of the normative Masoretic text, which reads here:

ותקח מרים הנביאה אחות אהרן את־התף בידה ותצאן כל־הנשים אחריה בתפים
ובמחלת

but the text of 4QPP breaks off in the middle of Exod. 15.21, for the space on the line would not allow for more than the opening words of Miriam's song. Then, for 4Q365 Fr. 6a and c, Sidnie White has suggested the following reconstruction:

1   בזית ע]

2   כי גאות] [לע]

3   גדול אתה מושיא א]

4   אבדה תקות שונה ונש]כה (ונשבת)

5   אבדו במים אדירים ש]ונה

6   ורוממנה למרוממם] [רות נתת]

7   [עו]שה גאות

[55] See the analysis by Tov, '4Q364–367', 57–9; 4Q364 agrees with the Samaritan Pentateuch (SP) in regard to the so-called 'harmonizing additions' of Gen. 30: 36 and Deut. 2: 8, though it does not agree with the SP in major details. Tov suggests that the author of 4QPP used the pre-sectarian layer of the SP (p. 64). 4Q365 agrees with the SP in respect to minutiae. The evidence for 366 and 367 is not sufficient for determining textual character.

[56] White, '4Q364 & 365', 218. Jubilees also has the same interlacing of exegesis and text.

[57] Ibid. 220.

White's translation is:

1. you despised (?)
2. for the majesty of [
3. You are great, a deliverer (?) [
4. the hope of the enemy has perished, and he is for[gotten] (or: he has cea[sed]) [
5. they perished in the mighty waters, the enemy (or: 'enemies') [
6. Extol the one who raises up, [a r]ansom . . . you gave (?) [
7. [the one who do]es gloriously. [⁵⁸

There are some similarities between what is found here as the Song of Miriam and Moses' Song of the Sea. George Brooke has noted that line 5 recalls Exodus 15: 10: 'they sank like lead in the mighty waters'; lines 2 and 7 perhaps reflect Exodus 15: 1, 'for he has triumphed gloriously'. The language of exaltation is found there also in Exod. 15: 2, 'and I will exalt him'. God is addressed in the second person singular in both songs: in line 1 here and in Exodus 15: 11–17.⁵⁹ The songs are both then songs of praise, intended to acclaim God's mighty deeds. Brooke suggests that this version of the Song of Miriam is intended to proclaim victory for the lowly, mainly on the basis of his reading of line 6 as: 'and he exalted her to the heights'.⁶⁰ While this is a very attractive proposal, perhaps it relies a little too heavily on a single Hebrew suffix and we do not know what or who has been extolled or exalted.

Brooke has implied⁶¹ that there is an interesting similarity between the text of this new version of the Song of Miriam and what Philo says in regard to the Therapeutae: Philo states that the combined choir of men and women sang hymns of thanksgiving to God the 'saviour', or 'deliverer', εἰς τὸν σωτῆρα θεόν. Here, God is called precisely that. It is interesting too that Philo mentions that there were indeed hymns of thanksgiving, in the plural (*Contempl.* 87). Philo, however, can write of 'hymns' in the plural, but insist that two choirs—one of men and one of women—sang the same song initiated by Moses. In *Agr.* 79–82, Philo indicates that in fact the women led by Miriam simply repeated the Song of the Sea composed by Moses: there was

---

⁵⁸ Ibid. 221–2; *DJD* xiii. 269–70.
⁵⁹ George Brooke, 'A Long-Lost Song of Miriam', *BAR* (May/June 1994), 62–5 at p. 63.   ⁶⁰ Ibid. 63–4.
⁶¹ Ibid. 65.

really only one song sung by both choirs, and here too he states the song was to God 'the only saviour' (τοῦ μόνου σωτῆρος). They sang in alternate refrains a melody that responded to one another's voices (*Agr.* 79). Philo understands Miriam as representing sense-perception that has been rendered 'pure and clean' and can therefore, with mind, provide hymns and sing blessings to God (*Agr.* 80). In this allegorical passage, it is clear that it is mind that is active in initiating and composing the song, and sense-perception (Miriam) provides an echoing response. In *Mos.* he states emphatically that there were indeed hymn*s* of thanksgiving to God (εὐχαριστικοὺς ὕμνους εἰς τὸν θεόν: 1: 180), not just one hymn, but this was indeed *one song* sung by two *choirs at the same time Mos.* 2: 256–7, with Moses as inspired initiator. Moses divides up the Israelites into male and female sections, and Moses leads the men and appoints his sister to lead the women. Therefore, Philo repeatedly insists on the one song of Moses and Moses' primary inspiration which was, to Philo, the 'beginning . . . of the prophecies of Moses influenced by inspiration' (*Mos.* 2: 258). Miriam does not herself take any initiative in leadership, but Moses 'appoints' his sister for the task (*Mos.* 2: 265), a task portrayed by Philo as being one of accurately echoing Moses' song. We can sum up Philo's position as being that there was *one song* (of Moses), sung by *two choirs* (headed by Moses and Miriam), which sang *two hymns* which were in fact bass and treble versions of the one song. In insisting on all of this, we may wonder whether Philo was forced to assert this view repeatedly against a tradition that there were indeed two inspired songs, with Miriam independently acting as a prophetic leader of inspired song.

In *Contempl.* there is a striking progression in terms of the singing in the meal context. Initially, the president sings hymns, new or old, and then there is individual singing of hymns by all the others who will participate in the meal (80). Only after this singing is the food brought in and eaten. After the food is consumed, two choirs, of men and women, form in the middle of the dining room and sing hymns, but after this they become one choir, singing hymns (85, 87). Here it is stated that after the crossing of the sea there was in fact one combined choir (and cf. 88), when Philo elsewhere insists on there being two. This is significant, for while Philo otherwise has outlined a hierarchical and gender-segregated Israel, with two choirs singing one song composed by Moses, in *Contempl.* he describes the Mareotic group as having one choir (men and women together), and yet still singing hymns, plural. While in *Mos.* the point of the composition of the song is to indicate that it is Moses' first instance of prophetic inspiration, in regard to the Mareotic group Philo states that 'both men and women were filled with inspiration and became a choir singing hymns of thanksgiving to God the Saviour' (87). There is a subtle but significant difference in what Philo states regarding the Mareotic group and what he states elsewhere, and it seems likely to me that he is in fact reflecting the notions of the group despite his own different viewpoint. There is one inspired choir, which sings hymns composed by Moses and Miriam. Miriam's own identity as a prophetess and composer of song would justify the *therapeutrides* using her as a model.

For the Mareotic group, though not actually for Philo, Moses—as inspired prophet—leads the men who have also in some way become struck by the rapture of divine inspiration. Miriam—as inspired prophet—does likewise with the inspired women. It appears to be a moment in which the Spirit is poured out on all of God's people, men and women, old and young, signalling their redemption, and perhaps pointing to the future in which God's Spirit would dwell with the righteous on earth (cf. Joel 3: 1–2).

Whether any song sung by the Mareotic group is identical to the one evidenced by 4Q365 is of course impossible to say. It should also be noted that, while Josephus tells us of one inspired song of Moses (not Miriam), he also notes a kind of general jubilation of the Hebrews who sang hymns all night in joyful revelry (*Ant.* 2: 346). Josephus seems to assume that the Hebrews themselves did not become inspired to compose songs, but only sang them in joy. It was Moses who actually made the composition of a new song. There may have been numerous alternative ways of understanding this important text.

Philo states that it is on the model of the combined choruses of Moses and Miriam, the Israelite men and women, that the choir of the devotees is based. In his description of the singing, there is no suggestion that Moses and the men—or the male members of the group—do the initiating and lead the hymns, and the women respond, echoing the men. Rather, there is a melodious intermixing of parts, with responses ('echoes and re-echoes') without real leadership (88)—they are separate but one choir (85). The result is 'harmonious concord'. Both men and women are 'filled with inspiration' and weave together hymns, melodies, harmonies, initiations, and repetitions, in a way that Philo finds truly musical and majestic. Here, despite himself and his views of women, Philo seems to have been carried away by what he has experienced. He lets on that women are inspired. We may surmise that these women found the prototype for their own inspired activity in the figure of Miriam, who not only led women in inspired song, but was a 'prophet' in her own right. As such both men and women are drawing on Wisdom, the inspiring spirit of God, which animates them to sing and dance in joy until the new day dawns. There is no mediation of women's access to God through men, or through institutional structures. Since both men and women are filled with God's spirit, men and women become fulfilled, and unified in spirit. Here we may find the foundation of their recognition of themselves as being part of one spiritual family, redeemed from the body's cravings, and attachment to the body itself.

MIRIAM'S WELL

One intriguing possibility which arises in all this discussion is that older traditions about women recorded in the Hebrew Bible were still preserved in folkloric tradition, and that these stories could also be changed and adapted to different circumstances. Indeed, it is precisely this type of folkloric counterbalance to the traditions selected by final Jerusalem priestly compilers of Hebrew Bible that we find later in the Haggada. Such folkloric traditions and alternative interpretations were incorporated into numerous biblical paraphrases, of which we now only have a small sample. An interest in Miriam comes through in one such biblical paraphrase: Pseudo-Philo's *Biblical Antiquities*. Like the Pentateuchal paraphrases found among the Qumran documents, this text proceeds with numerous omissions and additions, some of which may be found in later talmudic literature or midrash. It was ascribed to Philo of Alexandria probably some time in the Middle Ages, though it is now thought that it was originally composed by another Jewish writer in Hebrew or Aramaic some time in the latter part of the first century CE, and then translated into Greek and Latin.[62] In this text, Miriam predicts Moses' birth when the Spirit of God comes to her and she 'sees' a dream (*Bib. Ant.* 9: 9–10, cf. 9: 15). Such a motif connects directly with Numbers 12: 6, where YHWH addresses Miriam and Aaron and claims that if there is a prophet 'among you' (i.e. Aaron and Miriam?), he speaks to such a person 'in a dream'. Miriam here has a dream, which enables her to predict the birth of Moses. The prediction of Moses' birth identifies Miriam as a prophet long before Moses is one, and explains why Miriam is suddenly called a 'prophet' in Exodus 15: 20.[63] Curiously, Josephus also mentions that Moses' role as redeemer is predicted through a dream, but here it belongs to Moses' father Amram (*Ant.* 2: 212–17). Of course, it is by no means certain that the biblical textual tradition preceded that of the apparent modifications of such biblical paraphrases; the biblical text may be seen rather to be a literary freezing of certain strands of a diverse oral tradition, and one which aims to relegate Miriam to a secondary, and marginal, place. If alternate traditions were known in Alexandria, and utilized in the spirituality of certain Jewish groups, this should not be a surprise.

In the *Biblical Antiquities* also there is a repeated motif of 'Miriam's well' (*Bib. Ant.* 10: 7; 11: 15; 20: 8), which appears later in rabbinic literature as an important symbol.[64] As Louis Ginzberg described it, it is the miraculous spring which flows out of the rock of Horeb (Exod. 17), and was eventually positioned in front of the Tabernacle, where it sent out twelve streams of water.[65] 'Miriam's well' was revealed through the prophetic merits of Miriam, but in fact it dated back to the second day of creation. It was built like a rock colander, and out of it came water which the Israelites drank during their long sojourn in the wilderness. It moved around with them, and rested just outside the Tabernacle. The water was miraculous,

---

[62] See discussion in Cheryl Anne Brown, *'No Longer be Silent': First Century Jewish Portraits of Biblical Women* (Louisville, Ky.: Westminster and John Knox Press, 1992), 19–28; Daniel J. Harrington, in Charlesworth (ed.), *Old Testament Apocrypha*, ii. 297–377; Levison, 'Prophetic Inspiration', n. 69 on pp. 328–9.   [63] In Ex. Rab. 1: 22 Miriam has a vision.

[64] Ginzberg, *Legends*, iii. 50–4, 307–8, nn. 119–35.

[65] Ibid. iii. 53, n. 129, citing t.Sukk. 3: 11–13.

causing trees watered with it to bear fruit constantly. It was fra-
grant and provided sweet-smelling grass for the poor to lie down
on. Eventually, it came to a permanent rest in the Sea of Galilee
(visible from Mount Carmel), and could effect magical cures for
those who were able to get to it. The symbolism of healing pure
water from the deepest reaches of the waters below the earth has
an extraordinarily evocative power. It is significant that it is
Miriam, a woman, who is able to reveal the well, which is really a
kind of fountain of pure (living) water. Miriam is therefore associated with an everlasting well which will never dry up. Philo
states that the spring gushing forth from the rock of Horeb symbolizes Wisdom (*Mos.* 1: 181–6, 188–90, 210–11, 255–7; *Fug.*
183–7), the feminine dimension of God. In the Christian Gospel
of John, such imagery is used to indicate the sustaining spiritual
power of God, identified with the Logos/Jesus (John 4: 10–14; 7:
38–9).[66] When Philo writes of the symbolism of Jacob's well
(which appears as a motif in John 4: 6, contrasting with the
spiritual fountain Jesus offers the Samaritan women), he writes
that the well is a symbol of knowledge, for it goes deep, and is
hidden away and found with difficulty (*Somn.* 1: 6). Whatever
the possible allusions, the story of Miriam's well points to her
agency as revealer of hidden waters running deep, and may
possibly have been known to this group of women who extolled
Miriam as their inspired prototype.

Did the Mareotic group understand themselves to be 'drunk'
with the spiritual drink of Miriam's well? If Miriam's well was
believed by some to have been positioned just outside the
Sanctuary, sending forth twelve streams, and the twelve loaves
of the table of shewbread were positioned inside the sanctuary,
then bread and water are spatially linked. Unfortunately, Philo
does not tell us anything regarding the prototype for the water
drunk in the special meal of the Mareotic group, but he does give
us some clue that the water itself was understood to be as
significant as the bread. He states that water is drunk, rather than
wine, because it is what is permissible for priests when
sacrificing (74). This alludes to the fact that priests were to

---

[66] See also 1 Cor. 10: 1–4, where Paul insists that the Hebrews were baptized
into Moses in the cloud and the sea, and then ate the same spiritual food (manna)
and drank the same spiritual drink (the water from the rock), identifying the
rock as Christ.

abstain from wine during Temple service (cf. *Ebr.* 126), and indicates that those participating in the meal saw themselves as priests 'for a lifetime' on duty in the Temple. Also, in the 'sacred symposium' (71) of the Mareotic group, the participants drink 'the most translucent water (διαυγέστατον ὕδωρ)' (73). This identifies the water as what we might consider the most purified water possible, apparently to be distinguished from the regular spring water they drink as a rule (37). The water they drink during the meal is not given a symbolic meaning by Philo, but may have been given such a meaning by the group.

Strangely enough, there are records of a device created or described by a Jewish woman named Miriam/Maria which was designed to distil water and other liquids to create 'divine water'.[67] All the information about her is embedded in obscure alchemical treatises, particularly that of a fourth-century alchemist named Zosimos, who identifies her as being Miriam, the sister of Moses.[68] Both Moses and Miriam were considered to have been among those who authored alchemical treatises. It is likely that this Miriam was indeed a real woman inventor or transmitter of devices useful for alchemy, who lived in Alexandria in the first century CE. Her invention, the so-called *balneum Mariae*, which was drawn by Zosimos on the basis of Miriam's design, was used until quite modern times in alchemical practice and chemistry. Miriam's device could have been used to distil pure water from sea water (which would extract salt as a residue). In Miriam's own alchemical/mystical writings, of which there seem to have been three, water seems to have been of key interest; she associates water with the soul.[69] What was the relationship between early Jewish alchemy and the allegorizing school of exegesis in Alexandria, in view of such tantalizing evidence? Whatever it was, it seems clear that women were active in both.

[67] F. Sherwood Taylor, *The Alchemists: Founders of Modern Chemistry* (London: Heinemann, 1951), 38–43; Jack Lindsay, *The Origins of Alchemy in Graeco-Roman Egypt* (London: Frederick Muller, 1970), 240–52. The term 'divine water' would later on in alchemy actually refer to a number of different liquids which had the power of acting upon metals, not distilled water.

[68] See Pierre E. M. Berthelot, *Collection des anciens alchemistes grecs* (Paris: Masson, 1888), 60.

[69] In the writings of Ibn Umail, *Kitab al-Habib*, quoted in Lindsay, *Origins of Alchemy*, 249.

REDEMPTION FROM THE BODY

All the elements of the forty-ninth-day festival point to the group celebrating redemption from the body. It may be significant that the festival of the forty-ninth day takes place throughout the night, which usually represents the time when bodily senses and desires were considered to be the strongest, and when a certain satisfaction of the needs of the body was permissible (cf. *Contempl.* 27, 34). Having satisfied the body at night by the simple meal, during the rest of the night the group triumphs in its victory over it. The unified choir singing hymns of thanksgiving to God represents this victory, which cannot be sustained fully in a permanent state, but only on every forty-ninth evening. Ordinarily, the Mareotic group are in their little houses, alone, where they compose songs (29), bodily separate from one another. In the normal seventh-day meeting, separation between men and women is still required. Philo can insist on women's virtue because of this separation, which is still maintained to a degree at the beginning of the sacred symposium. But in the celebration of the forty-ninth evening, Philo's rhetoric of women's modesty collapses, as does the separation between the sexes. They place themselves 'in the middle (κατὰ μέσον) of the dining room (τὸ συμπόσιον)' in two choirs. The choir of women and the choir of men each has its own leader: 'the leader and chief (ἡγεμὼν . . . καὶ ἔξαρχος) is selected for each one as being the most honoured and also most musical' (83). Ultimately, the separation into two choirs of men and women is overcome. The resulting single choir is born of inspired singing, in which it seems that the body is completely transcended, for gender separation is no longer required. As Engberg-Pedersen has noted, in this progression, 'night and all it stands for has now been finally conquered'.[70] Engberg-Pedersen notes also how at the end of the night-long session of singing and dancing the *therapeutai* and *therapeutrides* stand with their faces *and whole body* turned to the east (*Contempl.* 89). He notes also how Philo's language of the waves being separated and then coming together in the Red Sea (87) parallels the separation of the men and women and then their coming together in a single choir.[71] The culmination of the

[70] Engberg-Pedersen, 'Philo's *De Vita Contemplativa*', 60.
[71] Ibid. 60.

mystical enterprises of the group in general are pointed to already in the early part of the text, as we have seen: 'they are seized by a heavenly passion—just like the Bacchic revellers and Corybants—(and) are inspired until they see the object of desire. Then through their longing for the deathless and blessed life, they consider their mortal life to have already ended' (*Contempl.* 12–13). As Engberg-Pedersen states: 'The therapeutic life as consummated at the great feast is the deathless and blessed life so far as human beings can attain to this. It is a life that is no longer mortal.'[72] On this night, they have died to the body and live in the soul. They have been redeemed from 'Egypt', these priests in the true Temple who can eat of the twelve loaves of self-control, drink the purest water (of the soul?), and sing hymns of thanksgiving with divine inspiration.

Overall then, in this chapter, we have explored dimensions of the group's spirituality and musical/mystical enterprise. It is worthiness of the soul which permits entry into the most excellent portion of the priests. Inspiration and adeptness in the doctrines are valued and the body—inscribed with sexual difference—does not count very much. The Temple of God is where the attendants of God gather to see him and sing his praises, full of thanksgiving at their triumph over the body. In other words, in terms of a contemporary phenomenological appraisal, the Mareotic group work themselves into an altered state of consciousness that is very common in many human societies and is well-documented in anthropological and scientific studies of 'religious' experiences. This state is usually referred to as a trance.

In his classic study, *Ecstatic Religion*, I. M. Lewis identified that 'trance states can be readily induced in most normal people by a wide range of stimuli', including 'music and dancing'.[73] This is especially the case when accompanied by psychotropic or alkaloid drugs or by 'such self-inflicted or externally-imposed

[72] Ibid. 62.
[73] Ioan M. Lewis, *Ecstatic Religion: A Study in Shamanism and Spirit-Possession*, 2nd edn. (London and New York: Routledge, 1989), 34, and see also for numerous intriguing case studies: Ernst Arbman, *Ecstasy, or Religious Trance, in the Experience of the Ecstatics and from the Pscyhological Point of View*, 3 vols. (Stockholm: Svenska Bokförlagt, 1963–70).

mortifications and privations as fasting and ascetic contemplation'. Natural endorphins in the human brain have been shown
to be released by trance induction,[74] which gives the person in
the trance an experience of bliss. Cultural and theological factors
will come into play whenever a person interprets the experience
of the trance state. The Jewish philosophers Philo describes in
Contempl. are examples of people in the ancient world who were
adept at inducing the trance state in themselves; those who participated in the Dionysiac rites did likewise, though via quite
different means, as Philo himself identified. While Philo distinguished between the 'sober' and the 'non-sober' types of trance
states, his distinction actually rests on his decisions about the
nature of virtue. It is more virtuous to reach the state via asceticism, music, and dance than it is via over-indulgence and wine.
Since God wants virtuous behaviour, he rewards those who
practise it with the sight of his light, a sight that is ultimately
denied to everyone save a few. That the men and women of the
Mareotic group strive to 'see God' through a life that is one of
self-effacing virtue and are rewarded accordingly is Philo's
whole point in *Contempl.* They are rewarded by becoming
friends of God, dwelling in his company in the heights of pure
bliss, because their virtue is unsurpassable.

---

[74] N. Ahlberg, 'Some Psycho-Physiological Aspects of Ecstasy in Recent
Research', in Nils G. Holm (ed.), *Religious Ecstasy* (Stockholm: Almqvist &
Wiksell, 1982), 63–73.

Conclusion

'And so thus, everything is explained, everything falls into place . . . Psychologically perfect. But there is no proof . . . No proof at all . . .'

. . . .

A little smile hovered on his pain-twisted lips.
'You would have made a good archaeologist, M. Poirot. You have the gift of re-creating the past.'[1]

But indeed from what is in [Philo's] very accurate investigation of the life of our ascetics it is very clear not only that he knew but also accepted the divine and reverent matters of the apostolic men around him, who were from the [nation of] Hebrews (therefore, it would appear, being very Jewish, they still kept most of the old customs).
                    (Eusebius, *Hist. Eccles.* 2: 15: 2)

Eusebius of Caesarea read Philo's *De Vita Contemplativa* through a dense cloud of Christianity, and any anomalies could be explained by considering them 'old customs'. More recently, since the discovery of the Dead Sea Scrolls, the elusive Therapeutae have sometimes been read through a different cloud, and configured as a branch of the better known Essene school of Judaea, anomalies explained away by their being an Alexandrian branch of the school, or by Philo's twists on sources describing Essenes. This study attempts to clear the air, to sever them from associations with more famous religious movements and to see them in the context of first-century Alexandrian Jewish philosophy. I have explored various subjects, looking for clues, but ultimately this study can provide no empirical proof. When Christie's Hercule Poirot sets out his case in front of a tense audience of suspects, someone generally confesses to clinch the accuracy of his cool reconstruction of events. In the case of a scholarly investigation of the past, especially of this nature,

---

[1] Agatha Christie, *Murder in Mesopotamia* (London: Harper Collins, 1936 and 2001), 347–8.

we do not have this confirmation after our sleuthing. Philo, presented with this analysis, would be sure to correct it.

Overall, we have reconfigured the Therapeutae as one of the ascetic, contemplative groups that formed part of the philosophical school of Jewish allegorical exegesis in first-century Alexandria. The allegorical school of exegesis had been strong for over 150 years, and had developed into groups which favoured different interpretative norms. The Therapeutae are illustrative of one of these groups: the extreme allegorizers. Philo chose to present this particular group as indicative of the virtue of the Jews to an audience of Romans, in Rome, during the course of his representations there in 41 CE. He shared much in common with this group in terms of the acceptance of norms of allegorical exegesis. He differed with them regarding the praxis of Jewish law, calendar, asceticism of the young, celibacy, and was uncomfortable about the women. The Mareotic group were not the only Jewish ascetics living in and outside Alexandria in the first century CE. The women of the group were not the only Jewish women philosophers and exegetes. Philo's decision to use them for his rhetorical purposes gives us evidence for wider phenomena.

In particular, the focus in this study has rested on issues of women and gender in the rhetoric of *Contempl.* and in the group to which *Contempl.* points. As with the study of women in antiquity in general, so with this study: we do not have named individuals, but rather small clues that enable us to get a sense of many women engaged in matters our sources refer to in passing. Only the model of 'Skepsis' or the mysterious woman alchemist Miriam may point to actual individuals, but the women of the Mareotic group give us the strongest evidence of a small collective that represents the tip of the iceberg. By considering the parallels of women in philosophy generally, especially among the Pythagoraean school, and by noting the activity of women elsewhere in Judaism, we can begin to get a better impression of the true situation of the Jewish women philosophers in Alexandria.

This branch of the 'extreme allegorizers' lived a life of extraordinary asceticism, linked with meditation on the scriptures—interpreted to reflect realities of the soul's journey to God—and musical composition. They met together every seventh day for instruction, and then every forty-ninth evening at a dinner in which the bread and water they drank were interpreted in line with deliverance from the body's desires (Egypt). The bread from the table of shewbread in the Temple and the eating of it symbolized the triumph of self-control, after which men and women could join together in a choir. They used music and dance to attain a trance-state in which they believed they experienced a vision of God's light.

In line with the anti-materialist ethos of the group, the body and its inscribed gender were devalued. Both men and women formed the senior group, as both men and women were among the 'dailies', or junior members of the group responsible for maintaining the seniors and the community. The juniors honoured the seniors as parents in common. Divisions existed between males and females until the celebration of the triumph over the body at the ritualized feast of redemption on the forty-ninth day. For the rest of the time the community was in training, working to subdue the pull of the material world. While the name 'Therapeutae' was problematized in this study, in order to break conceptual links, the conclusion reached is that θεραπευταί conforms to a constellation of cultic terms used in *Contempl.* which reflect the usage of the group, since they saw themselves as imitators of Moses: the great suppliant and attendant of God.

This cultic usage of terms should probably not be considered exclusive or sectarian. The words θεραπευταί and θεραπευτρίδες mean 'attendants', those who attend the gods or God. While the term would have been known to Philo's audience, it has not generally been known to modern readers, who have read the term as a sectarian name. We may continue to use the customary Latin designation 'Therapeutae' (masculine plural, functioning as gender-inclusive) or perhaps 'Therapeutics', as some prefer, but we should not lose sight of the real meaning lying beneath such words. Both the self-designations of the group—'the attendants (of God)' or 'suppliants (of God)'—would have made a claim: the practitioners of this ascetic, spiritual path had gone away from normal life to serve God in his Sanctuary, understood symbolically. Ultimately, both men and women saw themselves not only as attendants or suppliants but as priests in this Temple. We saw in Philo's comments on contemplative ascetics how he can use this terminology for their quest to serve (and see) God.

These ascetics—and Philo may once have been one—could be individual or living in community, extreme or moderate allegorizers. All of these may have shared the terminology of both Philo and the Mareotic group for their enterprises, drawn from allegorical tradition, but they should probably not be lumped together as a cohesive movement. Attitudes to the Law, to the Temple, to women, to calendar, or to all kinds of other matters may have varied. Asceticism of many kinds was being practised in the philosophies of the Graeco-Roman world, the origins of which may be traced to the East. A particular kind of Alexandrian Jewish asceticism, linked with allegorical exegesis, forms part of a wider picture of philosophical asceticism that would ultimately flow into Christian practices and exert a profound influence on Western history.

In the classic terminology used of Alexandrian Judaism, it is clear then that this group is 'Hellenized'. But to what extent is this a helpful observation? John Barclay has recently examined the different types of Hellenization abounding in Ptolemaic and Roman Egypt and pointed out that one cannot subsume them into one homogeneous category. Given that Jews may have constituted about a third of the population of Roman Alexandria,[2] all types of positions are probable. People adopted Greek customs and ideas in various ways, for various reasons, and to various degrees.[3] In cases of the most extreme assimilation, such people effectively ceased to be Jews any longer. In low assimilation, Jewish customs were preserved in the context of Jewish neighbourhoods which had little contact with the city outside.[4] More difficult to assess is what Barclay defines as 'cultural convergence' in surviving literature, but, as we saw, the evidence of Artapanus, Aristobulus, and Aristeas, as well as Philo, tells of a Judaism that could be very clearly conceptualized in Greek terms.[5] For the Mareotic community, allegorical exegesis might easily lead beyond cultural convergence to total 'Hellenization'. Given the position of 'extreme allegorizers' the distinction between Jewish allegorical philosopher and non-Jewish Pythagoraean or

[2] Modrzejewski, *Jews of Egypt*, 73.

[3] Barclay, *Jews*, 82–124.

[4] Barclay classifies the 'Therapeutae' among those who were in the 'low assimilation' category, ibid. 118–19.

[5] Ibid. 125–80.

Neoplatonist might have been difficult to discern. However, for the members of the Mareotic group they were clearly Jews, the true disciples of Moses, with a spiritual focus very heavily reliant on scripture. If they shared Philo's understanding of the etymology of the word, they would have seen themselves as the true Israel: those who see God. They were the opposite of apostates. They took allegorical interpretation as being the only true or real way to deal with scripture, the literalists being 'provincial' and, basically, wrong in their interpretations. Had they replied to Philo, they may have argued that his continual observance of the Law's literal meaning—while still advocating an allegorical understanding—only tied him into the world and ultimately left him unable to grasp the true bliss he craved.

While little can be verifiable, this study proceeded on the basis of two primary axioms: first, that Philo's text was highly rhetorical and, secondly, that what he described was true. The truth of Philo's account has been questioned by the assertion that *Contempl.* conforms to the genre of a utopian fantasy. However, it is one of the main features of such fantasies that the utopian group be located far away at the edge of the known world. Philo's Therapeutae exist just outside one of the great metropolises of antiquity, on a busy lake, and are connected with the city. The community was not located far out into the Indian Ocean, or in Scandinavia. Without this essential feature of remoteness, there seems no reason to categorize it as a utopian fantasy. *Contempl.* is clearly a *bios theoretikos*, created as a partner to a *bios praktikos*, which concerned the Essenes of Judaea. Since the Essenes were a real group—attested by two further first-century witnesses and probably also by the Dead Sea Scrolls—then likewise so were the Therapeutae.

Unless there is sound comparative evidence that can be utilized to assess the historicity of an account, one cannot assess the reliability of individual units of information. A sceptical approach that would doubt the veracity of certain information in *Contempl.* would be reliant on an underlying theoretical or unconscious anti-historical epistemological framework, but would ultimately be an arbitrary decision on the part of the observer. Since *Contempl.* is the only text with information about the Therapeutae, it is simply impossible to proceed with a historical study on the basis of an assumption that only some of the comments by Philo are true and some are not, because there are no outside criteria that could be brought to bear on individual elements to make an assessment of veracity in each instance. Either one uses the axiom that Philo presents us with falsehood and therefore there is no 'history' to be presented here or one proceeds with the axiom that Philo presents truth and goes from there. This is not to say in fact that Philo may not have made some things up, but only that we cannot prove he did or did not do so given the current state of evidence.

Proceeding on the basis of an axiom which asserts that what Philo states is true is not meant to indicate that the truth he presents is simple. Truth may be half-true, or shaped truth. A major part of the truth about the group may have been omitted. The audience has been invited to fill in gaps in ways that may create a false image. We cannot read *Contempl.* as a straightforward repository of factual information, because of the way that Philo's rhetoric has shaped the presentation. Not only was it Philo's aim to present a *bios theoretikos*, but it was also his aim to present an ideal of Jewish excellence that would impress an audience not composed of Jews, and not composed—apart from the opposing contingent—of Alexandrians. It has been argued here that this work was created as part of a strategy to convince the Emperor Claudius of the Jewish case in Alexandria. It formed one section of a long work 'On Virtues' in which *Legat.* was the first part, a curious 'palinode' the second, a treatise on the virtue of *bios praktikos* (the Essenes) the third, a treatise on the virtue of a *bios theoretikos* (the Therapeutae) the fourth, and, probably, a treatise on the virtue of the *bios logikos* (Moses and Judaism as a whole) the fifth. The political context in Alexandria, and Philo's involvement in it, generated a series of works aimed at showing to people of importance that 'perfect good' was to be found within Judaism, in its diverse parts. Chaeremon's work on the Egyptian priests seems to come from the other side of the Alexandrian dispute, and it addresses very similar themes.

No historian should read Philo's text without being alert to the rhetorical dimension, and we have been much concerned to understand it. However, rhetoricity does not invalidate historicity. To set up a binary opposition between 'rhetoric' and 'historical reality' is absurd: much of what we know about the past is embedded in texts that were written with a rhetorical purpose. If a witness is clearly biased, and an argument is powerfully at work, this does not mean that the source is impossible to use for historical reconstruction. Rhetoricity is not necessarily connected with falsehood or fantasy. It is very easy to adopt an ultra-sceptical approach to ancient history, and to question whether anything happened as it has been described as happening, or to doubt the veracity of certain accounts. The point is that the rhetoric itself is a powerful tool to use in the uncovering of historical truth. While Philo gives us 'truth' he gives it to us bent in all kinds of ways so that we do not recognize what we are seeing. With proper awareness, the rhetoric gives us a means to unbend it, at least in part, as long as we use it to strike at reality rather than let the rhetoric use us as Philo intended.

Throughout this study we have been much occupied with context: the context of Philo within the political and social traumas of first-century Alexandria; the context of the Therapeutae within the allegorical school of Jewish philosophy; the context of Philo's statements on women and gender within the discourse of *philosophia*, and so on. The work of contextualizing the text, and the group to which it points, can go on further. Most importantly, it would be very interesting now to consider points of comparison between the Therapeutae and other Jewish groups, especially the Essenes, or early Christian communities. Much more could be delved into, particularly in regard to asceticism and allegorical traditions. Others may wish to open up dimensions of *Contempl.* that remain locked in the present analysis. This study has been tightly constructed, and is itself an exercise in rhetoric: it is an argument proceeding point by point to convince an audience of other scholars and students of ancient history of the veracity of a particular historical presentation. Those who do not find it convincing may not share some of my underlying presuppositions, or may bring different evidence to bear on the material that will nuance some matters, or challenge the soundness of others, or find the logic flawed. We are all Poirots in this, as we engage our minds as best we can in the task of bringing the dark regions of the past into the light, and argue long and hard about what we see.

Partial Translation of Philo of Alexandria, *De Vita Contemplativa*

This translation by Joan Taylor translates the relevant parts of De Vita Contemplativa *on the basis of the Greek text of Philo given by F. H. Colson, Philo ix (Loeb Classical Library; Cambridge, Mass.: Harvard University Press, 1941), 112–68. For textual issues and alternative translations, see Colson's notes. Summaries of portions of the text left untranslated appear in italics within brackets.*

1. I have discoursed on Essenes, who were zealous for and who worked hard at the active [philosophical] life, excelling in everything or—at least to say it more moderately—in most parts. Going on directly, and indeed carrying on in accordance with the plan [of my subject] I will say what is required about those who embrace contemplation [as a philosophical lifestyle]. I will not add [anything] of my own for the sake of making [my account] better, which is customary for all the poets and chroniclers to do for want of good [historiographical] practices, but will absolutely go about [telling] the actual truth, even though I know the most skilled speaker would grow weary of telling it [like this]. But nevertheless we must persevere and fight on to the end, for the superlative virtue of the[se] men should not be a reason to strike dumb those who rightly think that nothing good should be passed over in silence.

2. The intention of the philosophers is immediately apparent by the name [given to them], for they are truly called '[devoted] attendants',[1] male and female, either because they profess medical skill [to attend/treat the sick] better than in the cities, for that [of the cities] attends bodies alone, while theirs [attends] souls which have been conquered by terrible and nearly incurable diseases, which are inflicted by pleasures and desires and griefs and fears, by covetous acts and follies and unrighteousness, and the countless multitude of other passions and evils—or else because they have been instructed by Nature and the sacred laws to attend [as cultic servants] the Being who is better than a Good, purer than a One, and older than a Monad.

3. Who among those who profess piety is worthy of comparison? (*3–9: Discusses comparisons: people who revere the elements; worshippers*

---

[1] For the meaning of the Greek word *therapeutai/trides*, see Ch. 3.

of heavenly bodies; worshippers of demi-gods; worshippers of different images; worshippers of Egyptian gods.)

10. But these people indeed infect with foolishness not only their own compatriots, but also those [living in regions] nearby, and they remain incurable for they are incapable of sight, the most vital of the senses. And I talk not of the body, but [the sight] of the soul, which alone gives knowledge of truth and falsehood.

11. But the [devotedly] attending type of people, who are before-hand taught always to see, desire the vision of the Being, and would pass over the sun perceived [by sense] and never leave this company leading to perfect happiness.

12. And those who are going about [devoted] attendance, not from custom, or from advice or recommendation of anyone, but because they are seized by a heavenly passion—just like the Bacchic revellers and Corybants—are inspired until they see the object of desire.

13. Then through their longing for the deathless and blessed life, they consider their mortal life to have already ended, and they abandon their belongings to sons or daughters or even other relations, voluntarily giving them an advance inheritance, while those who do not have close family [give] to companions and friends. For it is right that those who have readily received the seeing wealth should leave behind the blind [wealth] to those who are blind still in mind.

14. The Greeks sing the praises of Anaxagoras and Democritus, because, smitten by longing for philosophy, they let the[ir] property be grazed by sheep. I admire the[se] men indeed, this being superior to money. But how much better are those who do not let creatures consume the[ir] property, but set [right] the needs of people—relatives or friends—so from wanting they are made wealthy. For that action [of Anaxagoras and Democritus] is inconsiderate—in order that I not say 'mad' of men that Greece admired—but this [of benefiting relatives and friends] is sober, and examined with good sense above measure.

15. (*Writes about how Democritus inflicted poverty on his own relations.*)

16. How much better and more wonderful then are those who are driven by impulses for philosophy no less [ardent than Democritus and Anaxagoras], but who have preferred magnanimity to carelessness, giving away their belongings, but not wasting them, in order that both others and themselves would benefit. On the one hand they supply [people] ungrudgingly with resources, and on the other they [benefit] themselves in the [life] of philosophy.

17. (*Care of money and possessions consumes time, cf. what Hippocrates said: 'Life is short but art is long.' Injustice/unrighteousness is bred by thought of the means of life and making money, and righteousness is furthered by the opposite.*)

18. Then when they have rid themselves of their belongings, no longer enticed by anything, they flee away without turning around, leaving behind brothers/sisters, children, wives, parents, numerous relations, friendly companions, and the native areas in which they were born and raised, since the attraction of familiar things indeed has a great power to entice.

19. And they do not move into another city, like the unfortunate or worthless slaves who beg to be sold by their owners, exchanging masters, not procuring freedom for themselves. For every city, even the best governed, is full of noise and innumerable disturbances which no one who has ever once been led by Wisdom can endure.

20. Outside [city] walls, they pass their time in cultivated or uncultivated land, pursuing solitude, not because they are practising any contrived misanthropy, but because the custom of mixing with dissimilar things is [something] they know [to be] unprofitable and harmful.

21. Now then the type of people [I describe] is in many parts of the inhabited world, for it was necessary that perfect good be shared by the Greeks and the Barbarians. But in Egypt, in each of the 'nomes' as they are called, it is superabundant, and especially around Alexandria.

22. The best of them from anywhere set off as to a homeland settlement, to a very suitable place which is above Lake Mareotis, lying upon a flattish, low hill, very well situated, because of safety and temperate air.

23. The safety is supplied by the encircling dwellings and villages. And the continual breezes which arise from both the lake which flows into the sea and the open sea nearby [result in] the pleasant temperature of the air. For those [breezes] of the sea are slight, but those [coming] up from the lake are stronger, so the mixture creates a very healthy climate.

24. The little houses of those who have come together are very frugal, providing shelter against the two most urgent things: against the blazing [heat] of the sun, and the chilly [cold] of the air. They are neither close together, like those in the towns—for close neighbourbood is troublesome and displeasing to those who are zealous for solitude and pursue it—nor far apart, because of the sense of community they adhere to and [also] in order that, if robbers make an attack, they may help one another.

25. In each there is a sacred room, which is called a reverence-place and place-for-one, in which they solitarily perfect the mysteries of the holy life. They take nothing [into it]—no drink, no food, nothing necessary for the needs of the body—but [only] laws, oracles declared through prophets, hymns, and other [writings] which increase and perfect understanding and piety.

26. Always then, without forgetting, they keep the memory of God. So indeed in dreams nothing else is dreamt of apart from the beauty of

the divine attributes and powers. In fact, many [of them] call out the famous decrees of the sacred philosophy in [their] sleep while dreaming.

27. They are accustomed to pray twice every day, at sunrise and sunset. When the sun rises they ask for a 'fine day', the 'fine day' being [that] their minds will be filled with a heavenly light. In the second instance they pray that the soul, being entirely relieved from the disturbance of the senses and being in its own council and court, may follow the way of truth.

28. The entire interval from morning until evening is for them an exercise, for they philosophize by reading the sacred writings and interpreting allegorically the ancestral philosophy. They consider the words of the literal text to be symbols of Nature which has been hidden, and which is revealed in the underlying meaning.

29. They have also the writings of men of old, those who began the school. They left behind many [written] recollections of the form of the interpretations [they used]. These [writings] are sort of like models used [by the group] in order to imitate the method of the practice [of allegorical interpretation]. Therefore, they do not contemplate [scripture] only, but also compose psalms and hymns to God in all kinds of metres and melodies which they have to write down in dignified rhythms.

30. So each of them separately, alone by themselves, practises philosophy for six days in the above-mentioned places-for-one. They do not cross over the main door [of the dwelling] or even see it from a distance. But they come together as a common group on the seventh days, sitting in order of 'age', with the proper figure, 'having the hands inside': the right hand in between chest and chin, and the left hand lowered along the thighs.

31. The most senior person (*presbutatos*), who is very experienced in the doctrines, then comes forward and discourses, with a composed appearance and quiet voice, and with reason and thoughtfulness. He does not show cleverness with words like the rhetors or the current Sophists, but closely examines the accuracy in the thoughts, and interprets [these] so that they do not sit at the points of the ears, but come through the hearing into the soul, where they remain secure.

32. This common reverence-place into which they come together on seventh days is a double enclosure: one part is set apart for men, and the other [is set apart] for women. For indeed also women customarily participate in listening [like the men], having the same zeal and purpose.

33. The wall between the areas rises upwards from the ground up to three or four cubits in the form of breastwork, but the upper section going up to the roof is wide open. [This arrangement is] for two reasons: so that the modesty which is becoming to the female nature be preserved, and so that, by their sitting in earshot, everything is easily audible, for nothing obstructs the voice of the speaker.

34. They first lay down self-control as a certain foundation stone of the soul [and then] they build the other virtues [on it]. None of them would ever eat food or drink before sunset, since they have decided that philosophizing is appropriate to the light [of day], but the needs of the body [are appropriate] for the darkness [of night]. They have allotted one to the day and a small part of the night for the others.

35. And some—for whom the yearning after knowledge has settled more completely—do not think of food for three days. Others are so [busy] enjoying themselves relishing the doctrines abundantly and lavishly supplied by Wisdom that in fact they hold out for twice the time, and only after six days taste necessary food. They are accustomed to live on air, just like the race of grasshoppers are said [to do]; their song, I guess, makes the lack tolerable.

36. They consider the seventh day to be something all-sacred and all-festive, thinking it worthy of special honour. [On this day], after the care of the soul, they also nurture the body, just as they of course also release the cattle from their continuous labour.

37. However, they do not eat anything expensive, but plain bread with a seasoning of salt which the more extravagant flavour with hyssop. Drink for them is running water [from a stream or spring]. For since Nature has made hunger and thirst mistresses over us mortal types of people, they appease them away, not laying favour on them, but [eating and drinking] the necessary things without which life could not be [sustained]. On this account, they eat just so as not to be hungry, and they drink just so as not to be thirsty, avoiding [complete] satisfaction as an enemy and plotter against both soul and body.

38. As for the two forms of protection—clothing and housing—we have already spoken concerning housing: that it is undecorated and rough, each one built only for urgent things. Clothing is likewise very simple. [It is made] for a defence against cold and heat, and consists of a cloak of woolly skin in winter, and an *exomis* or linen cloth in summer.

39. They entirely practise simplicity [of life], knowing pride is the origin of falsehood, and simplicity of truth, each [state—truth and falsehood—] having the essential nature (*logos*) of [being] a spring. For the many forms of evil [flow] out of falsehood, and the abundant forms of good, both human and divine, flow out of truth.

40. I wish also to speak of their common meetings and the cheerful pastimes of symposia, in contrast to the dining pastimes of others. (*41–58: Discusses how other sorts of people get drunk and rave like dogs, argue, fight, mutilate people, and sleep. He expresses disapproval of the expensiveness of banquets, the type of banquets 'prevalent everywhere' in which there is 'Italic expensiveness and luxury emulated by both Greeks and Barbarians who arrange things for ostentation rather than for festivity' (48) and the practice of having effeminate male slaves to wait on the*

table. He notes two symposia in which Socrates took part, Xenophon's and Plato's, that people may point out as being better.)

58. But even these compared with the [banquets of] others, that is of those of us who embrace the contemplative life, will seem a joke. (*58–63: In Xenophon's banquet there are flute girls and entertainers, and in Plato's banquet the talk is all about sensual love.*)

63. For all these enticing things, which are able by the novelty of thought to distract the ears, are superfluous to the students of Moses, who, having learnt to love truth from first youth, despise [these pastimes at symposia], and they continue on [undeceived].

64. So since these well-known symposia are full of nonsense, themselves self-disgraced—that is if anyone does not pay heed to mere opinion and the wide report about them which now may purport [them] to be successful—I will contrast [them with the symposia] of those who have dedicated their personal lives and themselves to the understanding and contemplation of the facts of Nature, according to the sacred instructions of the prophet Moses.

65. First of all, these people assemble on [every] seventh seventh-day, holding in awe not only the simple number of seven, but also the square [of it]. For they know its purity and eternal virginity. And it is also the eve of the great special day which the number fifty has been assigned; fifty being the most holy and natural of numbers, since it is the square of the right handed triangle which is the origin of the composition of the whole universe.

66. So then they come together clothed in white, radiant with the utmost seriousness, when a certain person from the 'dailies'—as it is the custom to call those performing these services—gives a sign. Before they recline, they duly stand in order in a row, with their eyes and hands lifted up to heaven. The eyes have been trained to see things worth looking at, and the hands are clean of income, and are not defiled by any gain. They pray to God that they might meet according to his mind and that their feast will be pleasing [to him].

67. After the prayers the seniors recline following the order of [their] admission. They do not consider as seniors the ones who are old in years and aged, but still they may be regarded entirely as 'children' if they have come to love the practice only recently. They are those who from early youth have matured and grown up in the contemplative part of philosophy, which indeed is the most beautiful and godly.

68. Women eat together [here] also. They are mostly elderly virgins. They strongly maintain the purity, not out of necessity, as some of the priestesses of the Greeks [do], but out of their own free will, because of a zeal and yearning for Wisdom, which they are eager to live with. They take no heed of the pleasures of the body, and desire not a mortal offspring, but an immortal one, which only a soul which is loved by God

is able to give birth to, by itself, because the Father has sown in it lights of intelligence which enable her to see the doctrines of Wisdom.

69. The [order of] reclining is divided, with men by themselves on the right, and women by themselves on the left. Surely no one by chance supposes that [they have] mattresses, which are not in fact expensive but still softer for people of good birth and erudite [conversation] who are trained in philosophy? [No indeed], for [the couches] are rough beds of cheap wood, upon which are altogether frugal strewings of local papyrus, slightly raised at the bend of the arm [so that] they can lean on them. For while they modify the Laconian harsh way of life a little, always and everywhere they practise noble contentment, and they hate with all their might the charms of pleasure.

70. They are not served by slaves. They believe utterly that the ownership of servants is against Nature. For she has given birth to all free, but the unrighteousness and greed of some who zealously seek the source of evil, inequality, have bound [people] up and fastened on the more powerful a power over the weaker.

71. In this sacred symposium, there is as I said no slave, but free people serve, and they fulfil the requirements of servants not by compulson or by enduring orders, but, with voluntary free will they anticipate quickly and willingly [any] requests.

72. For it is not any free people who happen to be [selected] for these services, but the juniors from among those in the assembly. They are chosen on merit with all care, which is fitting for the manner of good character and good birth of those eager to reach the summit of virtue. They are just like real children who are affectionately glad to be of service to fathers and mothers. They consider [the seniors] their parents in common, more closely connected with them than by blood, since, for those who think rightly, there is no closer connection than goodness. And they come in to serve with their tunics ungirt and hanging down so that there is nothing in their appearance to suggest an image of a slave.

73. In this symposium—I know that some hearing [this] will laugh, but they are people who do things worthy of tears and lamentation— wine is not brought in on those days, but [only] the most translucent water. [It is] cold for most of them, but warm for the weaker of the seniors. The table is also free from meat, and upon it [are] loaves of bread, along with a seasoning of salt. There is also hyssop as a relish, ready for those of a more delicate constitution.

74. Just as right reason dictates abstinence from wine for the priests when sacrificing, so also for these [people] for a lifetime, for wine is a drug of foolishness, and many expensive things to eat [just] stir up that most insatiable of animals: desire.

75. And such are the preliminaries. Now, after the guests have reclined in the order I have described, the serving people stand in order

ready to attend. When a silence is established among everyone—'And when is there not (a silence)?!' someone might say; but it is even more than before, so that no one ventures to make a sound or even to breathe too forcefully—the president seeks out a certain matter in the sacred scriptures or indeed explains something put forward by someone. He is not at all thinking to put on a good show, for he does not grasp for fame through cleverness in discourses, but rather [has] a desire to perceive certain things more clearly, and, having perceived [them], not to withhold [his perceptions] from those who—even if they are not in fact quite as perceptive as he is—still nevertheless have a similar desire to learn.

76. He rightly goes slowly with the teaching, lingering over and dwelling on it with repetitions, imprinting the thoughts on the souls [of his hearers]. For the mind of those listening is unable to follow the interpretation of one who goes too quickly, and with breathless rapidity, and it fails to comprehend what is said.

77. The listeners [with eyes and ears fixed] upon him, remain listening in one and the same position. They indicate comprehension and understanding with nods and glances, and [indicate] praise of the speaker with happy expressions and the gradual turning around of the face. [They indicate] incomprehension with a gentler movement of the head, and by pointing with the finger of the right hand. The juniors standing by pay no less attention than the people reclining on couches.

78. The interpretations of the sacred scriptures are through the underlying meanings [conveyed] in allegories. For these men, all the law book seems to be like a living being, with a body made up of literal words, and the invisible mind of the wording constitutes its soul. The soul above all begins to consider the things similar to it. As it were through a mirror of names, it sees the transcendent beauty of concepts which are reflected [there], bringing what is perceived naked into light for those able, with a little reminding, to see the unseen things through the seen.

79. When then it seems to the president that the speech has reached its goal by good aiming, and it seems to the others that the hearing [has also], [there is] clapping from all the audience, who are looking forward to what is still to follow.

80. Then the [president] stands up and sings a hymn composed to God, either a new one of his own composition or some ancient one [composed] by the poets of old, for they have left behind many [songs] in many metres and melodies: hexameters, trimeters, hymns of processions, [hymns] relating to libations, [hymns] relating to the altar, for standing [in a chorus] and for [choral] dancing, well measured out for turning and twisting. After him, in fact, the others according to order take their turn at singing. Everyone else listens in total silence, except

when they need [to sing] closing lines and themes. For then all men and all women sing aloud.

81. When each person has finished a hymn, the juniors bring in the above-mentioned table, upon which the most all-pure food is [set out]: [loaves] of leavened bread, along with a seasoning of salt mingled with hyssop. This [arrangement] is in deference to the sacred table in the vestibule of the holy Temple sanctuary. For upon this [table] are loaves and salt, without flavouring, and the bread is unleavened, and the salt is not mixed [into the bread].

82. For it was appropriate that the simplest and purest food be allotted to the most excellent portion of the priests, as a reward for services, while others would zealously seek the same [kind of food], but hold off from the [Temple loaves], in order that their betters might have precedence.

83. After the dinner they celebrate the sacred [eve] all night. And the night festival is celebrated in this way. They all stand up together and, first, place themselves in the middle of the dining room in two choirs, one of men and the other of women. The leader and chief is selected for each one as being the most honoured and also most musical.

84. Then they sing hymns to God composed of many metres and melodies, singing all together, then again antiphonically and harmonically, tapping time with hands and feet, engaging in procession, then continuous song, and in the turns and counter-turns of choral dancing.

85. When each of the choirs has sated itself by itself—as in the Bacchic rites they drink the liquor of the god's love—they blend together and become one choir from out of two, a memory of the one established of old by the Red Sea, by reason of the wonderful works there.

86. (*Describes the story of the parting of the Red Sea.*)

87. Seeing and experiencing this [salvation], which is a work greater than in word, thought and hope, both men and women were filled with inspiration and became a choir singing hymns of thanksgiving to God the Saviour. The men were led by Moses the prophet, and the women by Miriam the prophetess.

88. On this [model] most of all the choir of the [devoted] attendants —male and female—is based. They sing with [canonic] echoes and re-echoes, with men having the bass parts and women the treble, combined together, and resulting in a really musical harmonious concord. The thoughts are lovely, the words are lovely, the choral singers are majestic, and the purpose of the thoughts and the words and the choral singers is piety.

89. So they are drunk [in this way] until dawn, with this beautiful drunkenness, with no heavy head or dozing, but [rather] they are roused more awake than when they came into the dining room. Then they

stand with eyes and their whole bodies [turned] to the east, and when they see the rising sun, they stretch out their hands up to heaven, and pray for a 'bright day' and truth and clearness of reasoning. And after the prayers they go back into each their own reverence-place, again to ply their trade and cultivate the use of philosophy.

90. So then let this suffice for matters of the [devoted] attendants who embrace contemplation of Nature and what it contains, and of those living in soul alone. They are citizens of heaven and also world, and are recommended to the Father and maker of all by virtue, which has procured them God's friendship, as a very appropriate reward for their goodness: a gift better than any good fortune and reaching to the very peak of bliss.

APPENDIX 2

De Migratione Abrahami 86–96

86. As it is an advantage to be good and morally noble, so is it to be reputed such. And, while the reality is better than the reputation, happiness comes of having both. For very many, after coming to Virtue's feet with no counterfeit or unreal homage and with their eyes open to her genuine loveliness, through paying no regard to the general opinion have become the objects of hostility, just because they were held to be bad, when they were really good.

87. It is true that there is no good in being thought to be this or that, unless you are so long before you are thought to be so. It is naturally so in the case of our bodies. Were all the world to suppose the sickly man to be healthy, or the healthy man to be sickly, the general opinion by itself will produce neither sickness nor health.

88. But he on whom God has bestowed both gifts, both to be morally noble and good and to have the reputation of being so, this man is really happy and his name is great in very deed. We should take thought for fair fame as a great matter and one of much advantage to the life which we live in the body. And this fair fame is won as a rule by all who cheerfully take things as they find them and interfere with no established customs, but maintain with care the constitution of their country.

89. There are some who, regarding laws in their literal sense in the light of symbols of matters belonging to the intellect, are overpunctilious about the latter, while treating the former with easy-going neglect. Such men I for my part should blame for handling the matter in too easy and off-hand a manner: they ought to have given careful attention to both aims, to a more full and exact investigation of what is not seen and in what is seen to be stewards without reproach.

90. As it is, as though they were living alone by themselves in a wilderness, or as though they had become disembodied souls, and knew

neither city nor village nor household nor any company of human beings at all, overlooking all that the mass of men regard, they explore reality in its naked absoluteness. These men are taught by the sacred word to have thought for good repute, and to let go nothing that is part of the customs fixed by divinely empowered men greater than those of our time.

91. It is quite true that the Seventh Day is meant to teach the power of the Unoriginate and the non-action of created beings. But let us not for this reason abrogate the laws laid down for its observance, and light fires or till the ground or carry loads or institute proceedings in court or act as jurors or demand the restoration of deposits or recover loans, or do all else that we are permitted to do as well on days that are not festival seasons.

92. It is true also that the Feast is a symbol of gladness of soul and of thankfulness to God, but we should not for this reason turn our backs on the general gatherings of the year's seasons. It is true that receiving circumcision does indeed portray the excision of pleasure and all passions, and the putting away of the impious conceit, under which the mind supposed that it was capable of begetting by its own power: but let us not on this account repeal the law laid down for circumcising. Why we shall be ignoring the sanctity of the Temple and a thousand other things, if we are going to pay heed to nothing except what is shewn us by the inner meaning of things.

93. Nay, we should look on all these outward observances as resembling the body, and their inner meanings as resembling the soul. It follows that, exactly as we have to take thought for the body, because it is the abode of the soul, so we must pay heed to the letter of the laws. If we keep and observe these, we shall gain a clearer conception of those things of which these are the symbols; and besides that we shall not incur the censure of the many and the charges they are sure to bring against us.

94. Notice that it says that wise Abraham had good things both great and small, and it calls the great ones 'property' that is, realities, which went by entail to his legitimate son alone. The small ones it calls 'gifts' and to receive these the base-born sons of the concubines are deemed worthy (Gen. 15: 5, 6). The former correspond to natural, the latter to positive laws.

95. I admire also all-virtuous Leah, because when Asher was born, symbol of counterfeit wealth the outward and visible, she cries, 'Happy am I, for the women will call me happy' (Gen. 30: 13). She aims at being favourably regarded, thinking praise due to her not only from thoughts masculine and truly manly, by which the nature that has no blemish and truth impervious to bribes is held in honour, but also from those which are more feminine, which are wholly at the mercy of appearances and powerless to understand anything presented to contemplation outside them.

96. It is characteristic of a perfect soul to aspire both to be and to be thought to be, and to take pains not only to have a good reputation in the men's quarters, but to receive the praises of the women's as well.

Epitome of Chaeremon the Stoic
'On the Egyptian Priests'

Epitome from Porphyry, De Abstinentia *4: 6–8, translated by Pieter Van der Horst in* Chaeremon: Egyptian Priest and Stoic Philosopher *(Leiden: Brill, 1987), 17–23. Used by permission of Prof. Van der Horst and Brill Academic Publishers, Leiden.*

6. Chaeremon the Stoic tells in his exposé about the Egyptian priests who, he says, were considered also as philosophers among the Egyptians, that they chose the temples as the place to philosophize. For to live close to their shrines was fitting to their whole desire of contemplation, and it gave them security because of the reverence for the divine, since all people honoured the philosophers as if they were a sort of sacred animals [sic]. And they were able to live a quiet life, as contact with other people occurred only at assemblies and festivals, whereas for the rest the temples were almost inaccessible to others. For it was requisite that those who approached them should have purified themselves and abstained from many things. This, too, is as it were a common law of the Egyptian temples. They renounced every employment and human revenues, and devoted their whole life to contemplation and vision of the divine. Through this vision they procured knowledge; and through both a certain esoteric and venerable way of life. For to be always in contact with divine knowledge and inspiration keeps them far from all kinds of greediness, represses the passions, and incites them to live a life of understanding. They practised frugality and restraint, self-control and endurance, and in all things justice and freedom from avarice. Their disinclination for social contact made them impressive. During the time of the so-called purifications and fasts they did not even have contact with their nearest kinsmen and those of their own blood, nor with almost anyone else when they were in contemplation, except with those who were pure and fasted together with them for the necessary duties, or with those who divided among themselves the rooms of purification and fasting which were inaccessible to those who were not pure and which were set apart for the religious services. But the rest of the time they moved more easily among those who were of their order, but they did not associate with anyone who stood wholly outside their religion. They were always seen near the gods, or rather their statues, either carrying or preceding them in a procession or setting them up with order and dignity.

And each of these acts was no empty gesture, but an indication of some allegorical truth. Their gravity was also apparent from their behaviour. For their way of walking was disciplined, and they took care to have a quiet look, so that they did not blink when they wanted to do so. They seldom laughed, and when it did occur, it went no further than a smile. They always kept their hands within their dress. And each had a symbol indicative of the rank he had obtained in the hierarchy, for there were several ranks. Their diet was frugal and simple, for as to wine, some did not drink it at all and others drank only very little of it, for they alleged that it caused injury of the nerves and dizziness of the head, which impedes research, and they said that it induced sexual desires. In the same way they were also cautious with respect to other things: they did not use bread at all in the periods of purification and fasting; and outside these periods, they ate it with hyssop, which they cut into pieces, for they said that hyssop reduces the great strength of it (sc. the bread). They abstained from oil for the most part, the majority of them even entirely. And if sometimes they used it with vegetables, they definitely took only a little, just enough to mitigate the taste (sc. of the vegetables).

7. They were not allowed to touch foods or drinks that were produced outside Egypt. A great opportunity for luxury had been excluded in this way. As to the products of Egypt itself, they abstained from all kinds of fish, and from such quadrupeds as had uncloven hoofs or had toes or had no horns, and also from such birds as were carnivorous. Many of them, however, even entirely abstained from all animals. And in periods of fasting and purification all of them did so; then they did not even eat an egg. But also as to other kinds of food they practised a not unexceptionable rejection; e.g. they rejected the consumption of (female) cows, and of such male animals as were twins, or blemished, or piebald, or of unusual shape, or tamed (considering them as having been already consecrated by their labours), or those resembling animals that are honoured—whatever imitation one may think of—of one-eyed, or those that verged on a likeness to the human form. There are innumerable other observations in the art (concerning these animals) of the so-called calf-sealers, observations which even result in systematic treatises. Still more elaborate (are the rules) concerning birds; for instance, that a turtle-dove should not be eaten. For they say this bird is often seized by a falcon that dismisses it thereafter, thus giving it its deliverance as a due reward for the intercourse. In order not to come into contact with such a bird without perceiving it, they shunned the whole species.

These are some of the religious observances that were common to all, but there were others which varied according to the class of priests and were proper to each individual god. But the periods of purification and fasting observed by all (priests) were clean. This was the period when they were to perform something pertaining to the sacred rites. Then they spent a number of days in preparation, some forty-two, others less, but never less than seven days. And during this time they abstained from all animal food, from all vegetables and pulse, but above all from sexual intercourse with women, for (needless to say) they never at any time had intercourse with males. They washed themselves three times a day with cold water, *viz.* when they rose from bed, before lunch, and before going to sleep. But when they happened to have an ejaculation during their sleep, they immediately purified the body in a bath. In other daily matters they also used cold water, but not so very much. Their bed was woven from the branches of the palm-tree, which they call *bais*, and a well-smoothed cylindrical piece of wood which was their pillow. They exercised themselves in enduring hunger and thirst and paucity of food during their whole life.

8. A testimony to their self-control is that, though they practised neither walking nor swinging exercises, they lived without disease and were energetic enough for average activities. Therefore they took upon themselves many burdens in the performance of their religious rites and many services which required more than ordinary strength. They divided the night for the observation of the heavenly bodies, and sometimes for ritual, and the day for the worship of the gods in which they sang hymns to them three or four times, in the morning [and in the evening], when the sun is on the meridian, and when it is descending to the west. The rest of the time they spent with arithmetical and geometrical speculations, always trying to search out something and to make discoveries, and in general always busy with the pursuit of learning. In winter nights also they were occupied in the same activity, being awake because of their love of learning, since they need not care for earning a living and are free from that bad master, great expense. Their limitless and incessant labour bears witness to the endurance of these men, the absence of desire to their self-control. It was considered by them to be most ungodly to sail from Egypt, because they were on guard against foreign luxury and pursuits. For this appeared to them to be lawful only to those who were compelled to do so by reason of requirements of the royal court. There was, indeed, a strong reason for them to remain faithful to the ancestral customs, for if they were convicted of trespassing even in a minor matter, they were excluded (sc. from the temples).

The true philosophizing was found among the prophets, the priests who had charge of the sacred vestments, the sacred scribes, and also the astrologers. But the rest—the crowd of priests, shrine(?)-bearers, temple-wardens, and assistants—practise the same rite of purification for the gods, yet not with such great accuracy and self-control. Such are the things testified about the Egyptians by a man who was a lover of truth and an accurate writer, and who was among the Stoics a very clever philosopher.

BIBLIOGRAPHY

Abrahams, Ethel, *Greek Dress* (London: J. Murray, 1908).

Adler, Ada (ed.), *Suidae Lexicon,* 5 vols. (Stuttgart: Teubner, 1967–71).

Adler, Rachel, ' "A Mother in Israel": Aspects of the Mother-Role in Jewish Myth', in Rita M. Gross (ed.), *Beyond Androcentrism* (Missoula, Mont.: Scholars, 1977), 237–55.

—— 'The Virgin in the Brothel and Other Anomalies: Character and Context in the Legend of Beruriah', *Tikkun*, 3/6 (1988), 28–32, 102–5.

Ahlberg, N., 'Some Psycho-Physiological Aspects of Ecstasy in Recent Research', in Nils G. Holm (ed.), *Religious Ecstasy* (Stockholm: Almqvist & Wiksell, 1982).

Alexandre, Jr., Manuel, *Rhetorical Argumentation in Philo of Alexandria* (Atlanta: Scholars, 1999).

Allison, Dale C., *Jesus of Nazareth: Millenarian Prophet* (Minneapolis: Fortress, 1998).

Almond, Philip C., 'Buddhism in the West: 300 BC–AD 400', *Journal of Religious History*, 14 (1987), 235–45.

Alston, Richard, 'Houses and Households in Roman Egypt', in Ray Laurence and Andrew Wallace-Hadrill (eds.), *Domestic Space in the Roman World: Pompeii and Beyond* (Portsmouth, RI: Journal of Roman Archaeology, 1997), 25–39.

—— 'Philo's *In Flaccum*: Ethnicity and Social Space in Roman Alexandria', *Greece and Rome* 44 (1997), 165–75.

Amar, Zohar, 'The Ash and the Red Material from Qumran', *DSD* 5 (1998), 1–15.

Amir, Yehoshua, 'The Term Ἰουδαϊσμός: A Study in Jewish-Hellenistic Self-Identification', *Immanuel*, 14 (1982), 34–41.

Amundsen, D. W., and Diers, C. J., 'The Age of Menarche in Classical Greece and Rome', *Human Biology*, 41 (1969), 125–32.

Anderson, Bernhard W., 'The Song of Miriam Poetically and Theologically Considered', in Elaine R. Follis (ed.), *Directions in Biblical Hebrew Poetry* (Sheffield: JSOT, 1987), 285–96.

Ankersmit, Franklin R., 'Historiography and Postmodernism', in Brian Fay, Philip Pomper, and Richard T. Vann (eds.), *History and Theory: Contemporary Readings* (Oxford: Blackwell, 1998), 175–92.

Annas, Julia, 'Plato's *Republic* and Feminism', *Philosophy* 51 (1976), 307–21.

Anon., *The Archaeological Sites of Alexandria (331 BC—1801 AD)* (Alexandria: The Alexandria Preservation Trust Historical Map Series, No. 1, 1992).

Appleby, Joyce, Hunt, Lynn, and Jacob, Margaret, *Telling the Truth about History* (New York and London: W. W. Norton & Co., 1994).

Arbman, Ernst, *Ecstasy, or Religious Trance, in the Experience of the Ecstatics and from the Pscyhological Point of View*, 3 vols. (Stockholm: Svenska Bokförlagt, 1963–70).

Archer, Leonie J., 'Notions of Community and the Exclusion of the Female in Jewish History and Historiography', in Leonie J. Archer, Susan Fischler, and Maria A. Wyke (eds.), *Women in Ancient Societies: 'An Illusion of the Night'* (London: Macmillan, 1994), 53–69.

Attridge, Harold, Elgvin, Torleif, Milik, Jozef, *et al.* (eds.), *Discoveries in the Judaean Desert XIII: Qumran Cave 4. VIII: Parabiblical Texts, Part 1* (Oxford: Clarendon Press, 1994).

Aune, David E., *Prophecy in Early Christianity and the Ancient Mediterranean World* (Grand Rapids, Mich.: Eerdmans, 1983).

Baer, Richard A., *Philo's Use of the Categories Male and Female* (Arbeiten zur Literatur und Geschichte des hellenistischen Judentums, 3; Leiden: Brill, 1970).

Bagnall, Roger S., 'The People of the Roman Fayum', in Morris L. Bierbrier, *Portraits and Masks: Burial Customs in Roman Egypt* (London: British Museum, 1997), 7–15.

——and Frier, Bruce W., *The Demography of Roman Egypt* (Cambridge: CUP, 1994).

Barclay, John M. G., *Jews in the Mediterranean Diaspora: From Alexander to Trajan (323 BCE–117 CE)* (Edinburgh: T. & T. Clark, 1996).

——'Paul and Philo on Circumcision: Romans 2: 25–9 in Social and Cultural Context', *NTS* 44 (1998), 536–56.

Barker, Margaret, 'The Temple Measurements and the Solar Calendar', in George Brooke (ed.), *Temple Scroll Studies* (Sheffield: JSOT, 1989), 62–6.

Bar On, Bat-Ami (ed.), *Engendering Origins: Critical Feminist Readings in Plato and Aristotle* (Albany: State University of New York, 1994), 1–96.

Barraclough, R., 'Philo's Politics: Roman Rule and Hellenistic Judaism', *ANRW* 2: 21: 1 (1984), 417–553.

Barzanò, Alberto, 'Tiberio Giulio Alessandro, Preffetto d'Egitto (66/70)', *ANRW* 2: 10: 1 (1988), 518–80.

Basore, John W. (ed. and tr.), *Seneca, Moral Essays* (Loeb Classical Library; Cambridge, Mass.: Harvard University Press, 1965).

Beard, Mary, 'The Sexual Status of Vestal Virgins', *JRS* 70 (1980), 12–27.

—— 'The Roman and the Foreign: the Cult of the "Great Mother" in Imperial Rome', in Nicholas Thomas and Caroline Humphrey (eds.), *Shamanism, History and the State* (Ann Arbor: University of Michigan, 1994), 164–90.

—— 'Re-reading (Vestal) Virginity', in Richard Hawley and Barbara Levick (eds.), *Women in Antiquity: New Assessments* (London and New York: Routledge, 1995), 166–77.

—— North, John, and Price, Simon, *Religions of Rome*, 2 vols. (Cambridge: CUP, 1998).

Beckwith, Roger, 'The Solar Calendar of Joseph and Asenath: A Suggestion', *JSJ* 15 (1984), 90–111.

—— *Calendar and Chronology, Jewish and Christian* (Leiden: Brill, 1996).

—— 'The Temple Scroll and its Calendar: Their Character and Purpose', *RQ* 69/18 (1997), 3–20.

Bell, H. I., 'Alexandria ad Aegyptum', *JRS* 36 (1946), 130–3.

Bell, Rosamund, *Simple Yoga Techniques* (London: Marshall Publishing, 1998).

Bennett, Judith M., 'Feminism and History', *Gender and History*, 1 (1989), 251–72.

—— 'Women's History: A Reply to Bridget Hill', *WHR* 2 (1993), 173–84.

Berchman, Robert M., *From Philo to Origen: Middle Platonism in Transition* (Chico, Calif.: Scholars Press, 1984).

—— 'Arcana Mundi: Prophecy and Divination in the *Vita Mosis* of Philo of Alexandria', *SBL Seminar Papers* (1988), 401–9.

Bergmeier, Roland, *Die Essener-Berichte des Flavius Josephus: Quellenstudien zu den Essenertexten im Werk des jüdischen Historiographen* (Kampen: Kok Pharos, 1993), 41–7.

—— 'Der Stand der Gottesfreunde: Zu Philos Schrift "Uber die kontemplative Lebensform"', *Bijdragen: International Journal in Philosophy and Theology*, 63/1 (2002), 46–70.

Berthelot, Pierre E. M., *Collection des anciens alchemistes grecs* (Paris: Masson, 1888).

Bhandarkar, Devadatta R., *Ashoka*, 4th edn. (Calcutta: University of Calcutta, 1955).

Bickerman, Elias, 'La Chaîne de la tradition pharisienne', in id., *Studies in Jewish and Christian History*, ii (Harvard: Heinemann, 1979), 256–69.

Billings, Thomas H., *The Platonism of Philo Judaeus* (Chicago: University of Chicago Press, 1919).

Birnbaum, Ellen, *The Place of Judaism in Philo's Thought: Israel, Jews and Proselytes* (Atlanta: Scholars, 1996).

Birnbaum, Ellen, 'Philo on the Greeks: A Jewish Perspective on Culture and Society in First-Century Alexandria', *SPA* (2001), 37–58.

Blair, Elena Duvergès, 'Women: The Unrecognized Teachers of the Platonic Socrates', *Ancient Philosophy*, 16 (1996), 333–50.

Bloedow, Edmund F., 'Aspasia and the "Mystery" of the Menexenos', *Wiener Studien* (Zeitschrift für Klassiche Philologie und Patristic, Neu Folge), 9 (1975), 32–48.

Blundell, Sue, *Women in Ancient Greece* (Cambridge, Mass.: Harvard University Press, 1995).

Bock, Gisela, 'Women's History and Gender History: Aspects of an International Debate', *Gender and History*, 1 (1989), 7–30.

Bohak, Gideon, *Joseph and Asenath and the Jewish Temple in Heliopolis* (Atlanta: Scholars, 1996).

—— 'Theopolis: A Single-Temple Policy and its Singular Ramifications', *JSJ* 50 (1999), 3–20.

Borgen, Peder, *Philo of Alexandria: An Exegete for his Time* (Leiden: Brill, 1992).

—— Fuglseth, Kaare, and Skarsten, Roald, *The Philo Index: A Complete Greek Word Index to the Writings of Philo of Alexandria* (Leiden: Brill/Grand Rapids, Mich.: Eerdmans, 2000).

Bos, A. P., 'Philo of Alexandria: A Platonist in the Image and Likeness of Aristotle', *SPA* 10 (1998), 66–86.

Bourdieu, Pierre, 'The Berber House', in Mary Douglas (ed.), *Rules and Meanings: The Anthropology of Everyday Knowledge* (Harmondsworth: Penguin, 1973), 98–110.

Bowman, Alan K., *Egypt Under the Pharaohs 332 BC–AD 642, from Alexander to the Arab Conquest*, 2nd edn. (London: British Museum, 1996).

—— and Rathbone, Dominic, 'Cities and Administration in Roman Egypt', *JRS* 82 (1992), 107–27.

Box, Herbert, *Philo Alexandrinus, On Flaccus* (New York: Arno, 1979).

Boyarin, Daniel, *Carnal Israel: Reading Sex in Talmudic Culture* (Berkeley, Calif.: University of Califormia Press, 1993), 181–93.

Breasted, James, *Development of Religion and Thought in Ancient Egypt* (Philadelphia: University of Pennsylvania Press, 1940, repr. 1972).

Brodribb, Somer, *Nothing Mat(t)ers: A Feminist Critique of Postmodernism* (North Melbourne: Spinifex, 1992).

Brooke, George (ed.), *Temple Scroll Studies: Papers Presented at the International Symposium on the Temple Scroll, Manchester, Dec. 1987* (Sheffield: JSOT, 1989).

—— 'A Long-Lost Song of Miriam', *BAR* (May/June 1994), 62–5.

Brooten, Bernadette J., *Women Leaders in the Ancient Synagogue:*

Inscriptional Evidence and Background Issues (BJS 36; Chico, Calif.: Scholars, 1982).

——*Love between Women: Early Christian Responses to Female Homoeroticism* (Chicago and London: University of Chicago Press, 1996).

Brown, Cheryl Anne, *'No Longer be Silent': First Century Jewish Portraits of Biblical Women* (Louisville, Ky.: Westminster and John Knox, 1992), 19–28.

Burns, Rita J., *Has the Lord Spoken Only through Moses? A Study of the Biblical Portrait of Miriam* (SBL Diss. Series, 84; Atlanta: Scholars, 1987).

Burr, Viktor, *Tiberius Iulius Alexander* (Bonn: R. Habelt, 1955).

Burrus, Virginia, 'Chastity as Autonomy: Women in the Stories of the Apocryphal Acts', *Semeia*, 38 (1986), 101–35.

Canaan, Tawfiq, 'Der Kalendar des palästinischen Fellachen', *ZDPV* 36 (1913), 266–300.

Carlier, Caroline, 'Sur un titre latin du *De Vita Contemplativa*', *SPA* 8 (1996), 58–72.

Casson, Lionel, *Libraries in the Ancient World* (New Haven and London: Yale University Press, 2001).

Chamonard, Joseph, *Délos VIII: Le Quartier du Théâtre* (Paris: E. de Boccard and École française d'Athenes, 1922).

Charbonneaux, Jean, Martin, Roland, and Villard, François, *Hellenistic Art (30–50 BC)*, tr. Peter Green of *Grèce hellenistique* (New York: G. Braziller, 1973).

Charlesworth, James H. (ed.), *Old Testament Pseudepigrapha*, 2 vols. (London: Darton, Longman & Todd, 1985).

Chesnut, Randall D., 'Revelatory Experiences Attributed to Biblical Women in Early Jewish Literature', in Amy-Jill Levine (ed.), *'Women Like This': New Perspectives on Jewish Women in the Greco-Roman World* (Atlanta: Scholars, 1991), 107–26.

Chitty, Derwas J., *The Desert a City: An Introduction to the Study of Egyptian and Palestinian Monasticism under the Christian Empire* (London and Oxford: Mowbrays, 1966).

Christie, Agatha, *Murder in Mesopotamia* (London: Harper Collins, 1936 and 2001).

Clark, Gillian, *Iamblichus: On the Pythagorean Life* (Liverpool: Liverpool University Press, 1989).

Clark, S., 'Aristotle's Woman', *History of Political Thought*, 3 (1982), 177–91.

Cohn, Leopold, Wendland, Paul, and Reiter, Siegfried, *Philonis Alexandrini opera quae supersunt*, vi (Berlin: George Reimer, 1915).

Cole, Susan Guettel, 'Could Greek Women Read and Write?' *Women's Studies*, 8 (1981), 129–55.

Collins, Adela Yarbro, 'Aristobulus', in James H. Charlesworth (ed.), *Old Testament Pseudepigrapha* (London: Darton, Longman & Todd, 1985), ii, 831–42

Collins, John J., 'Artapanus', in James H. Charlesworth (ed.) *Old Testament Pseudepigrapha* (London: Darton, Longman & Todd, 1985), ii, 889–903.

Colson, Francis H., and Whitaker, George H. (eds.), *Philo*, 10 vols. (Loeb Classical Library; Cambridge, Mass.: Harvard University Press, 1929–62).

Comber, Joseph, 'The Verb *therapeuō* in Matthew's Gospel', *JBL* 97 (1978), 431–4.

Conybeare, Frederick C., 'Philo concerning the Contemplative Life', *JQR* 7 (1894), 755–69.

——*Philo About the Contemplative Life* (Oxford: Clarendon Press, 1895; repr. New York: Garland, 1987).

Corley, Kathleen, *Private Women, Public Meals: Social Conflict in the Synoptic Tradition* (Peabody, Mass.: Hendrickson, 1993).

Corrington, Gail Paterson, 'Philo On the Contemplative Life: or, On the Suppliants (The Fourth Book on the Virtues)', in Vincent L. Wimbush (ed.), *Ascetic Behavior in Greco-Roman Antiquity* (Minneapolis: Fortress, 1990), 134–55.

Cosson, Anthony de, *Mareotis, Being a Short Account of the History and Ancient Monuments of the North-Western Desert of Egypt and of Lake Mareotis* (London: Country Life, 1935).

Cotter, Wendy, 'The Collegia and Roman Law: State Restrictions on Voluntary Associations, 44 BCE–200 CE', in John S. Kloppenborg and Stephen G. Wilson (eds.), *Voluntary Associations in the Graeco-Roman World* (London and New York: Routledge, 1996), 74–89.

Coventry, Lucinda J., 'Philosophy and Rhetoric in the Menexenus', *Journal of Hellenic Studies*, 109 (1989), 1–15.

Cross, Frank, and Freedman, David Noel, 'The Song of Miriam', *JNES* 14 (1955), 237–50.

Dalby, Andrew, 'Levels of Concealment: The Dress of the *hetairai* and *pornai* in Greek Texts', in Lloyd Llewellyn-Jones (ed.), *Women's Dress in the Ancient Greek World* (London: Duckworth and Classical Press of Wales, 2002), 111–24.

Dalman, Gustaf, *Arbeit und Sitte in Palästina*, 7 vols. (Gutersloh: C. Bertelsmann, 1928–39).

Daumas, François, and Miquel, Pierre, *De Vita Contemplativa* (Les Œuvres de Philon d'Alexandrie; Paris, Éditions du Cerf, 1963).

Davies, Glenys, 'Clothes as Sign: The Case of the Large and Small Herculaneum Women', in Lloyd Llewellyn-Jones (ed.), *Women's Dress in the Ancient Greek World* (London: Duckworth and Classical Press of Wales, 2002), 227–41.

Davies, Philip, and Taylor, Joan E., 'On the Testimony of Women in 1QSa', *DSD* 3 (1996), 223–35.

Dawson, David, *Allegorical Readers and Cultural Revision in Ancient Alexandria* (Berkeley, Calif.: University of California Press, 1992).

Delcor, Mathias, 'Is the Temple Scroll a Source of the Herodian Temple?' in George Brooke (ed.), *Temple Scroll Studies* (Sheffield, JSOT, 1989), 67–89.

Delia, Diana, 'The Population of Roman Alexandria', *Transactions of the American Philological Association*, 118 (1988), 275–92.

Delling, Gerhard, 'The "One who sees God" in Philo', in Frederick E. Greenspahn, Earle Hilgert, and Burton L. Mack (eds.), *Nourished with Peace: Studies in Hellenistic Judaism in Memory of Samuel Sandmel* (Chico, Calif.: Scholars, 1984), 28–33.

Demand, Nancy, 'Plato, Aristophanes and the *Speeches of Pythagoras*', *Greek, Roman and Byzantine Studies*, 23 (1982), 179–84.

Dillon, John, 'Philo and the Greek Tradition of Allegorical Exegesis', *SBL 1994 Seminar Papers* (Atlanta: Scholars, 1994), 69–80.

Donceel, R., and Donceel-Voute, P., 'The Archaeology of Khirbet Qumran', in Michael Wise *et al.* (eds.), *Methods of Investigation of the Dead Sea Scrolls and the Khirbet Qumran Site* (New York: New York Academy of Sciences, 1992), 27–31.

Drummond, James, *Philo Judaeus or the Jewish Alexandrian Philosophy in its Development and Completion*, 2 vols. (London: Williams & Norgate, 1888; Amsterdam: Philo Press, 1969).

Dunbabin, Katherine M. D., 'Triclinium and Stibadium', in William J. Slater (ed.), *Dining in a Classical Context* (Ann Arbor: University of Michigan Press, 1991), 121–48.

Dutt, Sukumar, *Buddhist Monks and Monasteries in India: Their History and Contribution to Indian Culture* (London: George Allen & Unwin, 1962).

Ehlers, Barbara, *Eine vorplatonische Deutung des sokratischen Eros: Der Dialog Aspasia des sokratikers Aischines* (Zetemata, 41; Munich: Beck, 1966).

Eingartner, Johannes, *Isis und ihre Dienerinnen in der Kunst der Römischen Kaiserzeit* (Leiden: Brill, 1991).

Ellis, Simon, 'Late-Antique Dining: Architecture, Furnishings, Behaviour', in Ray Laurence and Andrew Wallace-Hadrill (eds.), *Domestic Space in the Roman World: Pompeii and Beyond* (Portsmouth, RI: Journal of Roman Archaeology, 1997), 41–51.

Elm, Susanna, *'Virgins of God': The Making of Asceticism in Late Antiquity* (Oxford: Clarendon Press, 1994).

Empereur, Jean-Yves, *A Short Guide to the Graeco-Roman Museum Alexandria* (Sarapis: Alexandria, 1995).

——*Alexandria Rediscovered* (London: British Museum Press, 1998).

Engberg-Pedersen, Troels, 'Philo's *De Vita Contemplativa* as a Philosopher's Dream', *JSJ* 30 (1999), 40–64.

Étienne, S. 'Réflexion sur l'apostasie de Tibérius Julius Alexander', *SPA* 12 (2000), 122–42.

Exum, Cheryl, 'Mother in Israel: A Familiar Story Reconsidered', in Letty M. Russell (ed.), *Feminist Interpretation of the Bible* (Oxford: Blackwell, 1985), 73–85.

Falk, Nancy Auer, 'The Case of the Vanishing Nuns: The Fruits of Ambivalence in Ancient Indian Buddhism', in Nancy Auer Falk and Rita Gross, *Unspoken Worlds: Women's Religious Lives* (Belmont, Calif.: Wadsworth, 1989), 155–65.

Fay, Brian, Pomper, Philip, and Vann, Richard T. (eds.), *History and Theory: Contemporary Readings* (Oxford: Blackwell, 1998).

Fehrle, E., *Die kultische Keuschheit im Altertum* (Giessen: Alfred Töbelmann, 1910).

Feldman, Louis H. 'The Orthodoxy of Jews in Hellenistic Egypt', *JSS* 22 (1960), 215–37.

——(ed. and tr.), *Josephus ix* (Loeb Classical Library; Cambridge, Mass.: Harvard University Press, 1981).

——'Josephus' Portrait of Moses. Part Three', *JQR* 83 (1993), 301–30.

Ferguson, John, *Utopias of the Classical World* (London: Thames & Hudson, 1975).

Festugière, Andre J., 'Sur une novelle édition du "De Vita Pythagorica" de Jamblique', *Revue des Études Grecques*, 50 (1937), 470–94.

——*Contemplation et vie contemplative selon Platon*, 4th edn. (Paris: J. Vrin, 1975).

Fiorenza, Elisabeth Schüssler, 'Text and Reality—Reality as Text: The Problem of a Feminist Historical and Social Reconstruction Based on Texts', *Studia Theologica*, 43 (1989), 19–34.

——'The Rhetoricity of Historical Knowledge: Pauline Discourse and its Contextualizations', in Lukas Bornkamm, Kelly del Tredici, and Angela Starthartinger (eds.), *Religious Propaganda and Missionary Competition in the New Testament World: Essays Honoring Dieter Georgi* (Leiden: Brill, 1994), 443–69.

——*In Memory of Her: A Feminist Theological Reconstruction of Christian Origins*, 2nd edn. (London: SCM, 1995).

Forster, Edward M., *Alexandria: A History and a Guide* (Gloucester, Mass.: Peter Smith, 1968).

Foucault, Michel, *The Use of Pleasure: The History of Sexuality 2*, tr. of *L'Usage des plaisirs* (Paris: Éditions Gallimard, 1984; Harmondsworth: Penguin, 1992).

Fox, Robin Lane, *Pagans and Christians* (Harmondsworth: Penguin, 1987).

Fraade, Stephen, 'Ascetical Aspects of Ancient Judaism', in Arthur

Green (ed.), *Jewish Spirituality from the Bible through the Middle Ages* (New York: Crossroad, 1986), 253–88.

Frank, Georgia, 'Miracles, Monks and Monuments: The *Historia Monachorum in Aegypto* as Pilgrims' Tales', in David Frankfurter (ed.), *Pilgrimage and Holy Space in Late Antique Egypt* (Leiden: Brill, 1998), 485–505.

Frankfurter, David (ed.), *Pilgrimage and Holy Space in Late Antique Egypt* (Leiden: Brill, 1998).

Fraser, Peter M., *Ptolemaic Alexandria*, 3 vols. (Oxford: Clarendon Press, 1972).

Friedman, Mordecai, 'Babata's Ketubba: Some Preliminary Observations', *IEJ* 46 (1996), 55–76.

Friedmann, Meir (ed.), *Seder 'Eliyahu Rabbah we-Seder* (Vienna: Achiasaf, 1902).

Früchtel, Ursula, *Die Kosmologischen Vorstellungen bei Philo von Alexandrien: Ein Beitrag zur Geschichte der Genesisexegese* (Leiden: Brill, 1968).

Gaca, Kathy L., 'Philo's Principles of Sexual Conduct and their Influence on Christian Platonist Sexual Principles', *SPA* 8 (1996), 21–39.

Gager, John G., *Moses in Greco-Roman Paganism* (Nashville, Tenn.: Abingdon, 1972).

Gaisford, Thomas (ed.), *Etymologicum Magnum* (Oxford: E. Typographico Academico, 1848).

Gardner, Jane F., *Women in Roman Law and Society* (London: Routledge, 1986 and 1990).

Garnsey, Peter, *Social Status and Legal Privilege in the Roman Empire* (Oxford: Clarendon Press, 1970).

Geytenbeek, Anton C., *Musonius Rufus and Greek Diatribe* (Assen: Van Gorcum, 1965), 51–62.

Gfrörer, Alfred, *Philo und die Alexandrinische Theosophie* (Stuttgart: E. Schweizer, 1831).

Ginzberg, Louis, *The Legends of the Jews*, tr. Paul Radin (Philadelphia: Jewish Publication Society, 1937–66).

Glenn, Cheryl, 'Sex, Lies and Manuscripts: Refiguring Aspasia in the History of Rhetoric', *College Composition and Communication*, 45 (May 1994), 180–9.

Glucker, John, *Antiochus and the Late Academy* (Gottingen: Vandenhoeck & Ruprecht, 1978), 174–92.

Goldin, Judah, *The Song of the Sea: Being a Commentary on a Commentary in Two Parts* (New Haven and London: Yale University Press, 1971).

Gooch, Paul, *Jesus and Socrates: Word and Silence* (New Haven and London: Yale University Press, 1996).

Goodblatt, David, 'The Beruriah Traditions', *JJS* 26 (1975), 68–85.

Goodenough, Erwin R., *The Jurisprudence of the Jewish Courts in Egypt: Legal Administration by the Jews under the Early Roman Empire as Described by Philo Judaeus* (New Haven: Yale University Press, 1929).

—— *By Light, Light: The Mystic Gospel of Hellenistic Judaism* (New Haven: Yale University Press, 1935).

—— *The Politics of Philo Judaeus: Practice and Theory* (New Haven: Yale University Press, 1938).

—— *An Introduction to Philo Judaeus* (Oxford: Basil Blackwell, 1962).

Goudoever, J. van, *Biblical Calendars* (Leiden: Brill, 1961).

Green, Arthur (ed.), *Jewish Spirituality from the Bible through the Middle Ages* (New York: Crossroad, 1986).

Gruber, Elmar R., and Kersten, Holger, *The Original Jesus: The Buddhist Sources of Christianity* (Shaftesbury: Element, 1995).

Gruen, Erich S., 'The Origins and Objectives of Onias' Temple', *Scripta Classica Israelica*, 16 (1997), 47–50.

Guignebert, Charles, *Des prophètes à Jésus: Le Monde juif vers le temps de Jésus* (Paris: La Renaissance du livre, 1935).

Gundry-Volf, Judith, 'Celibate Pneumatics and Social Power: On the Motivations for Sexual Asceticism in Corinth', *USQR* 48 (1994), 105–26.

—— 'Controlling the Bodies. A Theological Profile of the Corinthian Sexual Ascetics', in R. Bieringer (ed.), *The Corinthian Correspondence* (BETL 125; Leuven: Leuven University and Peeters, 1996), 499–521.

Haas, Christopher, *Alexandria in Late Antiquity: Topography and Social Conflict* (Baltimore and London: Johns Hopkins University Press, 1997).

Habicht, Christian (ed.), *Altertümer von Pergamon 8.3: Die Inschriften des Asklepieions* (Berlin: Walter de Gruyter, 1969).

Hallett, Judith M., 'Women's Lives in the Ancient Mediterranean', in Ross Shepard Kraemer and Mary Rose D'Angelo (eds.), *Women and Christian Origins* (New York and Oxford: OUP, 1999), 13–34.

Halperin, David, 'Why is Diotima a Woman?' in id. *One Hundred Years of Homosexuality and Other Essays on Greek Love* (New York: Routledge, 1990), 113–51.

Hammond, Nicholas G. L., *The Genius of Alexander the Great* (Chapel Hill, NC: University of North Carolina Press, 1997).

Hanson, Ann E., 'Village Officials at Philadelphia: A Model of Romanization in the Julio-Claudian Period', in Lucia Criscuolo and Giovanni Geraci (eds.), *Egitto e storia antica dall'ellenismo all'età araba: bilancio di un confronto* (Bologna: CLUEB, 1989), 429–40.

Harmon, Austin M. (ed.), *Lucian* (Cambridge, Mass.: Harvard University Press, 1961).

Harris, Harold A., *Greek Athletics and the Jews* (Cardiff: University of Wales Press, 1976).

Harris, William V., *Ancient Literacy* (Cambridge, Mass.: Harvard University Press, 1989).

Harrison, Verna E. F., 'The Allegorization of Gender: Plato and Philo on Spiritual Childbearing', in Vincent L. Wimbush and Richard Valentasis (eds.), *Asceticism* (New York: OUP, 1995), 520–34.

Hauptman, Judith, *Rereading the Rabbis: A Woman's Voice* (Boulder, Colo.: Westview Press, 1998).

Hawley, Richard, ' "Pretty, Witty and Wise": Courtesans in Athenaeus' *Deipnosophistai* Book 13', *International Journal of Moral and Social Studies*, 8 (1993), 73–91.

—— 'The Problem of Women Philosophers in Ancient Greece', in Leonie Archer, Susan Fischler, and Maria Wyke (eds.), *Women in Ancient Societies: 'An Illusion of the Night'* (Basingstoke: Macmillan, 1994).

Hay, David, 'Philo's References to Other Allegorists', *Studia Philonica*, 6 (1979–80), 41–75.

—— 'References to Other Exegetes in Philo's *Quaestiones*', in David M. Hay and Ernest S. Frerichs (eds.), *Both Literal and Allegorical: Studies in Philo of Alexandria's Questions and Answers on Genesis and Exodus* (Atlanta: Scholars, 1991), 81–97.

—— 'Things Philo Said and Did Not Say about the Therapeutae', *Society of Biblical Literature Seminar Papers*, 31 (1992), 673–83.

—— 'Putting Extremism in Context: The Case of Philo, *De Migratione* 89–93', *SPA* 9 (1997), 126–42.

—— 'The Veiled Thoughts of the Therapeutae', in Robert M. Berchman (ed.), *Mediators of the Divine: Horizons of Prophecy, Divination, Dreams and Theurgy in Mediterranean Antiquity* (Atlanta: Scholars, 1998), 167–84.

Hayward, C. T. Robert, 'The Jewish Temple at Leontopolis: A Reconsideration', *JJS* 33 (1982), 429–43.

—— 'Philo, the Septuagint of Genesis 32: 24–32 and the Name "Israel": Fighting the Passions, Inspiration and the Vision of God', *JJS* 51 (2000), 209–26.

Heinemann, Isaak, 'Therapeutae', *Pauly's Realencyclopädie der classische altertumswissenschaft*, 5a (1934), 2335–8.

Hengel, Martin, *Judaism and Hellenism*, tr. John Bowden of *Judentum und Hellenismus*, 2 vols. (Philadelphia: Fortress, 1981).

Henry, Madeleine A., *Prisoner of History: Aspasia of Miletus and her Biographical Tradition* (New York: OUP, 1995).

Heyob, Sharon Kelley, *The Cult of Isis among Women in the Graeco-Roman World* (Leiden: Brill, 1975).

Hill, Bridget, 'Women's History: A Study in Change, Continuity or Standing Still?', *WHR* 2 (1993), 5–22.

Hirschfeld, Yitzhar, 'The Archaeology of the Community of Hermits', *Cathedra*, 99 (2001), 197–201.

Hobson, Deborah, 'Women as Property Owners in Roman Egypt', *Transactions of the American Philological Association*, 113 (1983), 311–21.

—— 'The Role of Women in the Economic Life of Roman Egypt: A Case Study from First-Century Tebtunis', *Echos du Monde Classique/Classical Views*, 28 (1984), 373–90.

Hoek, Annewies van den, *Clement of Alexandria and his Use of Philo in the* Stromateis: *An Early Christian Reshaping of a Jewish Model* (Leiden: Brill, 1988).

—— 'The Catechetical School of Alexandria and its Philonic Heritage', *HTR* 90 (1997), 59–97.

—— 'Philo and Origen: A Descriptive Catalogue of their Relationship', *SPA* 12 (2000), 44–121.

Hoff, Joan, 'Gender as a Postmodern Category of Paralysis', *WHR* 3 (1994), 149–68.

—— 'A Reply to My Critics', *WHR* 5 (1996), 25–30.

Honigman, Sylvie, 'Philon, Flavius Josèphe, et la citoyenneté alexandrine: Vers une utopie politique', *JJS* 48 (1997), 62–90.

Horsley, Richard A., 'Spiritual Marriage with Sophia', *VC* 33 (1979), 30–54.

Horst, Pieter van der, 'The Role of Women in the Testament of Job', *Nederlands Theologisch Tijdschrift* 40 (1986), 273–89.

—— *Chaeremon: Egyptian Priest and Stoic Philosopher* (Leiden: Brill, 1987).

Husson, Geneviève, *Oikia: Le Vocabulaire de la maison privée en Égypte d'après les papyrus grecs* (Paris: CNRS and Sorbonne, 1983).

Huzar, Eleanor, 'Alexandria ad Aegytpum in the Juleo-Claudian Age', *ANRW* 2: 10: 1 (1988), 619–68.

Ilan, Tal, *Jewish Women in Greco-Roman Palestine* (Peabody, Mass.: Hendrickson, 1996).

Irigaray, Luce, 'Sorcerer Love: A Reading of Plato, *Symposium*, "Diotima's Speech"', in ead., *An Ethics of Sexual Difference*, tr. Carolyn Burke and Gillian C. Gill (Ithaca, NY: Cornell University Press, 1993), 20–33.

Irwin, K. G., *The 365 Days* (London: George Harrap & Co., 1965).

Jahn, Otto, 'Socrate et Diotime: Bas-relief de bronze', *Annales de l'Institut Archéologique*, 13 (1841), 1–24.

Jantzen, Gerald J., 'Song of Moses, Song of Miriam: Who is Seconding Whom?', *CBQ* 54 (1992), 210–20.

Jarratt, Susan C., 'The First Sophists and Feminism: Discourses of the "Other"', *Hypatia*, 5 (1990), 27–41.

Jaubert, Annie, 'Le Calendrier des Jubilés et de la secte de Qumran: Ses origines bibliques', *VT* 3 (1953), 250–64.

—— 'Le Calendrier des Jubilés et les jours liturgiques de la semaine', *VT* 7 (1957), 35–61.

—— *La Date de la cène: Calendrier biblique et liturgie chrétienne* (Paris: Gabalda, 1957).

Jensen, Christian, 'Ein neuer Brief Epikurs', in *Abhandlungen der Gesellschaft der Wissenschaften zu Göttingen Philologisch-Historische Klasse*, 3/5 (Berlin: Weidmannsche Buchhandlung, 1933), 1–94.

Jones, Arnold H. M., *The Criminal Courts of the Roman Republic and Principate* (Oxford: Basil Blackwell, 1971).

Kasher, Ariyeh, *The Jews in Hellenistic and Roman Egypt* (Tubingen: J. C. B. Mohr (Paul Siebeck), 1985).

—— 'Synagogues as "Houses of Prayer" and "Holy Places" in the Jewish Communities of Hellenistic and Roman Egypt', in Dan Urman and Paul V. M. Flesher (eds.), *Ancient Synagogues: Historical Analysis and Archaeological Discovery* (Leiden: Brill, 1995), i. 205–25.

Kashnir-Stern, Alla, 'On the Visit of Agrippa I to Alexandria in AD 38', *JJS* 51 (2000), 227–43.

Kasser, Rodolfe, *Les Kellia, ermitages coptes en Basse-Egypte* (Geneva: Éditions de Tricorne, 1989).

Kelly-Gadol, Joan, 'The Social Relation of the Sexes: Methodological Implications of Women's History', *Signs*, 1 (1976), 813–23.

Kent, Susan Kingsley, 'Mistrals and Diatribulations: A Reply to Joan Hoff', *WHR* 5 (1996), 9–18.

Kerkeslager, Allen, 'Maintaining Jewish Identity in the Greek Gymnasium: A "Jewish Load" in *CPJ* 3.519 (= P. Schub. 37 = P. Berol. 13406)', *JSJ* 28 (1997), 12–33.

—— 'Jewish Pilgrimage and Jewish Identity in Hellenistic and Early Roman Egypt', in Frankfurter (ed.), *Pilgrimage and Holy Space in Late Antique Egypt* (Leiden: Brill, 1998), 99–225.

Kimelman, Rueven, 'The Shema' and its Rhetoric: The Case for the Shema' being more than Creation, Revelation and Redemption', *Jewish Thought and Philosophy*, 2 (1992), 111–56.

Klinghardt, Matthias, 'The Manual of Discipline in the Light of Statutes of Hellenistic Associations', in Michael Wise *et al.* (eds.), *Methods of Investigation of the Dead Sea Scrolls and the Khirbet Qumran Site: Present Realities and Future Prospects* (New York: New York Academy of Sciences, 1992), 251–70.

Kloppenborg, John S., and Wilson, Stephen G. (eds.), *Voluntary Associations in the Graeco-Roman World* (London and New York: Routledge, 1996).

Kock, Theodor (ed.), *Comicorum Atticorum Fragmenta*, 3 vols. (Leipzig: Teubner, 1980–8).

Koerte, Alfred (ed.), *Menandri Quae Supersunt* (Leipzig: Teubner, 1959).

Koester, Craig R., *The Dwelling of God: The Tabernacle in the Old Testament, Intertestamental Jewish Literature and the New Testament* (Washington, DC: Catholic Biblical Association of America, 1989).

Koester, Helmut, 'Associations of the Egyptian Cult in Asia Minor', in Peter Scherrer, Hans Taeuber, and Hilke Thür (eds.), *Stein und Wege: Festschrift für Dieter Knibb zum 65 Geburtstag* (Vienna: Osterrichisches Archäologisches Institut, 1999).

Kraemer, Ross Shepard, 'Ecstasy and Possession: Women of Ancient Greece and the Cult of Dionysus', in Nancy Auer Falk and Rita Gross (eds.), *Unspoken Worlds: Women's Religious Lives* (Belmont, Calif.: Wadsworth, 1989), 45–55.

—— 'Monastic Jewish Women in Greco-Roman Egypt: Philo Judaeus on the Therapeutrides', *Signs*, 14 (1989), 342–70.

—— 'On the Meaning of the Term "Jew" in Greco-Roman Inscriptions', *HTR* 82 (1989), 35–54.

—— *Her Share of the Blessings: Women's Religions Among Pagans, Jews, and Christians in the Greco-Roman World* (Oxford and New York: OUP, 1993).

—— 'Women's Judaisms at the Beginning of Christianity', in ead. and Mary Rose D'Angelo (eds.), *Women and Christian Origins* (New York and Oxford: OUP, 1999), 50–79.

—— and Mary Rose D'Angelo (eds.), *Women and Christian Origins* (New York and Oxford: OUP, 1999).

Kroeger, Richard and Catherine, 'An Inquiry into the Evidence of Maenadism in the Corinthian Congregation', in Paul J. Achtemeier (ed.), *Society of Biblical Literature Seminar Papers 1978*, ii (Missoula, Mont.: Scholars, 1979), 331–8.

Lake, Kirsopp, *Eusebius, The Ecclesiastical History*, i (Loeb Classical Library; Cambridge, Mass.: Harvard University Press, 1926).

Lamberton, Robert, *Homer the Theologian: Neoplatonist Allegorical Reading and the Growth of the Epic Tradition* (Berkeley and Los Angeles: University of California Press, 1986).

Lambropoulou, Voula, 'Some Pythagoraean Female Virtues', in Richard Hawley and Barbara Levick (eds.), *Women in Antiquity: New Assessments* (London: Routledge, 1995).

Leach, E. R., 'A Possible Method of Intercalation for the Calendar of the Book of Jubilees', *VT* 7 (1957), 392–7.

Lefkowitz, Mary R., and Fant, Maureen B., *Women's Life in Greece and Rome* (London: Duckworth, 1982).

Levick, Barbara, *Claudius* (New Haven and London: Yale University Press, 1990).

Levine, L. I. (ed.), *Ancient Synagogues Revealed* (Jerusalem: Israel Exploration Society, 1982),

Levison, John R., 'Prophetic Inspiration in Pseudo-Philo's *Liber Antiquitatum Biblicarum*', *JQR* 85 (1995), 275–96.

——'Inspiration and the Divine Spirit in the Writings of Philo Judaeus', *JSJ* 27 (1996), 271–323.

Lewis, Ioan M., *Ecstatic Religion: A Study in Shamanism and Spirit-Possession*, 2nd edn. (London and New York: Routledge, 1989).

Lewis, Naphtali, ' "Greco-Roman Egypt": Fact or Fiction?', in Deborah H. Sandmel (ed.), *Proceedings of the Twelfth International Congress of Papyrology* (Toronto: A. M. Hakkert, 1970), 3–14.

Lewy, Hans, *Sobria Ebrietas: Untersuchungen zur Geschichte der antiken Mystik* (Giessen: Töpelmann, 1929).

Lewy, Julius and Hildegard, 'The Origin of the Week and the Oldest West Asiatic Calendar', *HUCA* 17 (1942–3), 1–152.

Lichtman, Allan J., and French, Valerie, *Historians and the Living Past: The Theory and Practice of History* (Arlington Heights, Ill.: Harlan Davidson, 1986).

Liebeschuetz, John H. W. G., *Continuity and Change in Roman Religion* (Oxford: Clarendon Press, 1979).

Lieu, Judith M., 'Circumcision, Women and Salvation', *NTS* 40 (1994), 358–70.

Lindsay, Jack, *The Origins of Alchemy in Graeco-Roman Egypt* (London: Frederick Muller, 1970), 240–52.

Llewellyn-Jones, Lloyd (ed.), *Women's Dress in the Ancient Greek World* (London: Duckworth and Classical Press of Wales, 2002).

Lobel, E., Roberts, C. H., Turner, E. G., and Barns, J. W. B., *The Oxyrhynchus Papyri Part XXIV* (London: Egypt Exploration Society, 1957).

Lucius, Ernst, *Die Therapeuten und ihre Stellung in der Geschichte der Askese: Eine kritische Untersuchung der Schrift* De vita contemplativa (Strasbourg: F. Bull, 1879).

Lutz, Cora E., *Musonius Rufus: 'The Roman Socrates'* (New Haven: Yale University Press, 1947).

McIlraith, Donald A., ' "For the Fine Linen is the Righteous Deeds of the Saints": Words and Wife in Revelation 19: 8', *CBQ* 19/8 (1999), 512–27.

MacMullen, Ramsay, *Enemies of the Roman Order* (Cambridge, Mass.: Harvard University Press, 1966).

——*Roman Social Relations* (New Haven: Yale University Press, 1974).

Maiuri, Amedeo, *Nuova silloge epigrafica di Rodi e Cos* (Florence: Le Monnier, 1925).

Malherbe, Abraham J. (ed.), *The Cynic Epistles* (Missoula, Mont.: Scholars, 1977).

Mangey, Thomas, *Philonis Judaei opera quae reperiri potuerunt omnia*, ii (London: G. Bowyer, 1742).

Marrou, Henri I., *A History of Education in Antiquity* (London: Sheed & Marou, 1956).

Mason, Steve, 'Greco-Roman, Jewish and Christian Philosophies', in Jacob Neusner (ed.), *Approaches to Ancient Judaism*, NS iv (Atlanta: Scholars, 1993), 1–28.

——'*Philosophiai*: Graeco-Roman, Judean and Christian', in John S. Kloppenborg and Stephen G. Wilson (eds.), *Voluntary Associations in the Graeco-Roman World* (London and New York: Routledge, 1996), 31–58.

Mattila, Sharon Lea, 'Wisdom, Sense Perception, Nature and Philo's Gender Gradient', *HTR* 89 (1996), 103–29.

Mayhew, Robert, 'Aristotle's Criticism of Plato's Communism of Women and Children', *Apeiron*, 29 (1996), 231–48.

Meier, Johann, *The Temple Scroll* (Sheffield: Sheffield Academic Press, 1985).

Mélèze-Modrzejewski, Joseph, *The Jews of Egypt: From Rameses II to Emperor Hadrian* (Philadelphia: Jewish Publication Society of America, 1995).

Ménage, Gilles, *Historia Mulierum Philosopharum* (*History of Women Philosophers*), ed. and tr. Beatrice H. Zedler (Lanham, Md.: University Press of America, 1984).

Mendels, Doron, 'Hellenistic Utopia and the Essenes', *HTR* 72 (1979), 207–22.

Mendelson, Alan, *Secular Education in Philo of Alexandria* (Cincinnati: Hebrew Union College, 1982).

Mernissi, Fatima, *The Harem Within: Tales of a Moroccan Girlhood* (Toronto: Bantam, 1995).

Meunier, Mario, *Femmes pythagoriciennes: Fragments et lettres de Théano, Périctioné, Phintys, Mélissa et Myia* (Paris: Guy Trédaniel, 1932; repr. 1980).

Meyers, Carol, *Discovering Eve: Ancient Israelite Women in Context* (New York and Oxford: OUP, 1988).

Milik, J. T., *Dédicaces faites par des Dieux (Palmyrie, Hatra, Tyr) et des thiases sémitiques à l'époque romaine* (Institut Français de Beyrouth: Bibliothèque Archéologique et Historique, 2; Paris: Guethner, 1972).

Mingazzini, Paolino, 'Su due oggetti in terracotta raffigurante Socrate', *La Parola del Passato: Rivista di Studi Antichi*, 134 (1970), 351–8.

Minnen, Peter van, 'Berenice, a Businesswoman from Oxyrhynchus: Appearance and Reality', in Arthur M. F. W. Verhoot and Sven P.

Vleeming (eds.), *The Two Faces of Graeco-Roman Egypt* (Leiden: Brill, 1998).

Moeller, Walter, *The Wool Trade of Ancient Pompeii* (Leiden: Brill, 1976).

Momigliano, Arnaldo, *Claudius: The Emperor and his Achievement*, tr. W. D. Hogarth (Oxford: Clarendon Press, 1934).

Montserrat, Dominic, 'P.Lond.Inv. 3078 Reappraised', *Journal of Egyptian Archaeology*, 76 (1990), 206–7.

——'An Edition, with Translation and Commentary, of Thirty Unpublished Papyrus Texts of the Roman Period from Oxyrhynchus', thesis, University College London, 1991.

——*Sex and Society in Graeco-Roman Egypt* (London and New York: Kegan Paul, 1996).

Morgenstern, Julius, 'The Calendar of the Book of Jubilees, its Origin and its Character', *VT* 5 (1955), 37–61.

Morris, Jenny, 'The Jewish Philosopher Philo', in Emil Schürer, *The History of the Jewish People in the Age of Jesus Christ (175 B.C.–A.D. 135)*, iii/2, rev. and ed. Geza Vermes, Fergus Millar, and Martin Goodman (Edinburgh: T. & T. Clark, 1987), 809–70.

Musurillo, Herbert A., *The Acts of the Pagan Martyrs: Acta Alexandrinum* (Oxford: Clarendon Press, 1954).

Neusner, Jacob, *The Philosophical Mishnah*, 4 vols. (Atlanta: Scholars, 1989).

——*Judaism as Philosophy: The Method and Message of the Mishnah* (Columbia, Fla.: University of South Florida Press, 1991).

——'The Mishnah's Philosophical Method: The Judaism of Hierarchical Classification in Graeco-Roman Context', *SPA* 3 (1991), 192–206.

——*The Transformation of Judaism from Philosophy to Religion* (Urbana and Chicago: University of Illinois Press, 1992).

Nock, Arthur D., *Conversion: The Old and the New in Religion from Alexander the Great to Augustine of Hippo* (Oxford: OUP, 1933).

——'Philo and Hellenistic Philosophy', in Z. Stewart (ed.), *Essays on Religion and the Ancient World*, 2 vols. (Cambridge: CUP, 1972), 559–65.

O'Neil, William M., *Time and the Calendars* (Sydney: Sydney University Press, 1975).

Osborne, Catherine, *Eros Unveiled: Plato and the God of Love* (Oxford: Clarendon Press, 1994).

Osiek, Carolyn, 'The Family in Early Christianity: "Family Values" Revisited', *CBQ* 58 (1996), 1–24.

Padel, Ruth, 'Women: Model for Possession by Greek Daemons', in Averil Cameron and Amélie Kuhrt (eds.), *Images of Women in Antiquity*, rev. edn. (London: Routledge, 1993), 3–19.

Perelman, Chaim, and Olbrechts-Tyteca, Lucie, tr. John Wilkinson and Purcell Weaver, *The New Rhetoric: A Treatise on Argumentation* (Notre Dame, Ind.: University of Notre Dame Press, 1969).

Petrie, W. M. Flinders, *Hyksos and Israelite Cities* (London: Egypt Exploration Society, 1906).

Pomeroy, Sarah B., 'Feminism in Book V of Plato's *Republic*', *Apeiron*, 8 (1974), 32–5.

——*Goddesses, Whores, Wives, and Slaves: Women in Classical Antiquity* (London: Pimlico, 1975; 1994).

——'*Technikai kai Mousikai*: The Education of Women in the Fourth Century and in the Hellenistic Period', *American Journal of Ancient History*, 2 (1977), 51–68.

——'Women in Roman Egypt: A Preliminary Study based on Papyri', in Helene B. Foley, *Reflections of Women in Antiquity* (New York: Gordon Bread/Science Publishers, 1981).

——*Women in Hellenistic Egypt from Alexander to Cleopatra* (New York: Schocken, 1984).

——'Women in Roman Egypt: A Preliminary Study based on Papyri', *ANRW* 2.10.1 (1988), 708–23.

——*Families in Classical and Hellenistic Greece: Representations and Realities* (Oxford: Clarendon Press, 1998).

Préaux, Claire, 'Les Continuités dans l'Egypte gréco-romaine', *Actes du Xe Congrès internationale de Papyrologiques* (Warsaw: Zaklad Narodowy Im. Ossolinskich, 1961), 231–48.

Radice, Roberto, *La filosophia di Aristobulo: I suoi nessi con il 'De mundo' attributo ad Aristotele* (Milan: Vita e Pensiero, 1994).

Rainbow, Paul, 'The Last Oniad and the Teacher of Righteousness', *JJS* 48 (1997), 30–52.

Ramazangolu, Caroline, 'Unravelling Postmodern Paralysis: A Response to Joan Hoff', *WHR* 5 (1996), 19–23.

Remus, Harold, 'Voluntary Association and Networks: Aelius Aristides at the Asclepieion in Pergamon', in John S. Kloppenborg and Stephen G. Wilson (eds.), *Voluntary Associations in the Graeco-Roman World* (London and New York: Routledge, 1996), 126–43.

Rengstorf, K. H., '$\mu\alpha\theta\eta\tau\dot{\eta}s$', in Gerhard Friedrich (ed.), *TDNT* iv. 432–45.

Riaud, Jean, 'Les Thérapeutes d'Alexandrie dans la tradition et dans la recherche critique jusqu'aux découvertes de Qumran', *ANRW* 2: 20: 2 (Berlin and New York: Walter de Gruyter, 1987), 1189–1295.

Richardson, G. Peter, 'Philo and Eusebius on Monasteries and Monasticism: The Therapeutae and Kellia', in Bradley H. McLean (ed.), *Origins and Method: Towards an Understanding of Judaism and Christianity: Essays in Honour of John C. Hurd* (Sheffield: *JSOT* Press, 1993), 334–59.

——and Heuchan, Valerie, 'Jewish Voluntary Associations in Egypt and the Roles of Women', in John S. Kloppenborg and Stephen G. Wilson (eds.), *Voluntary Associations in the Graeco-Roman World* (London and New York: Routledge, 1996), 226–51.

Richlin, Amy, *The Garden of Priapus: Sexuality and Agression in Roman Humor*, 2nd edn. (New York: OUP, 1992).

Richter, Gisela, *The Portraits of the Greeks*, 3 vols. (London: Phaidon, 1943).

Ridgway, Brunilde S., *The Severe Style in Greek Sculpture* (Princeton: Princeton University Press, 1970).

Riley, Denise, *'Am I that Name?': Feminism and the Category of 'Women' in History* (Minneapolis: University of Minnesota, 1988).

Robinson, Bernard P., 'The Jealousy of Miriam: A Note on Num. 12', *ZAW* 101/3(1989), 428–32.

Robinson, James M. (ed.), *The Nag Hammadi Library in English* (San Francisco: Harper, 1988).

Rodziewicz, Mieczslaw, 'Alexandria and the District of Mareotis', *Graeco-Arabia*, 2 (1983), 199–216.

——'Taenia and Mareotis: Archaeological Research West of Alexandria', *Annual of the Egyptian School of Greek and Roman Studies*, 1 (1990), 62–78.

Romm, James S., *The Edges of the Earth in Ancient Thought: Geography, Exploration and Fiction* (Princeton: Princeton University Press, 1992).

Rosenau, Pauline Marie, *Post-modernism and the Social Sciences: Insights, Inroads, and Intrusions* (Princeton: Princeton University Press, 1992).

Roussel, Pierre, *Les Cultes égyptiens à Délos du IIIe au Ier siècle avant J. -C.* (Nancy, Paris: Berger-Levrault, 1916).

Rousselle, Aline, *Porneia: On Desire and the Body in Antiquity*, tr. Felicia Pheasant (Paris: Presses Universitaire de France, 1983; Oxford: Basil Blackwell, 1988).

Rowlandson, Jane, 'Beyond the Polis: Women and Economic Opportunity in Early Ptolemaic Egypt', in Anton Powell (ed.), *The Greek World* (London and New York: Routledge, 1995).

Rowlandson, Jane (ed.), with Roger Bagnall *et al.*, *Women and Society in Greek and Roman Egypt: A Sourcebook* (Cambridge: CUP, 1998).

Runia, David T., *Philo of Alexandria and the Timaeus of Plato* (Leiden: Brill, 1986).

——*Philo in Early Christian Literature* (Assen: Van Gorcum, 1993).

——'The Reward for Goodness: Philo, *De Vita Contemplativa* 90', *SPA* 9 (1997), 3–18.

——'Philo of Alexandria and the Greek Hairesis-Model', *VC* 53 (1999), 117–47.

Russell, David A., *Criticism in Antiquity*, 2nd edn. (London: Bristol Classical Press, 1995).

Safrai, S., and Stern, M., *The Jewish People in the First Century: Historical Geography, Political History, Social, Cultural and Religious Life and Institutions*, 2 vols. (Assen: Van Gorcum, 1976).

Saloman, R., 'Epigraphic Remains of Indian Traders in Egypt', *Journal of the American Oriental Society*, 111 (1991), 731–6.

Sanders, E. P., *Jewish Law from Jesus to the Mishnah: Five Studies* (London: SCM, 1990).

——*Judaism: Practice and Belief 63 BCE–66 CE* (London: SCM, 1992).

Sandmel, Samuel, *Philo of Alexandria: An Introduction* (New York and Oxford: OUP, 1979).

Sawyer, Deborah, *Women and Religion in the First Christian Centuries* (London: Routledge, 1996).

Saxonhouse, Arlene, 'Classical Greek Conceptions of Public and Private', in Stanley I. Benn and Gerald F. Gaus (eds.), *Public and Private in Social Life* (London and Canberra: Croom Helm, 1983), 363–84.

Schäfer, Peter, *The Hidden and Manifest God: Some Major Themes in Early Jewish Mysticism*, tr. Aubrey Pomerance (Albany, NY: State University of New York, 1992).

——'Research on the Hekhalot Literature: Where do we Stand Now?' in Gabrielle Sed-Ranja (ed.), *Rashi, 1040–1990: Hommage à Ephraim E. Urbach* (Paris: Cerf, 1993).

Schaff, Philip, and Wace, Henry (eds.), *Library of Nicene and Post-Nicene Fathers Series III, Athanasius: Select Works and Letters*, iv (New York, 1924; repr. Peabody, Mass.: Henrickson, 1994).

Schefold, Karl, *Die Bildnisse der antiken Dichter, Redner, under Denker* (Basle: Benno Schwabe, 1943).

Schoene, Alfred (ed.), *Eusebi Chronicorum libri duo*, ii (Berlin: Weidmann, 1875–6).

Scholem, Gershom G., *Major Trends in Jewish Mysticism* (New York: Schocken, 1941).

Schroeder, Leopold von, *Pythagoras und die Inder: Eine Untersuchung über die Herkunft und Abstammung der Pythagoreischen Lehren* (Leipzig: O. Schulz, 1884).

Schwank, Benedikt, 'Neue Funde in Nabatäerstädten und ihre Bedeutung für die neutestamentliche Exegese', *NTS* 19 (1983), 429–35.

Schwyzer, Hans-Rudolf, *Chairemon* (Leipzig: Harassowitz, 1932).

Scott, Joan Wallach, 'Gender: A Useful Category of Historical Analysis', *American Historical Review*, 91 (1986), 1053–75.

——*Gender and the Politics of History* (New York: Columbia University Press, 1988).

—— 'Deconstructing Equality-versus-Difference: Or, the Uses of Poststructuralist Theory for Feminism', in Marianne Hirsch and Evelyn Fox Keller (eds.), *Conflicts in Feminism* (New York: Routledge, 1990), 134–48.

Seland, Torrey, 'Philo and the Clubs and Associations of Alexandria', in John S. Kloppenborg and Stephen G. Wilson (eds.), *Voluntary Associations in the Graeco-Roman World* (London and New York: Routledge, 1996), 110–25.

Setälä, Päivi, 'Brick Stamps and Women's Economic Opportunities in Imperial Rome', in Arina Angerman, Geerte Binnema, Annemieke Keunen, Vefie Poels, and Jacqueline Zirkee (eds.), *Current Issues in Women's History* (Routledge: London and New York, 1989), 61–74.

Sgarbi, Romano, *Problemi linguistici e di critica del testo nel De Vita Contemplativa di Filone alla luce della versione Armena* (Milan: Istituto Lombardo di Scienze e Lettere, 1992).

Shaw, B. D., 'The Age of Roman Girls at Marriage: Some Reconsiderations', *JRS* 77 (1987), 30–46.

Sherk, Robert K., *The Roman Empire: Augustus to Hadrian* (Cambridge: CUP, 1988).

Shroyer, Montgomery J., 'Alexandrian Jewish Literalists', *JBL* 55 (1936), 261–84.

Simon, Marcel, *Jewish Sects at the Time of Jesus*, tr. James H. Farley of *Les Sectes juives au temps de Jésus* (Paris: Presses Universitaires de France, 1960; Philadelphia: Fortress, 1967).

Simpson, Peter, 'Aristotle's Criticism of Socrates' Community of Wives and Children', *Apeiron*, 24 (1991), 99–114.

Sissa, Giulia, 'The Sexual Philosophies of Plato and Aristotle', in Paula Schmitt Pantel (ed.), *A History of Women in the West*, i. *From Ancient Goddesses to Christian Saints*, tr. Arthur Goldhammer of *Storia delle donne in Occidente*, i. *L'Antichità* (Rome and Bari: Gius. Laterza & Figli Spa, 1990; Cambridge, Mass.: Belknap of Harvard University Press, 1992), 46–81.

Slater, William J. (ed.), *Dining in a Classical Context* (Ann Arbor: University of Michigan, 1991).

Sly, Dorothy, *Philo's Perception of Women* (Brown Judaic Studies, 209; Atlanta: Scholars, 1990).

—— *Philo's Alexandria* (London and New York: Routledge, 1996).

Smallwood, E. Mary (ed. and tr.) *Legatio ad Gaiam* (Leiden: Brill, 1961).

—— *The Jews under Roman Rule from Pompey to Diocletian: A Study in Political Relations* (Leiden: Brill, 1981).

Smelik, Klaas A. D., and Hemelrijk, Emily, ' "Who Knows Not What Monsters Demented Egypt Worships?": Opinions on Egyptian Animal Worship in Antiquity as Part of the Conception of Egypt', *ANRW* 2: 17: 4 (1984), 1853–2337.

Smith, Jonathan Z., 'The Prayer of Joseph', in Jacob Neusner (ed.), *Religions in Antiquity: Essays in Memory of Erwin J. Goodenough* (Leiden: Brill, 1970).

Smith, Morton, 'Palestinian Judaism in the First Century', in Moshe Davis (ed.), *Israel: Its Role in Civilization* (New York: Jewish Theological Seminary of America, 1956), 67–81.

Smith, N., 'Plato and Aristotle on the Nature of Women', *Journal of the History of Philosophy*, 21 (1983), 467–78.

Snyder, Jane McIntosh, *The Woman and the Lyre: Women Writers in Classical Greece and Rome* (Carbondale and Edwardsville, Ill.: Southern Illinois University Press, 1989).

Spelman, Elizabeth, *Inessential Woman: Problems of Exclusion in Feminist Thought* (Boston: Beacon, 1988).

Stephens, William H., *The New Testament World in Pictures* (Nashville, Tenn.: Broadman, 1987).

Sterling, Gregory, 'Philo and the Logic of Apologetics', *Society of Biblical Literature Seminar Papers 1990* (Atlanta: Scholars, 1990), 412–30.

—— ' "The School of Sacred Laws": The Social Setting of Philo's Treatises', *VC* 53 (1999), 148–64.

—— 'Ontology versus Eschatology: Tensions between Author and Community in Hebrews', *SPA* 13 (2001), 190–211.

Sternbach, Ludwik, 'Indian Wisdom and its Spread beyond India', *Journal of the American Oriental Society*, 92 (1972), 97–123.

Stone, Lawrence, *The Past and the Present Revisited* (London: Routledge & Kegan Paul, 1987).

Strachan-Davidson, James L., *Problems of Roman Criminal Law*, 2 vols. (Oxford: Clarendon Press, 1912).

Stradonitz, Reinhard Kekule von, 'Die Bildnisse des Sokrates', *Abhandlungen der preussischen Akademie der Wissenschaften philosophische-historische Klasse* (1908).

Szesnat, Holger, ' "Mostly Aged Virgins": Philo and the Presence of the Therapeutrides at Lake Mareotis', *Neotestamentica*, 32 (1998), 191–201.

—— 'Philo and Female Homoeroticism: Philo's Use of γύνανδρος and Recent Work on Tribades', *JSJ* 30 (1999), 140–7.

—— ' "Pretty Boys" in Philo's *De Vita Contemplativa*', *SPA* 10 (1998), 87–107.

Takacs, Sarolta, *Isis and Sarapis in the Roman World* (Leiden: Brill, 1975).

Taylor, F. Sherwood, *The Alchemists: Founders of Modern Chemistry* (London: Heinemann, 1951), 38–43.

Taylor, Joan E., *Christians and the Holy Places: The Myth of Jewish–Christian Origins* (Oxford: Clarendon Press, 1993).

—— The Immerser: John the Baptist within Second Temple Judaism (Grand Rapids, Mich.: Eerdmans, 1997).

—— 'A Second Temple in Egypt: A Reconsideration of the Evidence for the Zadokite Temple of Onias', *JSJ* 29 (1998), 1–25.

—— and Davies, Philip R., 'The So-Called Therapeutae of *De Vita Contemplativa*: Identity and Character', *HTR* 91 (1998), 3–24.

—— and Higham, Thomas, 'Problems of Qumran's Chronology and the Radiocarbon Dating of Palm Log Samples in Locus 86', *Qumran Chronicle* 8/1–2 (Aug. 1998), 83–96.

Tcherikover, Victor A., *Hellenistic Civilisation and the Jews* (New York: Jewish Publication Society of America, 1959).

Thesleff, Holger, *Pythagoraean Texts of the Hellenistic Period* (Abo: Abo Akademie, 1965).

Thundy, Zacharias P., *Buddha and Christ* (Leiden: Brill, 1993).

Tod, Marcus, 'Sidelights on Greek Philosophers', *Journal of Hellenic Studies*, 77 (1957), 132–41.

Tov, Emanuel, 'The Textual Status of 4Q364–367 (4QPP)', in Julio Trebolle Barrera and Luis Vegas Montaner (eds.), *The Madrid Qumran Congress: Proceedings of the International Congress on the Dead Sea Scrolls, Madrid 18–21 March 1991*, i (Leiden and Madrid: Brill and Editorial Complutense, 1992), 43–82.

Treggiari, Susan, *Roman Marriage: 'Iusti Coniuges' from the Time of Cicero to the Time of Ulpian* (Oxford: Clarendon Press, 1991).

Trible, Phyllis, 'Bringing Miriam out of the Shadows', *Bible Review*, 5/1 (Feb. 1989), 14–25, 34.

—— 'Subversive Justice: Tracing the Miriamic Traditions', in Douglas A. Knight and Peter J. Paris (eds.), *Justice and the Holy: Essays in Honor of Walter Harrelson* (Atlanta: Scholars 1989), 99–109.

Turnebus, Adrien, *Philonis Iudaei in libros Mosis, de mundi opificio, historicos, de legibus; eiusdem libri singulares* (Paris: Apud Adr. Turnebum typographum regium, 1552).

VanderKam, James C., 'Calendrical Texts and the Origins of the Dead Sea Scroll Community', in Michael Wise *et al.*, *Methods of Investigation of the Dead Sea Scrolls and the Khirbet Qumran Site* (New York: New York Academy of Sciences, 1992), 371–88.

—— *Calendars in the Dead Sea Scrolls* (London and New York: Routledge, 1998).

Vaux, Roland de, *Archaeology and the Dead Sea Scrolls* (London: British Academy and OUP, 1973).

Vellacott, Philip (ed.), *Euripides, The Bacchae and Other Plays*, rev. edn. (Harmondsworth: Penguin, 1973).

Vermes, Geza, *Jesus the Jew: A Historian's Reading of the Gospels*, 2nd edn. (London: SCM, 1983).

Vermes, Geza, and Goodman, Martin (eds.), *The Essenes according to the Classical Sources* (Sheffield: Sheffield Academic Press, 1989).

Vermeule III, Cornelius C., 'Socrates and Aspasia: New Portraits of Late Antiquity', *Classical Journal*, 54 (1958), 49–55.

Vidman, Ladislav, *Sylloge inscriptionum religionis Isiacae et Sarapiacae* (Berlin: Walter de Gruyter, 1969).

Völker, Walter, *Fortschritt und Vollendung bei Philo von Alexandrien: Eine Studie zur Geschichte der Frömmigkeit* (Leipzig: J. C. Hinrichs, 1938).

Waithe, Mary Ellen (ed.), *A History of Women Philosophers: Ancient Women Philosophers 600 B.C.–500 A.D.* (Dordrecht and Boston and Lancaster: Martinus Nijhoff, 1987).

Walker, Susan, 'Women and Housing in Classical Greece: The Archaeological Evidence', in Averil Cameron and Amelie Kuhrt (eds.), *Images of Women in Antiquity*, rev. edn. (London: Routledge, 1993), 81–91, 304–5.

Wallace-Hadrill, Andrew, *Houses and Society in Pompeii and Herculaneum* (Princeton: Princeton University Press, 1994).

Walter, Nikolaus, *Der Thoraausleger Aristobulus: Untersuchungen zu seinen Fragmenten und zu pseudepigraphischen Resten der Jüdisch hellenistischen Literatur* (Berlin: Akademie-Verlag, 1964), 35–123.

Wegner, Judith Romney, 'Philo's Portrayal of Women: Hebraic or Hellenic?', in Amy-Jill Levine (ed.), *'Women like this': New Perspectives on Jewish Women in the Greco-Roman World* (Atlanta: Scholars, 1991), 41–66.

Weitzman, Stephen, *Song and Story in Biblical Narrative: The History of a Literary Convention in Ancient Israel* (Bloomington, Ind.: Indiana University Press, 1997).

Wells, Louise, *The Greek Language of Healing from Homer to the New Testament* (BZNW 83; Berlin and New York: de Gruyter, 1998).

Wender, D., 'Plato: Misogynist, Paedophile and Feminist', *Arethusa*, 6 (1973), 75–90.

Wendland, Paul, 'Die Therapeuten und die philonische Schrift vom beschaulichen Leben', *Jahrbücher für classische Philologie, Suppl.* 22 (1896), 693–772.

White, Hayden, *Metahistory: The Historical Imagination in Nineteenth Century Europe* (Baltimore and London: Johns Hopkins University Press, 1973).

—— 'The Historical Text as Literary Artifact', in Brian Fay, Philip Pomper, and Richard Vann (eds.), *History and Theory* (Oxford: Blackwell, 1998), 15–33.

White, Sidnie, '4Q364 & 365: A Preliminary Report', in Julio Trebolle Barrera and Luis Vegas Montaner (eds.), *The Madrid Qumran Congress: Proceedings of the International Congress on the Dead Sea*

Scrolls, Madrid 18–21 March 1991, i (Leiden and Madrid: Brill and Editorial Complutense, 1992), 217–28.

Wilcken, Ulrich, *Urkunden der Ptolemäerzeit* (Berlin and Leipzig: Walter de Gruyter, 1922).

Williamson, Ronald, *Jews in the Hellenistic World: Philo* (Cambridge: CUP, 1989).

Wimbush, Vincent L. (ed.), *Ascetic Behavior in Greco-Roman Antiquity: A Sourcebook* (Studies in Antiquity and Christianity; Minneapolis: Fortress, 1990).

Winston, David, 'Iambulus: A Literary Study in Greek Utopianism', Ph.D. thesis, Columbia University, New York, 1956.

——'Iambulus' *Islands of the Sun* and Hellenistic Literary Utopias', *Science Fiction Studies*, 3 (1976), 219–27.

——*Philo of Alexandria: The Contemplative Life, The Giants and Selections* (Classics of Western Spirituality; New York and Toronto: Paulist, 1981).

——'Was Philo a Mystic?', in Joseph Dan and Frank Talmage (eds.), *Studies in Jewish Mysticism* (Cambridge, Mass.: Association for Jewish Studies, 1982).

——*Logos and Mystical Theology in Philo of Alexandria* (Cincinnati: Hebrew Union College Press, 1985),

——'Philo and the Contemplative Life', in Arthur Green (ed.), *Jewish Spirituality from the Bible through the Middle Ages* (New York: Crossroad, 1986), 198–231.

——'Philo's Mysticism', *SPA* 8 (1996), 74–82.

Wintermute, O. S., 'Jubilees', in James H. Charlesworth (ed.), *Old Testament Pseudepigrapha* (London: Darton, Longman & Todd, 1985), ii, 35–142.

Wire, Antoinette Clark, *The Corinthian Women Prophets: A Reconstruction through Paul's Rhetoric* (Minneapolis, Minn.: Fortress, 1990).

Wise, Michael, Golb, Norman, Collins, John J., and Pardee, Dennis (eds.), *Methods of Investigation of the Dead Sea Scrolls and the Khirbet Qumran Site: Present Realities and Future Prospects* (Annals of the New York Academy of Sciences, 722; New York, 1992).

Witt, R. E., *Isis in the Graeco-Roman World* (London: Thames & Hudson, 1971).

Wolfson, Elliot R., *Through a Speculum that Shines: Vision and Imagination in Medieval Jewish Mysticism* (Princeton: Princeton University Press, 1994).

Wolfson, Harry A., *Philo: Foundations of Religious Philosophy in Judaism, Christianity and Islam*, 2 vols. (Cambridge, Mass.: Harvard University Press, 1947).

Wriggins, Sally Hovey, *Xuanzang: A Buddhist Pilgrim on the Silk Road* (Boulder, Colo.: Westview Press, 1996).

Yadin, Yigael, *Finds from the Bar Kokhba Period in the Cave of Letters* (Jerusalem: Israel Exploration Society, 1963).

Yonge, Charles D., *The Works of Philo Judaeus, the Contemporary of Josephus, translated from the Greek* (London: Henry G. Bohn, 1854–5; repr. Peabody Mass.: Hendrickson, 1993).

Zabin, S., ' "Iudeae benemerenti": Towards a Study of Jewish Women in the Western Roman Empire', *Phoenix*, 50 (1996), 262–82.

Zeitlin, Solomon, 'Some Stages of the Jewish Calendar', in id., *Studies in the Early History of Judaism*, i (New York: Ktav, 1973), 183–93.

—— 'The Book of Jubilees and the Pentateuch', in id. *Studies in the Early History of Judaism*, ii (New York: Ktav, 1974), 147–64.

—— '2 Maccabees 6, 7A and Calendrical Change in Jerusalem', *JSJ* 12 (1981), 58–60.

Zerubavel, Eviatar, *The Seven Day Circle: The History and Meaning of the Week* (Chicago and London: University of Chicago, 1985).

INDEX OF GREEK TERMS*

* including words transcribed into English letters

GENERAL INDEX

Page numbers in italics denote illustrations